Bard   FICTION PRIZE

Bard College invites submissions for its annual Fiction Prize for young writers.

The Bard Fiction Prize is awarded annually to a promising, emerging writer who is a United States citizen aged 39 years or younger at the time of application. In addition to a monetary award of $30,000, the winner receives an appointment as writer-in-residence at Bard College for one semester without the expectation that he or she teach traditional courses. The recipient will give at least one public lecture and will meet informally with students.

To apply, candidates should write a cover letter describing the project they plan to work on while at Bard and submit a C.V., along with three copies of the published book they feel best represents their work. No manuscripts will be accepted.

Applications for the 2012 prize must be received by July 15, 2011. For further information about the Bard Fiction Prize, call 845-758-7087, or visit www.bard.edu/bfp. Applicants may also request information by writing to the Bard Fiction Prize, Bard College, Annandale-on-Hudson, NY 12504-5000.

Bard College PO Box 5000, Annandale-on-Hudson, NY 12504-5000

COMING UP IN THE FALL

Conjunctions:57
KIN
Edited by Bradford Morrow

Our ancestors, our parents, our siblings, our spouses, our children, our children's children. Family trees, pedigrees. Forebears, descendants. Now our joy and sanctuary, now our burden and bane, family is the cradle from which we spring, the collective from which we set out into the world, and the people we're buried beside at our journey's end. Nothing is more familiar, nothing more ineffable than the emotional prism, the blood knot that con-stitutes family. We can try to leave them. They can disinherit us. But there is no dispelling DNA, no true exile from that which binds us with our kin.

In *Conjunctions:57, Kin*, over two dozen contributors, includ-ing Noy Holland, Joyce Carol Oates, Rebecca Back, Karen Hays, and Micaela Morrissette, explore the intricacies of family ties and the labyrinthine nature of kinship.

One-year subscriptions to *Conjunctions* are only $18 (two years for $32) for more than seven hundred pages per year of contemporary and historical literature and art. Subscribe or renew online at conjunctions.com, or mail your check to *Conjunctions*, Bard College, Annandale-on-Hudson, NY 12504-5000. For questions or to request an invoice, e-mail conjunctions@bard.edu or call (845) 758-1539.

CONJUNCTIONS

Bi-Annual Volumes of New Writing

Edited by
Bradford Morrow

Contributing Editors
Walter Abish
Chinua Achebe
John Ashbery
Martine Bellen
Mei-mei Berssenbrugge
Mary Caponegro
William H. Gass
Peter Gizzi
Robert Kelly
Ann Lauterbach
Norman Manea
Rick Moody
Howard Norman
Joan Retallack
Joanna Scott
David Shields
Peter Straub
John Edgar Wideman

published by Bard College

EDITOR: Bradford Morrow
MANAGING EDITOR: Micaela Morrissette
ASSISTANT MANAGING EDITOR: Coleen Murphy Alexander
SENIOR EDITORS: Robert Antoni, Peter Constantine, Brian Evenson,
 J. W. McCormack, Pat Sims, Alan Tinkler, Teresa Vilardi
COPY EDITOR: Pat Sims
WEBMASTER: Brian Evenson
ASSOCIATE EDITORS: Jedediah Berry, Alice Gregory, Jessica Loudis, Eric Olson,
 Judi Smith
ART EDITOR: Norton Batkin
PUBLICITY: Mark R. Primoff
EDITORIAL ASSISTANTS: Charlotte Benbeniste, Andrew Durbin, Kianoosh
 Hashemzadeh, Nicole Nyhan, Emma Smith-Stevens

CONJUNCTIONS is published in the Spring and Fall of each year by Bard College, Annandale-on-Hudson, NY 12504. This issue is made possible in part with the generous funding of the National Endowment for the Arts, and with public funds from the New York State Council on the Arts, a State Agency.

SUBSCRIPTIONS: Use our secure online ordering system at www.conjunctions.com, or send subscription orders to CONJUNCTIONS, Bard College, Annandale-on-Hudson, NY 12504. Single year (two volumes): $18.00 for individuals; $40.00 for institutions and overseas. Two years (four volumes): $32.00 for individuals; $80.00 for institutions and overseas. Patron subscription (lifetime): $500.00. Overseas subscribers please make payment by International Money Order. For information about subscriptions, back issues, and advertising, contact us at (845) 758-1539 or conjunctions@bard.edu.

Editorial communications should be sent to Bradford Morrow, *Conjunctions,* 21 East 10th Street, New York, NY 10003. Unsolicited manuscripts cannot be returned unless accompanied by a stamped, self-addressed envelope. Electronic and simultaneous submissions will not be considered.

Conjunctions is listed and indexed in Humanities International Complete and included in EBSCO*host.*

Visit the *Conjunctions* website at www.conjunctions.com and follow us on Facebook and Twitter.

Cover design by Jerry Kelly, New York. Cover photograph by Ken Prior of an undulatus asperatus cloud formation near Schiehallion Mountain, Perthshire, Scotland, November 4, 2008. Reproduced by kind permission of the photographer. The editor is grateful to Ian Loxley of the Cloud Appreciation Society (http://cloudappreciationsociety.org) for assistance in obtaining this image.

Available through D.A.P./Distributed Art Publishers, Inc., 155 Sixth Avenue, New York, NY 10013. Telephone: (212) 627-1999. Fax: (212) 627-9484.

Printers: Edwards Brothers

Typesetter: Bill White, Typeworks

ISSN 0278-2324

ISBN 978-0-941964-72-2

Manufactured in the United States of America.

TABLE OF CONTENTS

TERRA INCOGNITA
THE VOYAGE ISSUE
Edited by Bradford Morrow

EDITOR'S NOTE. 7

Benjamin Hale, *The Minus World* 8

Susan Steinberg, *Spectacle*. 40

James Morrow, *Fixing the Abyss* 53

Kyra Simone, *Seven Stories from the Palace of Rubble*. 74

Howard Norman, *Radio from the Cities*. 79

Stephen Marche, *Leaving Alberta* 91

Cathy Park Hong, *Three Poems* 100

Kathryn Davis, *Descent of the Aquanauts*. 105

Charles Bernstein, *Recalculating* 119

Alexandra Kleeman, *The Brief History of Weather* 126

Joanna Scott, *De Potter's First Grand Tour Around
   the World*. 147

Donald Revell, *Two Poems* 166

Jonathan Carroll, *East of Furious* 167

Tim Horvath, *Altered Native* 183

Nomi Eve, *The Education of Benesh the Matchmaker* 187

Andrew Zawacki, *f/11* 205

Gabriel Blackwell, *The I and the It* 211

Robert Coover, *The Box*. 221

Barney Rosset, *China* 228

Ryan Call, *The Artificial Stork*. 260

Julia Elliott, *Regeneration at Mukti*. 267

Peter Gizzi, *Modern Adventures at Sea* 285

Andrew Ervin, *Under the Boardwalk* 289

Cole Swensen, *On Walks: Rousseau* 297

John Madera, *Notes Toward the Recovery of Desiderata*. 302

G. C. Waldrep, *Three Poems* 318

Karla Kelsey, *Aftermath*. 322

Marc Nieson, *The Fortunes of Cities*. 328

Peter Straub, *The Ballad of Ballard and Sandrine* 340

NOTES ON CONTRIBUTORS. 378

EDITOR'S NOTE

YOU WILL TRAVEL THROUGH parts north here, as you accompany Gauguin to Greenland, wend your way from Eskimo Point through rural Alberta. The wartime world of Mauthausen and the all but forgotten theater of China are also on the itinerary, places in which, for all the tragedy, horror, and despair inherent in their histories, the fundamental, irrepressible whimsy of the human spirit thrives. Imaginary places—or are they?—such as *The Beneath* and an Amazon River endowed with secret passageways and trapdoors and forbidding lovers intent upon devouring each other are also ports of call in this issue into terra incognita. But then there are the Jersey Turnpike and the Waikiki Tiki Motor Lodge, equally territories that stretch the normal into the liminal and from there into worlds that are essentially and only dreamed about—mind trips, if you will.

The act of voyaging, journeying, migrating from the known toward something not known or at least unfamiliar is older than literature itself. It's hard to think of any classic author who hasn't been drawn to such narratives, dispatches from elsewhere, travelogues that give us sharp images from remote loci real or imagined where the compass needle swings in circles. From Homer to Calvino, Swift to Chatwin, Ovid to the Shakespeare who wrote *The Tempest*—an endless group of literary explorers has traveled these unmapped paths and *Terra Incognita* hopes to add a little to that grand canon.

By the way, the photograph on the cover of this issue, taken by Ken Prior, is an astonishment. I encountered it in a doctor's waiting room, in an issue of *Time* magazine that featured an article about the discovery of a new cloud formation, the undulatus asperatus. Thanks to Ken and everyone at the wonderful Cloud Appreciation Society for allowing us to include it here. And for those of you with your heads appropriately positioned in the clouds, you might consider joining the society. Very small cost, very large cumuli.

—Bradford Morrow
April 2011
New York City

The Minus World
Benjamin Hale

"I SAW THIS DOCUMENTARY? About DARPA?" Greg obligingly nodded him to go on. Megan was watching the ceiling. Peter had spent the evening nervously shoving conversation across anxious waves of silence. "You know DARPA? Defense Advanced Research Projects Agency. They're involved with all kinds of black helicopter shit, like training spies to do ESP, invisibility shields, the Montauk Project, all that shit, but OK, so they've developed this thing called the Exo-atmospheric Kill Machine—it's this satellite with a really, *really* fucking powerful laser on it that can just zoom in on anybody anywhere in the world and kill them from outer space. One second you're walking around, hum-de-dum, doing your thing, then all of a sudden, zzzzt, you're dead. That's our fucking tax dollars at work."

Megan was lying on the couch with her bare feet in Greg's lap and Peter sat hunched on the edge of a chair, rapidly bouncing his leg on the ball of his foot. Since they'd gotten home from dinner he'd been sucking down glass after glass of orange soda so quickly the original ice cubes hadn't had time to melt. It was getting late. Megan gave Greg a meaningful-seeming look that Peter couldn't interpret.

"I really don't think they have the capability to do that," said Greg.

"Do *not* be a fool," said Peter. He could feel how agitated his voice was. It had a quivery edge of emotion that he couldn't swallow. "It's the fucking government. They have the money, they have the power. Do *not* be naive."

"I'm going to bed," Megan said to Greg.

It was the first night Peter would be staying with Greg and Megan. They had picked him up from South Station that afternoon and taken him out to dinner in Boston, then come home and talked for a while. Greg had had a beer with dinner, and that's it. Megan was pregnant, and Peter of course was not drinking. The air was awkward with sobriety.

Peter kept on trying to think of interesting things to say. Every time he tried to make conversation Megan looked at him like he was crazy.

During his exit interview, Robin had told Peter he needed a fresh start. Robin was the counselor-therapist woman. She was nice to him but he never believed anything she said. She always did the therapist thing of being nice to you but not getting remotely emotionally involved. Her face was round and so deliberately earnest-looking that there was obviously nothing earnest in it at all. She was wearing this sort of low-cut shirt, and Peter's eyes kept getting stuck in her cleavage. During the interview she shrugged up the shawl thing she was wearing and wrapped it across herself, and Peter wondered if she'd noticed him looking at her breasts. She probably had. Peter had finally learned that women are better at knowing when you're looking at their breasts than you think they are. He was a little embarrassed but it wasn't like he was ever going to see her again. This was his exit interview. She told him he needed a fresh start.

Yeah, well. Peter was edging up on the realization, the main part of him had already admitted it, but out of fear he'd not yet let his conscious mind admit it, that there is no such thing as a fresh start. Not in life. In a Nintendo game, if you fuck up beyond the hope of ever pulling your shit together again you can always press the reset button, and you're back at the beginning, and Mario is little again and running down the brick pathway ready to encounter the mushrooms and the turtles, but you, playing him, now know exactly when and where the dangers will come. When the mushrooms and the turtles slide onscreen from the right-hand edge of the TV, you will be ready for them. At least until you get to the last place where you died. Life is not like that. No matter how badly you fuck up, you cannot ever press the reset button and start over. All you can do is pull the plug.

Peter needed help. His parents wouldn't help him anymore, his sister wouldn't help him, his ex-girlfriend Gina wouldn't help him, his friends wouldn't help him and he wasn't sure he had any more friends. Other relatives were out, too. All of the possible people who might help Peter had been overfished, like an empty sea that has no more fish in it. But Greg, Greg had fish left for him.

As soon as we can, Peter promised himself, we will pay Greg back for the many times he's helped us when we didn't deserve it.

(Ever since he was a kid, Peter had always talked to himself using the first-person plural. The "we" was always the external, rational voice talking to him, Peter. Superego talking to id. He only did this in his head, though, or out loud when he was alone. If people had heard him talking to himself in the first-person plural they might think he was crazy.)

9

"As soon as I can," he said to Greg, "I will pay you back for this."
"Don't worry about it," said Greg, and went upstairs to bed to join his wife (the word wife still sounded weird) in bed.

Greg clearly didn't expect to ever be repaid. Part of Peter also knew he'd probably never repay him.

"We have to pay him back," said Peter to himself when he was alone. "We have to pay him back."

Greg's wife disliked Peter. She had her reasons.

Most people disliked Peter. Peter disliked Peter. Even Greg disliked him oftentimes, although he always helped him. Greg "loved" him. Some people still loved Peter. He wasn't sure about his mom, but his dad loved him. His sister loved him. Even his ex-girlfriend loved him. But, coming to the point, they wouldn't give him any money.

Greg wasn't giving him any money, either. Just a place to stay, rent free and indefinitely, and a job, which with time and patience and work and saving and not fucking up would turn into money. Greg was doing the whole teaching him to fish instead of giving him fish thing. Peter had never been any good at fishing. He was good at staying up all night doing drugs and playing Nintendo. That he could do.

Greg had gone upstairs, said goodnight and turned off the light. It was dark all over the house except for the weak white kitchen light above the sink. Greg and Megan's house was in Somerville, Massachusetts. This was the first time Peter had ever been to Massachusetts. He'd been on a Greyhound all day and the previous night, and hadn't really slept at all except for little naps in the bus seat for the last, like, thirty hours. Megan had made up the futon bed for him in the basement. There was a futon in their unfinished basement that Peter was going to sleep on until he had enough money to move out. Which was probably going to take a while. The basement was full of boxes and Christmas ornaments and vacuum cleaners and things like that, and a futon. Peter and Greg had stayed up talking a while after Megan went to bed. Megan was really, really pregnant. They had gotten married like a year ago. Peter hadn't been there. Unless a miracle happened, like finding a magic bag of money that always has money in it, Peter was probably going to still be staying in the basement when their kid was born. This was the newest of the various reasons Megan disliked Peter.

It was a little after midnight. Peter wasn't tired at all. Peter had a meeting with his prospective employer tomorrow morning at eight.

"Why so early?" he'd asked his brother.

"They've already been working for two hours by then," said Greg. "They get to the lab around six. They have to start working that early because the fishermen bring in the catch even earlier than that."

The job was driving this truck with a tank full of salt water on it from the marine biology lab at MIT to the docks in New Bedford to pick up all the squid the fishermen hauled in along with the fish. The fishermen just threw the squid back and kept the fish, but MIT needed squid to run experiments on. So he was supposed to get there early in the morning, before the boats come in, ask them to give him their squid, then drive back to MIT, deliver the squid. He would be paid by the squid.

Greg said he had put the word in for Peter. He said they weren't interviewing anybody else. The job was as good as his, this interview was basically a formality. He said they'd been trying to get students to do it, but none of them wanted the job because it didn't pay that much and you had to get up at three in the morning to do it. Greg said he'd seen the thing for the job on the job-posting thing, the bulletin board, in the student quad cafeteria whatever area for weeks and weeks and nobody had torn any tabs off it. So he went to the marine biology lab and asked the guys who worked there what the job was and what it entailed and how much it paid and stuff like that. And then he asked them if they'd mind giving his younger brother Peter a job.

"What did you tell them?" said Peter.

"Not everything. I said you were in kind of a tough spot and needed to make some money, get back on your feet."

"What do you mean back?"

"I told them you'd be a reliable worker. So please don't embarrass me."

So they didn't know everything. Everything was that Peter was a twenty-six-year-old addict with ten thousand dollars of credit card debt, a criminal record and no college degree, who'd been living in a halfway house in Illinois until last week. But now he was here. So?

Actually, that wasn't everything, not even close. But those were the big things.

OK, so we have to be there at eight. It takes like twenty minutes to get there. OK, so let's get up at seven. That means we should go to bed now.

Peter opened his brother's liquor cabinet. Inside it was a sight that amazed and ashamed Peter, a sight that probably always would: a bunch of bottles of liquor that were half full, three quarters full . . .

11

you know, bottles that have been opened, but aren't empty. Greg was the kind of person who could pour himself a glass of Scotch or whatever, drink it, and then stop drinking, and go to bed or whatever, instead of drinking until either there was nothing left to drink or he physically couldn't drink anymore.

Peter got a glass out of the cupboard and poured himself about three fingers of what looked like expensive Scotch. He looked at it, set it down and poured another finger. He took a sip, put the glass back on the kitchen counter and started looking around the kitchen for something he could turn into a funnel to pour the Scotch back into the bottle with. He ripped a page out of a *National Geographic* with a picture of whales on it and rolled it into a funnel. He stuck the skinny end into the neck of the bottle and dumped the glass into the fat end. The page instantly got all damp and floppy. Some of the blue ink from the whales slid off the page and got in the Scotch, tiny ribbonlike clouds of whale-colored ink in the Scotch. Oh no. We're fucking this up. The whisky was running down the sides of the bottle and getting all over his hands and the counter. While Peter was doing this it occurred to him that his mom had a funnel that she used for cooking somehow. A funnel had some sort of cooking-related function. Remember we used to play with it when we were a kid? When we would make potions? Peter had once covered it in aluminum foil and worn it as a hat when he was the Tin Man for Halloween, and Greg had been the Scarecrow and Lindsay had been Dorothy. There was no Cowardly Lion. This led to the thought that Greg and his wife had a pretty nice house and everything, full of grownup stuff, and they cooked, and they might have an actual funnel somewhere in the kitchen, one that was made for being a funnel, made out of metal or plastic or something. But it was too late now.

He put the stopper back in the bottle, wiped the bottle and the counter off with a paper towel, put the bottle back in the liquor cabinet, thought about how weird it was that they even had a liquor cabinet and if they had a fucking liquor cabinet they probably had a fucking funnel, then he looked in the liquor cabinet and realized there was in fact a funnel *in* the liquor cabinet, washed the glass and dried it and put it back in the cupboard, went downstairs, set the alarm clock Megan had given him for seven, took off his clothes, got in bed and stared at pink tufts of fiberglass insulation stapled to wooden beams in the basement wall until the alarm clock went off.

As soon as he hit the button that shut off the buzzer he was suddenly incredibly sleepy. He heard Greg and Megan moving around upstairs. He fought his way into the same clothes he'd worn the day before, went upstairs, pissed, splashed water on his face and combed his hair with his hands. His skin looked pink and puffy, and his eyes were narrow and swampy looking. The whites of his eyes were dull gray. He joined them in the kitchen.

"How'd you sleep?" said Megan.

"Bad," said Peter.

"I'm sorry."

She was making coffee. Their coffeemaker looked like a spaceship. Greg and Megan were both healthy, good-looking people. Greg had always dated girls who were way above Peter's looks-bracket. Megan had stubby fingers and bug eyes and skin and hair right out of commercials for skin and hair products. She looked like a pregnant woman on TV. Some pregnant women get fat feet and things like that. But Megan just had a perfectly compact, round belly, like she had a beach ball under her shirt. It looked like when she gave birth it would just kind of make a harmless popping sound like the sound of a cartoon bubble popping, and then she'd go back to exactly what she looked like before.

"You want a ride to the campus?" said Greg. "I'm going to my office early anyway."

Fuck. We can't say no. There's no point. We're going to the same place anyway, it doesn't make any sense for us to walk now.

He'd planned on smoking cigarettes while he walked to the campus, and if Greg drove him that meant he wouldn't get to do that and he probably wouldn't have time for a cigarette until after the interview.

"Thanks," said Peter.

They were eating bagels and cream cheese. Peter couldn't eat anything. He was hungry, but he couldn't eat anything. He drank four cups of coffee and afterward was light-headed and slightly nauseous.

Greg was reading the newspaper.

"Can I have the funny papers?" said Peter. Greg slid the cartoon page out of the newspaper and gave it to him. Peter gulped coffee and read *The Far Side* first, then *Calvin and Hobbes*, then started working his way through the other ones that are never, ever actually funny, like *Hägar the Horrible*.

"So," said Megan. "Are you going to start looking for a place soon?"

"Megan?" said Greg.

"Well, yeah," said Peter. "I'll be out of here pretty soon."

Greg read the newspaper, ate his bagel and began to fiercely ignore their conversation.

"I figure maybe a couple weeks," said Peter. "Depends on when I get my first paycheck and stuff like that. Really soon though."

"Where are you thinking of living?"

"Well, OK, this one time? I was driving by this storage place. You know, where they have all these storage lockers? I once helped a friend of mine move his shit out of one of those things. Some of them are pretty big inside. His was temperature controlled too, so it was even warm in there. You know what the rent for those things is? It's like fifty bucks a month. And I thought, fuck, man, I could just rent one of those and live in it. Just put a mattress in it or something, a thermal sleeping bag, maybe get one of those electric camping lanterns. There you go. Super-cheap place to stay."

"What about taking showers?" said Megan.

"Thought of that. I'd take showers in the locker room at the rec center. Just like once or twice a week. I read this thing about how modern Americans take way too many showers anyway. It kills the good bacteria. You don't really need to shower more than once a week."

Greg folded his newspaper.

"You're not going to live in a storage locker," he said.

"Why the fuck not?" said Peter.

After breakfast Greg drove him to the campus. Greg was thirty years old. He worked in a chemistry lab at MIT where he did something that involved testing chemicals on rats. Their sister, Lindsay, was twenty-five. She was in her first year of law school. Peter was twenty-six, and he was nothing.

"Go in there and ask, they'll tell you where it is."

"OK," said Peter. The car door was open and Peter was halfway out of it. The car was making a soft, mildly irritating bong-bong-bong sound because the door was open.

"I'm going home after I finish in the lab," said Greg. "If you wait around till then I can give you a ride back, but it'll be a while. I don't know how long you'll be. You can walk around and explore the campus if you want. Or you can go to Cambridge. There are bookstores and coffee shops, you can kill a day there. Or you could come by my office before noon, we can get lunch. Or you could just walk home, it's not that far."

Peter started to freak out a little. Greg was giving him too many options. Too many choices to make. When Peter started to get freaked out, when he started to feel like a loosely put-together thing unraveling uncontrollably in every direction, he tried to use a trick they'd taught him in therapy: try to boil everything down to just one decision at a time. Just choose between one pair of options, then go on to the next one. Either this or that. Pick one. Next decision.

"I don't know," said Peter.

"Well, if I don't see you later I'll assume you went home. OK?"

That made things a little easier. Peter walked up to the building. It was early and not many people were on the campus yet. It was October. The weather was wet and bleak and made the grass look greener. It was a cold morning. It was ugly out. Or beautiful. Whatever. It wasn't either. He never thought of a day as beautiful or ugly. He knew what beautiful and ugly days were supposed to look like, but he didn't really care about the weather.

He could see a clock on another building. We should buy a watch, he thought. He had about five minutes. He lit a cigarette and realized that it might take a while to find the place he was supposed to find—that he might not be able to just walk in and instantly be there. So if we smoke this cigarette, we might be late for the interview.

Decision: He put out the cigarette even though he'd only just lit it, and went inside. Decision made. He had analyzed the situation, weighed the options, and made a decision, like an adult.

"Can you please tell me where the marine biology lab is please?"

Peter was embarrassed by how small and weak his voice sounded. He was trying to be polite. The girl behind the desk didn't hear him.

"I'm sorry?"

She craned her neck and slightly tilted the flap of her ear toward him with her finger. She was a sweet-looking pudgy girl. She was drinking coffee, or some kind of hot drink in a paper cup that steamed up her glasses. Maybe it was tea.

"Can you please tell me where the marine biology lab is?"

"Which one?"

"Um. I don't know. The one where they do stuff with, um, squid?"

"Do stuff with squid?"

"You know, do like, experiments? Study them?"

She looked at something on her desk, somehow figured out what he was talking about, gave him directions. His shoes were wet and they squeaked on the hard vinyl floor. The halls were dark and he didn't see anyone else in the building. He found the right room eventually. He didn't know what time it was when he knocked on the door. He was probably late. Nobody answered. He opened it and stuck his head inside.

"Hello?"

He was afraid of raising his voice too much.

The marine biology lab was all tile, plastic, stainless steel surfaces, garishly bright, and smelled like brine and fish. The best thing Peter had in his bag of experience to compare it to was a seafood grocery store. It smelled more nautical than the sea itself. The sea-ness of the smell of the sea was compacted here, concentrated. The smell was sickeningly thick.

Peter hadn't bothered to dress up for the interview or anything. He figured they wouldn't expect somebody applying for a job that was basically just driving a truck to wear a suit and tie to an interview. He'd look silly if he did. Plus he didn't have any nice clothes anyway. Peter was wearing jeans, a button-down borrowed from his brother, and a smoky-smelling Goodwill denim jacket. It turned out he wasn't under- or overdressed. The scientists in the lab wore jeans and T-shirts. Peter was met by a woman in her late twenties, not much older than Peter. She shook his hand. She was wearing a fleece pullover. She had blunt features and blonde hair she wore in one thick braid behind her head. She looked like a Viking woman. She looked like Hägar the Horrible's wife.

"Peter Cast?" she said.

"Yeah, hi."

"Emma. Nice to meet you."

She had a friendly, slightly husky, lower-register voice. Something about her made Peter wonder if she was a lesbian. The phrase "lesbian Viking" popped up in his mind and stayed there.

"You're Greg Cast's brother, right?"

Not many people were in the room, just four or five what looked like grad students sitting around looking at paperwork. Two of them were huddled over an old computer with a green-on-amber screen display.

"So you're ready to start getting up wicked early in the morning?"

"If that's what I gotta do," said Peter, trying to sound game, the kind of guy who liked getting up at three in the morning to drive a truck. He wasn't really ready to start doing anything.

She led him to a big cylindrical tank with an open lid. The lip of the tank came up to their chests. Its sides were thick, pale green metal. The insides were smooth wet ceramic. An air filtration pump thing beside it made a low white humming noise. It was full of squid. They varied in size—some were the size of a hand span, the biggest ones looked about ten inches, maybe a foot long. The squid aimlessly darted around inside the tank. Their head flaps undulated, they

16

languidly propelled themselves through the water with their pumping tentacles like slow-motion darts. It was at once fascinating, beautiful and ridiculous to see how gracefully they moved, until they bumped their stupid heads into the sides of the tank. Some of them swam around a lot, some of them just floated. They looked bored.

Emma unhooked a long mesh net from a holder on the wall and dipped it in the tank. She swirled it around slowly, causing the squid to come alive with agitation, shooting every which way, bouncing off the walls, making the water wobble and churn.

Emma snagged a couple of squid in the net and brought them out of the water. The heavily sagging net drooled water back into the tank. The squid hung limp and slimy in the net, weakly writhing their tentacles, trying to move their poor boneless bodies, totally out of their element. Emma dragged her hand in the tank to wet it, reached into the net and grabbed one of them. Just like that. She held it by its tubular, torpedo-shaped head. She dropped the net back in the tank. The squid's slick, shiny body was red and gold, like an apple, flecked with metallic sparkles. The thing wiggled its tentacles, dangling feebly in her hand. Its flat, weird yellow eyes glistened dimly, like silver foil, like dirty sequins. It was disgusting and a little terrifying. The smell was overpoweringly putrid, almost gagging.

"These are the guys we're after," said Emma. "Want to hold it?"

Peter hoped this wasn't some kind of test. Because no fucking way was he going to touch the squid. If that was the case he'd just find some other job, one that didn't involve squid-touching.

Emma dropped the squid back in the tank. They walked around the lab while she explained the experiments they were running on the squid. Some of the squid were separated in smaller tanks. Peter listened to her talk and nodded comprehendingly and didn't understand any of what she was saying.

She showed him the truck. It was behind the building, through a back door, parked at the bottom of a delivery ramp. It was an F-450 with a huge rectangular metal tank in the bed. There was an aluminum ladder bolted to the side of the truck bed, leading up to the rim of the tank. Peter climbed the ladder and looked inside. It was about half full of salt water.

"We have to change the water once in a while. It's not ideal, but it's what we've got right now. Basically, we need as many squid as we can get."

She explained the job to him. Drive to New Bedford, get there around six, when the fishermen bring in the first catch. Get the squid. Bring them back. There were maps, directions, instructions. She gave him the keys to the truck and watched him drive it around the parking lot a few turns to make sure he could maneuver the vehicle.

"A lot of the squid are going to die," said Emma. "They go into shock, and they're dead by the time you make it back from New Bedford. So you gotta get the squid back as soon as you can. The dead ones are no good. We can only experiment on live squid. We pay you for every live squid you bring back."

"So—you want me to speed?"

"No," said Emma. "Definitely not. We're not asking you to do anything illegal. I'm just saying, the longer you spend on the road, the more squid are going to die on your way back. We pay by the living squid. Interpret that however you want."

The phrase "by the living squid" finally replaced "lesbian Viking" in Peter's head. Of course she was saying, in a winking way, in a, I'm not actually saying this but yes I am saying this kind of way: yeah, speed.

"You're hired," she said, and gave him a tight handshake that made Peter self-conscious about his own feeble handshake. He thought of the limp, slimy squid in her hand. She sent him to accounts and payroll to sign tax forms and other formal documents. For technical reasons he had to be signed on as a contractor. To make the paperwork simpler or something. No benefits. So he pocketed the keys, followed her directions across the campus to payroll, got lost a couple times, asked directions, found it, signed a bunch of stuff, went outside, chose a marble staircase to sit at the top of that overlooked one of the main lawn quad whatever areas of the campus and smoked three cigarettes in a row, lighting the second off the first and the third off the second while watching the campus come to life, the students shuffling across the damp grass in their coats and hats with cups of coffee and satchels and backpacks, on their way to their first classes presumably, or labs or wherever they were going. These kids were in their late teens and early twenties. Later they would probably go on to work on projects like satellites with giant lasers that kill people from outer space, and make a lot of money. While Peter, who was six, seven years older than they were, would continue being broke and desperate. What he felt toward these kids walking across the grass while he sat on the steps smoking wasn't quite hate or resentment. There was too much self-loathing mixed into his feelings for that. It requires more self-respect to hate and resent, it takes enough self-confidence to believe that they've been blessed and you've been gypped by a capricious universe. No, Peter mostly blamed himself. He'd started the game with two hundred dollars same as anyone else, but had bungled it in bad moves and reckless investments. How do other people do it? How do other people navigate the world so easily, as if they already know the way, and never feel unmoored, lost, frantic, like their compasses have been fucked up by too much holding a magnet under them to watch the needle spin and spin, searching for a north that seems to be everywhere at once?

"Sometimes I think about just not talking for a while," Peter said to Greg at lunch. Greg took him to lunch to celebrate his getting a job. Peter thanked him effusively, even though it wasn't really an unusual thing for Greg to buy him lunch, because Peter had no money. They were eating at a nice-ish place in Cambridge. Their table had a tablecloth and a flower arrangement on it. Greg ordered a calamari appetizer as a joke. The breaded calamari rings were tough to chew. They didn't really taste like anything. The sauce they came with was good, but the calamari itself tasted like nothing. "I mean, like, not talk for a long time. Like six months or a year or something. I heard that Buckminster Fuller did that. He just decided not to talk for like a year."

"Why would you do that?" said Greg. "What good would that do?"

"Just to be silent," said Peter. Peter was slightly self-conscious about sitting in this restaurant, being ragged and dirty looking and reeking of smoke. The undersides of his cuticles were perpetually dirty. At some point in his life he'd acquired yellowish-gray rims of filth around his fingernails that never went away no matter how much he washed his hands. "You know, to figure shit out in my head until I'm ready to talk again."

"If you can't figure shit out talking, why do you think you'd be able to figure it out not talking? What have you got to figure out anyway?"

"What I'm going to do with my life."

"Plus it would be difficult logistically."

"What do you mean?"

"I mean, OK, say you walk into a store, you need to buy something. How do you communicate with the guy at the counter?"

"I'd carry a notepad and a pen around with me everywhere."

"If you're not talking for some Zen, self-searching reason, if you're writing everything down and showing people the notebook, wouldn't that mean you'd actually be spending way more effort just to communicate with people? What's so Zen about that? It's ridiculous.

You're just inconveniencing everybody else for no reason."

Peter felt cornered. He had ordered a cup of coffee with his club sandwich. He'd only eaten half the sandwich, and that was a labor, but had asked the waitress for three coffee refills. The cup was pretty small. With each refill he ripped open a sugar packet and dumped a fresh silken thread of sugar into the coffee, then separated the flaps of the sugar packet along the glued seams, flattened it and tore it into strips, which he wadded into tiny balls with his fingers. When he ran out of sugar packets he went to work on the flower arrangement, fastidiously denuding the daisies of their petals and wadding those into tiny balls too.

"Um," said Peter. "I guess so. I mean, you know. I don't, um. Shit. I don't know."

"It sounds like you haven't really thought this through."

Half the daisies in the glass flute of water were now naked, sad-looking yellow circles on sickly thin stems. A pile of weird debris had accumulated on the tablecloth next to Peter's plate, wadded-up bits of pink sugar-packet paper and daisy petals.

"Quit fucking with their flowers."

"Sorry."

Peter's hands shot back from the half-stripped flower arrangement. He put his hands in his lap like a reprimanded child. Then he started unwadding the tiny balls he'd made.

"I don't think I'm gonna do it anyway. The not-talking thing, I mean. Not right now anyway."

Greg smiled deftly and nodded, like a therapist being nicely encouraging, only Greg did it with condescending irony.

"I think that's a good plan."

Peter did manage to sleep a little that night. Emma had said it was a bit over an hour's drive from Cambridge to New Bedford, plan for an hour and a half, and he was supposed to get there before six in the morning. Plus the walk to campus took about twenty minutes. Peter didn't see why he couldn't just park the truck at Greg's house, but he hadn't thought to ask about it that morning. Maybe it had something to do with rules about campus vehicles off school property or something. We should ask about that. So that means we should get up at about three thirty to be on the safe side. Especially since it's our first day and we should leave some slack time in case we fuck something up. Eight hours counting backward from that means we should go to bed at seven thirty.

It didn't feel like it had been dark out for long when Peter went to bed. He lay there for four, five hours, not sleeping. Megan was watching TV upstairs, and the living room where the TV was was directly above the futon in the basement. The volume wasn't loud but he could almost hear what was happening on the TV. But he must have fallen asleep eventually, because the skull-grinding electric throb of the alarm-clock buzzer dragged him out of a nightmare he was having about a guy with his arms and legs cut off who was stuck inside a refrigerator shitting blood into a hole in the bottom of it. He opened his eyes and didn't know who he was or where he was. He saw the red digital numbers 3:30 glowing somewhere in the darkness outside of his body and didn't know what they meant. As he slowly recalled who he was, what was going on, and what he now had to do, he realized that he would probably never get used to this.

He doused himself with cold water and struggled with Megan's fancy, complicated coffeemaker, muttering "Fuck" over and over as he fiddled with levers and buttons. At last he was able to make it make coffee, but it tasted weird. He'd probably done something wrong. He poured it into one of their plastic travel-mug things and left for campus in the utter dark. The streets were empty, and as silent as the streets of a semiurban place like Somerville get. The sidewalks and buildings were dull orange from the streetlights. It was cold. Peter turned up the collar of his denim jacket and hugged it to himself, shivering. He walked with hunched shoulders and a quick, short, screw-tight gait, slurping the weird-tasting coffee and smoking cigarettes in contiguous succession while he walked, concentrating on his feet. He had a headache that came at him in fuzzy broken radio waves of pain and his thoughts were like a screeching horde of freaked-out bats flapping around frantically, going nowhere. A part of him still worried constantly about whether he would ever feel that life was still worth living if he could never get drunk or high again. He hoped there would come a time when he had no desire to get fucked up, and wouldn't even think about it, and would be totally fine with being sober, but he doubted it would ever happen. It was like being offered the choice between a death sentence and life in prison. It's like, I'll choose life, I guess.

He found the truck parked by the delivery ramp by the back door to the marine biology lab. He climbed up into the truck. It was battered and clunky, everything in it rusty, oily smelling, puffy shreds of foam poking out of cuts in the bench seat, sticky hand-grime coating the steering wheel. He started the engine, switched the heater on full-blast, turned on the radio. He unfolded the sheet of yellow notepaper on which he'd written the directions to the commercial fishing docks, smoothed it out on the dashboard. As he drove the truck, he could both hear and feel the great quantity of salt water sloshing around in the tank in the back of it. If he stopped too abruptly at a light he felt the water heave against the front of the tank, and heard it splash over the sides. He wondered why there wasn't a lid on it or something. It was a particular feeling of strange calm, driving a giant truck around in the middle of the night, completely alone— not sadness or loneliness, but a warmer feeling, a tingling-bellied melancholy. For the most part he found his way, cautiously easing the enormous vehicle into the turns. He was pathfinding, trying to memorize the route. There was one hard-to-find turn that he fucked up and had to double back to take. He lost five or ten minutes, but learned that part of the route much better. Once he'd climbed onto the highway he was fine. He sat back in the seat and breathed easier, turned up the radio and twisted the dial, the green needle scrolling back and forth along the FM band, looking for anything halfway decent. The airwaves were clogged with Alanis Morissette, Bush, Live, Collective Soul, fucking *Moby*. Comfortably south of Boston the highway began to cut through areas less and less urban, and more fields and trees appeared to his sides as the landscape opened up. He passed other cars from time to time, but mostly it was just trucks out on the highway, twinkling juggernauts of roaring engines and sighing gaskets. The last long stretch of the drive was on a smaller highway, through rural country that surprised Peter. He was surprised by the bucolic pleasantness of this part of Massachusetts—being a Mid-westerner, Peter thought of the whole Northeast as a place paved over from one massive metropolitan area to the next, cities and suburbs connected by stark gray spiderwebs of industry. The sky was no longer black, still dark but gradually lightening. He could make out cows standing in clusters in green and brown fields off to the sides of the road. Like a lot of things in New England, Peter was realizing, the cows were more ideal, more picturesque than they were in other parts of the country. Back home in Illinois the cows were all nondescript dull brown ones—but these cows were the classic black-and-white kind, cartoon cows, the kind of cow a child would draw if you asked a child to draw a cow. They looked like what cows are supposed to look like. Peter appreciated that. He liked clouds that were fluffy, fire engines that were red, and cows that were spotted black and white.

Soon the sky had brightened into morning light, though because it was overcast the dawn was a more gradient process than usual. He could smell the sea. As he got closer to the shore, the forests and farmland fell away into more developed areas, houses, concrete. This looked more like what he expected of the East—a gray-and-brown place, metal and brick, drifts of mushy litter packed against the corners of the concrete barriers along the roadsides. The clouds looked slightly yellowish green, tortoise colored. He made it through New Bedford: an old town, all that stately New England stodginess, all the little architectural filigrees corroded by time and weather, more recently overlaid with colorless industry, which had also already gone largely to rust. And there was the sea.

He drove through the open gates of a chain-link fence and onto a wide asphalt blacktop by the docks. Rigging clinked against mast poles, the docks creaked, waves softly slapped against the seawall. The sky was cluttered with seagulls. The water was choppy and the green of oxidized copper, the line of the horizon between ocean and sky an indistinct gray smear. It was barely daybreak, and there were fishing boats anchored at the docks, already come in from their first catch, and more in the harbor that looked to be on their way in. Peter parked the truck as close to the docks as he could, killed the engine and stepped from the truck cab's soporific cocoon of artificial warmth into the sharply pointed cold of the morning, made colder by the sea. Here again was that overpoweringly putrid smell of fish and brine.

He walked timidly out onto the dock with his hands crammed in his jacket pockets. The boat lurched in the water. The boat was a huge, complicated piece of machinery, rigging, nets, enormous gears for releasing and dragging up the net. Everything on it was wet and filthy. Fish everywhere, slapping their bodies, dying on the embossed sheet-metal deck. Machinery creaked, squealed, hummed. Peter could hear the fishermen working on the boat, their boots clanging on the deck, their voices shouting over the din of machines. He was nervous about approaching them. He didn't quite know what to say, and was afraid they would make fun of him.

The dock swayed very slightly. In the boat, fishermen in caps and bright yellow foul-weather gear were sorting through fish on conveyor belts. On the conveyor belts and here and there all over the deck, fish flopped around, their mouths and gills gaping, their blank, disklike eyes seemingly looking at nothing. Peter found it a little amazing how long fish survive out of water. They take so long to die.

"Hey," Peter called down to the fishermen on the boat from where

23

he stood on the dock. They hadn't heard him. "Uh—hey? Um—?"

One of the men looked up at him. The others kept picking through the fish with their work gloves. There were rows of big blue plastic barrels, the size of garbage cans, full of fish, lined up on the deck alongside the conveyor belts. The men tossed some of the fish into the barrels, some back into the sea, and let some move past them on the conveyor belt and fall into a hole that emptied somewhere inside the hull of the ship. There seemed to be a system.

"Good morning," said the fisherman who had looked up at him.

"Um," said Peter, "I'm from the biology lab at MIT? Can we have your squid?"

This last sentence felt strange in Peter's mouth, but the fisherman was unfazed. Peter imagined fishermen as having big, bushy beards. A couple of the men on the boat did in fact have beards, but not this one. He did have a sharp New England accent, though. At least he had that.

They gave him their squid. Peter followed the fishermen's lead during the process of getting the squid. They had done this before and were used to people from MIT coming for their bycatch.

"Where's Emma?" said the man who'd spoken to him.

"I'm her new squid man," said Peter, and imagined a superhero named Squidman.

They invited Peter onboard. On the deck of the swaying anchored boat he stepped gingerly amid the dying fish, trying not to squish them. They were gross, alive, frightening. The fishermen largely ignored him, but Peter still felt inadequate and embarrassed among them. These were men who had real jobs, *really* real jobs, who got up before dawn and worked with their hands and knew how to do things. These were men who knew how to operate complicated machines, who knew how to do practical, useful things, who knew how to catch fish. There were fish out there in the ocean, and these guys got in their boat and went out there and got them and brought them back. Just like that. These were men who were not easily frightened, not easily overwhelmed. Some of the fishermen looked younger than Peter, and Peter was ashamed that he was as old as he was and didn't really know how to do anything useful.

Soon the wire handle of a heavy plastic bucket full of squid was sinking painfully into the flesh of his hooked fingers. The squid writhed and squirmed in the bucket. Their tentacles stretched, thrashed, suckers sticking to the sides of the bucket. It was like holding a bucket full of aliens. The smell was pointedly sickening. Peter tried to breathe through his mouth. Sometimes when you see animals that are hurt or trapped, you wonder what they're feeling. You wonder if they're in pain, if they're afraid. Peter found that it wasn't easy to do that with squid. It was hard to anthropomorphize them, to project human emotions onto them. They were just too scary, too weird looking.

Peter dumped the squid into the tank on the truck and went back for another bucket, and so on, feeling less uncomfortable with the task with each bucketful. He did the same with a few other fishing boats that were docked there that morning, and began to feel like an old hand. It was fascinating to watch these animals that were so helpless and awkward when slopped together in a bucket instantly come alive when he dumped them in the water, suddenly moving with otherworldly gracile ease. He got back in the truck and began the task of following the directions in reverse, which was harder, especially in New Bedford, a town he had even less familiarity with than Cambridge—as in, none—plus he'd driven in in the dark. But he felt good now. He was at work. The fishermen had understood, and helped him, and given him their squid. He turned the radio up and found a station that played a stretch of non-suck songs, and was back on the highway, looking at the trees and black-and-white cows standing along the fences.

On the fairly long and mindless drive Peter's mind fell into patterns of thinking about Gina, the way iron filings filter themselves into magnetically predictable patterns on a vibrating surface. Last fall and winter, before things completely fell apart, Peter and Gina had been living together in a squalid apartment in a fairly sketchy area of Humboldt Park. He was working twenty, thirty hours a week at a music store in Logan Square, and Gina was going to school part-time at UIC and waitressing at a steakhouse. There was this one time, though, when it was almost the end of the fall semester for her, and Gina had invited over a friend of hers from school and his girl-friend. Peter couldn't remember either of their names now. They'd only met that one time. They were nice people. Peter couldn't really remember anything about them. It was a Saturday afternoon in a Chicago December, which means it was brutally cold with an arctic windchill. The weather had been flirting with the idea of snowing all day. They had all holed up in Peter and Gina's apartment, smoking weed and drinking and playing Monopoly. Their apartment was on the second floor of a half-dilapidated wooden house that had been divided into dubiously up-to-code apartments. It was cluttered with desiccated houseplants with dust-coated leaves that the previous tenant had left, and poorly insulated and poorly heated, such that they spent that winter always draped in blankets and wearing hats inside, and had two space heaters going at once, cheap ones from the hardware store, metal boxes with grates of glowing orange filaments that hummed and made clicking and clinking noises, as if broken parts were rattling around loose inside them. And still it was fucking freezing in the apartment. Peter had landed on a trick that seemed like a good idea at first, which was to boil water. He'd been boiling a pot of water on the stove for mac and cheese, and noticed that the steam raised the temperature of the room. So he would keep a soup pot full of water boiling on the electric stove all afternoon and night until they went to sleep, filling the apartment with hot moisture, fogging it up like a bathhouse. It was strangely pleasant to breathe the warm, humid air; it felt good in the lungs and on the skin. It was probably good for all those half-dead houseplants too. One night both Peter and Gina passed out dead drunk—not an uncommon occurrence that winter—and forgot to turn the stove top off. When they woke up the next day, the pot was ruined, the red coil of the stove eye having burned away all the water and then gone to work on the pot itself, causing the Teflon coating to crackle and peel in curdled flakes, and turning the outside of the black pot a brassy, reddish-brown color. The insides of the kitchen windows were glazed with sheets of ice, thick as fingers.

They had been so much in love, remembering it made Peter almost physically sick with regret. Peter would always remember this one particular time, when he and Gina had first gotten together, when they were having sex, and they had looked into each other's eyes and said, "I love you," which they had just started saying to each other—there was something about that one time, it was hard to explain. It was hard to explain because it was such a common-place-sounding thing when you're describing it, something predictable, that anyone could experience, that anyone could say. That's one of the irritating tragedies about being a person these days, is that love is a clichéd emotion, sadly, something used to sell stuff, and it's hard to talk about it earnestly without sounding like somebody on daytime TV. But this feeling had happened to Peter exactly once in his life, then. It was a moment that, Peter felt, no matter if he and Gina stayed in love or not later on, would tie them together forever. He knew he might not have a moment like that ever again with anyone. In retrospect he was glad that it had happened to him at least once. But by the time the thing with her friends from UIC happened, Peter had lost all agency in their relationship. At first it had felt like they had been moving forward, together, at the same time, but by then, Gina was leading and Peter tottering along behind her every step of the way. She decided when they would have sex and how, she decided what they ate, what they were going to do, what they were going to watch on TV. Sometimes she even walked a pace ahead of him on the street when they were out together. Peter had relinquished any control, and was now helpless, dependent, a flaccid ancillary of capitulation to her. She removed the need for him to make decisions, she protected him, made him feel loved, safe, taken care of. And she had slid into nagginess, was always castigating him for something, sniping at his every fault, from his pitiful inability to ask his boss at the music store for more hours to what shirt he would wear, and whether or not he would button the collar. Once, when they were driving to a party, trying to follow some complicated, barely sensical directions a stoned friend had given them, Peter, who was at the wheel, had accidentally called Gina "mom." But Peter still loved her, even now. Since they broke up she had quit drinking on her own. He saw her the last time he was in Chicago, a few months ago, during the couple of days he had free between rehab and the halfway house. They had lunch together. The least intimate meal of the day. She had been impenetrably distant and polite. As if they were acquaintances. Gina hadn't seemed happy or unhappy. She was just flat. Flat as the green line of a dead person's heart monitor on a hospital show on TV. She wasn't the same person anymore. It was totally *Invasion of the Body Snatchers*, when the aliens replace someone you love with an eerily disaffected doppelgänger, a person who looks exactly like the person you love but who you know just, just isn't.

The people at the marine biology lab were a little disappointed with him when Peter made it back to Cambridge. Just a little, which was OK. Peter was used to people being disappointed with him. It turned out a lot of his squid had died on the way back. He hadn't realized how quickly they could die when they were in shock. Peter watched as the lesbian Viking marine biologist fished around in the tank for the squid with a long net. Standing on the ladder on the side of the truck, swishing the long, skinny net in the tank full of squid, she reminded him of one of those guys in Italy with the striped shirts and the hats who do the thing in the boats with the long poles. One net full at a time, Emma raised the squid dripping and squirming

27

from the water and carefully dumped them out into five-gallon plastic buckets that one of the grad students who worked in the lab held out for her. They counted the squid as they collected them. They were paying him five bucks a squid. He'd picked up almost forty squid at the docks that morning, but by the time he got back, apparently only eighteen of them were still alive enough to pay for. The ninety-dollar take that day was the first money he'd made since he got fired from the record store, almost a year ago, when he was living with Gina in Chicago. Emma told him to get the dead squid out of the tank and put them in these special buckets they used to throw away dead animals. As Peter stood at the top of the ladder in the cold, fishing with the net for dead squid, these sad-looking, bloated lumps of jellied fat, he wondered if he couldn't double-team the lab and make some money on the side by taking the dead ones to a Chinese restaurant or something. He didn't see why not. Maybe they wanted live ones too, like how you're supposed to cook lobsters alive. Squid are dead when you eat them, right? A dead squid's a dead squid. Maybe he could sell them to the restaurant where he ate calamari with Greg. He counted twenty dead squid. That meant his haul was overall more dead than alive. If he'd made it back with all the squid alive, he would have made almost two hundred dollars.

Peter finished putting the dead ones in the special buckets. Then it was like, well, guess it's time to go now. He walked through the building toward the front entrance, the way he'd come in the day before, and was in the sort of lobby area when he remembered that he'd wanted to ask Emma if it was OK to park the squid truck at Greg's house, so he didn't have to get up even earlier than crazy early to walk to campus and get the truck. He stopped in the middle of the floor of the lobby area and looked at the door. He'd heard once that there was a phrase in French, because they have a lot of phrases for those kinds of weird feelings that are hard to describe but are incredibly specific, for that weird feeling you get when you realize you just forgot to say something you'd meant to say to somebody before you left, and at the moment you realize this, you're not so far away from the place you just left that there's no point in going back now, but you *are* far enough away that if you did go back and say it, it would be kind of weird and awkward. Peter stood there for a moment, then turned around and started walking back to the lab, then thought, whatever, fuck it, we'll just try to remember to ask her about that tomorrow, and turned around again and started walking back toward the front door of the building. But then he had the thought that,

28

knowing him, he would probably also forget to ask tomorrow, and he should probably just ask now because he was already fucking here and it was fresh on his mind, so he turned around again and again stalled out when his increasing anxiety about facing the awkwardness of going back to the lab dragged him to a halt. Maybe we can write a note to ourselves on our hand, he thought, to remind us to ask Emma about the truck. Let's write it in permanent fucking marker, like a Sharpie, and if we write it today, then it'll probably still be there tomorrow, and even if it washes off a little then the mark will still be there, which will be enough to remind us. So he turned back around.

"Are you OK?" said the girl at the front desk who'd given him directions yesterday. "Can I help you?"

Peter realized that to an outside observer, such as the girl at the desk, he'd just been slowly staggering back and forth in the lobby of the building looking confused.

"Um." He walked up to the desk. The girl was drinking a hot liquid again that might have been coffee or tea. It steamed up her glasses. She was a little on the heavy side, but she was very sweet looking and had bright, smooth skin and Peter began to think she was kind of cute. Her glasses were ugly, though, and took away from her face. He tried to imagine what she would look like if she wasn't wearing the glasses. Peter hated it when he caught himself thinking things like this, because they made him feel like an asshole. He couldn't help it, they just popped in there. When Gina broke up with him, a period of time began that started with a time of utter darkness, during which he got fired from the music store and evicted from the apartment and crashed his car, then went to rehab, and then the halfway house, and now this, and during that whole period of his life, that kind of thing—girls, love, maybe even sex, that stuff—had been so far out of the question that there was no point in even thinking about it at all, except for small things he almost couldn't help, like looking at Robin's breasts during his exit interview.

"You look like you're looking for something," said the girl at the desk. She smiled bigly at him in a way that suggested she might want to talk to him in a friendly, non-I'm-at-work way.

"Are you drinking coffee or tea?"

She gave him a look that wasn't an are-you-crazy look, just a low-grade jitter of the needle on her what-the-fuck-o-meter.

"That's why I was trying to decide back there. I mean what, not why. When I was walking back and forth."

29

"What?"

Peter wondered if he was trying to flirt with her. If so, that coffee/tea thing was a train wreck of an opening line.

He remembered that he'd wanted to write a note on his hand with a permanent marker.

"I mean, hey, uh. Can I borrow a pen?"

She offered him the gnawed-on Bic that was in her hand.

"Actually, do you have like a, a permanent marker, like a Sharpie or something?"

She glanced at a mug on the desk that was Garfield's head and full of pens. She found a black Sharpie in it and gave it to him. Peter uncapped the marker and thought about sniffing glue when he was really young. He held the wet, sweetly stinky point of the marker poised above his palm, but had totally forgotten what he was supposed to write on it. He stood there a while trying to remember, couldn't, and just pretended to write something on his hand while worrying about how obviously fake the gesture was, gave her back the marker, and slowly wandered out the door like a zombie looking for brains. He figured that from now on he should probably just leave out the back door to the parking lot to avoid her.

So Peter went home and spent most of the day drinking coffee and watching TV and making the air in the house crackle with uncomfortable tension between him and Megan, who sat at the kitchen table sorting through baby shower presents, such as baby clothes and one of those things with the big, brightly colored beads on it that you can push around on the metal things.

In the afternoon Megan went upstairs to take a nap, and when she'd been up there long enough to assume she was asleep, Peter silently poured himself a generous swallow of vodka from Greg's liquor cabinet, and as soon as it was in him Peter instantly felt calmer and happier than he had in a year.

The next morning he was surer on his feet with the fishermen. Peter had slept well that night. He still didn't like getting up at three thirty in the morning, but he felt less like death warmed over, and made the drive to New Bedford in significantly less time than the day before. Then it was down to the docks, say hello to the yellow-jacketed soaking men in the boats, the same situation and same faces, dump the squid in the truck and he was off, hauling fucking ass down those adorable little New England highways to get the squid to the lab alive. His foot kept the pedal planted to the floor, the engine roared and all those trees and fences and black-and-white cows wailed past him like he was playing Tempest and flying through space, hell yeah, warp speed, motherfucker, we are on a *mission*.

And when he got back to the lab, the scientists were pleased. Emma the blunt-faced Scandinavian counted thirty-two, we repeat *thirty-two* living squid out of the fifty or so he'd brought back. That meant a hundred and sixty bucks in his pocket. That could pay for at least two months' rent in a storage locker. At this rate maybe it wouldn't be so long after all till he could move out of Greg and Megan's basement. He was getting good at this. He cheerfully fished the dead squid out of the tank, stuffed them himself into the special dead animal buckets, no longer icked out by it all, and before leaving he even remembered to ask Emma if he could park the squid truck at Greg's house so he didn't have to get up so early. She said no, because of some rule about school-owned vehicles being parked off campus property. OK, whatever. At least he asked.

In the hallway he took a pull of vodka from the water bottle full of vodka and 7UP he'd brought with him, to give him the courage he needed to talk to the girl at the front desk in the lobby.

He smiled at her when he was in the lobby. She smiled back.

"Hi, weirdo," she said. Peter figured there was a high probability she was flirting with him.

"What do you mean, weirdo?"

"You act weird. So what did you write on your hand yesterday?"

"Nothing. I just pretended to write on my hand."

"I know. I could tell."

He explained to her about the squid truck, told her about the job. He made her laugh. There is no better feeling in the world than making someone laugh. Her name was Amy. She thought the whole situation was kind of funny. She wasn't wearing those ugly glasses today, and she really was pretty cute. She was a senior at MIT. Working the desk in this building was her work-study job. It was ridiculously easy, she said. All she had to do was just sit here for four hours on weekday mornings. She mostly just did homework. She also said she was in "biochem." Peter asked her if she knew his brother, Greg. She blanked on him till he said, "Mr. Cast?" (Greg wasn't the kind of PhDickhead who wants everybody to call him "doctor.") Of course she knew him. First she seemed a little impressed that Greg was his brother, and then Peter thought he saw something behind her eyes wonder what Gregory Cast's brother was doing driving the squid truck, as if she expected the brother of a young professor at MIT to be making something of his life. But she seemed to find the fact that Peter was a loser kind of charming. Maybe it was refreshing to meet him, considering all the other guys she met around here were probably hyperambitious type-A types who didn't expect to be crashing in their brothers' basements and getting up at three thirty in the morning to drive a truck full of squid when they were twenty-six. That's what Peter told himself, though admittedly he was counting unhatched chickens. Then he surprised himself by throwing himself off a cliff and asking if she wanted to get a cup of coffee sometime.

"Or tea," he added. She laughed. That was clever. Peter had actually successfully said something that sounded cool and was flirty and kind of clever. She said yes. If she had said no, then Peter really would have had to start leaving the building through the back door. But she said yes. She said she was free tomorrow afternoon. With her logistical guidance, they arranged to meet at a coffee shop in Cambridge at three in the afternoon tomorrow. Peter left the building in a state of elation.

His days at this job would apparently be oddly structured: getting up insanely early in the morning, then a few hours of frenzied activity, then a long stretch of time between getting off work and letting exhaustion take him under in which he had nothing to do. Walking around and drinking the vodka and 7UP from his water bottle, he wandered the campus, he wandered the town, he wandered. He went back to Greg and Megan's house and stole more vodka when Megan wasn't looking. He took the whole bottle into the basement and, with his mind racing with energy, he spent the afternoon drinking by himself in the dark basement while pacing around in circles until he passed out on the futon.

When the alarm woke him up at three thirty Peter was beyond hungover. A hangover doesn't even adequately suggest what he was feeling. It was an evil black cloud. There should have been flies buzzing around his head. He tried to get out of bed and fell on the floor. In the bathroom his eyes were so heavy-lidded and bloodshot it looked as if he'd been punched in the face, twice. He got in the shower, even though he didn't have time for a shower, and took a shower anyway, his logic going something like, maybe if I take a shower, time will stand still and at the end of this shower it will still be now. He downed a glass of water and puked it out half a minute later. Hair of the dog, he thought, and twisted open another bottle of vodka, gulped down a few shots, and instantly felt a hell of a lot better. He dumped half the vodka in the bottle into his water bottle, filled up the rest with 7UP and he was off, feverishly smoking cigarettes and speedwalking through the dark, empty streets of Somerville and Cambridge, occasionally unscrewing the cap of his water bottle and taking a sip of his tepid vodka-7UP mixture, trying not to think about how late he was, there's the truck, keys, ignition, let's go.

The fishermen at the docks smelled something funny with him, maybe literally, though Peter figured the general ambient stench of the fish was enough to mask any alcohol on his breath. It was like the fishermen knew there was something too buoyant about him today, too gung-ho-let's-do-this. He wasn't his usual anxious, timid, exhausted self. His usual self? How would they even know? This was only his third day on the job.

There was the usual haul of forty, fifty squid in the bycatch buckets. Back in the truck now, vroom, vroom, tearing ass down the highways back to Cambridge as fast as humanly possible, making up for time, working every twitch of horsepower the clunky old truck had in it, doing eighty, ninety, edging up on a hundred miles an hour, which he could do because there were almost no other cars on the road yet, the sun coming up perceptibly later today as it was still quite dark, barely daybreak, though it was hard to tell because the sky was overcast again, a sheet of hammered iron with the newly risen sun a fuzzy white blot in it. And again on the drive back his mind careened back to Gina. Peter thought, in a swirly-headed half-hungover, half-drunk way, about the girl he was supposed to get coffee with later that day, in the afternoon, and figured that today he definitely should leave the building through the back, one, because of the state he was in, and two, because of some sort of like, groom not seeing the bride before the wedding type reason. He would have time to go home, go back to bed, catch a desperately needed chunk of beauty rest before his "coffee date" with Amy. This "coffee date" officially made Amy the first girl who had shown any interest in him at all since Gina dumped him. Amy wasn't as good-looking as Gina, and there was no way she was as good. He would have traded anything to be with Gina again, though of course he had nothing of any value to trade. He again remembered that time in the winter, in December, when those people, the couple, these friends of Gina's from school, were hanging out with them on a Saturday afternoon, celebrating the end of finals, or something. They played Monopoly on the floor, everybody in socks and hats and draped in blankets with the two space heaters roaring and clinking and water boiling on the stove, and still it was cold. Peter was the ship. Peter was always the ship, because when they were kids, Greg had always gotten to choose first because he was the oldest, and he always chose the top hat, because, duh, it was the coolest piece, and Lindsay had always gotten to choose next because she was a girl, and she always chose the dog for some reason, which left Peter as usual with the leftovers, and he always chose the ship because he thought it was the next-coolest piece after the top hat, and being the ship became a private tradition with him when he played Monopoly. They smoked a couple bowls and drank hot cider and rum, though they didn't have all that much rum left, and when that ran out they broke into the beer, and when they ran out of beer they sat for a while around the game board, having crapped out on the game and long ago forgotten whose turn it was, discussing who would brave the elements and death-march it the three long blocks down the street to the store to get more beer. The wind was rattling the sides of the house and the temperature hovered somewhere in the ballpark of zero. Peter volunteered. The guy, the friend of Gina's from school, offered to go with him, help him carry the beer back, but Peter waved him off, said, Don't worry, man, I got it. They pooled their cash and Peter crammed the ball of ones, fives, and tens into the pocket of his coat, which he squeezed on over a hoodie, a sweater, and a scarf. Outside, the streets had that desolate, moondust look that very, very cold days sometimes have, puddles fossilized opaque and white into the sidewalk cracks, the wind sifting powdery old snow in wispy waves across the road. He hadn't worn gloves, and he alternated the hand he was smoking with—when his right became numb he'd stuff it in a pocket and switch to the left, then go back to the right when the left was numb. Instead of going to the store to get more beer, he found himself ringing the bell at Dominick's place. Dominick lived on the next street over, halfway between their apartment and the store. Looking back on it, Peter supposed that one could call this building a "crack house," but Peter simply thought of it as Dominick's place. Then he was inside Dominick's place, stamping his boots, shaking off the cold, though it was cold inside the house too, colder than Peter and Gina's apartment. And then Peter was forking over to Dominick all the cash he had just been given.

And now a cow was standing in the road. Peter saw it, of course, and knew what it was. It was a cow, one of those picturesque black-and-white New England cows, and it was standing in the road, in the middle of the lane that Peter was currently driving in. It might have been that Peter was going so fast that he wouldn't have had time to stop anyway, but Peter didn't even brake. The sight of the cow just confused him. The few long fractions of seconds that passed between seeing the cow and hitting the cow with the squid truck were just like, hey, that's not supposed to be there. That cow is supposed to be over *there*, behind the fence, with the other cows.

The cow made a hideous noise that was a combination of mooing and being hit by a truck, rolled into the air and smashed the glass of the windshield. Peter was stomping on the brake and the accelerator at the same time, the truck was on its side now, and now, after maybe blacking out for a moment, Peter was heaving open the driver's side door, pushing it against gravity, realizing how drunk he was and wondering how badly he was hurt. His hands were shaking. He crawled out of the wreck as fastidiously as he could. He put a hand to the side of his head, which hurt, and his fingers came back red. It was almost unbearably painful to inhale breath, which maybe meant he had broken a rib or two against the seat belt, and one of his knees seemed to be so fucked up he could hardly walk—one leg of his jeans was dark red and he didn't even want to look at it. OK, so. What now?

He saw where the cow was lying in the road, and limped over in that direction. Several hundred gallons of salt water had splashed onto the road, along with a loose streak of diffusely strewn chunks of metal and the dust and crumbs of blue-green glass blasted scattershot across the asphalt. The cow was alive. It was lying on its side in a puddle of blood made thinner by the water. It was wet—its hide was sleek and glossy with blood and water. Blood trickled from its open mouth, and its chest rose and fell like bellows, the air rushing in and out of the mouth and nostrils. Its shiny black eyes were desperate and scared. All around them, draped bizarrely over the body of the cow and lying inert in useless, slimy piles of tentacles, were the squid. The squid, in perhaps a collective dying gesture, had all released their ink sacs, and had covered this whole scene with their ink. The water and the cow's blood and Peter's blood mixed with the oily, briny-smelling squid ink. The runny puddles of ink had rainbows swirling in them. It was about six in the morning.

Peter sat down on the shoulder of the road, and watched the cow dying and the squid dying.

A farmer, presumably, a man who at least looked like a farmer, who looked to be in his fifties maybe, in heavy rubber boots and a mackinaw, had hopped over the wooden fence by the roadside, the fence that separated what was supposed to be the car space from what was supposed to be the cow space. The glittering stardust of shattered glass crunched under his boots as he approached the scene. With his hands on his hips, he looked at the dying cow, and looked at the squid flopped pell-mell across the road, squirming their tentacles and squirting their ink into the blood and water. He went to Peter, and offered him a hand.

It had been dark in that crack house in Chicago, even darker for Peter because his eyes were still adjusting to the indoors. The only light on was in the kitchen, where he could see a couple of plump Hispanic girls sitting at the table, smoking and talking rapidly in Spanglish, and a bunch of thuggish-looking black dudes were sitting in the living room in their puffy, metallic-gloss coats. They were all drinking forties they kept in their laps and some of them were smoking. They paid no attention to Peter. Some of the guys Peter recognized and some he didn't. The couple of guys on the couch were playing Super Mario Bros. on a dusty, beat-up-looking NES, the original console, which you didn't see much anymore even then, passing the controller back and forth between them, switching turns when Mario died, which happened often because they sucked. Peter watched them play Nintendo while Dominick was counting the money, going into the kitchen, coming back with Peter's crack. The guys playing Super Mario were drunk and high and not putting much effort into it. The only sounds in the room were beer swishing around in bottles when somebody took a swig, the music on the game, and the silly *boing!-boing!-boing!* noises Mario made when he jumped. Soon Peter was also high and sitting on the couch, and thinking about how weird it would be if there was a loud *boing!* sound when a person jumped in real life. They were on one of the underground levels, with the "scary" Mario music, that goes *do-do-do-do-do-doot. . . . do-do-do-do-do-doot . . .* Peter held his lighter to the pipe and felt that hot, corrosive, acrid froth in his lungs and the beautiful feeling that went with it. In a way, smoking crack makes you feel like when you get the star of invincibility in Super Mario. Suddenly the music speeds up really fast and you're flashing with inner energy and anything that touches you dies. And then it wears off, and you're back to being normal Mario—the same as before, but now you feel less than you should be, or could be. Peter watched them playing the game: Mario kept sliding off the bricks and falling into chasms, getting killed by the plants that go up and down in the tubes, just running right the fuck into the turtles and mushrooms. Peter was getting irritated watching them play. It's like, dude, come *on*, it takes a pretty fucking remedial player to let Mario get killed by a fucking mushroom. When they finally exhausted all of Mario's lives and got a Game Over, Peter asked if he could play. They gave him the controller, and watched him sail through World 1-1, as he had done so many thousands of times since his childhood that the landscape of the first level was etched in his brain, in his soul, he probably could have literally done it with his eyes closed, going by sound and muscle memory alone, collecting every coin and bumping every secret box, getting every 1-up mushroom, fire flower and invincibility star to be got. When he came to the end of World 1-2, just to show off, he entered the Minus World. The guys on the couch were astounded. They had seriously never seen that shit before. "The fuck you doin', motherfucker?" said the guy next to him. "All walkin' through rocks and shit?" Peter glowed with pleasure, with pride. The Minus World is a glitch in the game at the end of World 1-2. At the end of the level—the very, very end, where the green tube is that you go into to leave the level—you can stand on top of the tube, crouch jump, move slightly to the right and moonwalk into this secret space, and it looks like you're gliding right through a solid brick wall and into the space where the three Warp Zone tubes are, and there's this hidden tube you can go down that takes you to . . . the Minus World. It takes you to World –1, World –2 and so on. The Minus Worlds are a bunch of fucked-up, unfinished or rejected levels that the programmers left floating around in the game, and some of them are almost, what, like, *psychedelic*. Mario swims through a water level of black water where all the tubes are neon pink, shooting fireballs at neon blue plants and yellow squid, and there are these big blank blue rectangles where there's simply nothing there, like a hole in the universe of Super Mario. It's as if Mario has traveled to the distant, frayed edges of space and time. He must look into the void. It's a little frightening. At some point in *this* world, the Plus World, the world outside, it had begun to snow, and snow in earnest, coming down in thick, heavy clumps of snowflakes so big they were almost snow*balls*. The snow was piling up in the corners of the windows, and the house acquired that still, densely muffled acoustic quality a house gets when it's covered in snow. The guys on the couch had become enrapt in watching Peter play the game, and Peter himself was in a shamanlike trance, his mind had been sucked into its vortex, he had fully broken through the living membrane and entered the pixilated otherworld. Being high on crack probably helped this. He took hits off the pipe in between worlds, when Mario pulled down the flag and entered the castle and the game tallied up his coins as fireworks went off. He was being cheered on now, all the guys were rooting for him. He was racing, racing through the game, heart pattering, the controller hot in his hands, the buttons getting slippery with sweat under his thumbs. He was winning. He was going to beat the game. He was a star. He was a hero.

Then someone stood in front of the TV.

Peter loosed a warbling, inarticulate shriek and ducked his head to see the screen.

He looked up, refocused his eyes on the Plus World, and was genuinely astonished to realize that the person who stood between him and the Nintendo was Gina. Astonished wasn't even quite the right word for it. It was more like, like cognitive dissonance, a feeling of seeing a certain thing in a context so unfathomably out of place that it simply *does not register*, and your subconscious spends a few seconds doubting whether you're really seeing what you're seeing before your conscious mind can catch up.

"What the *fuck* are you *doing* here?" said Gina.

Uh-oh: language. Brain problem. Brain-related problem. Language receptors not good right now.

"What?" said Peter.

Peter blinked, trying to think. The game screen still left a rectangular wake of light in his vision. Gina was covered in snow. She was wearing snow boots, a coat, a hat, a scarf. He flicked a glance outside. Snow. It was dark out. What time was it? The past was trickling back to him.

"I'm getting more beer," he said.

Peter had been sort of planning on smoking a little bit here and then going to the store and buying the beer with his credit card. He wasn't exactly sure if he had any credit left, but that was a bridge he'd cross when he came to it.

He tossed aside the controller and stood up. Head rush. His knees were trembly and weak. He realized he was very hungry.

"OK," he said. "Let's get the beer."

"Forget the fucking beer." She was furious, but quiet, almost whispering. She was afraid of the guys who hung out here. "Dan and Jessie left a long time ago. You were gone for *five—hours*. I was *so* worried."

"Uh—" Peter looked around the room. Everyone was staring at him. He didn't know where to put his hands.

38

"What the fuck were you thinking?" said Gina. "Do you still have the money we all gave you?"

Peter must have known, somewhere in there, that hours, and not minutes, were passing. Later, he thought the whole thing was kind of like the *Star Trek: The Next Generation* episode where Captain Picard dies in this world, and then he wakes up in another world, and lives out a full, happy life as a flute maker on a rustic, primitive planet, and then dies in that world and wakes up again just a couple seconds later onboard the *Starship Enterprise* again. Only this was sort of the opposite of that. Only it wasn't really like that at all, actually, because when Peter had entered into a separate time-space, into the Minus World, real time was still going on without him just like normal, and Gina had been embarrassed, at first, when he was taking so long, and then embarrassed and nervous and scared when he'd kept on not showing up and it had begun to snow, and then mortified as her friends gave up on him and were putting on their coats and leaving, and then Gina had been stomping around for hours, panicked and desperate, in subzero weather and rapidly accumulating snow, calling his name in the streets, calling out his name as if he were a lost child.

Spectacle

Susan Steinberg

ONCE IT WAS UNDERWATER I thought of.

Once I was gripped by thoughts of underwater.

Because my father once said, when I shouldn't have been listening, what if all the earth's water were drained.

Because my father once said, when I was too young to deal with it, it would be wild.

He said there'd be ships and planes and cars and bodies.

It made me afraid for years.

I was afraid to drive across bridges.

I could only think of the water below, the cars and bodies inside it.

By which I mean my body inside it inside of a car.

I imagined ways to see what was down there.

I wanted to have X-ray vision.

It went on and on, this want.

But I was over it now.

Not over the want of X-ray vision, but the want of seeing in water.

Because now I thought of the space between the clouds and sun.

Of what things were in that space.

Of what happened in that space.

This was the space I thought of now.

The space, I mean, I was gripped by now.

Because I knew a girl who died in that space.

It was years before and she died in a plane.

It made me afraid of flying.

I avoided flying for years.

To say I went nowhere for years.

But today there was somewhere I needed to be.

Today I was going to visit a friend.

Because today I was brokenhearted and needing to visit a friend who lived what felt like across the world.

And so I had to fly to see him.

And so there I was, suspended.

And so there I was watching our shadow on the backs of clouds.

40

And I was thinking of ways to think about clouds.
I was thinking of some original ways.
Because what you think, I think, is white and high.
And white and high says nothing of clouds how I think of clouds.
And as we went higher,
And when the shadow was smallest,
And when there was no shape, but just a point,
And when there was no point,
The flight attendant's skirt made a sound.
She was standing at my row.
She said are you all right.
I knew I didn't seem all right.
I knew it was wrong not to seem all right.
I knew better than to seem this way.
The flight attendant needed something.
She needed me to seem all right.
Even if I didn't feel all right.
She needed me different from my father who never seemed all right.
She didn't know, of course, my father.
She didn't know, of course, the sad places my sad brain went when she gave me the look that said please be all right.
But I knew how to seem all right.
I knew how to push things deep into my gut.
I knew how to play a role that was always all right.
I could do this for her.
I could do this now.
I knew how to play a role that was not a girl.
The role was not a guy.
But it was always all right.
Because my father was never once all right.
And I took after him in some, but not all, ways.
And no one wanted to see the ways in which I did.
So I stopped thinking of what it was I was thinking that was making my face all wrong.
So I stopped thinking of the clouds.
So I stopped thinking of this guy I loved.
It was too much to think.
I was brokenhearted, too much to think.
There was this guy and he was wrong for me.
My father would have been enraged.
He wanted something more for me.

He made this clear he wanted something more.
The flight attendant wore too much makeup.
It was orange and stopped where the face stopped being a face.
There was a time I wore too much makeup.
It was back then I wore too much.
It was part of my performance back then.
I was performing something obscene back then.
I was feeling like a showgirl then.
I was feeling like a show for you.
I would dance in my head for my father.
And I would dance for his friends in my head when he had friends.
I was not a nice girl.
I was a very nice girl.
I was not very nice.
There were things I did.
The flight attendant said are you all right.
I said it's my head.
She said your head.
She was how I used to be.
By which I mean she was still obscene.
By which I mean her shirt was too tight.
The snaps were straining and I could see skin between the snaps.
I couldn't help but look at her skin.
This made her obscene, not me.
She was the one whose shirt was too tight.
She was the one who got it all wrong.
She was the one who lived in that space between the clouds and sun.
She was the one who walked back and forth in that space between the clouds and sun all day.
There was a very fine line between giving orders and taking orders.
There were very fine lines between me and her.
The lines were no different from the lines that held each thing in place.
She didn't yet know the right things to ask.
She said what about your head.
That was not the right thing to ask.
The right thing to ask was what can I get you.
The right thing to ask was how does the plane stay up.
The right thing to ask was who on this plane can't I trust.
The right thing to ask was and then what.

The world revolved around her empty brain.

And I lived in the revolution.

We all lived in the revolution.

The right thing to ask was and what did you do when you found out the girl died.

The answer is I lost my shit.

But the question is what did you do.

Enough to say I lost it.

Because her initials were G. O. D., this girl, and I knew her from school.

Enough to say this is why I lost my shit.

Enough that she was flying home from study abroad, and the plane exploded, and everyone died, and the plane parts crashed to the ground.

And the body parts crashed to the ground.

And the people on the ground looking up were crushed.

Is why.

Enough.

I was too young to deal with this then.

I tried to deal with it then.

I tried to deal with it by not flying.

I tried to deal with it by taking pills.

I tried to deal with it by dropping out of school.

The right question was what did you do.

Because her initials were G. O. D., and I found this alarming.

But what was it you did.

Because we took a class together sophomore year.

And just because.

I am nowhere near where I want to be.

I have lost the flight attendant.

I have lost the stiff sound of her skirt.

She was just standing there, orange faced and stiff, waiting for an order, hers or mine, but I can't remember what I needed from her, what she needed from me.

I have lost her face and it was just days ago I saw it.

It was just days ago she stood at my row making me feel not like a girl and how is it my mind is replacing it with other things.

But how is it so many things.

Like the sun in the morning, the sun in the evening.

Like the sky between the sun and sun.

The leaves that turned too bright that year.

And we walked through leaves and dirt on our way to class.

Sophomore year which was a hundred years ago already.

Sophomore year and it was me and this girl and her two blonde streaks and I thought at first she would be too cool.

She was not, as it turned out, too cool.

She was cool, but it turned out I was too.

Because I knew how to be from watching girls.

Because I knew from watching guys as well.

The way they stood there.

And the girls just stood there.

We wore schoolgirl skirts from the Goodwill.

We wore guys' sweaters and black tights.

We were too old for schoolgirl skirts.

The Goodwill was on the corner of North and Harford, and no one wanted to be there.

People shopped there because they were either poor or cool.

The poor people bought serious clothing.

I watched a woman buy a wedding dress there.

I wasn't judging as she held the dress up to herself.

I wasn't judging that she was by herself and holding up this tattered, yellowed dress.

I was poor too but I was not the kind of poor that counted as poor.

We bought schoolgirl skirts and ran north back to school.

There were no leaves on North.

There was brick and endless brick.

There were guys who wanted to mess you up.

They wanted to get you hooked on drugs.

We were already hooked on drugs.

We weren't hooked but we were something else.

The guys said sister.

They said let's see you smile.

They said let me ask you something.

They said look at that ass.

They said you make me hard.

We said fuck you.

We ran the way back to school.

Leaves fell like snow at school and we were not the right kind of poor.

We had philosophy class, and I didn't understand philosophy.

The professor wore a red velvet jacket.

I couldn't follow his ideas.

What's there, what's not there; I couldn't follow.

Instead she and I passed notes on how bored we were, how hungry we were.

Instead we passed drawings of the professor.

There was this guy in class who called himself the mystic.

He was an asshole who predicted things at lunch.

Like he predicted a girl would drop out of school.

And he predicted a professor would kill herself.

He was an asshole this guy and only he called himself the mystic.

He wore a hat made of old socks sewn together.

He'd go into a trance at lunch.

We called the trance the so-called trance.

We called the guy the misfit.

He'd roll his eyes into his head and we'd try not to laugh.

We didn't try not to laugh.

We laughed in his dumbass face.

We drew pictures of him in philosophy.

He once intercepted one of the pictures.

He said some shit like you fuckers.

He did some thing like shake his head.

This was long ago and who cares about this dumbass.

I'm lost.

Let me get back to the subject.

Let me get the subject back.

The flight attendant and her orange face, her stiff skirt, her snaps nearly popping on her shirt.

And me and my needs.

She said what about your head.

I said what.

Listen.

I'm ready to talk about the guy I love.

I'm ready to tell you what happened.

I'm ready to talk about his eyes.

I'm ready to talk about his teeth.

It wasn't real love.

Not with him I mean.

I fell in love with myself.

I was a girl worth falling for.

Unlike many girls.

Unlike the girl from sophomore year.

Unlike the flight attendant who was more a woman than a girl.

She said what about your head.

She said what can I do.

But the right thing to ask her was how does the plane stay up.

She could tell I was not all right.

She could tell by the way my hands were on my head, my head pressed to the window, that I was in no way all right.

I just needed to be a few nights with my friend.

Because I needed this friend to tell me to stop.

I needed this friend to tell me that I could stop.

Stop what.

The window felt like it could crack.

It felt like my head could have pushed a way through the window.

I felt like my father must have felt mornings after nights.

I must have looked how he often looked.

He often looked on the verge of cracking into tiny bits, of being swept up into the wind.

When I was gripped by thoughts of underwater I thought first of X-ray vision.

I thought next of submarines.

I thought next of me in a submarine, my face pressed to the window.

But next I thought of the windows cracking.

And next I thought of water rushing in, of fish rushing in, of shells and sand and plants and cars and planes and people long forgotten or now forgotten or never known.

The flight attendant had the thinnest hips and I could never love a face like hers.

It turned out I liked something else.

It turned out I liked what my father liked.

A little edge, a little something off.

I said my head was suffering from the pressure.

I said my head felt like it would combust.

I said I was all right.

She said can I help, and I said you could bring me a drink.

She looked at me like who was I.

I just sometimes played this arrogant role.

It was not always nice this role.

It was neither girl nor guy.

It was both girl and guy.

It was sometimes girl and sometimes guy.

Just because I knew how to be both him and her.

Just because.

There was a fine line between.

I said did you hear me.
She said we need to level out.
She said I'll be back to take your order.
She gave me a look like you're an asshole.
I stared her down.
I said forget it.
I said I don't need your help.
I said I don't need anyone's help.
But later, in the airport, waiting for a cab, the ground was cold and wet and I felt small and snapped into something old.
When the guy said do you need help I said yes.
I don't like to say this but I said yes.
Perhaps because I needed help.
Perhaps because I needed a guy to help.
He was missing a tooth, and I never liked to see this.
It reminded me of something from when I was a kid, a cartoon or something, and then, as a kid, I tried not to cry.
He said how can I help.
I said you tell me.
He said do you need a cab.
I said I need something else.
He said what do you need.
I said I need your advice.
I need help I said.
I was in need I said.
I was a mess I knew.
I wanted to be intercepted, whisked off, brushed off.
He said I can help you to get a cab.
And I rode in the cab to my friend's place where I would drink my friend's whiskey.
And I would tell my friend what I told the toothless guy because it was my friend I was supposed to tell, my friend who could help, I realized in the cab, and not the toothless guy.
I had gotten confused.
There are too many characters in this story.
There are too many stories in this story.
The guy at school was not a mystic.
There were no mystics.
There were people who knew shit and people who didn't.
And the people who knew shit only knew shit because they were smart.

47

And the people who didn't only didn't because they didn't care.

There are too many people, too many bodies, too many parts to play.

When the plane exploded I became afraid.

I was gripped by the space between the clouds and sun.

I was consumed by what could happen in that space.

They described it as a fireball.

Try to picture that.

They described it as a spectacle.

It's impossible for me to picture.

All I can see is a rain cloud or something.

All I can see is this rain cloud spinning in place for a second before it burst.

The guy I loved was too much like my father.

Where did that come from.

God.

He had short hair and a fat face and he was too much like my father.

Because his shoes, as well, were never tied.

Because his shirts, as well, were always stained.

When we met he seemed more in control.

When we met I wanted to be controlled.

It was at a party at someone's house.

I was dancing wildly and he was watching me dance.

And I had forgotten for the moment about the sky.

And I was ready for something I didn't know what.

After the party, we were standing outside and he was looking at my mouth.

And he drove a big car and I needed him to tell me get in and he did.

And I needed him to drive the car fast and he drove the car as fast as he could.

Then one thing, another, another another.

My friend said yank him out like a rotting tooth.

He said change your perspective.

I was drinking his whiskey and he refilled my glass and refilled my glass until tiles in the floor became lovely things.

Stop thinking of the eyes, the mouth he said.

Start thinking of the stains on his shirts he said.

Start thinking of the crazy shit he said.

He said yank him out.

But I was like how.

I meant what tool would I use.

I imagined a tiny clamp, a tiny hook.

I said what tool.
I was drunk.
You're too literal he said.
Fuck you I would have said.
If what.
If the ceiling hadn't turned lovely too.
If I weren't being such a dumbass girl.
If I weren't being two tits a hole and a heartbeat.
I was such a girl sometimes.
Meaning I was such a guy.
On the runway I felt unafraid.
We were going really fast and I didn't care.
I imagined how my hair would have blown were the window cracked.
I imagined how my skin would have blown back into my hair.
And my teeth would have blown through the back of my head.
I wasn't yet thinking of how we would push upward.
I wasn't yet thinking of that space between the clouds and sun.
I was thinking of the guy I loved.
It wasn't love.
It was just a performance.
And how terrible not getting what you want.
Like when I wanted things as a kid and my father said no.
Like when he said no no no.
About every last thing, no and no and no.
Like when I wanted the guy to drive faster.
And he pulled over.
And I wanted my head in his lap.
I was thinking of his hands on my head.
And then we lifted.
And I didn't care.
And when the shadow of us was huge, then not,
And when the shadow of us was just a point,
And when there was no point,
The flight attendant needed something.
So I changed for her.
Because I felt like it.
Because I was ready for the fireball.
I was ready to land in the broken bones of a stranger standing on the ground.
I was ready to be a person remembered or forgotten or never known.

The right thing to ask was does one fly.
Or does one drop.
Or.
My father had said no study abroad.
No way he said.
Waste of money he said.
But he had no money then.
He was jobless then.
He was brainless then sitting on the curb outside the house near North he would lose.
How terrible not getting what I wanted.
Terrible the cigarette stuck to his lip.
The house like a mean face behind him.
The windows as eyes and so on.
He was still drunk from the night before.
He sat on the curb a hole in his pants and was like no way.
He was like waste of money.
He was like get lost.
He was like no way no fucking way get lost.
But I stood there for a while thinking he might change his mind.
But he went into the house.
I walked away.
School was so boring.
I didn't care about philosophy.
I sat by the window counting leaves.
I wrote notes about the teacher's red velvet jacket.
I didn't care about what's there what's not.
At lunch the misfit called our skirts stupid.
He said we looked like children.
He made no sense.
He said you look like perverts.
I said shut the fuck up.
I said what's with this guy.
I said someone tell him to shut the fuck up.
And she laughed and I said what.
I said I'm serious and she laughed even harder and I said what.
And then I was laughing too hard.
Her initials were not G. O. D.
No.
They were just G. D.
I never knew her middle name.

But whatever.

G. D.

G. fucking D.

I wasn't cut out for certain things.

I lost my shit.

On cloudy days I watched the sky.

On every day I watched the sky.

And nothing happened except sun and other stars.

And the planes that did their thing and I did mine.

And nothing happened except once.

There was the one day I was watching the sky.

I heard the plane that day before I saw it.

And I saw it emerge from above the clouds.

And it was flying too low, and the roar it made made me scared.

And I swear it was coming for me.

And I swear I could see the pilot's face, see the look on the pilot's face.

And I thought to duck below something, to hide below something, but there was nothing to hide below.

I was in the kitchen.

And it was coming for the kitchen window.

And I watched it coming for me.

And I started to cry.

And then what.

Nothing.

It shot across the sky like any plane.

Like any day, the sky full of planes.

Like any cloudy day.

Like any anything day.

I felt amazing.

I took a shower.

I went to a party.

I met this guy who would be all wrong.

The misfit could have told me all of this.

Because he knew a few things about my future.

Like how I was the girl who would drop out of school.

And a professor really would kill herself.

That was an awful day, the kids all crying.

It was an awful mess, just everyone crying.

Pills, of course, and I'm still too young to deal with this.

Pills, of course, as women do.

Susan Steinberg

It was an awful day, the kids just crying.
The misfit crying like a kid.
The misfit making a spectacle of himself.
But that was a different day.
That was a different day, the misfit crying.
The misfit predicting the fireball.
The misfit saying don't go abroad.
And when I thought for a second he was right,
And when I thought for a second how uncool,
And when I thought for a second I loved this girl,
And when I ate my lunch,
And when I said misfit,
And crumbs sprayed out,
And she laughed her ass off.
And I laughed my ass off.

Fixing the Abyss
James Morrow

> *Language speaks. If we let ourselves fall into the*
> *abyss denoted by this sentence, we do not go tum-*
> *bling into emptiness. We fall upward, to a height.*
> *Its loftiness opens up a depth. The two span a*
> *realm in which we would like to become at home,*
> *so as to find a residence, a dwelling place for the*
> *life of man.*
>
> —Martin Heidegger

TO THIS DAY NO ONE CAN SAY precisely why a remorseless and rei-
fied nihilism visited itself upon Western civilization in the second
decade of the twenty-first century. Being neither a trained philosopher
nor a credentialed historian, but merely a creator of depleting and
socially irresponsible horror films, I cannot hold forth authoritative-
ly on the coming of the abyss. As a member of that cadre of accomplished pessimists deputized to explore the belly of the beast, however, I believe that my recollections are worth setting down—to say
nothing of my therapist's conviction that, if I fail to complete this
memoir, my dreams will never be devoid of demons again.

The most viable theory of the rift's origins attributes it to a conjunction of five disparate events. I allude not only to the wholesale
abandonment of reason, under cover of Jesus, by several major political parties in the industrialized democracies of Europe and North
America, not only to the ballooning of thermonuclear-weapon stock-
piles in the United States and Russia following a convulsion of nostalgia for the Cold War, but also to the realization by the priestly
caste that they could once again impose their carnal requirements on
nonconsenting children without running afoul of the civil courts, as
well as to the ontological transmogrification of suicide bombing—
from despicable terrorist act to rarefied genre of performance art—by
the hipper sectors of the Islamic blogosphere. Finally, of course, we
must factor in the delivery by Dr. Dudley Yarborough, comparative
literature professor at the Pennsylvania State University, of his three
hundredth stand-up lecture titled "Mutually Assured Deconstruc-
tion," keyed to his professionally lucrative and intractably tenured

conviction that morality, truth, beauty, and knowledge are illusory notions at best, overthrown in the previous century by perspectivism, poststructuralism, hermeneutics, and France.

We do know that the beast first stretched its jaws in proximity to Dudley. No sooner had he finished saying, "As Baudrillard has noted, it is no longer relevant to say that the real world 'exists,'" than a fault line opened down the middle of 102 Willard. Although no earthquake stronger than 3.7 on the Richter scale had struck central Pennsylvania since the late Cretaceous, the class naturally assumed they were witnessing a seismic event, but when cobra-size flagella emerged from the rupture, along with rivulets of a tarlike substance that was certainly not lava, plus a stench suggestive of Dover Beach at low tide, everyone realized that the phenomenon would not be easily named. Yarborough himself proved unequal to the crisis. According to his students, he simply stared dumbfounded at the gulf, a stick of chalk pressed against his mustache and a frown coalescing around his wire-rimmed glasses.

Luckily, the situation was redeemed by a returning-ed student, Brenda Lutz, a thirty-four-year-old divorcée who'd resolved to get her BA despite juggling two jobs and the responsibilities of single motherhood. Brenda had the presence of mind, first, to organize an evacuation of the entire building and, second, to alert the administrators in Old Main that an abyss had arrived and they might want to look into it. "Though no one should presume to discuss the event coherently," Brenda informed President Clapham's one and only reachable plenipotentiary, "for logocentrism is dead, and we have lost all fixed vantages from which to make sense of the world, or so Professor Yarborough, following Derrida, tells us." Before the day was out, the entire campus population had been relocated to the outskirts of town with the loss of only one life, the victim in question being Lewis Thornhill, a romantically inclined sophomore who fancied himself a latter-day Young Werther and, *mutatis mutandis*, hurled himself into the void.

While the recrudescent religiosity of the West's secular republics certainly contributed to the cataclysm, as did the renaissance of the arms race, the institutionalization of clerical rape, and the aestheticization of suicide bombing, I must lay most of the blame at Yarborough's feet. It's all very well for a scorched-earth, skepticism-squared ethos to enrapture Ivy League humanities departments, but when *épistémologie noire* comes to America's land-grant universities, we know we're all in a lot of trouble. In my view Sheila Kittman's Senate

Subcommittee on Postmodern Irruptions was well within its rights to deny Yarborough a place on our team. He'd done enough damage already.

You will recall that, shortly after the coming of the widening gyre, Governor Abelard arranged for the Pennsylvania National Guard to lower into its gullet a live video camera and concomitant floodlight, the whole arrangement connected to a twenty-mile length of coaxial cable. Although the void soon proved hostile to this probe, pulverizing the camera with a flagellum shortly after the cable had paid out, the broadcast lasted long enough to afford the world a three-second glimpse of an amoeboid something-or-other lying at the bottom of the pit. The PBS commentator floridly described the beast as "the Minotaur of our disordered Zeitgeist, raging at the nexus of a vertical labyrinth," but the public never warmed to that epithet. The label that stuck issued from Drexel Sprite of the Nowhere Network, who dubbed the amoeba Caltiki, after the mucilaginous monster featured in that classic 1959 Eurotrash feature *Caltiki - il mostro immortale*, codirected by Riccardo Freda and an uncredited Mario Bava, the supreme master of Italian horror cinema. Let me hasten to note that my presence on the exploration team had nothing to do with my unauthorized *Caltiki* sequels and everything to do with the fact that, in the words of Boing Boing blogger Justin Felix, my oeuvre suggests "the sorts of irredeemably meaningless movies Vladimir and Estragon might have made if they'd had a 16mm Bolex at their disposal."

Slowly, inexorably, the rift expanded, growing at the rate of thirty meters per day. By Thanksgiving a dozen evacuated communities had plummeted into the gulf, including State College, Lemont, Boalsburg, and Pine Grove Mills. Although there were predictable instances of severe melancholics interacting fatally with the phenomenon, inevitable suicide pacts by cliques of clinically depressed adolescents, and unavoidable casualties among homeless persons, farm animals, and woodland creatures, it claimed remarkably few lives. (Fortunately the void did not manifest itself in Utah, Nevada, or some other state with a high self-slaughter rate.) Still, there was no question that Caltiki had to be stopped before FEMA ran short of resources and humanity ran out of places to hide.

Although the catastrophe was obviously metaphysical in nature, I can hardly fault the US Army Corps of Engineers for attempting a technological fix. Not only did they have the manpower, to say nothing of a three-billion-dollar appropriation from Senator Kittman's subcommittee, they were also receiving advice around the clock from BP, a corporation that, having successfully capped the Deepwater Horizon oil well in the spring of 2010 after despoiling the Gulf of Mexico for over a hundred days, could boast of considerable experience in these matters. Impressed by the army's assets, several prominent technocrats went on record with predictions that the abyss would be stitched together within a month. But Caltiki was having none of it. The flagella snapped the web of steel girders like matchsticks, leaving the monster free to pursue its cryptic agenda.

I felt equally hopeful when I learned from CNN that President Trilby, exercising her authority under the Unitary Executive War Powers Act, had implemented a policy of "strategic neutralization." The principle was perfectly sound. We all know from high school chemistry that a pool of sulfuric acid may be rendered inert by adding sodium hydroxide to create an exothermic reaction whose end products are sodium sulfate and water, that is, $H_2SO_4 + 2NaOH \rightarrow Na_2SO_4 + 2H_2O$. It seemed logical to suppose, therefore, that Caltiki might be paralyzed through copious applications of sentimentality, to wit, *Nihilism + Schmaltz → Insipidity + Tears*. And so it was that thousands of Smurfs and Care Bears were thrown into the pit by preschool children bused in from every state in the union, even as their parents dumped wheelbarrow loads of garden gnomes, Charles Dickens novels, and Mother's Day cards, along with ten thousand emergency DVD transfers of Shirley Temple movies. When this gesture proved futile, Disney World was dismantled in toto, shipped to central Pennsylvania on flatcars, and surrendered in an epic gesture of propitiation, despite raucous protests from the Florida tourism industry. Plans were under way for sacrificing the Alamo stone by stone when President Trilby declared that her administration was abandoning its appeasement policy, a decision that occasioned jubilation throughout the state of Texas.

Shortly after the ingestion of Bellefonte, Senator Kittman's subcommittee arranged for a vanguard of Navy SEALS to reconnoiter the first two miles of the shaft. They returned bearing a fount of useful information. Rappelling gear would not be necessary, for the void boasted a narrow footpath spiraling ever downward like grooves in a rifle barrel. Besides hiking boots, utility belts, Kevlar jumpsuits, and thermal long johns, our exploration team would also do well to wear pith helmets, as the overhanging crags were continually releasing what one scout described as "gobbets of incandescent oatmeal." The outriders found that they could palliate the omnipresent stench by donning face masks of the sort used by Muscovites during the peat-fire season. As for laptops, digital cameras, iPads, cell phones, and other portable electronic devices, we might as well leave them at home. There was no WiFi in the abyss, and the amoeba made a point of using its psychokinetic abilities to fry any lithium batteries borne deeper than a hundred yards into its domain.

On the night before our scheduled descent, the members of our intrepid quartet got to know one another over pints of Yuengling in the saloons of Altoona, a metropolis that, lying a mere nine miles from the gulf's leading edge, was scheduled for evacuation over the next seventy-two hours. Barhopping across the bewildered city, traveling incognito to avoid interrogation by the news media, hauling packs jammed with clean socks, flashlights, sleeping bags, MREs, and potable water, we soon realized that none of us fully understood how the idea of negotiating with Caltiki had first come about. I opened my CosmoBook and trolled the Internet, soon satisfying our collective curiosity. Although President Trilby wanted the world to believe that the policy had originated with her staff, even as a liberal think tank called the Montesquieu Institute likewise attempted to claim credit, it turned out that the godmother of our adventure was one Rhonda Scoursby, a Unitarian Universalist minister from Nashua, New Hampshire, whose YouTube video had gone so promiscuously viral that it inevitably came to the White House's attention.

"My intuition tells me that the beast does not intend to be causing so much damage," said Reverend Scoursby, speaking into her fourteen-year-old son's digital camera. "This is almost certainly a case of cross-cultural misunderstanding. The proper plan of action is clear. We must assemble a team of crack nihilists and send them on a journey to the center of the void, their goal being to communicate with the amoeba and find out what it wants."

At the last minute Dudley Yarborough attempted to join our fellowship, no doubt seeking expiation for his sins, but the rest of us quickly agreed that, when it came to playing hardball with the abyss, he simply wasn't in our league. To the end we remained a community of four—spindly Egon Spackle, lead vocalist of the notorious *métal hurlant* band Shit Sandwich; brilliant Helga Arnheim, prominent public intellectual and author of *Das Nichts*, a Brechtian play about Josef Mengele's career at Auschwitz-Birkenau; elfin Myron Solomon, avant-garde mathematician and inventor of that distressing set of hypothetical numbers known as "division-by-zero resultoids"; and my overweight self, Jerome Mallow, perpetrator of such deplorable

instances of cinematic Grand Guignol as *The Blood-Brain Barrier,
AtroCity, Entrails, Entrails II, Teleology Lost, The Heat Death of
the Universe, Ragnarök,* and *Ragnarök: The Sequel,* not to mention
my five smash-hit homages, *Disillusionment of Caltiki, Resentment
of Caltiki, Dionysian Revels of Caltiki, Bitter Wisdom of Caltiki,*
and *Caltiki Fucks the World.*

Typical moment from a Jerome Mallow film: Near the beginning
of the third act of *AtroCity,* a freckle-faced adolescent walks into a
McDonald's restroom, takes a piss, washes up, and avails himself of
the blow-dryer—thereby triggering a blast of heat that melts the
flesh from his hands. Ligaments seared away, the little finger bones
fall to the tiled floor with a crisp tinkling sound. We worked very
hard on the foley track. You can understand why the team needed
me.

Our journey began on the twentieth of October. I must confess I was
hoping we'd be home by Halloween, when I was scheduled to give a
live prime-time interview on the Nausea Channel in conjunction with
a forty-eight-hour marathon of films by horror auteurs Herschell
Gordon Lewis, George Romero, David Cronenberg, and, yes, Jerome
Mallow. The audience, I feared, would not regard my service on the
expedition as a sufficient excuse for a no-show, for most of them had
sided with the rift and didn't want to see it healed. But I had no control over the situation, each pair of coordinates on Caltiki's gullet
marking a point of no return, and I resolved to put self-promotion out
of my mind and concentrate on the odyssey at hand.

The first two days passed uneventfully, albeit unpleasantly, our
descent haunted by the foul odor of the amoeba's breath and the per-
cussive ploppings of the incandescent globules on our pith helmets.
Although our flashlights shone brightly enough to guide our footsteps, the gloom grew so thick it became a palpable presence, an entity that feasted on light and excreted dung of infinite mass. The
gelatinous walls glistened with an ectoplasmic excrescence, like the
skin of an immense snail, even as the path mysteriously acquired an
asphalt paving. With our every downward tread, the flagella increased
in number and thickness, and by the morning of day three these
undulating extrusions had so proliferated as to suggest a plantation
of sea anemones thriving at the bottom of the Mariana Trench.

Day four brought an unexpected sight: a Swiss chalet embedded in
the sticky walls, its front porch extending far enough to provide a

platform for a wooden crossing gate. Had the horizontal barrier not been on fire, we could have easily climbed over it, but as things stood we were stymied, the flames soaring upward to form an impassable rampart—and yet, paradoxically, the red tongues did not consume their fuel.

A fiftyish man with rheumy eyes, pallid skin, and feral hair hobbled onto the balcony of the chalet. His mustache was as broad and thick as the paintbrush he might have used to touch up the gingerbread ornamentation hanging from the eaves. He radiated unwellness, remaining upright only with the aid of a cane.

"I am the guardian of the first gate!" he screamed. "Be gone, decadent mortals!"

"Good God, it's Friedrich Nietzsche!" gasped Egon, who knew a thing or two about philosophy, having dropped out of Harvard before dropping out of Western civilization. "Zarathustra himself, everybody's favorite Antichrist—the one who foresaw Caltiki's coming!"

"Prescient I was when alive, and prescient I am today!" Nietzsche said, corroborating Egon's praise. His thick German accent evoked the way Werner Krauss would have sounded in *The Cabinet of Dr. Caligari* if it had been a talkie. "In my own immortal words, 'Man would sooner have the void for his purpose than to be void of purpose'!"

"Please quench the fire," Helga said. "We're on a vital mission."

"Truths are illusions whose illusory nature has been forgotten!" Nietzsche declared.

"The whole world is counting on us," noted Myron.

"Our metaphors have been worn smooth like guineas effaced by too much handling! Our words now operate as mere metal and no longer as coins!"

"Leave this dude to me," Egon whispered to the rest of us. "January the third, 1889, Turin, the Piazza Carlo Alberto, Herr Doktor Nietzsche witnessing a coachman savagely beating his horse."

"I've heard that anecdote," Helga said. "Nietzsche hugs the poor animal and weeps like a motherless child."

"Go for it," I told Egon.

"Take no prisoners," Myron said.

Stepping as close to the fire as he could without igniting his long hair, the lead vocalist of Shit Sandwich held his flashlight like a microphone, cleared his throat, threw back his shoulders, and, fixing on the philosopher, sang with an intensity of feeling such as I'd not experienced since Alanis Morissette covered "Fever Dream" over the

credits of *Entrails II*. As far as I could tell, Egon performed all three
stanzas without a whiff of irony or one iota of irreverence.

> *Oh Danny boy, the pipes, the pipes are calling*
> *From glen to glen, and down the mountainside*
> *The summer's gone, and all the flowers are dying*
> *'Tis you, 'tis you must go and I must bide.*
>
> *But come ye back when summer's in the meadow*
> *Or when the valley's hushed and white with snow*
> *'Tis I'll be here in sunshine or in shadow*
> *Oh Danny boy, oh Danny boy, I love you so.*
>
> *And if you come, when all the flowers are dying*
> *And I am dead, as dead I well may be*
> *You'll come and find the place where I am lying*
> *And kneel and say an "Ave" there for me.*

The effect on Nietzsche was immediate and dramatic. His lower
lip trembled uncontrollably. Tears squirted from his eyes like jets
from a child's water pistol. His sobs reverberated off the walls of the
rift, which for all their pulpiness produced a credible echo.

Like a wizard wielding his staff, Nietzsche raised his cane high,
then aimed it at the flaming crossing gate. Instantly the fire went
out, and the arm flew upward, assuming a forty-five-degree angle.

"If you reach the monster, please don't reveal that I let you pass
without a fight," Nietzsche said, wiping his tears with his sleeve.
"Tell it that, after a ferocious battle, the four of you wrestled me to
the ground. Once I realized I was defeated, I insisted that you crucify
me on the balcony of my chalet."

"As you wish," Egon said.

"Assure the beast that I still regard pity as the smile of slavery,"
the philosopher begged us. "Say nothing of 'Danny Boy.'"

We nodded synchronously.

"Perhaps you'd like to come along," Helga suggested. "We could
use a man of your formidable intellect."

"What better ambassador to the abyss than Friedrich Nietzsche?"
Myron said.

"Zarathustra does not desert his post!" the philosopher insisted.
"Now and forever, I shall remain true to my Kantian duty, even if
Kant himself was a *schnorrer*!"

Marching forward, we passed beneath the raised gate without mishap, whereupon it dropped back into place. Before continuing on our way, we faced Nietzsche and permitted him to set us straight about a thing or two.

"Harken, Jerome Mallow, from whose *Bitter Wisdom of Caltiki* I have derived much aesthetic satisfaction!" shouted Nietzsche, gesturing toward the gate with his cane. The arm once again burst into flames. "To you I say, 'He who fights with monsters should look to it that he himself does not become a monster!' Hear me, Helga Arnheim, who has pondered the dark heart of the devil Mengele! To you I say, 'When you gaze into the abyss, take care that the abyss does not gaze into you!' Listen, Egon Spackle, troubadour of unpalatable truths! To you I say, 'It's all very well to make music, but now I challenge you to turn your own life into a work of art, as I have done!'" Exiting the balcony, the philosopher slipped into the gloom of his chalet. "Heed my words, Professor Solomon, mathematician *extraordinaire!*" he called from out of the shadows. "To you I say, 'Your lust for knowledge is in truth a yearning for hell! Once you have exhausted all of nature with your science, you will next seduce damnation itself—a conquest that will leave you as hungry as ever, begging the universe for one more crumb!'"

The four of us exchanged complex scowls whose meaning, *pace* Derrida, was unequivocal. Nietzsche might be a bona fide genius, but he was also a bit of a windbag, if not a megalomaniac. It was probably just as well he'd elected to remain behind.

Collectively, we drew forth our kerchiefs, wiping the sweat of the circumscribed inferno from our brows. We slaked our thirst with swigs from our canteens, extended our walking poles, and, with the fire at our backs and Caltiki still to come, continued on our way.

What animal goes on four legs in the morning, on two legs at noon, and on three legs in the evening? Doubtless you recall the Riddle of the Sphinx. Surely you remember that the solution is man. Yes, correct, *nolo contendere*: But then there are those animals that travel on six legs at all times, morning, noon, and evening—and also in the dead of night.

Can you guess what particular hexapodal creature presided over the second barrier on the black-brick road to Caltiki? Cineasts will immediately think of "*Them!*", the quintessential 1950s giant-insect movie, featuring Edmund Gwenn and James Whitmore coping with a colony of immense ants, but that is not the right answer. Litterateurs might say T. S. Eliot, who famously desired to be a pair of ragged claws scuttling across the floors of silent seas—and yet that reply must also be disqualified, crustaceans being eight legged. This leaves only one possible solution.

The instant I clamped eyes on the immense vermin, over five feet long from head to rectum, I knew who he was. Ever since acquiring the movie rights to *The Metamorphosis* from Kurt Wolff Verlag—a major headache, let me tell you—I'd felt an intense rapport with this insect. And, indeed, I was the abysmonaut to whom he first spoke.

"Jerome Mallow, we meet at last!" cried the cockroach in voice evocative of the creaking diabolical mechanism that Kafka had devised for *In the Penal Colony*. "I want you to know I'm one of your most devoted aficionados. That said, I cannot let you pass."

This time our way was blocked by a ferocious helix of steel wire, its razor-sharp barbs grinning in the beams of our flashlights. The insect sentinel lay crouched atop his dwelling place: a battered, corroded Quonset hut protruding from the surrounding membrane like a rusty nail holding a blintz to a dartboard. His segmented antennae moved up and down with the rhythmic alternations of a timpanist working his mallets.

"We have an appointment with the void," I said. "Kindly remove your wire."

"Nowhere in the cinema of pessimism does *Disillusionment of Caltiki* find its equal," said the insect. "I'm sorry you never found funding for *The Metamorphosis*. You would've done me proud. Please go away."

"Is that who I think it is?" Helga Arnheim asked, pointing toward the vermin. "*Als Gregor Samsa eines Morgens aus unruhigen Traumen erwachte—*"

"One and the same," I said.

"I want you all to depart this instant," Gregor Samsa declared.

"You want us to depart—and you desire something else as well," I said.

The cockroach's antennae stopped twitching. He regarded me with both compound eyes. "And what might that be?"

"You know, my dear Gregor."

"Do I?"

"Climb down!" I commanded.

Limb by spindly limb, the vermin scrabbled from the roof of the Quonset hut to the ground. At one point his abdomen crashed against the corrugated tin shell, sending forth a reverberation like a bell calling pilgrims to some incomprehensible rite.

The instant Gregor attained his front yard, I threw myself upon him. Wrapping my arms around his carapace, I accorded the insect an impassioned embrace. He smelled of decaying eggs and festering fish heads. Gagging, I pressed my lips to his thorax, his mouth parts, his many-lensed eyes. I kissed the symbolic apple that his father, in an act of inordinate cruelty, had lodged in his back. At first my colleagues simply stood and stared, simultaneously appalled and appreciative—but then they too lavished affection on Gregor, tenderly stroking his every mound and crevice. For the better part of an hour, caresses were bestowed and reciprocated, moans exuberantly traded, bodily fluids luxuriantly exchanged.

"Until you four came down the road, my life was utterly barren," the cockroach told us. "How can I ever repay you?"

We told him how, and there followed an event so remarkable that I hope to put it in a movie one day. With surprising aplomb Gregor clamped his mouth parts around one end of the steel wire and began drawing it into his body, inch by inch, foot by foot, an image suggesting nothing so much as a reverse-motion shot of a spider releasing a filament of silk from its spinneret. A harsh and bitter meal, to be sure—and yet Gregor seemed to thrive on it: a ringing vindication, I decided, of Nietzsche's assertion that we are strengthened by every ordeal short of annihilation. As we tramped past the Quonset hut and continued on our way, the insect reared back, balanced himself adroitly on his cloaca, and, having assumed a posture evocative of multiarmed Kali, waved at us with all six of his legs.

"Farewell, Gregor!" I cried, glancing toward the gesticulating cockroach. "We'll explain to Caltiki that you didn't let us go without a fight!"

"No—don't!"

"No?"

"Tell the beast the truth—tell him I wouldn't let you go without a kiss!" Gregor insisted. "Godspeed, Jerome Mallow! I hope we get to make our movie sooner rather than later!"

As our fellowship continued its descent, fissures appeared beneath our feet, and soon the asphalt sheathing dissolved into chunks resembling the lowest grades of bituminous coal. Even as our path crumbled, it also narrowed, until we found ourselves walking along a precarious ledge, hemmed by the membrane on one side and open air on the other: a seven-mile drop to Caltiki's brow or brain or whatever dorsal aspect it presented to the world. Egon Spackle and I advanced with particular caution, fearful that, having made our contributions to the quest—the beguiling of Nietzsche, the seduction of Gregor Samsa—we were now considered expendable by whatever arcane powers lay behind the abyss.

We rounded a corner. A bungalow appeared, plated in gold and studded with gemstones. The dazzling edifice spanned the lane and extended into the void, defying gravity by means of foundational flying buttresses. The sign on the front door read, ENTER OF YOUR OWN FREE ENTERPRISE, which is exactly what we did, forthwith finding ourselves in a room opulently appointed with a Persian rug, Tiffany lamps, and a suede sofa of such apparent softness it suggested a therapeutic mud bath.

Seated at a poker table swathed in green baize, our host made lucid pantomimic gestures, inviting us to assume the four empty chairs. He was a vigorous man in middle age, with a costly tan and an auburn toupee. We sat down as instructed, whereupon our host, still saying nothing, provided each of us with a thousand dollars in blue, red, and white chips. Silently he dealt a game of five-card draw, then opened for eighty dollars. Everyone stayed in. Myron requested one card. Egon, Helga, and I each drew three. The dealer stood pat, subsequently wagering his entire stack of chips. I dropped out, having no faith in my pair of eights. Helga likewise left the game, as did Egon. Myron matched the dealer's extravagant investment.

Speaking for the first time, our host said, "Take today's lesson to heart, gentlemen," then showed his hand: a ten-high straight. "Gamble only with other people's money, but keep the winnings for yourself."

"Although in this particular instance," Myron noted, revealing his diamond flush, "the winnings are moving in an unexpected direction."

Our host scowled and snorted. "The rear door to my cottage is locked, and I've hidden the key where you'll never find it. Try climbing over the fucking roof, and I'll push the ejector button, hurtling you into the void. In short, I'm the best and brightest of the rift's guardians. You might as well turn around and head back to Altoona."

"Not before we learn who you are," said Myron, raking in his pot.

"Roscoe Prudhomme. You've never heard of me. I'm not in the same fucking pantheon with your Nietzsche or your Kafka or your Marquis de Sade, but as the principal architect of the most insidious and socially useless financial instrument of all time, I can say I've made my contribution to nihilism's ascent."

Prudhomme went on to explain how, way back in 1994, he and two dozen of his fellow JPMorganers were enjoying an off-site weekend in Boca Raton when—everyone having tired of the yacht parties, bikini-model parades, and $3,000 double magnums of Cristal—the conversation turned to the government's pesky requirement that a bank must keep billions of inert dollars on hand in case its clients, be they corporations or countries, began defaulting on their loans en masse. Inevitably the JPMorganers posed a challenge to themselves. Might they design a financial product certain of protecting them from the slings and arrows of unreliable borrowers even as it freed up vast quantities of capital?

"And suddenly I had it!" Prudhomme cried. "An unprecedented sort of third-party contract that would allow us to erase all risk of unpaid loans from our books and put it on the ledgers of nonfinancial institutions like indemnity companies and pension funds!"

"I don't know what you're talking about," I said.

"Neither do I," Egon said.

"Neither does anyone else," Prudhomme said. "That's the fucking beauty of it."

"But you were a *bank*," Helga said. "You were *supposed* to have risk on your books."

"I'll never forget that sunny day in Boca Raton," said Prudhomme, ignoring Helga's admonishment. "The excitement was electric. It was like working on the fucking Manhattan Project. They should put a plaque on the wall, like the one at the University of Chicago commemorating the first self-sustaining nuclear chain reaction. 'In this conference room the credit-default swap was born.'"

"But you forgot to ask a crucial question," Myron noted. "What if one of those compliant third parties didn't have the money to pay up? Obviously this would create—dare I say it?—a chain reaction, one default leading to another, with investors bailing out left and right. You should have foreseen that, Roscoe."

"Actually we did foresee it, but we went ahead and started selling our swaps anyway—how's *that* for state-of-the-art cynicism?"

"If you're such a hotshot financier, why aren't you on Wall Street right now, making a million dollars a day?" Helga asked. "Why do you waste your time down here?"

"Because I'm fucking *dead*, that's why," Prudhomme replied. "Not long after the crash of 2008, my conscience got the better of me. I decided I'd created a Frankenstein monster, guaranteed to increase the sum of misery in the world, so I put a fucking bullet through my brain. In recent months I've come to regret that decision. My guilt has all but evaporated. Knowing he'll be hanged in the morning has the effect of wonderfully concentrating a man's mind, but the abyss does an even better job."

"Unlike my friends, I *do* know something about derivatives," Myron told our host. "It happens that you're talking to the inventor of division-by-zero resultoids. You want my advice? Forget your pathetic little investment strategies. Forget swaps, futures, options, hedge funds, arbitrage, endorsements in blank, collateralized debt obligations, marked-to-market assets, and securitizing your grandmother." The mathematician unfurled his fingers and patted the breast pocket of his jumpsuit. "I happen to be carrying a blueprint for the most lucrative financial instrument since the popes were peddling their eschatological insurance policies back in the Middle Ages."

"Myron Solomon, am I right?" said our host, his astonished jaw swinging open. "I read about you in *Discover*! It's a pleasure to meet you, sir"—the banker seized the mathematician's hand, shaking it vigorously—"a pleasure and a privilege!"

"I detested that *Discover* profile," Myron said. "The reporter was a chucklehead."

"Dr. Solomon, you'll be interested to know that, before too long, the Poker Tournament of the Millennium will occur at this table." Prudhomme tapped the baize with his index finger. "Fifteen successive days of Dallas Balls-to-the-Wall, a five-hundred-million-dollar buy-in, no limits on bets or raises. The late, great Ken Lay of Enron is in the rec room right now, playing Pac-Man and raring to go. We're still waiting for the incomparable Keating to die—Charlie Keating of that gorgeous savings and loan swindle—likewise the inimitable Madoff. Bernie's son hanged himself a while back—maybe you heard, terrible tragedy—so he'd be the logical fifth, but Mark refuses to play cards with his dad. Do you understand what I'm offering you, Dr. Solomon? Your friends must go home, but you can have a piece of the action."

"I don't want a piece of your damn action. I want—"

"I know what you want. All right, Myron. Very well. Give me the blueprint, and I'll give you the key to the back door."

"Give me the key to the back door," Myron retorted, "and I'll give you the blueprint." From his vest pocket he produced a business envelope, dangling it in front of Prudhomme like a felinophobe tormenting a domestic shorthair with a catnip mouse. "You know about pyramid schemes, Roscoe, including the innovations wrought by your friend Madoff. My device is three times as lucrative, four times as sustainable, and five times more difficult to regulate. It's called a tesseract scheme."

"A tesseract scheme?" said Prudhomme, rising from his chair. "As in the famous four-dimensional hypercube?"

"I'm impressed with your knowledge of higher mathematics," Myron said.

"When the credit-default swap emerged from my brow, I was the smartest guy in the room," Prudhomme said.

Approaching a particle-board bookcase, the financier withdrew an ostensible Ronald Reagan biography, then flipped back the cover to reveal that it was in fact a cedarwood receptacle. From the compartment he removed a gold key, then pressed it into Myron's palm. Casting me a freighted glance, Myron indicated with his eyes that I should vacate my seat and sidle toward the back door. Nonchalantly I repositioned myself as my fellow explorer had requested.

Prudhomme rubbed his hands as if lathering a bar of soap. He retrieved the envelope, broke the seal, and removed a single sheet of paper. "This had better be good," he said, unfolding the page.

"Now!" Myron cried, delivering the key into my possession with a deft lateral pass.

I jammed the implement into the hole, rotated my wrist, pulled open the door. Helga leaped out of her chair and sprinted through the jamb, followed by Egon, Myron, and me.

"Wait a minute!" shouted Prudhomme. "This doesn't look like a tesseract scheme! This looks like a goddamn chess problem!"

"It *is* a goddamn chess problem!" Myron cried as the four of us raced along the path.

"Come back here, you generation of vipers! You fucking velociraptors! You scumbag Trotskyites!"

"So long, sucker!" Myron replied. "We'll give your regards to Caltiki!"

For a full half hour we frantically pursued the twisting bore of the void, our boots pounding the crumbling asphalt, our flashlights etching silvery veins on the throbbing walls. Only after the last echo of Prudhomme's curses died away did we dare decelerate, our mad dash becoming a steady jog and then a brisk walk.

James Morrow

The following day—weary and hungry, dazed and bewildered—we arrived at the bottom of the abyss. Huddling together in Caltiki's mammoth shadow, drawing what solace we could from one another's company, we strove to project a manifest deference toward the object of our quest. As large as Gregor Samsa's Quonset hut, the thing was indeed an amoeba: a quivering, gunky, funky, one-celled spheroid of protoplasm, evocative of the very mass of cow intestines from which Freda and Bava had fashioned their original *Monstro Immortale*. A dozen tentacle-like pseudopods radiated from the amoeba's great blobby core. Its food vacuole held an unlit marijuana joint as large as a canoe.

"You may address me as Your Lordship," the behemoth said in a thunderous voice, its power to intimidate diminished only slightly by an endearing lisp. "I shall address you however I see fit."

"We are honored to be in Your Lordship's presence," I said.

"You are surely among the greatest and most powerful beings in the galaxy," Helga said.

"If not the universe," Egon said.

"Cut the bullshit," Caltiki said.

"Yes, Your Lordship," Egon, Helga, and I replied in unison.

"I apologize for all the mess topside," the monster continued. "There was probably an easier way to get your attention than devouring a college town and the adjacent communities, but I couldn't think of one."

"The damage estimates begin at around three billion dollars," Myron noted.

"So sue me."

"We wouldn't dream of it, Your Lordship," I said.

"You obviously have much to teach us," Helga said.

"Stop it," Caltiki admonished us, igniting the spliff with a firebrand. "Sycophancy does not become you. Don't hide your light under a bushel, O my guests. You got past Nietzsche, an accomplishment worth bragging about. Allow me to salute you." The monster proceeded to do just that, gesturing respectfully with all twelve of its pseudopods. "You circumvented the cockroach. Very resourceful. You outfoxed Roscoe Prudhomme. Most impressive. In short, you have proven yourselves worthy of an audience with the abyss. Would you like to hear my thoughts on why your species is in so much trouble?"

"Indeed," I said.

"Oh, yes," Egon said.

"Quite so," Myron said.

68

"You have our complete attention," Helga said.

Caltiki sucked in a profligate portion of cannabis smoke. "We'll begin with a history lesson. For the past twenty-five hundred years, every time a great sage was born into your world, the same three mystics mounted their camels and rode to the nativity site bearing gold, frankincense, and myrrh. But who, really, were these magi? They were Zoroastrians, that's who, Persian astrologers, keepers of a philosophic tradition tracing all the way back to 600 BC—and the proprietors of the single worst idea your human race has ever devised."

"The single worst?" Helga echoed, transfixed.

"I refer to the notion that all sentient souls can be neatly sorted into the saved and the lost—the enlightened and the benighted, the virtuous children of Ormazd and the vicious adherents of Ahriman." Caltiki took another toke. "The gold, frankincense, and myrrh were simply a ruse for getting past the midwives and reaching the cradles of Plato, Christ, and the rest. In every case, Balthazar, Caspar, and Melchior bent over the newborn infant and whispered their poisonous dichotomy into his little ear. 'Ormazd versus Ahriman, Ormazd versus Ahriman, Ormazd versus Ahriman . . .'"

"The whole weltanschauung gets resurrected in the third century AD as Manichaeism," Helga explained to our fellowship.

"The sands of time make their inexorable descent," Caltiki said. "The babies become adults, strutting one by one onto the stage of history. Plato and his students, tidily dividing the population of Athens into clever Socratics and clueless Sophists. Jesus and his apostles, merrily separating eternity-bound sheep from eternally damned goats. Mohammed and his followers, deftly pitting believers against infidels. Descartes and his disciples, coolly sundering the biosphere, thinking humans on one side, unfeeling animals on the other. Marx and his coterie, confidently cleaving Homo sapiens into a capitalist bourgeoisie and its proletarian victims. Need I go on? O my guests, from an amoeba's perspective it's a mighty bizarre way to look at the world—and by the evidence of your history it's a rather bloody way as well. If Nietzsche had appreciated what Zoroaster was *really* about, he would never have chosen him as his mouthpiece. Thus spake Caltiki."

Silence settled over the abyss, a quietude so complex and dense it fully befitted the magisterial amoeba before whose throne we stood. At last Helga spoke.

"It would appear that we find ourselves at a crossroads," she told our fellowship.

"Somehow we must progress past dualism," I said, realizing for the first time that I was in love with Helga.

"Sign me up," said Egon.

"Hear, hear!" said Myron. "Though I cannot imagine how we'll go about it."

"I would invite you to ponder the material cause of your sickness," the monster said. "An effective cure normally requires a correct diagnosis. Look at your own naked bodies in the mirror. What do you see? A radical form of bilateral symmetry, that's what. Dualistic arms, legs, ears, nipples, buttocks. Submit yourself to an autopsy, and it's the same story. Dualistic lungs, kidneys, auricles, ventricles, cerebral hemispheres. Thus spake Caltiki."

"No *wonder* we're all Manichaeans at heart," Helga said, heaving a sigh. "It's bred into our bones. What a brilliant analysis, Your Lordship!"

"Don't patronize me."

"I'm not," Helga said. "I really believe you're onto something."

"Even if we accept your conclusion, I don't see what we can do about it," I said. "We can't turn ourselves into asymmetrical invertebrates like you."

Myron said, "Though when I consider recent breakthroughs in genetic engineering, I sense that something along those lines might be arranged."

"The ingenuity of humans never ceases to amaze me," Caltiki said. "Still, you won't be going monolateral anytime soon, and meanwhile the abyss is gaining on you. If you're serious about climbing out of your hole, you might start by attempting some cognitive restructuring vis-à-vis your local giant amoeba from hell."

"I'm sure I speak for the whole group when I say we're willing to give it a try," Helga said.

"You think of me as a creature apart—am I right?" said Caltiki. "An anomalous monster, possibly malign, possibly benevolent in a *Star Trek* sort of way, but always a monster. Horse manure. Grow up, people. There are no creatures apart. There are no monsters. Read your Darwin. I'm an amoeba, for Christ's sake. A particularly large amoeba, but still an amoeba. Tunnel deep into the earth, and you'll discover my living relatives. Study the fossil record, and you'll come upon my extinct ancestors. My line is legitimate. Domain, *Eukaryota*. Kingdom, *Amoebozoa*, Phylum, *Tubilinae*. Genus and species, *Amoeba proteus*. My pedigree is entirely in order—and so is yours. In fact, if you look back far enough into the mists of time, you'll find that amoebas, people, petunias, and all other creatures are intimately and materially and perhaps even spiritually connected, though I've never liked that word 'spiritually.' Whenever I hear it, I sense another dualism on the wing."

"Caltiki means to say we're all DNA-bearing eukaryotes under the skin," Myron explained to me, as if I didn't know, which I didn't. "Now, I suppose one *could* argue for a primal dichotomy between eukaryotes and prokaryotes, but at the end of the day even *they're* on the same continuum."

"As for my epithet, *Monstro Immortale*—what an absurdity!" Caltiki said. "When it comes to eluding death, O my guests, I'll have no greater success than you." The amoeba inhaled a cloud of euphoriant. "And that is all I know. Thus spake Caltiki. This interview is over."

"Just one more question, Your Lordship," Myron said. "As we march back to the surface, will we have to deal with the three guardians again?"

"You won't have to *march* at all," Caltiki replied, lifting up three of his pseudopods to reveal a hole about the diameter of the wishing well in my most erotic movie, *Snow White and the Seven-Year Latency Period*. "Have your forgotten your Heidegger? Go ahead, O my guests. Take the plunge. You can trust me."

We hesitated for a protracted interval, our vociferous debate punctuated by periods of nonverbal fretting. In the end we decided the amoeba was telling the truth, and so we held hands, closed our eyes, and made the leap.

The rest of the story is not mine to tell, except in the most trivial sense—yes, we did fall upward, returning to Altoona unharmed, and, yes, I did get back in time for my live appearance on the Nausea Channel. But now the narrative belongs to Homo sapiens per se. The ball is in our collective court. We'd better not take the Manichaean bait again. The moving pseudopod writes and, having writ, moves on.

Ever since the great gulf sealed itself, we four explorers have been fighting the good fight on behalf of asymmetry. I have nothing but praise for Myron Solomon's best seller, *What to Do until the Amoeba Comes: A Personal Inquiry into the Modern Malaise, with Answers in the Back of the Book*. No less impressive are Egon Spackle's recent efforts. After dissolving Shit Sandwich and reforming the band

71

as Cheerful Despair, he produced a hit album, *Krapp's Penultimate Tape*, including a half dozen songs that invite the listener to apprehend the world from an amorphous invertebrate's perspective. But I must reserve my supreme encomiums for the encyclopedic, three-part, nine-hour antidualism play written by my new bride, Helga Arnheim-Mallow. Winner of the Pulitzer Prize, *Fixing the Abyss* is a thoughtful and nuanced celebration of that rare bird the genuine monist, a breed of thinker that historically includes, by Helga's reckoning, Epicurus, Isaac Newton, Percy Bysshe Shelley, the fourteenth Dalai Lama, and nobody else. Rumor has it that Dudley Yarborough, the scholar who brought us the void, has just incorporated *Fixing the Abyss* into his syllabus.

As for my own answer to the amoeba's challenge, I am pleased to report that my film adaptation of *The Metamorphosis*, music by Egon Spackle, is cleaning up at the box office. If this trend continues, the profits will be sufficient to underwrite *Caltiki in the Most Plausible of All Possible Worlds*, which I believe is my best script ever. True, the critics savaged my decision to give Gregor Samsa's story an obliquely happy ending, but I believe that Kafka—who had a better sense of humor than most movie reviewers—would forgive me.

Before dropping dead, Gregor meets one of his contemporaries, Raymond Dart, the South African anatomist who discovered the first *Australopithecus* fossils, those unequivocal links between human beings and extinct anthropoid apes. Thanks to Professor Dart, Gregor learns that he isn't quite as alienated as he believed. Domain, *Eukaryota*. Kingdom, *Animalia*. Phylum, *Arthropoda*. Class, *Insects*. Order, *Blattaria*. And so on.

"So you see," says Dart, anticipating what Caltiki will tell our expedition one hundred years later, "there are no creatures apart. There are no monsters. You are not alone."

"Cold comfort that," Gregor says.

"Do you think you're the only entity on earth to experience existential dread?" says the anatomist to the insect. "Do you think you're the sole being in the Western world who's had an encounter with nothingness? Get over yourself, Gregor. Yes, what I'm dishing up is cold comfort, but that's better than nobody giving you any sort of comfort! I'm making an effort here!"

For some reason, these remarks strike Gregor as hysterically funny, and Dart starts laughing as well. Soon the insect and the anatomist are hugging, kissing, and guffawing up a storm. A veritable deluge of salt water spills from the dying cockroach's eyes, flowing forth into the theater—*The Metamorphosis* is being exhibited in 3-D and Tactiloscope—an event that initially proves disconcerting to the audience. But in time they realize there's no cause for fear and trembling. It's only a movie. Even the most nihilistic filmmaker would not drown his own customers.

And so they sit back and relax, bathed in an unfathomable sadness while swimming in a river made of Gregor Samsa's enigmatic tears, until at long last the strange currents bear everyone safely home.

Seven Stories from the Palace of Rubble
Kyra Simone

COUNTY FAIR

HE HOPES TO FLY a giant helium balloon a record twenty-five miles into the earth's atmosphere and parachute down. This is a moment worthy of fanfare. Six teenagers stand with their heads spinning. A farmer throws down his pillow, a quarry worker lets his shoulders go weak, a communist boss kneels down in the street and begs the man in the balloon to stop. The crowd calls out to him with weary arms, "Fly off to new realms," they cry. This is what life has been like. Mothers make kites out of junk-mail leaflets searching for missing people. They fly them over houses that have fallen off the market. A lemon drops from the sky into the hands of the assistant who counts new shapes. She works for the chief. She is busy in his saddle. As he thrusts her the usual afternoon earthquake, tops spin, lakes threaten to flood, postmen ring doorbells with overwhelming force. Hunters drop their shotguns and explode with dreams of mounting their wives on walls. "This is no Sunday in the park," thinks the assistant. She spent her school years studying maps of the chief's insides, and now, as he approaches nuclear disarmament, she finds herself quietly lost, unequipped for the weapons of Europe. After twenty-five years of extraordinarily bad news about childhood obesity, the balloon inflates and floats away, leaving the gondola with the man inside, on the ground. In Moscow, when this sort of thing happens, it is not unusual for a man to throw his face in a barrel. Today, a bit breezy. Tonight, clear, light winds. Tomorrow, plentiful sunshine.

FOREIGN AFFAIRS

On an empty coast in the days of shock, the old queen bathes beneath a cloud of uncertainty. Here is a place known for its spectacular wildlife and robust children, hooligans, mosaics, a land of distress.

Here is a queen as queens must be: parties, hotels, interviews, blood-baths. "What shall I eat today?" she says to a minnow. "Which memory of which man, which country, which ocean." There are spare professors and men who look through telescopes, gamy Gypsies, and tough-shouldered champions, veal boys from the streets who are tender as the night. Until Mr. Ten Percent arrives in his steamroller, holding a portrait of his mother and a sign that points east, a man still trying to skip to the next paragraph. He has the look of smooth rides across muggy shores, eyes that remember throwing rocks at one another. "This isn't random," says the queen, "we've been meeting here for a decade of beheaded Mondays." Mr. Ten Percent scratches an *X* on a piece of church that lies between them. The queen understands that it is his heart. "In this country, symbols matter," she says. "Let's play a record," says Mr. Ten Percent, and they dance on the water to the echoes of what other people are thinking. Miles away, a dress hangs on a bush in the clearing. It burns beside the footsteps of the wife who has set it on fire. Pilgrims search factories for shards of glass. They see their images in them, now just cubist sketches of ruined towns.

WHEN LANGUAGE IS GONE FROM BODIES

On the radio, a man tells the story of a mythical rabbit, who was beaten so badly, he split in two and became twins. The sailor tilts in his chair and listens to the legend, touching the patterns of animals he has killed and tattooed across his chest. His hands are graveled from wrestling anacondas. His boat sails through sunken rings of fog, passing lost thoughts of the pinching collar, or eyes transfixed by the watch on the wrist, and the shrinking of the spirit that can result. Long-gone relatives take off their corsets in the distance, realizing that the shadows of electrical wires are the same as winter branches that have let their leaves fall. The sailor's table is set with a feast; the nightingale waits to land upon his shoulder. "Here we are truly in another world," he says, collecting the feathers of his winged companion. "And look, I can still make a blanket of your anxiety." The sailor picks up a postcard, each day left blank. His mind is swimming with fish, moving blindly toward a green light. The world is full of magnificent things. Ravishing dancers linger in costume, dinosaur skeletons emerge from boys' heads, meadows lie punctuated with discarded glass. Oh to wander light-headed, through a gallery of faces, and be blown untraceably from one island to the next. There are many kinds of time that exist: the long, slow, repetitive cycle and the fleeting moments of bodily motion. One day, he may dock his boat in a desolate cove known for rare whales, and find no creatures. Instead, a rare woman will come out to greet him, a goddess among a forgotten population of five.

PAWNS TALK OF SCARS

A woman and a girl bake bread in the barren field of a stadium. Their voices are unusually soft today. Later, they will nap on stolen furniture. They will build cities with stacks of paper that have flown from office windows—recipes for disaster, catalogs of wounds to be filed away in coffins. Tonight they will lie there for a lifetime. Cows may triumph the fields, little things may die as they sleep. The skirts of fate wish to fly up and reveal something, but they are held down with cinder blocks, dreams of jammed highways that will never reach the future. Outside, crowds gather daily to peer at lists posted on high walls. They clench their jaws and point at empty houses. The famously slow clock ticks in the center of town: another never-ending moment of desire, another year of cars speeding away. The woman waits before her oven. Her arms are crossed; she stands like a Greek myth on a burning stage. "I care little for birds," she says to the girl, "I am in the business of rhinoceros skin." As time passes, the girl begins to paint on the stadium pillars, pictures of places where they enjoy science, and eulogies. She escapes through the legs of an overthrown chair and kicks an old trophy into the empty field. "Yoo hoo! Mother! I've left the house, like thousands have done!" Beyond the walls of the auditorium, abandoned cars go for short drives. A cabby waits with a scar on his face. The girl gets in. "You are the thing I have always wanted!" she says, as they take off for the north. It snows. The crowd laughs. History still breathes through dark houses in dry lands. The woman knows her bread will not be eaten.

WORLD BUSINESS

The virgin stands at the edge of the Atlantic, unveiling herself before a million stars. She looks for something in the vessels before her—a flood, a call, some message of the irreparable beauty coloring each heart, each wave, blue. On the other end of the galaxy stars look like numbers, companies, pieces of advertisements, lost icons of a sluggish world. "I'm nothing unusual," she calls out to passing lights. "What kind of business can we do each other?" If she dangles too low from the diving plane, will wings emerge from the small of her back, will fins grow from her green demising body, or will she sink with doubt in the dark oceans of youth? She could easily become that drowning passenger, fallen from the ambitious balloon; another crashed human imagination in search of a strange, uncompassed voyage. Battered or dead, she wonders what she will mourn for if, at the end of all this, all these dreams of romance and aviation, she fails to leap from the edge. At her feet, the caterpillar makes no move to advance his technology as he lies still and lets a descending moth gouge him in the shoulder. There it is: no exit either. Here is a game in which failure trumps death, and every frightened heart is a small stopping of history. There will be mountains of them ticking at the end of the world, treacherous and imaginary as the lost slopes of Atlantis.

MUSEUM

A lone wolf strides through an ancient town. He is a slip of a thing, walking articulately with the grace of a dancer, standing in the wind at the edges of cliffs. But the lives of wolves haven't lost their bloodiness. His upper body still casts a long, heroic shadow; his tail still ends in a daggerlike thrust. In town, he visits buildings waiting to be excavated, and bows to antique people too rare to behead. An old woman in a window is singing the blues. She is illuminated from afar as the only square of light. The wolf stops to listen and look up at her for a while, letting his mind run through the poppy fields patterned on her dress, calculating the sharpness of glass objects in her eyes. To be sure she has a beak for a face. Her hair blows across it like silver on the wind, and how her old songs are full of sad news. The wolf keeps walking, knowing that her light will go out like all the others.

Kyra Simone

She will become a statue eroding on some beach in a dream, a silenced relic in an empty museum, a detail in a painting most people pass by. Up ahead, other animals scatter from the wolf's path. Horses and beetles, even dangerous creatures in the marshes, envelope themselves or drown as he comes near. In a mirror lying on the ground, the wolf catches a glimpse of his own image, and for a moment knows what frightens the others: the eyes of eternity and the slow jaws of kings. But he will soon wander off from the mirror and the town, in search of another simple, absent, tragic adventure. Decades before, his face is found on a piece of fallen alabaster, from a map of the heavens painted on the ceiling.

PALACE OF RUBBLE

A breaking wave collapses on the bank before two half-naked women on white Arabian horses. The water moves with a pulse at the edge of the planet. It sucks in invisible creatures and spews them out again over the desert, a sick coast that never fully swallows anything. "The truth is, we don't have enough liquor," says the older woman. "We were promised jubilation," says the younger. The two plain Americans are luxuriously undressed, but there is nothing in their pockets and no paintings growing in their heads. They've spent the day at the mansion, strewn over staircases that lead nowhere and men with rifles passing through for a slow dance. The king's piano has died in the ballroom, crumbling like an elephant kneeling down to sleep. The air suggests bald men changing tires dripping with used oil, not roses. One day, these women will huddle inside trailers and teach six-year-olds how to make barbed-wire fences. But today, they will only watch foreign swans on a foreign marsh. The younger woman removes the last piece of cloth remaining on her body and puts on a helmet some soldier has left on the beach. "How beautiful it is," shouts the other, looking up at her. "I love it," the young one sings back. Here is a response like many others, immediate and makeshift. For the first time, they stop counting the days and wonder if they will grow old in this scorching, isolated, windowless place. The world is a widening palace of ruined freedom, but here at least there are no happy crowds to puff at in the dust.

78

Radio from the Cities
Howard Norman

IT WAS THE NIGHT John Lennon died. I was living and working in
Eskimo Point, Northwest Territories, near Hudson Bay, on December 8, 1980. Hours earlier in the arctic's crepuscular daylight, the Inuit
pilot, Edward Ominiq, had stood next to his Cessna on the hard-
packed snow landing strip, which was sprinkled with crushed coal
for traction, and remarked, "I'm going south to Canada." Edward was
about sixty years old. Leaning back against his plane he then shouted
desperate-sounding implorations in his language (his mouth open in
wind-muted anguish like Edvard Munch's *The Scream*), the Quag-
miriut dialect spoken along Hudson Bay. It had begun to snow hard.
The sky was shifting behemoth dark clouds west to east. Edward was
addressing Sedna—I distinctly heard her name—the ancient spirit who
controls the sea and to some extent the air over the land and sea. For
centuries Sedna has comported herself with severe, unpredictable
moodiness, exhibiting an uncanny repertoire of punishments and
even lethal retributions for the cruelties, greed, spiritual trespasses of
humankind. To say that Sedna can be capricious is to say there are
stars in the sky. Consequently, the Inuits' relationship with Sedna is
provisional; she has to be appeased daily. Edward Ominiq was trying.
His attempt was both mesmerizing and disturbing. He had worked
himself up half to tears. I didn't know which particular trespass he
was apologizing and asking mercy for—with human beings there are
so many so frequently—or if I should even be looking at him. What
is decorum in the presence of such a dramatic and intimate petition
for mercy from invisible forces? All the while I helped his son, Peter,
load five electric guitars and sacks of mail into the cargo hold. The
guitars were going to Winnipeg for tuning and repair.

Yet something was very wrong here. Something was not going well.
Edward was staring at the horizon. Studying it. Peter in turn studied
his father's expression.

Edward kept repeating one phrase in Inuit, maybe twenty or twenty-five times, and finally I asked Peter what it meant. "It's my
father's biggest fear," he said, "his biggest worry. And it's the reason

79

he won't fly today—I'm sure of it."

"Would he mind if I know what it is?"

"It's hard to translate. But my father believes that radio airwaves—I'm not sure what word to use. Radio airwaves from cities can catch his plane and pull him like a fishing net. And he is very afraid of this. He doesn't want to be pulled down to a city—like Winnipeg. Like Montreal. He's seen cities in magazines and doesn't want to go there. He doesn't want to go where rooms are stacked up on each other, like in a hotel. He doesn't even like that rooms are stacked up on each other in the Churchill Hotel. He's seen that. He goes to Churchill a lot. He has bad dreams about having to sleep high up off the ground."

"He flies up in the air, though."

"Not the same to him. You won't figure it out. Just take it as fact. It's how he gets when he thinks Sedna is angry. He thinks she'll make radio airwaves from the cities, net him, and drag him off course and he'll have to land in a city and he'll never get out. He'll die in a city. He doesn't have a lot of fears, my father. But the ones he has, they're big. That's why he's so upset right now. That's why he's definitely not flying today. When he's like this I just step back. He's my father. I've seen this a lot of times."

"Now I understand why he'll fly south as far as The Pas but no farther—too close to Winnipeg. That's why the guitars would be put on somebody else's plane and sent on to Winnipeg, right? Or the train."

"See how much you can figure out in a day? One thing's for sure, my father's not flying today. Let's get the guitars off cargo, eh?"

Peter had a band called Nanook the Gook. The band's name originally was Turbulence (I wondered if it came from his father's experience in flying mail planes, or some inner turmoil Peter had experienced), but they had decided to change it when the Vietnam War was at full nightmarish cacophony, with daily reports on the CBC. In other words, they'd had this band for nearly fifteen years. The Vietnam War came to be called the first television war, but at the time in Eskimo Point there were no televisions; it was a radio war. "We're small brown people," Peter once said to me. "So were those Vietnam folks."

Anyway, I'd heard Nanook the Gook play four times and knew that their repertoire was exclusively the songs of John Lennon. Also, Peter, who was about thirty-five, wore round, wire-rimmed glasses when he played guitar and sang, no corrective lenses, just clear glass. He had ordered them through an advertisement for John Lennon

Granny Glasses he had heard on the radio or seen in a magazine. I think *Rolling Stone*. *Rolling Stone* was delivered by mail plane every three or four months.

Though they would never be written up in *Rolling Stone*, the band was, for a time, enormously popular throughout the scattered demographic of villages along the coast of Hudson Bay, with an intensely loyal following. Often Edward had flown them to gigs. I still have a number of reel-to-reel recordings of their covers of "Instant Karma," "Power to the People," "Woman Is the Nigger of the World," "Whatever Gets You Through the Night," "Nobody Told Me," "Don't Worry, Kyoko," "Working Class Hero." The band was heavy on guitars (they had recently taken on a new lead guitarist, who was seventeen), and Peter's voice made me suspect that his vocal coach might have been a seagull. In my recording of "Nobody Told Me," in fact, you can hear seagulls in the background.

I had been employed by the Oral History Project to translate life histories and folktales. In previous years I had worked under different sponsorship in Churchill, right on Hudson Bay. Now, at Eskimo Point, I was in the midst of translating a single complicated story. The working title I gave it was "I Hate to Leave This Beautiful Place." In broad outline, the story concerns a goose who falls into unmitigated despair, primarily exhibited by a high-pitched keening, a wailing lament that can be heard echoing across the stark tundra landscape: *"I hate to leave this beautiful place!"* repeated over and over and over. The bird itself was originally a man—a family man, with a wife and two children, a sculptor who had worked in soapstone, a great artist whose carvings of birds were everywhere admired. This man was known to have seldom left his home village of Padlei. Then one day he angered a powerful shaman, who changed him into a goose. It will be best to simply relate the story whole cloth, of course—and I will do that—but allow me to say here that in his incarnation as a goose, he must of course eventually migrate south, leave home, or else the arctic winter will kill him. In this story, melancholy is the intensifying element to the universal themes of mortality, longing, home, sanity—and the story contains, with Inuit philosophical generosity characteristic of their spoken literature, and without spelling it out, a meditation on what the world requires of and imposes on an individual, and how that individual comes to knowledge of himself or herself through indelible experience.

I hate to leave this beautiful place. I hate to leave this beautiful place.

81

The woman from whom I had originally heard the story and whom I was working with on a daily basis was named Lucille Amorak. Lucille was a wonderful poet, as well; late in her life her poems seemed to represent the spoken word and written word in equal measure; they had a willful informality. Here is one of my favorites:

GRUDGES

My aunt held a grudge—she forgot why.
My cousin held a grudge—he forgot why.
My father held a grudge—he forgot why.
Lots of things happened in the village,
lots of things.
People were born—people died—gulls
were everywhere all the time—
the beach and the big boulders on the beach
stayed put.
My cousin living in another village
held a grudge—she forgot why.
I held a grudge—it was because a seal
took a fish right off my line!
For a long time I held a seal grudge.
I don't hold that grudge anymore, but
at least I remember why I once did.
My other uncle held a grudge—he forgot why.
My other aunt held a grudge—it was
against me. I forgot why.
One day I walked over to her house and said,
"What's your grudge?" "I forgot," she said.
"It was fun holding it, " she said,
"then it wasn't."
We sat down for a meal. That was a while ago.
I forgot what we ate. My aunt was in
a pretty good mood, though—she laughed
a lot—I forgot what over.

As Lucille's family had never joined a church, there were no birth records, but she told me that her mother had told her that she had been born in 1913. Lucille Amorak was Peter's grandmother's sister. Every day we worked on the transcription and translation from seven o'clock in the morning until noon. This had been our schedule for three weeks running. We sat at her splintery table, in her one-room shack house, located next to the post office that flew a Canadian flag. The teapot was often on boil and each morning she would hold a piece of seal fat to the open end of a flask, tip the flask to soak the fat in whiskey. The work often went haltingly; my Inuit needed work, yet Lucille had "a lot of English," as she put it. We managed.

Anyway, at about 11 or 11:30 p.m. on December 8, I was reading, for the hundredth or so time, *The Carrier of Ladders*, a collection of poems by W. S. Merwin, in the stockroom of the Hudson's Bay Co. store, where I had a cot and washbowl, and shaved without a mirror—courtesy of Mr. Albert Bettany, store manager since 1955. They were spare quarters to be sure. But I had a space heater; it was probably about ten or fifteen degrees below zero out, Fahrenheit. Suddenly Peter walked right in, no knock on the door. "Hey—hey," he said. "Tommy's gonna be on the radio, eh?" Tommy was the drummer, Tommy Ipiuk, who was around thirty. I sat up from my cot, switched on the shortwave, and it came in clear. Turning the dial, I found NWT—Northwest Territories Radio. The weatherman, who was also a news broadcaster, was named Gabriel Omik. He alternated between English and Inuit; he had a wonderful, quirky manner and sometimes out of nowhere, for no discernible reason, would speak in a pretty good imitation of Humphrey Bogart.

One thing to know about Gabriel's show is that his weather report included recriminations. Let me explain. Through labyrinthine arctic gossip routes sustained to some degree by mail-plane pilots and the now-defunct telegram services and such, Gabriel received all sorts of information about the behavior of people in his listening region. This was the equivalent, say, of the Crime Report in the daily newspaper that serves the small hamlet where I live in Vermont, which archives the disparate incidents, often petty crimes, some harrowing, some ludicrous—loud talking late at night on the street to abuse of a homeless dog, jaywalking to drunk driving, mailboxes smashed in by drive-by teenagers bored to tears, and so forth—the cumulative effect being: *Look how much generally small-time criminal behavior can be fitted into any given day and night.* When I think of it, basically the same sort of sociology—stupidity, recklessness, killing of time—was experienced in arctic villages as well. The difference was, Gabriel Omik would chose a perpetrator to indict as having specifically insulted Sedna, pissed her off or agitated her in some terrible way or other. So that when Tommy Ipiuk got blackout drunk and took potshots at a neighbor's sled dogs, all but blinding one in its right eye, Gabriel Omik found out about it. "Now, word got to me that this stupid fellow named Tommy Ipiuk—who's a very cool drummer for Nanook the Gook and I've seen them play, they're great, they do all those John Lennon tunes—Tommy had a stupid dumb-ass night the other night, he shot at a neighbor's dog, and now Sedna is not happy, my friends, she is *not happy*, and there's a freakin' outrageous storm coming in from the Northwest, my friends. It's gonna blow the asshole out of a polar bear, it's gonna wail louder than Hendrix doing the national anthem at Woodstock, it's gonna tear into Inuit Territories and have a wild time. So thanks a lot, Tommy Ipiuk. And I mean, if you weren't such a fantastic drummer . . ."

As I listened to this riff on the relationship between human misjudgment and a threatening weather system, of the sort I had heard dozens of times—Tommy's fifteen minutes of infamy—Gabriel suddenly, with a sharp, sobbing intake of breath, interrupted himself: "Friends in the northern world, I—" And for a good long minute Gabriel could not speak. You could hear him trying to catch his breath. There were some weird sounds in the background. It sounded as if someone was breaking something. Then Gabriel said, "My friends—John Lennon was murdered tonight in the city of New York in the U.S." There was another long pause. "John Lennon was gunned down. John Lennon is gone."

I imagined then this radio message physically manifesting itself as a net and floating out in the air into eternity.

I remember it taking less than half an hour for the band to gather in my room. Tommy, Peter, a guitarist named Sam Bird, and William, a guitarist and keyboardist, sat in fold-down slat chairs and plugged in their guitars to the extension-cord socket connected to the auxiliary generator. Tommy set up the drum kit. Gabriel, in his NW Territories Radio studio, started playing John Lennon song after John Lennon song. Nanook the Gook jammed with the radio. And while I didn't write down all the titles, I do recall the first three, perhaps because Tommy could scarcely get through the band's cover of them, not because he did not know how to play them perfectly by heart, but for all his sobbing fits. Plus he was getting very drunk on whiskey. At one point in the evening Tommy said, "I'm such a fuck-up," and, drunkenly to be sure, went off in berserk fashion into a drum solo that must've lasted fifteen or so minutes, screaming with nearly catatonic repetition, "Sedna—pleeeeze, Sedna—pleeeze, Sedna—pleeeze!"

"You can't be thinking that shooting at those dogs had anything to do with what happened in New York," I said. "Tommy—"

He kicked over the drum set, threw the drumsticks at my face, then walked over and took a swing at me, which missed. He sat down on the floor. "What the fuck do you know?"

The long arctic night unfolded with whiskey, cigarettes, music, radio, and very little talking. Every once in a while I'd repair to another storage room and tune in a foreign station on the shortwave. The death of John Lennon was being talked about in so many languages it was mind-boggling. It was a murder translated everywhere.

I didn't know where exactly Gabriel was broadcasting from; it might have been Winnipeg. Some years later, and with no small amount of letter writing, I managed to acquire a copy of Gabriel's playlist of that night. It was obviously typed out on a manual typewriter. *Cold Turkey. I Found Out. Mother. Hold On. Working Class Hero. God. Imagine. Crippled Inside. Jealous Guy. It's So Hard. I Don't Want to Be a Soldier. Give Me Some Truth. Oh My Love. How Do You Sleep? Oh Yoko! New York City. Mind Games. I'm Sorry. One Day (At a Time). Bring on the Lucie. Intuition. Out of the Blue. Only People. I Know (I Know). You Are Here. Meat City. Going Down on Love. Whatever Gets You Through the Night. What You Got. Bless You. Scared. No. 9. A Dream. Surprise Surprise (Sweet Bird of Paradox). Steel and Glass. Beef Jerky. Nobody Loves You (When You're Down and Out). Just Like Starting Over.* (List smudged and incomplete.)

Nanook the Gook left the storage room of the Hudson's Bay Co. store at about 7:30 a.m. the following morning. Gone sleepless, by 8:00 I was again working with Lucille Amorak, who was suffering from a case of pneumonia that had been diagnosed at the small hospital in Churchill. Edward Ominiq had flown her there and back on a single day. That was preferable for Lucille, as she had no interest in staying at the Churchill Hotel either. As a result of her condition, Lucille was loudly short of breath, which infused her recitation of the folktale we were working on with a punctuated sense of urgency sentence by sentence, and when she raised her voice for emphasis, or shifted into the voice of this or that character, her voice caught and rasped, as if she would not reach the next word. She hacked and wheezed at times too. She often had to lie down and nap during a given day. After about a month—according to my notebooks right up to December 14—we got to the point where Lucille simply could not work on this story anymore. She was too exhausted both from pneumonia and the work's repetition. It was enough. I was fortunate to have lots of help with the translation from her husband and two nieces, who would go over the story and vocabulary lists, but finally we stopped on December 21. The CBC, BBC, stations out of Amsterdam, Vancouver, Paris, Prague, New York, Buffalo, all sorts of cities were still reporting the aftermath of John Lennon's murder and playing his songs. I asked Lucille Amorak if she had ever heard of John Lennon and she said, "I heard about him from Peter. He played me some songs. He sang some songs. I asked Peter if this John Lennon would be visiting and he said no he wouldn't." She poured us each a cup of tea, I closed my notebook, and we sat a long time saying nothing.

Peter announced that he needed to get down to New York in the United States, sit for a while in Central Park near the Dakota, "maybe even find some people to play some Lennon songs with." He had gotten hold of a copy of a map of New York from the library in Churchill. He had circled Central Park. As for employment, Nanook the Gook was definitely confined by winter itself—people just didn't travel much until spring. Still, the band made a little money and Tommy had previously saved up. I don't know the details of his finances but I do know that he definitely had his mind made up to get to New York and that he wanted the rest of the band to go with him, yet they had no such interest and this caused a deep rift. I was scheduled to leave from Churchill by train to Winnipeg. Trains had a fixed schedule on paper, but often that schedule was intervened and altered and canceled by blizzards. Perhaps depending on the degree to which Sedna was distraught. Probably I'd have to sleep high up off the ground for some nights in the Churchill Hotel.

The day before I left, Peter insisted that I walk with him about a quarter mile out of Eskimo Point to a frozen pond. It was cold as hell out and I was fighting off the flu and didn't really think it too wise to go with him, but I was persuaded by the fact that he was carrying his electric guitar and small amplifier and a battery protected against the cold inside some packing material. I had no earthly idea what he had in mind and didn't ask. When we reached the pond, a few ravens flew off, and there, out toward the center of the pond, which was vaguely outlined by a rise in snow along its bank, was a snowy owl. It was a big owl and held its ground and didn't move at all, except for a slight flutter of its wings and subtle head bobbing and its eyes closing and opening, not blinking, closing and opening with signal mysteriousness. The owl was almost camouflaged by the snow and snow light off the pond, but nonetheless, once you saw it you could glance away and locate it again, because it had not moved at all. Peter and I had not said a word to each other this whole time. Now he took out the battery from its wrapping, set the wrapping on the frozen ground, and situated the battery on top. He fixed the amp, then the guitar, to the battery, turned, and started to whine and echo the opening bars of "Whatever Gets You Through the Night" and I mean blasting it out over the tundra. The owl shifted only slightly and tucked its head deep into its shoulders and closed its eyes. It was sad and comical and a number of other things I can't describe. ". . . through the night, all right, all right." Peter had a voice that made Bob Dylan seem like Pavarotti but what did it matter really. He joyfully shouted, "I got my Eskimo freak on!"—wildly gyrating in classic rock-star style—wailing. He was torn up inside is what I thought. And I'd never before and haven't since seen tears actually flying from someone's face. When he finished the song in an exaggerated way he bowed to the owl and said, "I've played for this fellow eight or ten times, you know."

For well over a year, Gabriel blamed the worst arctic storms on Mark David Chapman, the sick creep who'd murdered John Lennon, though he blamed Inuit people in various locales for other trespasses and violations too. (In fact, it was on his program that I first heard warnings about pollution causing climate change—which was agitating Sedna almost beyond belief.) I never saw Peter again but did learn that he made it to New York in December of 1981 and got to play John Lennon songs with different musicians and singers gathered on the first anniversary of John Lennon's death in Central Park across from the Dakota apartment building. Apparently Peter got "caught up"—as his father put it—in the city for the rest of that winter. Early in the summer of 1982, he traveled by bus and foot to Flin Flon, Manitoba. From there Edward Ominiq flew him to Eskimo Point. Back home, almost immediately "spirits began using him." When this was said of someone, it meant many things, all of them malevolent. The way Edward put it was, "Peter was done in."

Though I'd once entertained the idea of writing a musician's biography of him, I admit that for years I had no news of Peter, no notion of his situation or even his whereabouts. Nor did I seek any of that out. I can claim only the slightest knowledge of his life after I saw him play "Whatever Gets You Through the Night" that bone-chilling bright day outside Eskimo Point. But when I finally returned to that village, one of his cousins suggested that I walk out to the old Eskimo cemetery and find Peter's gravestone. Naturally, I did that. Under his name and the years of his birth and death, it reads: Nobody Told Me There'd Be Days Like These.

There was a man who was the best carver of soapstone anyone ever saw. He lived in Padlei—he carved in Padlei. He never left Padlei, except to go out and find soapstone for his carvings. He knew where to find the best soapstone. Well, of course, jealous and envious carvers tried to follow him, but they never could. The moon had special affection for him. That's what people said. They said the moon helped him out. It was true. I believe it was true.

Anyway, anyway, anyway, one day this man carved a seal and seal hunter. One day he carved seagulls above a whale. One day he carved an owl. One day he carved a mother, father, daughter, son. One day he carved a woman sleeping. One day he carved a man sleeping. One day he carved a spirit figure. One day he carved a goose flying.

On the day he carved the goose flying, a shaman—very nasty fellow, very powerful fellow—this shaman arrived uninvited to Padlei. He sat near the man carving the goose, and when the work was finished, the shaman said, "Give it to me."

The carver said, "No."

"Why?"

"This one is promised to someone."

"Promise it to me now!" the shaman said. He was getting angry.

"No."

It began to snow. The shaman turned the carver into a goose. Everyone in the village of Padlei saw this happen. In past times they had seen this shaman turn people into seals, seagulls, whales, guillemots, foxes, bears, ravens. Those people never came back to the village either. They never came back. They went out into the distance and didn't return.

"Now I have the carving," said the shaman. "And soon it will be winter." Then the shaman flew through the air, holding the carving. He went out to meet the horizon. It didn't take him long.

"Look!" the carver's wife said. "Look—there!" When people looked to where she was pointing, they saw a flock of geese leaving in the southward direction.

"Look!" the carver's daughter said. "Look—there!" When people looked to where she was pointing, they saw another flock of geese lifting up from the earth. This flock flew off in the southward direction.

Sadness was in everyone's eyes. Sadness was on everyone's face. This is the truth of it.

"Look!" the carver's son said. "Look—there!" When people looked to where he was pointing, they saw another flock of geese going southward.

"Father," the carver's daughter said, "you have to join them."

"Father," the carver's son said. "My sister is right—you must leave."

"Husband," the carver's wife said, "if you stay you will die. The river ice will clasp you by your legs. Your wings will stop moving. Your eyes will close."

Hearing this, the carver flew over to a pond that was already freezing over. Everyone in the village stood along the edge. "Do I have sadness on my face?" he called out.

"You are a goose now," his wife said. "It is hard to tell."

"Look more carefully," he said.

"Oh, yes, now I see it," his wife said.

Everyone went back to their homes, except for the carver's wife, son, and daughter, who stayed by the pond. All night—all night, and then for five days and nights—everyone heard the goose crying loudly, "I HATE TO LEAVE THIS BEAUTIFUL PLACE! I HATE TO LEAVE THIS BEAUTIFUL PLACE! I HATE TO LEAVE THIS BEAUTIFUL PLACE! Night. Day. Night. Day. It was so loud that the wife, son, and daughter lost their hearing. Later their hearing came back, but as for right then, they were deaf. They saw the carver crying out but could no longer hear him.

Finally, he flew southward. In the spring he returned. He was still a goose. This was the shaman's fault. The carver was visited every day that summer by his family. They told him all the news of the village. When winter approached again, his family wondered, would he cry out, "I HATE TO LEAVE THIS BEAUTIFUL PLACE!" and soon he did. He cried it out for days and for nights.

"We'll stay by the pond," the carver's wife said. "We'll just have to lose our hearing each time. That is the truth of it."

After that, when anyone left the village of Padlei, they would say, "I hate to leave this beautiful place." This is the story of how that came about and why you hear people saying it and meaning it. The carver returned every spring for many years. For as long as a goose lives.

One day the carver's wife, son, and daughter were out walking.

89

They had wandered quite far from Padlei. "Look!" the daughter said, and when everyone looked in the direction she was pointing, they saw a figure holding still on the horizon. They walked to it. When they got close they saw it was the shaman. He was now made of soapstone. The carver's wife said, "He is clutching the carving of the goose that your father made!"

"It's rightly ours," the daughter said. She tried to pry it from the shaman's hands but could not. Then the son tried but he could not. Then the carver's wife began to wail loudly, "I HATE TO LEAVE THIS BEAUTIFUL PLACE! I HATE TO LEAVE THIS BEAUTIFUL PLACE!" Again and again—even louder than her husband had cried it. Through the night. All day the next day. Into the next night—until finally the shaman's hands cracked loose the carving and it fell to the ground. The daughter picked it up directly. They all returned home. This is the truth of it. (Told by Lucille Amorak.)

Leaving Alberta
Stephen Marche

LAST WEEK IN THE FIELDS just beyond the Tuscan Hills development on the outskirts of Yellowhead in Northern Alberta, six-year-old Sarah Ferguson, running downhill chasing a dandelion seed, stepped on a land mine and exploded. The developers hired a team to decipher the explosion but all they uncovered was other buried objects. *The Yellowhead Gleaner* published a complete list: antique guns and knives in small wooden boxes, ragged dresses folded under the roots of poplars, crucifixes and Jewish stars preserved in knitted bags or naked in the earth, and also "a tattered paperback book without inscription." I knew instantly that it was the copy of James Frazer's *The Golden Bough* that had belonged to Madeleine Parr. I could almost see the wrinkled Penguin cover and the paper so yellow and frail it wouldn't seem physically capable of supporting the masses of fine, linear notation in its limn-soaked margins. The developers of the Tuscan Hills have been digging up my youth out there in the middle of nowhere.

Yellowhead is slightly closer to Edmonton than to Fort McMurray, a town just large enough to warrant the high school I attended. I buried the stuff with a few others during the spring of 1989. The ceremony must have been a night in May, late in the month, because the ground had thawed but the university acceptance letters hadn't yet shivered their life openers into our mailboxes. I cannot separate the place from the time of my life I was living there, the time just before the end of school, far away and long ago. The prairies of Northern Alberta, to me, are a place longing to live, longing to be a place, as desolate and grand and inconceivably vast as youth. There are still unnamed lakes there. There are places where people genuinely are not.

The energy company where most of the town worked owned a chunk of the province the size of Florida, which it was just beginning to strip of the notorious bitumen, ravaging the wilderness into a pure inorganic nightmare flatland. At that time, the field where Sarah

Ferguson was to die belonged to nobody. A Ukrainian family had immigrated to Yellowhead with the standard deal that settled Western Canada—a free quarter section on the understanding that it had to be cleared or would revert to the Crown—but after a year's farming the family had found the land so poor they abandoned it.

My school, Marc Garneau High, siphoned kids from an hour and a half away in each direction. I knew at most fifteen of its seven hundred students. Marc Garneau was populated largely with farmers' sons and daughters, and my friends were all the internationalized children of the energy executives and technicians who chose not to live too close to the brutality of the oil sands. As the saying goes, everybody works in Fort McMurray but nobody lives there. We were the children of oil. We didn't mix with the children of soil. That was another saying. Our worldliness wasn't all pretense either. Our parents were always away, digesting the surface of the earth in great sloppy mouthfuls, or up in the air motivating the ethereal wraiths of finance needed to conjure the machinery onto the plains. We were in charge of ourselves.

For grade eleven and most of grade twelve my girlfriend was Trista Kim, the only Asian girl in Yellowhead. She dated me, I think, strictly because I had spent grades one through six in Hong Kong and was the only boy in a thousand-kilometer radius who didn't find her Asianness exotic. Trista was an interesting woman. She had the highest marks in math at Marc Garneau and four vestigial nipples—one was a real, full extra nipple, the others like tiny moles. The toothy smile she wore was so permanent it amounted to a mask—her cheerfulness so obviously a guise it grew seductively more mysterious with time.

The night of the ceremony, I had wandered over to Trista's superannuated bungalow, a place hardly ever bothered by her parents' presence. She kept it clean in their honor, like a tidy grave. Trista and I were so mature that we had broken up in April because we knew that in June, when the universities picked us, our futures would diverge forever. Imminent separation didn't prevent us from our ordinary high school activities, hanging out listening to music and fooling around. For Trista in 1989, the whole world had been rendered toxic by top-forty country and Celine Dion and Guns N' Roses, so she shut herself up in the bunkers of Talking Heads and Morrissey. Morrissey and Talking Heads provided all the food and fuel she needed, and she was unready, just yet, to open the door a crack and chance the postapocalyptic scene. I remember the night of Madeleine's ceremony we were listening, over and over, to the Smiths' *Hatful of Hollow.*

"Just another bush party," Trista said. "I mean that's what it will probably be, right? If a stranger stopped by in a car and walked into that field, he would think he was in the middle of a bush party."

"It will be a party in a bush," I said.

"It sounds just like another bush party. But maybe we should go to bush parties. Maybe we should be those kinds of people."

"I don't even know what kinds of people those are."

"They're the kind who go to bush parties. They get it all out of their systems. Probably we're heading for midlife crises."

Midlife might as well have been eternity. "Tell me exactly what she said to you again."

"I told you."

"Just tell me again. It's so cool."

"Madeleine called me over when we were all smoking cigarettes out by the front banisters. And she tossed her lovely head of blonde hair like a pony and patted her weird old book and she said, 'I know you need it to rain.'"

Madeleine Parr had told us that we needed it to rain. She was going to do for all of us what she had done for Sammy Mooncalf. Madeleine had arrived at the beginning of grade twelve, a stranger among the strangers, and in the winter, she began to date Sammy Mooncalf, a local boy who lived with his mother, a nurse at the Yellowhead hospital. Sammy hadn't even applied for university. He had promised his mother that he would graduate from high school; then off to the drills, to roughneck for a hundred grand a year until he was chewed up by the work like all the other local boys.

"They look so weird together," Trista said.

"Because he's Indian and she's white?"

"Yeah, I'm so racist but . . ."

"She's pretty white."

"Exactly. That's what I mean. I'm just a Korean girl but that creature is so, so white."

Madeleine Parr was a blonde of the type around which modern civilization is currently arranged: She had pretty handwriting and always walked like she had just left ballet class. The stock market runs so that men can put blondes like Madeleine in nice houses, and buy them nice clothes that they can wear out of their nice houses when they go to have their blonde hair kept blonde. Her father was one of those Connecticut Yankees who had wildcatted in Texas and then drifted north, chasing the next fortune—polished human dust but still dust, blown around the prosperous world.

"I saw Sam and Madeleine burying a dress together once," Trista said.

"That's what we're supposed to bring tonight, right? I'm supposed to bring a weapon and you're supposed to bring a dress? I would hate to commit a faux pas at the orgy."

Trista nodded. "I saw them burying the dress in the field by the railway tracks."

"How do you know it was a dress?" I asked.

"This was back in January, and they just laid it under the snow."

"You dug it up then?"

"Maybe." Trista smiled.

"When was this?"

"End of January. A very plain dress with that I'm-a-virgin off-white she wears so much."

I did not ask Trista what she had been doing in a car near the railway tracks in January, when we had been going out, attached by bonds of supposed loyalty. "Please, Please, Please, Let Me Get What I Want" started to play, the last song on *Hatful of Hollow*.

"Trista, honestly, can you figure out why we're listening to this weird blonde? Railway crossroads. Next it will be tarot cards."

"It began with 'The Waste Land,'" Trista said.

Right after we studied "The Waste Land" in advanced English, Sammy Mooncalf started driving into Fort McMurray, to the Boomtown casino, and driving away with huge sums of cash. His biggest night, I believe, was over ten thousand dollars, scythed from the craps table. In March, he bought himself a Ford F-150, which I imagine was the happiest moment of his life. I had inadvertently been responsible for uncovering why he was so lucky, when Madeleine left behind her copy of *The Golden Bough* at school and I picked it up. Every page had been underlined but the passages about the sexual rituals and vegetation, as I showed Trista and, through her, the rest of our friends, were crammed with notes in her cramped girlish handwriting, and they mentioned Sammy by name.

"What would you bring?" Trista asked. I knew then that we were going to go.

"My grandfather's gun."

"Why?"

"Because it's hideous," I lied. My grandfather, his soul a pocketful of violence, had returned from World War II with a grandiose understanding of the big hate. He worked his whole life in the tin shop at Canadian Pacific and handmade the pistol in his off hours.

"We have to go. We have to. It will be the final night of the smoothies," Trista said, grabbing her keys from the counter, jingle-jangling them.

Trista always called our group the smoothies. I think she meant to make fun of our snobbery, of our assumption that our childhoods in Saudi and China and our parents' money and our wide-open futures made us smoother than the rest of the kids at Marc Garneau. But the word was perfect in other ways for us, for that time and that place. We had been smoothed away, like the landscape had been smoothed away for the oil, religion and nationality smoothed away. Our smoothness craved roots, dirty roughness binding us into the earth. I did not need to ask Trista what she was bringing to the ceremony. She had already told me. The mourning dress from her Korean great-grandmother who had died on a ferry leaving Vancouver Island eighty years ago. A long strip of white, that was all she would show me. Was the white strip Trista's root as my grandfather's gun was to me? Or was Madeleine our root? I have wondered: By having us bury these fetishes, was Madeleine having us throw away our roots or offering us a way to reroot ourselves in our desolate Alberta youth?

Trista and I drove out of Yellowhead in silence. The edge of town, even then, was difficult to establish. No line, no sign, just the sleeping drama of machinery on the ever-outward-expanding construction sites, then a thinning of the houses and then hay bales. We had no trouble finding the spot. Two hundred yards or so from the road, a huge fire was roaring.

We parked, sat in the dark. Trista leaned over and kissed me with maximum adolescent tenderness, my hands automatically lifting to her breasts.

"We could stay here," she said.

"That's true. We could just watch the fire."

"Like a drive-in movie."

We kissed again but knew that we wanted the fire more than each other. We needed to see the burning in the dark field. We needed Madeleine.

The wild grasses, still soggy from thaw, matted our steps, the air mildly furious with spring. Madeleine Parr was sitting at the edge of the light, cross-legged, smeared with mud, in a ripped dress, her flared golden tresses coppered by the fire. Though she was busy guiding the bodies into their various positions, she smiled at Trista and me. I remember my initial reaction was identical to walking down the school highway. Oh look, there's Billy, there's Emmanuel, there's Sammy Mooncalf. It's just that they were all fucking in the flame-licked dark. And among them, among us, Madeleine Parr lounged like a tatterdemalion goddess, presiding over the orgy. I had sex four times, once with Madeleine, but all I remember is how grim it all was, how grim and workmanlike its pleasure, before we buried our fetishes and slipped into the night.

The administrative reaction was predictably severe because it was necessarily so futile. The school year being nearly over, our grades already with the universities, they could afford to expel us all without consequences. The purity of Yellowhead youth was at stake, and we were the smoothies. The principal and the teachers desired our outsiderly shame. And we were ashamed, though not for their reasons. It wasn't the sex. Who cared about sex? Our shame gushed because, by our participation in the ritual, we had admitted to each other how ferociously we needed the right schools to pick us, how we longed to succeed, how we desired the world and a place in it. Our faith embarrassed us. What had we been thinking? That Madeleine Parr was a witching woman who could fix our futures with dirty games? She had read Frazer, the chapter "The Influence of the Sexes on Vegetation," but I could read it too:

> For four days before they committed the seed to the earth the Pipiles of Central America kept apart from their wives "in order that on the night before planting they might indulge their passions to the fullest extent; certain persons are even said to have been appointed to perform the sexual act at the very moment when the first seeds were deposited in the ground." The use of their wives at that time was indeed enjoined upon the people by the priests as a religious duty, in default of which it was not lawful to sow the seed.

Madeleine Parr was our Pipiles priest. We did it all for her sake, for the sake of our belief that she knew how life worked, the signal blonde of civilization. What could be sillier?

*

I have my own daughter now. Four years old. Sarah Ferguson running in the hectic of her laughter, the world's young fizz, stepping, exploding—these gestures have not stopped scouring the sides of my brain. Nobody would be charged, I knew that. The police chief in Yellowhead is Billy Matteo, one of the few smoothies who stayed in town, who also happened to be one of the boys screwing in the dark, screwing his way into a future under the guidance of Madeleine Parr. For all I know, the land mine belonged to him. I do know that his father served in Korea. One of the bent and trembling girls of the field, Lauren Hill, just a year ago became the youngest justice ever appointed to the Superior Court of Alberta. I'm sure they all know about the explosion. We haven't spoken since the ceremony and who wants to start when it might involve criminal conspiracy?

Madeleine Parr is now an associate professor of religious studies at the University of Chicago. I found her e-mail address online and sent a link to the story in *The Yellowhead Gleaner*. Moments later, she IMed.

MP: I saw. The story made the Trib here even. How's your life?
SM: Surprisingly confused at the moment.
MP: Because of the girl.
SM: Because of the girl.

For a decent, stalemated while, we IMed back and forth about nothing much, the lives of our old friends, the distances of the various journeys that had spilled out from that burning night in that missing place, the journeys that had taken us from the field that belonged to nobody to wherever we were standing now. Madeleine hadn't heard that Trista was a vet in Arkansas. Had she seen the nipples? Had she remembered?

MP: It's amazing how it worked, isn't it?
SM: What worked?
MP: The ritual.
SM: How so?
MP: I just mean that everybody in that field that night "made it." Will Matteo is police chief in Yellowhead, did you know that? Trista Kim's a vet you tell me. Lauren Hill a judge. Mark Yerevan has six kids and a ranch.

SM: And you're a tenured professor.

MP: A testament to the power of faith? I believed I was the priestess for all of you.

SM: High school high priestess.

MP: And only in that place. Only in Alberta. I'll tell you I'm not a saint in Chicago.

SM: Didn't seem to work for Sammy Mooncalf, though.

Right after school, Sammy Mooncalf had joined the oil sands as a roughneck, earned his hundred grand a year, paid off his mom's house, snorted as much of the money as he could, and blew the rest on wrecked trucks until the crash that killed him at twenty-three. Four hundred people showed up for his funeral.

MP: The strange power of the burying ceremony is its connection to the unpredictable.

SM: Why was it so unlucky for Sammy then?

MP: I think luck may be a misleading word. And also he was lucky in his way. It was just not our way.

SM: What is our way?

MP: Ordinary middle-class life.

SM: His bad luck was our good luck.

MP: That's one way to handle it.

SM: And so Sammy and this little girl have to die so we can drive midlevel cars and own houses in decent neighborhoods and send our kids to reasonable schools.

MP: Is your life worth it?

She was apparently still my priest. She took my confession anyway.

SM: I don't know. I don't know if anyone else would say I was worth it. If I'm walking down the street now, even in sneakers and a T-shirt, cabs pull up to see if I want a ride.

MP: I know what you mean.

SM: Or this. My daughter fell out of her crib a year ago and I was holding her. The medics strapped her little body down to protect her neck but she wouldn't stop crying. And I was holding her hand the whole time we were driving and at the hospital it turned out her neck was fine but her arm was broken and I had been holding it the whole time. That's why she was crying.

MP: I know what you mean.

I knew that she did not know what I was trying to mean. It's not her fault either; I am essentially unpriestable. Madeleine and I chatted for the sake of chatting but we had nothing more to say.

Even though I haven't lived there for twenty years, I can tell you that nothing on earth is more beautiful than an Alberta June—its size beyond scale, beyond the vanity of human measurement, and its sloppy loveliness, its effortless splurge, paintbrush wildflowers nurtured by long-distance thunderstorms under an inconceivable sky. It is beautiful but it offers no comfort. It answers no questions either and gives no clues, no cures for the aching gamble under the surface of everything, in Alberta and elsewhere.

Three Poems
Cathy Park Hong

THE QUATTROCENTO

I hail an aerocab,
turn up my personalized surround sound
track: wistful to anthemic
to voice
      recognition
a song strains after a long
sweet spot of identification
      O parable diced three ways
      I want to share my thoughts
with you and formal
      you so wander outwards
      into the mesquite frontier preserved
in sprawl
      out on my cub rug, my domain
You are a friend, you are user
      friendly, a nod and the room brightens
to an aquarium of starfish, clean,
filtered
      of chimes and zither
the thip of pick against rack of strings
a sample of sounds free to share
included the versions
      of California would you like
an aerial footage of clouds
      the mild color of jicama recognize
your face in its formations
flattering, thriving before focus

      is a new commodity
the focus groups agree my attention lasts
as long as parents are concerned

100

trolling caused
two real deaths and the duration
of alarm lasts as long as
              recess bells drilling
for us to line near bars
              where we used to hang
ourselves in exit 5 now a rest
              stop, all towns now are rest stops
to a vanishing point
out the obvious, we're all going to
              the Cloud, haunted by a desire for abolition,
              a gobbet of flesh marooned
on the smooth, gleaming
surface of image
you can now feel the hologram
like skinned grapes in a haunted
              town after town where industry
was once material

              fall out is soft, invisible
snow, nieve, der schnee,
xui, noon means eye, lightly
              I speak in commands
and greetings, sometimes drive-by
flaming
we live accentless
              chat with me the voice
activation is on so too the translation
conversion of Euro
              to the falling currency
of American
fragments no longer subversive
              or choice of form but encoded
 I don't want to be a niche
              I want to be a yardstick
become the voice

of the carefree surfer riding the winter waves
              in his gimp suit
There is no moon, no night
where our minds can freshen up

unless I dim you out
    like a dimmer you prat what part of
my password is weak
    like your abs, you
half-eaten child living
    in a torso of live-cams
you think your head is legendary
everyone can see you

    see the brightest tree
of you, you everywhere
    your face I interface
massage into being, sprouting mouth
after raw mouth, lidless
nervous system, sunlit band
    width of one argonaut blood
cell recalling
ancestors surveying
    the bright, unbound
presence of the new world,
    trampling thrush
my heart fills with water
    swallowing it
whole.

SHEDS OF A NATION

Go, go, I breathe the air
    flossed with silence
moving me to melt

into any form what
    choice when they
finish your thought

did you mean numerous no
    numinous
when minds flood into minds
yet one creed molds

this town of giant convenience
        a white church
of blond wooden pews burning

a dark pile of something
        enough these terrors,
clarity, empathy, please

drop me onto a quiet coast
        dotted with sandpipers
the horizon hyphenates

are they UN forces no
        they are nudist bathers.
They have beached.
Dashed with amorous wet,

They call out like walruses,
these loafing rebels against
        the enhanced,
I see too much

Yet go, go into the unknown,
        smell the salt, rancid
scent of water, seagull,
grass tufts and listen,

the one with the sodden beard says
        undrape yourself,
you are not guilty to me.

ENGINES WITHIN THE THRONE

We once worked as clerks
        scanning voices from mothballed
pages into the clouds, all memories
outsourced except the fuzzy
        childhood bits when

103

Cathy Park Hong

I was an undersized girl with a tic,
they numbed me with botox
      I was a skinsuit
of dumb expression, just fingerprints
over my shame

      all I wanted was snow
to snuff the sun blades to shadow spokes,
muffle the drum of freeways, erase
      the old realism

but this smart snow erases
      nothing, seeps everywhere,
the search engine is inside us,
the world is our display

      and now every industry
has dumped whole cubicles, desktops,
fax machines into developing
      worlds where they stack
them as walls against

what disputed territory
      we asked the old spy who'd drunk
with Russians to gather information
the old-fashioned way,
we were warmed

by the goods of his tales,
it was like sitting by the television fire,
      and drinking iced cocoa
and remembering
ourselves in this vanishing

      frontier, in this new realism.
Finding shelter from the snow,
      I recalled his whoppers to you,
when you were half transparent
with depression.

Descent of the Aquanauts
Kathryn Davis

EVERYBODY THINKS IT'S going to be different for them, Janice said. The dinosaurs thought so too. She was on the porch of her rental duplex, busy smearing her thighs with suntan lotion, her tan an enviable deep golden-brown. By this time Janice had been at the shore for a month. Golden-brown was the color everyone craved, not only for their body parts but for their food.

The dinosaurs had small brains, one of the girls said. All of us were older now; we'd learned things in school. Everyone thought the sun went around the earth, then everyone thought the earth went around the sun. Who knew what they'd be thinking next? The moon came out of the place where the ocean is now. The moon came from outer space and the earth captured it in its orbit.

The moon, Janice said. The moon was what started all the trouble. She finished her thighs and started in on her arms. She took her time, squeezing the lotion out bit by bit and rubbing it into her skin in small circular motions; she was driving the little girls crazy. They'd promised their mothers they wouldn't go to the beach without her. You couldn't apply lotion on the beach—that was Janice's rule. If you waited until you got to the beach, sand would get in the lotion, spoiling your tan.

Janice informed everyone that after her husband arrived Friday they were taking a moonlit cruise on a luxury sailboat. She hadn't married the boyfriend with the two-tone car; he turned out to be unreliable, meaning he dumped her for someone better looking. The man she married was named Henry and everyone thought he was too nice for Janice. He had the appearance of an English gentleman, very delicate and pale, the way a hermit crab looks between shells. Henry treated everyone with kindness. One of the little girls said he asked to see her pee-hole, but it was common knowledge he liked Janice best.

After two people got married everything that had formerly seemed interesting became uninteresting—this was common knowledge too. Once you were married, romance and heartbreak were no longer an option. Where were the surprises? When she wasn't wearing a bathing suit, Janice wore a girdle under her clothes. She didn't have a pussy anymore, she had genitals. Her nipples disappeared in one big thing called a bosom.

You girls know nothing, Janice said, lighting a cigarette and blowing smoke rings. The sky was the usual color, a solid shade of blue that suggested everything worth seeing lay behind it. This was also true of the houses on either side of the street, two rows of identical white duplexes, like the semidetached brick houses back home. The only way you could tell the duplexes apart was by their awnings—Janice's was forest green with yellow stripes.

The curly-headed girl came walking down the stairs from the second floor with her raft under her arm. Have any of you ever *looked* at the moon? she asked. The raft was the same color green as the green of Janice's awning, the canvas so old and dry that until the girl got it into the water it made her skin creep. If you look at the moon you see it's something different from what they teach you, the girl said. She'd been planning to go to the beach alone but when she overheard Janice talking about the moon she couldn't resist joining in. Stars around the silver moon hide their silverness when she shines upon the earth, the girl said, quoting her favorite poet. Upon the black earth.

It used to be too dangerous to go on moonlit cruises, Janice continued. Once she got started she was unstoppable. The thing about the moon is how it makes things happen just by being there, like the way it can pull all the water on one side of the planet into a big bulge and then let it go. That's why there are tides.

I wish I could go on a cruise, someone said.

My dad says those cruises are highway robbery, said someone else.

It was a block and a half from the duplex to the boardwalk. The sidewalk was so hot the curly-haired girl could feel it through the soles of her flip-flops. The grass was yellow, the hydrangeas blue. The ocean was a wobbly sliver of light even brighter than the sky and shimmering like a mirage—she could hardly wait to get there.

The cruise is worth it, Janice corrected. Ab-so-tive-ly pos-i-lute-ly. She said it helped if you were a newlywed. She leaned forward to put out her cigarette on the sidewalk, and when she sat up everyone held their breath to see if her bosom was going to stay inside her suit. The thing I'm talking about happened long ago, Janice said. Not as long ago as the Rain of Beads but a thousand times worse. People used to think the Horsewomen were involved, only this was another group. They were older and they were human girls and they had a leader—

they called themselves the Aquanauts. Their leader was a girl who no longer cared what anyone thought about her. She no longer cared if everyone thought she was weird. During the week there were only women and children at the shore, just like now. The men came on the weekends. If the men had been there probably none of this would have happened.

People went to the shore then? someone asked.

You think vacation is something new? Janice laughed the laugh she'd been working on, one that was supposed to sound musical.

If the men were there it wouldn't have made any difference, someone said. I've heard about the Aquanauts. What happened had nothing to do with what sex people were.

Across the street the mother of one of the little girls had appeared in her driveway in a red bikini, a lit cigarette gripped between her lips as she hosed down her convertible. The mothers didn't pay Janice for keeping an eye on their daughters, but they made it worthwhile for her, occasionally inviting her and her husband to their parties. Otherwise Janice wouldn't have had any social life to speak of, she knew that, just as she knew the reason why had something to do with her being unsuitable in some way she couldn't put her finger on, but which she suspected had to do with the fact that she, unlike the mothers, spent so much time with their daughters. It would be different when she had a daughter of her own.

In the beginning the group was like Pangaea, Janice said—that was how they got their power. They were like one giant lump of land surrounded by a single giant sea. It wasn't until the lump broke into pieces that you could tell from the fossils how it used to be. One girl had a black locket that used to belong to another girl's mother, one girl had another girl's friendship ring. One girl stole. She stole Blue Boy from Pinkie in the pack of trading cards in another girl's cigar box, breaking up that treasured pair forever. Of course the girls didn't like each other equally. The coastline of Asia didn't dovetail exactly with South America. When they played Nancy Drew someone always got left out, frequently the girl who stole, who refused to be Bess, while the girl who didn't care what anyone thought of her was always George. She came from very far away and then one day she disappeared. In between she lived on the second floor of a duplex apartment at the shore.

When I say *girls*, Janice said, I mean *teenagers*.

How many girls were there? someone asked. By now everyone knew better than to ask their names.

107

What difference does it make? I don't know, Janice said. Maybe four. Maybe five. Not a big group.

I have a black locket, someone said.

Do you think I'm blind? said Janice. And don't everyone go telling me about your friendship rings.

A hot breeze gusted off the bay, riddled with flies. Janice swatted at them but they kept landing on her; they were attracted to the suntan lotion. If she knew who'd taken Blue Boy she wasn't saying.

The Aquanauts always waited until the families had left the beach and gone home, Janice said. It added to the girls' feeling of power to think of what was going on in the duplexes without them there. Everyone's bathing suit had a crotch full of heavy gray sand and you had to be careful not to make a mess in the bathroom when you peeled it off. On weekends the fathers mixed cocktails and opened cherrystones while the mothers mixed cocktail sauce. During the week the mothers did it all themselves. If you were a good girl you sat on the duplex porch with your mother while she painted your fingernails bright red to match hers. She drank a martini and you drank apricot nectar. The little sisters played with their Ginny dolls, the Ginnies who couldn't walk and the Ginnies who could, though you wouldn't really call what they did "walking."

By the time the girls got to the beach, the sun was on its way into the bay on the other side of the island, and the shadows of the boardwalk shops and amusement park rides had grown longer and longer, making the sand dark and cool. The two lifeguards had turned over their chair and their lifeboat and taken off their whistles, dreaming of kissing the same girls they'd spent the whole day protecting. The beach was empty except for the gulls and the things people left behind accidentally like wristwatches and shoes or on purpose like trash. The sand castles had been swallowed by the sea. It was low tide, the shadow of the top car of the Ferris wheel swinging back and forth at the edge of the water.

I like the black-haired lifeguard, said one of the older girls.

He likes you too, said another girl. I can tell.

What about the man with the metal detector? said the curly-haired girl's little sister. The man with the metal detector was always one of the last people to leave the beach. Her heart went out to him, with his over-tall red crew cut and the way the sleeves of his white short-sleeved shirt stuck out like fairy wings.

Don't be stupid, said someone else. This happened before any of us were born.

What difference does it make? said the curly-haired girl. It could have happened yesterday.

Every night it was the same thing, Janice said. The girls would wait until the beach was dark and then they would walk straight into the ocean and swim away from shore until they disappeared. Afterward they would sit under the boardwalk and get so drunk that by the time they came home and went to bed it seemed to all of them that they were like clothes tumbling around in a dryer.

One night something different happened. The girls didn't come back. The mothers were sitting on the duplex porches, smoking cigarettes and drinking cocktails. They were sitting in groups of two or three, the fathers still in the city. Some of the fathers also were sitting on their porches at home, drinking and smoking and listening to the hot summer wind moving through the crowns of the sycamore trees. The fathers weren't in groups; aside from the ones having affairs they were alone. There was a feeling of melancholy everywhere, the melancholy of being in a place apart from the person with whom you normally spent your time, thinking of her sipping her martini, picturing the lit tip of his cigarette traveling in darkness away from his lips and toward the ashtray. The sound in the other person's ears of a car turning onto the street where the two of you normally lived. The sound of the sea in your own ears. The feeling of melancholy was everywhere and it wasn't, generally, such a terrible feeling. Because everyone knew they were going to be reunited with the person they were missing, they could throw themselves into their melancholy moods.

There had been warnings. But people never heed warnings.

No one listened, and as more and more people stopped listening, more and more people stopped telling the truth. Even Madame X didn't tell the truth, having been designed that way by the Chamber of Commerce. Nothing will put a bigger damper on a family vacation than being told the world's about to end.

You've seen how she just sits there in her glass case in the arcade, Janice said, with her big glass eyes and her little plaster hands lifted like the pope's, waiting for the next coin to drop. That night she decided—no more lies. Supposedly it was one of the lifeguards who got the fortune, but he didn't take it seriously. The only thing lifeguards take seriously is looking good for girls. You don't belong here, the fortune said. You never have. Once the land stops getting in its way, the ocean is going to be everywhere.

Madame X told me I was lucky in matters pertaining to business and finance, someone said.

She told me I was going to meet a dark, handsome stranger, said someone else.

I bet she meant the lifeguard, said one of the little sisters.

Girls, Janice said, oh girls. For a moment she stared off into space like she was trying to collect herself. The parents didn't realize anything was different, she said, and she sounded angry. Not at first. If they'd been paying attention to the moon they might have had a clue, but they were too filled with feelings of nostalgia and self-pity, the way adults become after they've been drinking. The girls knew it was going to happen that night, though, and they were ready. Their leader said she hoped they'd said their good-byes. Everyone had brought her air hose, for all the good it would do.

It was late and the tide was as low as it gets. The girls didn't think they'd ever had to walk so far before arriving at the water. They walked and walked and walked and meanwhile the moon was practically on top of them, like they could touch it. Like they could stick a finger in one of the craters—you've all seen the moon do that.

My dad says that's just an optical illusion, someone said.

If your dad's such a genius, why did he ever have you? said someone else.

The curly-haired girl moved a little closer. I wouldn't dream of touching the moon with my two arms, she said. She was quoting the poet again but no one cared. They were too busy listening to Janice. Even the curly-haired girl couldn't leave. That was the thing about Janice—she made you want to know where she was taking you, even if you didn't want to go.

After what seemed like forever, the girls got to the water, Janice continued. There had been a sea breeze all day long. Now there was nothing except a feeling like something holding its breath. The girls waded in, enjoying the warm water on their feet and the burst of the first waves against their ankles, still warm but cooler, the shallow water mixing with water from the heart of the ocean, which was cold. The ocean is coldhearted; you don't have to be a genius to know that. It makes boats sink. It makes you watch where you put your feet. If you choose to swim at the end of the day after the lifeguards have left the beach you take your life in your hands. You know that, don't you? Janice gave everyone a piercing stare meant to drive her point home.

As usual the girls were dressed in identical black bathing suits with skirts and identical white rubber bathing caps that strapped under the chin. They looked like old ladies. They didn't enter the water like old ladies, though, splashing water up over the tender parts of themselves to lessen the shock. The girls plunged right in and kept on going. They ignored the jellyfish and the seaweed. They didn't look back. At their leader's command they dove under the first big breaker that came their way and rose up on the other side at the exact same time as meanwhile the whole idea of what a wave is fell apart behind them. For a moment they paused so everyone except the girl who was so nearsighted she couldn't see anything without her glasses had a chance to make eye contact with one another. Then they kept on swimming.

The girls had been preparing for this for a long time. At the shore they practiced in the ocean; at home they practiced in the bathtub. At first they just held their breath, but after a while they got so they could breathe underwater. The girls didn't really need the hoses anymore; they just brought them along for backup. People were eighty percent water, they figured. What made everyone think the moment our ancestors came out of the water and started to breathe air represented a step up the evolutionary ladder? Why did people always think things got better by moving forward? Why did people think that way? It was so limited! As if the surface was somehow better than everything else. As if *air* were king.

The girls rose on the next wave and felt themselves flung forward as the wave broke behind them. The further they got from shore the bigger the waves were becoming, rocking under them with more and more energy. It was like they were being pushed on a swing, higher and higher, getting swept up the side of a hill to stay for a split second at the top before being swept down into the valley below and then up again, the top even higher this time, the slope even steeper and the valley lower, until they found themselves at the top of a mountain of water the size of an alp. The moon was right there above them, drawing the ocean up to it. The girls practically banged their heads against its surface. Because of the moonlight everything looked like it was coated in silver, but you could see how dark the water was underneath the coating, so dark green it was almost black, and the moon itself was whiter than anything, whiter and smoother than an egg.

I've had that dream, someone said. I dream about those kinds of waves a lot.

It's an ancestral memory, Janice explained primly, as if she were mentioning something better left unsaid.

The girls didn't realize until they'd arrived at the top of that final

111

wave that one of their group was missing. You'd probably guess it was the girl with the bad eyesight, but you'd be wrong. The girl with the bad eyesight was right there treading water with the rest of them, waiting for the signal from the leader to dive under. No, it was another girl, one of the best swimmers. Unfortunately for her, or maybe fortunately—who can say?—she didn't always concentrate on what she was doing. She was careless, and when people are careless things go wrong.

Somewhere along the line, Janice said, the careless girl let herself get caught in a breaker that carried her back to the beach. The breaker curved over her head and thumped her from behind—that's the kind of thing that happens when you're thinking about something else, like for instance a boy. Then it churned her around and around before leaving her on her stomach in the sand together with a lot of broken clamshells and those little crabs the size of your thumbnail. Even though nobody was there to see her, the girl stopped to make sure her bathing suit was still in place before getting to her feet. Normally she didn't care about the way she looked, but this was different. The world was about to end and her friends had left her behind. They were going to survive and she was doomed. Plus she had to go home to her parents.

Except it didn't end, someone said. How can we be here if the world already ended?

I'm getting hot, said someone else. When do we get to go to the beach?

A lot of people died, Janice said. You've studied it in school. The world didn't actually come to an end, but it might as well have. It was like scientists predicted. Whole countries weren't there anymore. You've all seen the globe. It looked completely different.

Suddenly she yawned and stretched and stood up. Well come on, she said. What are you waiting for?

The beach was just a block and a half away but it always took longer to get there than it should. The little girls had to be herded along and there were lots of things to carry. Things got dropped and someone had to go back to pick them up. By the time they arrived at their usual spot—a good spot just to the left of the lifeguard stand with no one between them and the water—the sun was directly overhead. Janice screwed the umbrella into the sand while the older girls spread their towels as far from the umbrella and as close to the lifeguards as they could get. The beach was crowded. Everyone was talking at the top of their lungs about private matters like heartbreak and terminal illness. It was the only way to be heard over the sound of everyone else, not to mention the surf.

Hurry up! Hurry up! cried the little girls.

It's not like the ocean is *going* anywhere, Janice pointed out.

A seaplane flew past very low over the water, trailing a banner that said TAKE A MOONLIGHT CRUISE ON THE EVENING STAR.

Come Friday, Janice said, that's going to be me and my honey on that boat. She set up her beach chair in the pool of shade made by the umbrella and sank into it, letting out a sigh.

It was a very young coast. The little girls went off to play with their buckets and shovels in the shallows while the older girls began working on their tans. One minute there was no wind at all, the next minute it came gusting off the bay. Some sheets of newspaper drifted past, followed by a baby wearing nothing. The lifeguards whistled in a swimmer who'd ventured too far out.

People are such idiots, Janice said. She reached into her beach bag and withdrew her cigarettes and her sunglasses. You know they're still down there, she said, lowering her voice. The Aquanauts are still down there. They live in the deepest part of the ocean where it's so dark you can't see what they look like. They don't look the way they did before the Descent. They used to care how they looked. They used to shave their legs, for instance, things like that.

The curly-haired girl knew Janice was talking about her. She thought it was probably a good idea to like being looked at if you were a girl—it was probably key to survival. If you were a gorilla it was the other way around. Somewhere the girl had read that if you looked a gorilla in the eye it would strangle you.

Whatever we can't see has power over us, Janice said. Plus, as much as people seem to think so, the ocean isn't infinite.

When that immense wave broke it went everywhere. Almost everywhere, Janice corrected herself—emphasizing *almost*—but not quite. You can't even begin to imagine what it looked like. Luckily it was nighttime. If it had happened during the day it would have been even more terrifying. The whole sky was blocked out. Some people ran, some people got in their cars. They ran the way people do in horror movies, looking back over their shoulders while continuing to run forward, without any sense of direction or purpose. Of course it did no good. The only things with a chance of making it were the things living in the water. Even then, a lot of them didn't do so well.

But the Aquanauts were OK, right? someone said.

Look! said someone else, laughing. The tide was coming in and just as Janice was talking about the immense wave breaking, a small wave had broken and sent parts of itself up over the sand and onto the bottom edge of someone's beach towel. As the water crept up the beach it turned the white sand dark, pocking it with tiny holes where the sand crabs lived. Then it went back where it had come from. The air smelled like hot tar. The bucket-shaped things the little girls had been building got washed away along with other things like sheets of newspaper and flip-flops and cigarette butts.

Where do you think *you're* going? Janice asked the curly-haired girl.

The girl was heading out into the water with her raft under her arm.

Didn't you hear what I was just saying? Janice asked. About the Aquanauts?

So? said the girl. Vacation was a nightmare when you were a teen-age girl forced to live in a rented duplex so small and with such thin walls that the sounds and smells of your whole family not to mention the people downstairs like Janice and her husband were always *right there*. The curly-haired girl knew Janice and her husband could hear her feet walking across their ceiling. While they were having sexual intercourse they could hear her feet. Janice could hear her feet while Henry's penis went in and out of her.

Maybe you don't get it, Janice said. This is no joke. Because I've watched you—you're always one of the ones they have to whistle in.

At first the girls just spent their time playing, she explained. They couldn't believe how lucky they were. They were alive and they could go anywhere they wanted. They could explore the parts of the ocean where human beings had never been before, and they could swim through the top floors of skyscrapers or into places like maximum-security prisons or movie stars' mansions or the lion cage at the zoo, places that had always been off limits to ordinary people. It seemed like nothing could hurt them, either. Not even sharks or giant squids, and they didn't get sick with things like gill rot or white fin the way regular fish did.

But after a while it was like, what's the point? A lot of time went by. The water receded. The descendants of the people who hadn't died began reproducing. First they did it as a necessity. It was only later they started enjoying it. Soon things were back to the way they'd been before the wave. Houses got built, streets like this one with rows of duplexes. Someone put up a boardwalk. There was a penny arcade with a fortune-teller in a glass case. This was possible because it turned out the future still existed. It's the one we have now, in case you wondered.

A whole lot of time had gone by but the girls hadn't gotten any older. They were still girls. Even after everything that had happened to them, that part never changed. Eventually they found themselves back at their old beach. They recognized it from the shadow of the Ferris wheel down by the water.

Janice pointed and the little girls gasped.

Our beach? someone asked.

What did you expect? said someone else. That's how history works, or else Janice wouldn't know it.

The girls couldn't get out of the water to lie on the sand and work on their tans. If they got out of the water they couldn't breathe, and they missed the way the lifeguards used to look at them. They didn't want to stay girls forever. That's the main thing about girls, am I right? Janice held out her left arm and studied it critically, admiring her tan and the way her ring sparkled in the sun. Girls are always in a big hurry to take the next step, she said, the one about men and romance and marriage and babies. The girls drifted as close to shore as they could without being seen. They could hear the sound of baseball games on people's radios. The lifeguards were looking out to sea but the girls knew they weren't looking for *them*. Every girl was crying but the other girls couldn't tell because their faces were already wet.

It's their own fault, someone said. They were the ones who decided to live undersea. No one made them do it.

If they hadn't they probably would have died, said someone else.

They'd be dead now anyway, said the curly-haired girl. She turned her back on the group and began walking toward the water.

After Janice finished moving the umbrella and all the beach things from the path of the incoming tide, she spread herself out on her towel, flat and wide and brown like a gingerbread man. Except they aren't, Janice said. The girls aren't dead and they aren't ever going to die. You'd think that was a good thing, wouldn't you? But what if you wanted to take the next step, only you were doomed to be a teenage girl forever? It would make you angry, wouldn't it? It would make you more than angry. It would fill you with murderous rage.

The girls got to be immortal and it made them deadly.

At first there didn't seem to be anything to worry about. Sometimes people said they felt something swim by them in the ocean but that was all. Sometimes the girls would bump against someone but just barely—the girls called that "kissing." Of course they no longer wore their black bathing suits and their white rubber bathing caps—when a girl bumped into someone, the person could feel how seamless the girl's skin was. Their skin felt smooth and slippery like sausage casings. It wasn't really skin, though. It was more like a pod.

After a while the girls began to shoot right past us, not quite seeing us and just barely feeling the bump of us against their skin. It was like all we were to them was something that got in their way. It was like they hated us.

I've felt that, someone said. I thought there was a fish swimming by me.

My mom said it was nothing to worry about, said someone else. It's only the current.

By now the curly-haired girl had gotten past the breakers and was lying on her stomach on her raft, paddling away from shore. She could see the moon up ahead, preparing to shine once the sun got out of its way. Every night there were more planets; planets were being born somewhere in space, being calved off larger, older planets. This was the way of the universe, the old making way for the new. When she looked back, the lifeguard stand was like a dollhouse toy, Janice like a dollhouse doll. Over the boardwalk the sky had turned the color of beets, but right above her head it was still blue and getting darker, the weird blue of a newborn baby's eyes.

It was then that the girl sensed it—a disturbance in the water next to the raft, a feeling of a presence getting ready to move past her and then pausing, sensing her there as well. She could see a glimmer of skin just below the surface, a shudder in the current as the head came up beside her. Whatever it was smelled like fish but also like it had been buried in dirt and was starting to decompose.

She could see where the stories came from. The thing's eyes were large and lustrous as plums, and when they stared at the girl they were filled with an intention so forceful she knew she couldn't be imagining it. Until that moment neither one of them had any idea of the other's existence, like the way a baby is suddenly in the world, or a dead person out of it. The thing's gaze was fixed on a place right above the girl's head, the place where she knew her thoughts were visible.

Back on shore no one noticed anything. People were eating hot dogs and burying one another in the sand. They opened her up and there it was, someone was saying in a loud voice. A tumor the size of a grapefruit.

Janice rolled over. You're probably wondering how those girls got to be that way, she said. Because they started out the same as you and me, just like everyone else.

They were all somebody's darlings, Janice said. They got tucked in, they got presents. They got Suzuki method piano lessons. Also My Little Pony and Felicity the American Girl, horseback-riding lessons, religious training, ballet lessons, and pets. Also bedtime stories when the nights grew dark. Once upon a time there was a little girl who could be anything she wanted.

Later she couldn't remember she'd ever even had a mother or a father.

My mom and dad had *me*, said one of the little girls.

But what about that other girl? someone asked. The careless girl who got caught in the breaker?

She's the one who had to watch it happen, Janice said. She saw everything. The bad news is you're all descended from her. That's why you have trouble sleeping—and don't go trying to tell me you don't because I know what goes on here at night. The bedroom walls are like paper. The good news is it'll start getting better once you're older. Cocktails at five—that's the answer. If those mothers and fathers hadn't been drinking their cocktails when the wave broke—if they'd been able to see what was going on, the way the first spray was very light, almost unnoticeable, but that it was followed by a disturbance in the air that was everywhere and was a threat to the whole idea of air, to the idea of breathing air instead of water—if those mothers and fathers hadn't been drinking cocktails then we'd have gone insane long ago.

In our house my dad's the one who drinks, someone said.

My mom drinks soda, said someone else. But my granny drinks rubbing alcohol.

Suddenly the dark-haired lifeguard stood on the seat of his stand and began blowing his whistle over and over again, louder and louder, violently waving his arms, motioning toward shore.

Speaking of cocktails, Janice said. She looked at the sky and then she looked at her wrist. The sun is over the yardarm, she said; no one knew what she was talking about. She began gathering together the things they'd brought with them to the beach. Everyone was beginning to gather their things together—it was as if a signal had gone off somewhere.

We can't leave now, said the curly-haired girl's little sister. Even though she was often embarrassed by her older sister, she didn't want her to die. She remembered the time she dreamed her older sister

117

died and it was terrible. She couldn't stop thinking of Cinderella singing "A dream is a wish your heart makes."

Both lifeguards had jumped down from their stand and were dragging their boat across the sand and into the water.

Janice seemed affronted. The problem with humans is they think their children are *theirs*, she said. They think because their children came from their own bodies and cells they *own* them, like where we come from points to the future.

By now most of the people leaving the beach had stopped in their tracks and were turned to face the water. The lifeboat rose and fell as the dark-haired lifeguard rowed it through the breakers, the oars lifting and lowering like wings on either side.

Does anyone know who it is? someone asked.

The stuck-up girl, someone said.

It's that poetry girl, said someone else.

Of course the girl couldn't hear them, she was so far out to sea on her raft. My darling, my dearest, she said. She had no way of knowing who it was she was talking to. How long had she been out there? The sand at the water's edge was cold and hard, the galaxies revolving on their horizontal plane like a roulette wheel.

From the shore all anyone could see was the lifeboat, getting smaller and smaller.

Believe me, you don't want to be here when they bring her back in, Janice said. It's not like I didn't tell her. You have to watch out for your arms and legs if you go that far out. You all heard me, right? The last girl this happened to had bites out of her.

Recalculating
Charles Bernstein

You can't be part of the problem if you don't see how you're part of the solution.

"For a poem is not the Poetic faculty, but *the means* of exciting it in mankind."

—Poe, Drake-Hallek review

Information wants to be free—from personification.

As if all we are and do revolves around a hollow center.

Every poem is a model of a possible world that only comes into being when reading is active, activated.

The poem is a constant transformation of itself.

As in the poem plays you or you play the poem. Aces are witches, clubs beat the rhythm, spades are queens, and kings rule!

We didn't have it when we needed it, but got it once we didn't.

Postmodernism: modernism with a deep sense of guilt.

Language is an albatross, a sullen cross, a site of loss.

I think of Emma climbing the icy rocks of our imagined world and taking a fatal misstep, one that in the past she could have easily managed, then tumbling, tumbling; in my mind she is yet still in free fall, but I know all too well she hit the ground hard.

The hardest thing is not to look back, the endless *if onlys*, the uninvited *what could have beens*. I live not with foreknowledge but consequences; wishing I had foreknowledge, suffering the consequences of not.

119

Charles Bernstein

. . . how poems become sites for mourning—not in fixed ritual
repetitions (prescribed liturgy) but as mobile and specific areas for
reflection and projection, holding areas, havens. Not words received for
comfort but works actively discovered in the course of searching.

Not to "get over" (as a disease) but as a way of "living with" (as a
condition).

The nightmare reality that erupts in the daylight like burnt offerings at
a pizza parlor. You say skeleton, I say: *Can you say that again?* That's
no phallus, that's the election of my impotence, writ large. As in: *Me
transformo,* you pale face. *Me tranformo,* you the unexpected product
of a sudden revelation.

I love art so much . . . but it never returns the favor.

Poems are stuck in black and white, which means that every color
connected to a poem is proof of the inner life of words.

As surely as God invents the idea of God but also of godlessness.

Angels brush against spattered brushwork, gory purple eyes loom out
amidst hearts pierced by arrows.

Every misfigured thought a dialect of its moment. *(Say! Don't you
speak in a dialect too?)*

Sometimes I am disturbed even by my ability to function. I feel, at
times, a shell of myself; a shell of a shell of myself.

Each day I know less than the day before. People say that you learn
something from such experiences, but I don't want that knowledge and
for me there are no fruits to these experiences, only ashes. I can't
and don't want to "heal"; perhaps, though, go on in the full force of my
disabilities, coexisting with a brokenness that cannot be
accommodated, *in the dark.*

Right after Emma died I could not stand to look at the photos of her—
and there are lots, because she made so many self-portraits. I felt each
photo was a lie—flaunting her presence in the face of her being gone.

120

Charles Bernstein

Now I see that the photographs are what she left me—that she is present to me in the way these haunted and haunting works are present.

Whale on beach like wolf at wedding: Bark is bigger than bite but insulates tree.

—For Yunte Huang, after Charlie Chan

Poetry should be silent, unread, invisible, inconceivable. The true poem can never be written or heard.

Not ideas but the idea of ideas; not questions but the inadequacies of answers; not currency but *against the tides.*

Better a weak jaw than an iron fist.

Stalling is my inspiration.

It's what I'd like to undo that keeps me up at night.

The problem with teaching poetry is perhaps the reverse of that in other fields: Students come to it thinking it's personal and relevant but I try to get them to see it as formal, structural, historical, collaborative, and ideological. *What a downer!*

Orphaned by the world, with no home but there.

If you don't make a mistake thrice, how do you learn from it?

If x is x, then y is y and o, o.

So much of what we can't imagine we are forced to experience. And even then we can't imagine it.

I've got a chiasmus as big as all Detroit and as old as the Second Avenue el.

He had the honeyed lips of someone who'd been in poetry too long, whose idealism had years ago become a manner of speech and whose only aesthetic aspirations were for a revival of the ideas he had rejected in his youth, as if you could get a second chance to bite the apple of the

121

Charles Bernstein

new and not come out smelling like a candied turkey in a slow dance medley. It was a fork in the road, but he had always favored spoons; and now, facing the music to which he had never dared to listen, he dove into the waters he has always reviled, ready to be eaten alive by the sharks of his proudly arrogant misjudgments.

This is the difference between a sentence and paradise. A sentence comes to an end, paradise has no beginning.

China export: "NOT MADE IN CHINA" T-shirts
U.S. export: "NOT MADE IN AMERICA" T-shirts

It was the kind of day you read about in the movies.

What's unseen but said's as consequent as what's apparent but unspoken. Words perform for inner eye we o'erlook at pleasure's peril.

Listening for inaudible songs in a sonic sea, I lost my bearings, falling, uncaring, into traps of my own despairing.

Always treat advice with skepticism (especially this advice).

Freedom from ideology's ideology's designer jeans.

Ideology's veils are imaginary; the freedom from these veils delusional.

Universalism is moral; particularism ethical.

(But every apple has a core, every horizon a philosophic song . . .)

We are gathered at a site of dialogue. As chaotic as our discussion may sometimes seem, we are always making patterns with them.

Most of those patterns are lost in the dark matter of the mystic writing pad.

When I say "we" I don't mean everyone, or perhaps anyone else, just a sense of some collectivity beyond myself.

"We aced the shit out of that asshole."

My advice to young poets is always: Start your own magazine or press & publish your own work and those of your contemporaries whose poems seem most crucial for the art, as you perceive it. And respond as much as possible, through poetics and reviews, to this work. Articulate its values, value its articulations. The web certainly makes such publishing easier, but it does not solve the hardest part, finding a community of other poets that allows for active and intense exchange, not based just on location or prior friendship or like-mindedness, but on the qualities and quiddities of the work as it unfolds in time and space, on earth and in the heavens of our "image nations."

Our inalienable rights are inevitably alienated; in this way, capitalism seems to merge with destiny; or our fate, through a darkened glass, is projected onto the world of which we are sentient.

So then it's necessary to be reminded, from time to time, that hegemony is something to work for rather than only and ever to recoil against.

I've grown so accustomed to the dark that I can hardly imagine anything more than shadows.

The Jew is a textual construction.

You're not there even when you're there.
You're not gone even when you've went.
You're still near even when you're gone.

In poetics, nothing is new except the exaggerations.

Beauty lies, I have always thought; a wonderful deception while it lasts.

The Beach trilogy (a family saga over three generations): *Seagull with Broken Wing, Rocks in Basket, Shadows in the Sand* . . .

Elliptical poetry: language poetry's bark without its bite.

The absence of ornament is an ornament.

123

Charles Bernstein

Robin's "Wandering Jew or Nomad," cut from the leather back of his family's Salt Lake City rocker: valuable more for what it is than to look at it. But isn't that true of all of us? (Something to touch amidst the loss.)

Here's the message: *There is no message.*

I'm talking to you, you motherfucker.

You want a message, go to a massage parlor.

I hope I have your attention now.

Your message has been scrubbed because of possible contamination by a virus.

". . . a highly concentrated state of intoxication—a state which, like madness, frequently enables the victim to imitate the outward demeanor of one in perfect possession of his senses."

—Poe, *Pym*

It's always darkest at night. A darkness day can't touch.

But we learn to live with it or anyway it learns to live with us.

Think snow and see Boca.

Crane is not metrical so much as parametrical.

My palsied heart and I agree . . .

It may be impossible but the concept is that we articulate our judgments, preferences, and beliefs while being aware that these are not universally shared; this holds a special problem for those whose beliefs include a belief in the universality of their beliefs.

The cause of the cold is not the cold.

We live facing the blinding sun of the not-yet born, in the shade of the dead. Meaning is the liminal space where the dead live in us as we look toward the future.

Charles Bernstein

"It is all very confused but more confused than confusing."
—Stein, *To Do: A Book of Alphabets and Birthdays*

"Shadow, come, and take this shadow up."

Are we here yet?

For now, I go hour to hour . . .

If you are not part of the problem, you will be.

The Brief History of Weather
Alexandra Kleeman

> *The first requirement of architectural beauty is suitability to situation. A house should always seem to belong where it stands. If it looks forced upon an unwilling landscape, or if it is in any way antagonistic or uncomfortable because conspicuous or out of scale, then it fails in this first requirement.*
>
> —Emily Post, *The Personality of a House*

> *It is best to read the weather forecast before we pray for rain.*
>
> —Mark Twain, *The Maxims of Mark*

IN SNOW

WHEN A FATHER RETURNS to empty shelves, empty cupboards, and a family that can only sit there, parched, playing one of many games centered around counting to larger and ever larger numbers, he will retrieve the luggage that he has brought back with him, bring the brown suitcase, the suitcase with two brass latches, opening it up before our eyes to reveal that it is full of snow.

Before our eyes he opens it up, his hands slip back the two latches in clean sound, and then the snow seen against a silk lining, paisley printed, all the snow glaring back the lamps and shaming our house with the brilliance of the things that belong outside of it.

The snow is what sand would be if it could forget its material, if it could forget its hardness, roughness, if it could forget its own weight. And the snow is what we would be if we could forget ours. If we could become the things we pretend instead of merely pretending at them, playing over and over at a game of falling silent and soft from couch to floor, making ourselves silent and soft as we can, playing at being snow, playing until our elbows and sides are too sore to move.

Before our eyes he makes small motions at the contents of the suitcase, and the snow begins to fill out, piling the table and over the table to the floor. Then we are in up to our knees.

126

WE ARE THE WEATHER

The weather is beautiful through the windows of our house, you could take it for a painting. With an ear pressed to the window, it speaks, stutters, moist noises like someone in a form of forced sleep.

Right now it rains. Water throws itself against our windows, sideways with the force of the wind. It makes the things outside melt, dripping off gelatinous blots of their own color. How wonderful to be able to melt the shape from things that belong so smugly to themselves. To be the outside itself, or to reach for it and feel something without the flat touch of glass.

Father proclaims man and weather natural enemies, and suddenly we are. In motion his mouth laps at the air, takes into it the world we have been presented with and passes it out again, deformed. Pressed against tongue, teeth, the sounds fall out marked by indentations from human molars. They take shapes that imply our own deformation, that cause us to turn over the words in our own mouths, heavy and cold like a mouthful of marbles that taste of the hands of other children.

Father names the body of man a device for sculpting weather more weatherlike, less crazed, a device for disciplining the air. He walks out into the daylight shaking damaged equipment toward the mild sky. As hollow tubes spill from his arms, as springs jerk wildly, taut and loose, flinging themselves like a ruined cartoon body, knotted together and dancing. His voice going on without punctuation without pause about the ruined possibilities of his invention, his invention a device intended to transform one thing into another, that takes it away from itself and makes it one's own, as my father to the weather or my mother to her projects of paper and thread. In the partial daylight, a father fills up with shadow, standing as a silhouette of a machine shuddering up and down as it works, wobbly, clanking against itself, a machine for the production of heat and noise.

My father, certain that internal forms of weather can be used to influence the external. My father under the big sky, shouting at clouds. We watch him through a window.

We play rain, rubbing our hands and faces all over the smooth surfaces of the furniture.

Alexandra Kleeman

MEASURED FACTS

We have invented a meter to measure the accumulation of time, a machine capable of producing detailed descriptions of the air. We have invented a method of extracting still water from rain and for shaming sleet and slush into legible forms of precipitation, forms a child could draw.

The surface of our home is a single block of shatterproof plastic. There is a single flaw in the surface of our home through which we would enter or exit, a thing we rarely do.

Air enters the flaw of a body and presses through into ever-deeper regions, traveling from oral reservoir to tracheal passageway to the lungs, which resemble small rooms. This is illustrated in a diagram fixed to the dining-room wall, which is designed to remind us to keep food and air passages separate. In this diagram, a frog sits in a glass-sided tank. The frog is a cross section, and air is a blue arrow traveling into its body. In the diagram to its right, the arrow is red, and represents food traveling the same path to the lungs. I point to this second frog, which is dead.

"Many thousands of years ago, the world's surface was covered with small, thoughtless beings whose deaths held no consequences. In the terrible storms of lava and rain that occurred before the climate had come to a form of sense, they died and multiplied like a storm in themselves, flourishing haphazardly and then collapsing into a pit or whatnot where their lungs filled with the syrupy weight of their own liquefied ancestors. They lived like the weather, like a smattering of problems unforeseen but urgent, and they died too like the showers or sunlight: a brief seizure with no purpose, no understanding of their own duration."

A necessary flaw belongs somewhere between an error and a mistake.

Our device to control the weather fails to control anything at all.

DREAMING WATER

We play a game based upon the weather; it begins in the living room.
We stand in the middle, looking around. One player will ask, "Do
you think it's going to rain?" and the other will answer. I hold out
my hand.

"I think I feel some drops, just a few."

Look up at the ceiling, search it for clouds.
Describe the color of the clouds and their shape.
This one like a duck, that one like an anvil.

Demonstrate surprise.

Cirrus clouds indicate cold weather if they move from left to right.
Cumulus clouds indicate rain if they are gray, stacked, or have grown
taller throughout the day. Stratus clouds can bring snow flurries or
storms. A cloud shaped like an anvil impends.

Describe the direction of their movement. Describe their speed.
I open an imaginary newspaper.
   The newspaper opens like wings, makes their sound.
   Gray squares tremble against the air.

"It says there's a thirty percent chance."

We watch the ceilings, and the minutes remove themselves.

TO UNDO OR NOT TO DO

This device is a vaporizer. It is for clouds, sunshine, temperature, and
wind. It is also for plants and other living things.

When I say it is for them, I do not mean that it is good for them.

This device is heavier than almost anything. It has a case made of
metal stuck through with tubes leading from one place within it to
another. No matter how hard you lean against it, it does not sway.

129

No matter how hard you kick it, it does not respond to or do anything. Under no circumstances is it to be kicked or pushed.

When the rain falls, bit by bit it becomes broken. I watch the rain falling on it, falling on its body and its back, falling into the funnel from which it acts out, falling all over it so it makes a sound like a thousand drums and I know suddenly that as heavy as it is it is hollow past the shell. All is different kinds of gray. It gives off small stars as the rain knits it in water.

What our family has done, the rain undoes in a matter of minutes. The color of the sky and the ground, it undoes. Undone, the dryness and smooth feeling of the air. If it could undo also the year or two years that have come before, would we be as we were, or would we be something new, wetter?

I hold my ruined pet, looking out the window at the rain, the rain, the substance that would either bring my pet back, or turn it into something more distant, untouchable.

PLAY HOUSE

Outdoors, water soaks the ground and is lost. Indoors we live with rules that prevent things from becoming lost or broken, from leaking outdoors and coming loose.

These are obstructions that redirect absences before they unfold, closed spaces in which things are not forced to pass out of view in time like everything else, like a sudden dissipation replacing the light with its hollow or the objects of the day with their opposites, a flower with its absence or the shape of a pet with a thin, tasteless vapor. We pass these things from our view instead with willed movements away, we leave them by force and when we return to them in several minutes or hours or days, they remain.

In this way, our house resembles a life tied in a knot, or a passage of time spread out in all directions. There are long spaces unfilled by anything, then sudden clumps of familiar and unfamiliar strewn as in a salvage yard, portions that have "stepped to the side, safe, rather than eliminating themselves violently." Indoors we may construct

130

Alexandra Kleeman

our lives from tissue paper, from brittle thread, from confectioner's sugar, if we wish. Materials that crumble at the touch or sag under moisture live like magazine images beneath our ceilings, they will not wish to stir within our thick walls, repaired constantly with special tools we have made to preserve their form. We might be anyone, and our undoing just another thing rolling around like a marble through the halls, waiting to be found and left and lost and forgotten.

My mother sits, making small scratching motions with the fingers to coax the meanings from flat objects. I run from the room. I run back into the room. I run from the room and make small scratching motions at the wall, yielding little. I run through the house. I search for my father, to go to him for the words to fill these descriptions. He stands in front of the window practicing his speech. I run from the room. I run back into the room. These are the things we make possible in an environment salvaged from its own predisposition toward destruction.

NEVER HAVE I EVER

I lie in the center of the emptiest room of our emptiest house looking from right to left. The room breathes around me as I lie more like a floor than the flattest, deadest floor. Looking down over the belly, I see the sockets and lights rise up and down, up and down steadily, and I can make it breathe more quickly by breathing more quickly, until I feel dizzy and my head rolls over in circles.

We study the weather from within this house, and we are the weather within this house. Outside this house there are weather and weather patterns, stretching for miles in any direction. We cannot control the weather from within this house. But in this house we are working on it.

We study the weather in a house that keeps the weather out, we watch the weather outdoors from indoors, through the windows. We can see rain through the windows, sleet through the windows, hail, snow, partially cloudy, cloudy with a chance of thunderstorms, partially cloudy with isolated thunderstorms. We can see fog through the windows, but we cannot see what lies past it.

131

Indoors we have cataloged the indoors, named its parts, and recorded their number and location. We remove their ability to surprise us, even as they relieve us of our astonishment. It seems as though this indoors is held up by these numbers: If they were to become lost, it would vanish like pots and pans when one forgets they are playing house.

Weather covers the length of a wooden fence. It covers over our backyard and the backyards of our neighbors, who have all disappeared. Where did they disappear to, and how?

They disappeared like weather, like weather the day after weather.

UNTIL SOMETHING HAPPENS

We approach the cold like the water approaches the bottom of a hill. It makes itself felt through the holes in our airtight windows, six inches of solid plastic. He rolled everyone in thick acrylic fleece; I saw nothing but white and a small circle of mixed color. We roasted and ate large wheels of meat, meat being "the command given to another body, setting it in purposeful motion with knives and grinding." There was nothing to do and there was less of it every day, the husks of board games drained in the corner of every room, their only use brief and saddening. Pick it up, look for something new to appear printed on the reverse side, try to use the game pieces on another board, grow heavy, carry to another room, and leave in that corner, a new corner. The winter "like an abomination paralleled only by the flaccidity of spirit with which it has been met in response." The winter "the gravest threat to productive and life-affirming activity to enter these walls since the homequake of three autumns prior," but making a sound more like that of mice inching under the floorboards or of fire scratching at the outer shell. One night, they read and I look at pictures in a large atlas of other places to be. On other nights, I read and Father argues about great inventions of the past. Or we listen to forecasts over the radio.

The first idea was a house without weather, says Father. The same idea as a roof, but bigger. Better, he says. Mother looks up from her work. She is making a blue scarf out of woolen yarn, another blue scarf to add to the piles of blue scarves, hats, mittens, muffs that sit over there in the closet, getting older.

Alexandra Kleeman

PERCENTAGE OF CLEAR SKY

Of the types and the shapes. Of arranging them in groups by height, weight, or self-similarity. Of the types of children they once were and could someday give birth to. Other people and their ability to pass freely through the space that you take up, to pass to and through and away from it in a way that you were not designed to do.

Once upon a time other people were around. You could see them through the window. They were washing their minivans, vacuuming debris up from under the car mats. They were playing with a dog, or tousling its ears, or scratching the scruff of its neck under the collar. You could see from their faces that they loved soccer, or horses, or mornings. They had preferences for large things over small, or the opposite.

What happened inside their houses, besides a choreography of lights going on and off and, eventually, entirely off?

How did they know when to turn which lights on and off, and to what end?

Distance and knowledge are nearly the same thing. Or so my family tells me, demonstrating this by covering my eyes with small pieces of white paper and asking me to identify what I see. Children have been visible outside the window, playing in the snow as though unaware of its crystalline structure, each one fragile and irreproducible. I have watched the snow melt in their hands, though I have not felt it melt in my own.

ONLY SLIGHTLY

My mother watches the storm from the kitchen window of this house, watches the storm fall over roof and yard. It falls from the sky, through a fiberglass frame of approximately a foot in diameter, suspended outside the kitchen window by a hermetically sealed plastic pipe. The pipe's opening governed by vacuum pump, ending in an airtight seal.

When it rains good, clean rain, when it rains types of rain that we

133

have not encountered previously, or familiar types that can replenish our collections, then we will make it sleep, we will put it under ether.

I watch her at the window, loading a canister of gaseous substance, checking air pressure within canister and pipe, preparing the pump for operation and checking its parts for leakage and wear. At the peak of the storm, when the sounds of individual raindrops falling upon the roof are no longer distinguishable one from the other, she presses the button and the frame fills with mist.

My mother dons raincoat, gloves, galoshes, and an oversized hat. She opens the umbrella and steps outside, gingerly over the cobblestones, gingerly to the collection tank. The plastic frame is filled with droplets of water suspended in midair, shaped like downward momentum, but paused there. Paused. She takes the large glass jar from beneath her coat and fills it with sleeping rain. The cap again atop the jar.

We have learned that the weather cannot be kept outdoors and must be brought indoors, dragged indoors, before it brings itself indoors. We create the image of a house where the outside must ask to be let in, where it rings the bell and wonders what to do with its hands while it waits for someone to come to the door. Through such preemptive tactics we show it that, though it may cover the whole world, we cover the world inside our house.

When my mother comes back, she leaves the jar on the kitchen counter. The raindrops inside look sad or exhausted. They stir, but only slightly.

LEARNED MOTIONS

We maintain a constant temperature of seventy-three degrees within our house, counteracting temperature drops with baths and warm foods, counteracting rises in temperature with meals of ice and cold water.

We gather in photographs in triangular formations, the hands of the two larger on the shoulders of the smaller, as if we could become a single solid structure.

Twentieth-century physicist Arthur Worthington photographed drops of milk at their moment of impact with a hard surface, providing irrefutable evidence of "the deeply lodged gimpishness of nature at her core." While scientists had previously imagined the splash patterns of liquids to be regular, symmetrical, crystalline, the photographs taken within Worthington's laboratory revealed ragged blooms that threw themselves up into the air with "indiscrimination worthy only of a pratfall." They surged up upon impact, or seemed to reach outward with irregularly sized pseudopodia. With this material proof of their irregularity, naturally occurring phenomena entered the category of "trainable effects," like "the squelching and spattering sounds that emerge from a mouth in the process of doing other than generating meaningful speech" that we silence with practice and much cloth.

The walls of our house are to its space as the rules are to a game. In between lie air, and everything allowed. We run circles from the kitchen through the den through the bedrooms through the kitchen.

Controlling the weather will be the first step past building descriptions that cannot hold it in. It could be the first step out of this house that we have lived so far into and through.

MANY QUESTIONS

At dusk, we play a game of thought and guessing. This is recreation, which fills the spaces between moments of productive friction, moments in which we create. In the dusk, the space within takes on a color to which it is difficult to respond. We want to turn the lights on but it is too early, we want to keep them off but it grows too late. We want a space in which we could half do, do halfway, but we are forced to be one thing or another, except within the act of hoping.

Our family, like other collections, possesses a nested structure. My father has known the most and thus could know us better than we know ourselves: He could dream us and we would not know the difference. My mother has seen less and knows proportionately less, and I know the least possible. I could fold up into her, and her into him. We would live inside him like a house, one large white house with two tiny windows on the front. In this house we would have all the things we have now, but we would have no father.

The game is called Many Questions. It happens like this:

I'm thinking of an object, my father says.
Is it a refrigerator? asks my mother.

No, it is not, he replies.
Is it my kitten? I ask.
No, no, he answers.
Is it a stop sign? asks my mother.
It is not, he replies. Now, why in the world would I think of that?

THAT WHICH MEETS NO RESISTANCE

The first idea was to build a house free of weather. Mother says Father was sleepless for weeks, drawing plans for houses without doors, without windows, houses without pipes for outdoor water to enter, houses without any air inside at all.

The first idea was to build a house free of weather. But they discovered within the removal processes a secondary origin of weather. A house with nothing to resist—no rain, no wind—finds areas of resistance within, growing frustrated with its own stasis, shuddering and crumbling around its own stable shape. He formulated a rule: *The shelter that meets no resistance shall resist itself.*

It was many days ago that Father's rule was proven accurate and, conversely, that our house proved itself to be a rule. I curled around my warmth as the morning opened itself up, peacefully, without even drops of dew or the movement of birds outdoors. A sharp whine began from within the walls and floor, making items of furniture whine too, like a bomb about to go off. The things on the walls fell off during this whining, and the things on the tables fell with the onset of a chugging, painful sound from machines somewhere within the house. Around us, two gulps softly and one spasm like an attempt to hurl something from the throat. I said that it seemed the house felt we were alien but I was told that was unlikely. The machinery, built to withstand high winds and violent events, was simply buckling under the weight of very little; we would, through induced outer turbulence, regain the internal stillness that comforted our objects and our routines. The floor was on a tilt and I watched the round things roll away and out of the room, and the flat and square things slide more slowly toward a similar exit. In another room the refrigerator was on fire, burning up from inside, smelling at once like charred meat and plastic.

I open the freezer door and stare at the hail. It stays still in there. It looks back at me from next to the ice cream and some frozen peas, the hailstones beginning to stick to the freezer's artificial frost.

THE FIRST IDEA

From one room I looked for another room to hold me, to change the things around me and leave this sharp feeling behind me in the sharp air. A feeling might claw you open with the simple intention of freeing itself, and it would be no one's fault. I took the black marker from the top of the table.

One arrives at the map room, taking long steps through the shuddering hall. Charts of yesterday's weather and today's weather and tomorrow's weather cover the walls and windows. This is where we make the fiction of tomorrow's weather, which we hope to make fact, where we draw the weather on the maps, draw the future on their flat faces.

I drew storms on the maps of yesterday and today.

There had been no storms yesterday or today.

The world of the future will be "storm free, an environment designed for utter compatibility with the needs of the many, as determined through a survey reconstructing the median desires of a high-quality section of inhabitants." It will wheeze rather than roar. Instead of the storm, there will be a pocket of mild, warm wind. Instead of the rain, there will be light and additional light, filling every corner of the empty sky. Instead of hiding from it as one, we will scatter, walking aimlessly away from a central point to a peripheral.

I drew a storm with a warm front traveling north toward this house, a low-pressure center. I marked the origin of storm activity and the counterclockwise direction of wind flow around the low-pressure center.

LACK OF WIND

The clouds we make with the breathing machine are too heavy, and will not float in the air. For now, we strap a harness to them and hang them from the rafters, but we will run out of room, even in this house designed to substitute the sky.

A small, simple game played using words printed on white note cards, and a small black-and-white board. Mother takes a card from the top of the deck and reads it out:

Move back three spaces.

It is my turn, and I move the piece that stands for me three spaces backward on the board. Tiny, useless clouds roll by like tumbleweeds. Or would, if any wind blew within the walls of our house.

I look toward my sister.

It is Father's turn and I read it out:

Move back one space.

Father moves his piece back one space, and takes the first card off the top of the pile:

Move back two spaces.

Mother moves her piece back two spaces. She takes the next card from the top of the pile. But I take myself to the map room, where I draw angry storms all across the midwestern United States, and both coasts.

A SMALL, SIMPLE GAME

I wander us to the room where clouds are constructed, and now we sisters look upon the same machines with similar eyes. Surrounding us are the freezing chambers, the artificial breathers, the cloud molds and cloud cutters.

The first of our homemade clouds were made of real breath, sighed and heaved into the chambers through an air tube. These clouds were perfect and small and a child could name them, pretending that they were a pet cat or dog. These clouds achieved a maximum volume of 6.5 liters, the vital capacity of my father's lungs.

But larger clouds were required to replicate natural weather, and the artificial breathers were therefore invented to be larger than we were, and better than we were at accomplishing things they did not even want to accomplish. Like a huge plastic tube, a huge rubber lung, the mechanical breathers breathed all through the night, wheezing through dream after dream, collapsing themselves into flat rubber sacks and then drawing back up, well oiled and smooth, and filling the chambers with a strange, moist breath that congealed into weird uncloudlike shapes.

To achieve standardized clouds for my mother's experiments, we took these clouds that felt a little woolly, a little wet, and pushed them into the molds, making the shapes of cumulus, nimbus, cirrus, stratus, fog.

The day the machine broke, there was barely a real cloud in the sky. The blue stretched pale and cool over my father, arms full of machine scrap jostling as he strode around in sharp patterns like a ball striking against invisible obstacles, emitting liters of shouting. The blue opened up over layers and layers of empty space waiting to be filled up with big soft shapes that we had chosen. It gaped above as, at the end of the driveway, no longer shouting, he crumpled downward.

INSTEAD OF ONE

My sister is either older than me or younger than me.

She is either better than me or she is less good.

Under the right circumstances, she is able to put aside self-doubt and leap into action with reflexes that harken back to a more instinctual time, rescuing the child from the onslaught of truck wheels, train wheels, car wheels, saving the child's life and earning the respect of townspeople and journalists.

Or else she is unable to.

The utility of a sister stems from the longing for reinforcement, for an additional, aligned person inside the house to see what is happening and feel some way about it.

This has something to do with why we are fitted with two eyes instead of one.

Alexandra Kleeman

WE HAVE DREAMT FOR THEM

Approximately the same height, almost certainly the same age, we sisters crawl hand and knee down a sidewalk we have imagined to exist: three feet wide, five hundred feet long, siding past a series of miniature houses lined up like the silences in a single day. Preferring one and then the other, we invest in these houses one by one as though we were able to see only halfway through them, through the front facade in a cutaway view, and not all the way.

In the living room, at half size, in the transparent homes we have dreamt for them and placed in our own, we crawl on hands and knees to peer in at one and the next. We have made them of ice and they melt, but slowly. The object of the game is to resist seeing all the way through these glass walls to the familiar objects that lie beyond them, to the old armchair with a dun doily on each tattered arm. Mothers and fathers in these homes of glass turn toward us and smile small, shining, glass smiles, holding up their smiles and their hands in greeting, standing still among perfect stacks of sandwiches: white bread, peanut butter, bananas. This mother, whistling as she fills brown paper bags. That mother, waving at us with one arm, the other arm around the shoulders of a gigantic glass of milk.

At this, my sister stops suddenly and makes a motion as if to dive in and leave us separate, lonesome. I grab the back of her dress and hold tight but she is so hard to hold still, my hands finding no place to make of her a handle or a knot. She whines low and mournfully, signaling as though she would like to crawl inside. Small, silly sister. She has not seen that the spell of play lasts only so long as one pretends not to wish to grasp the things that we have played into being.

In one house, they make snowman versions of themselves, which come slowly to life and begin slowly a series of ordinary things that the family watches, entranced. The snowmen notice us watching, then all the inhabitants of the house turn to us and wave.

In another house, they invent a device to control the weather. When I look into this house and count the number of persons inside, I begin to cry.

The fact of two sisters allows an escape into situations that could not be accommodated by only one. With two, we may hide in the cupboard for hours pretending we are somewhere else entirely, without ever having to feel ourselves alone.

From the cupboard, I gaze at her and beckon her in. My knees hunched up by my ears.

The fact of two sisters allows for escape within a situation that is hostile or unfair. Certain species of cicadas lie dormant in their burrows for seven years of hibernation, before bursting forth to eat and eat and fly about in the air.

Certain species of birds time their own hatching to meet the soft new cicadas when they emerge.

I set the table, four plates and four sets of silverware, for our small, careful family.

With her face set in a shape of preoccupation, my mother removes the fourth plate and places it back in the cupboard.

I see my sister's face grinning back at me from the cupboard, a space so small I cannot imagine how I would fit with her in there.

EACH ONE LIKE THE NEXT

I can see my sister crouching in the living room, playing over some thing I cannot see.
  A toy?

The reasons for a sister are manifold, and if we could persuade her to speak she would give them for herself. The house is emptier every day, less populated, the doors all shut, the objects seem to disappear from tabletops. It is like a leak has opened up someplace we cannot see or sense, there has been no one to watch or be watched by. The eyes grow restless, finding faces in the folds of curtains, crockery, closets.
  For another, too few games can be played alone.

I played a game alongside my parents at breakfast. It began with all players picking up a section of the newspaper and opening it up at the fold. My father shakes it three or four times, with a disappointed sound. My mother begins with the headlines and then the little sections, then the longer articles. We went through it, piece by piece, until all was read. We consumed the little letters in their little blocks,

141

then we turned the page for the others.

My newspaper was imaginary, and I finished first.

I watch from the doorway, an empty frame. This door has been taken off its hinges to prevent it from being slammed shut. The resulting air flow, expelled at the velocity of anger, could shake a house to dust. The door has been taken off and taken where?

UNHABITED

A house at night should not be woken into alone, if other methods can be made available. The presence of a parent via effigy, by means of photograph or even an object that they have been seen to love, hate, or merely hold, may be presented to the darkened house as evidence of the presence, past or future, of others with an investment in your existence. The notion of a linkage between you and another, by means of structure or form, will impress the house and render it less likely to target you with unidentified sounds and shadows.

We play a game involving the description of the walls, but we are both so good at it that we cannot but fail to surprise each other.

Are there ghosts in the house, and if there were, how would they have gotten in? I tuck the quilt in under my feet, I close the closet door, and turn on three different night-lights. These things will yield, if not safety then an allusion to the idea of it. If there were ghosts in the house, how lonely would they be? With no one to see me I become like a vapor.

The emptiness within the house populates what lies beyond it. Lightning walks the plain like a tall, glowing man. He looks toward me and at once he is gone.

WE COULD DO IT ALONE

I explain to her the mechanics of daring. She must step outside the door. Outside the door, the day roils with temperatures that would touch our skin.

I explain it. Game play proceeds by turns, with each player advancing the series by one. One player's proposal for action on the part of another is balanced by a counterproposal for a different sort of action by a different person. She must step outside the door. But when will the action be performed? The emphasis is upon daring, not doing. If it were only about doing, we could do it alone, in our separate rooms, with the door closed. I explain to her that this process may bring joy nevertheless, though she remains impermeable to this point, sprawled sideways on the carpet and staring deeply into it.

As I watch her stare under the couch or into the cabinets, I imagine that she may be dissatisfied with the network of beings and objects that she is required to live among. Escape from the scale she was born into could be achieved by burrowing into phenomena of a different scale, belonging to the world of much larger or smaller things.

Our father, for example, has escaped us, has escaped deeper into the house or laboratory, to a position behind a final door through which the sounds of shouting are audible. Our mother proceeds laterally, walking her eyes around at their much greater height, as if in a walking form of sleep. They exist for their work, and are lost to us now.

Experienced by a much smaller being, this day would glow with the excess beauty of certain of its shorter intervals. The moment, for example, when a spoon fell from the table and onto the kitchen floor in the brilliance of an unlonely afternoon. Stretched to a beautiful length, the resulting sound would have rung out for nearly an hour, rung out like a force of nature, a piece of the air. We would not have had to think of a new game, living our joys in the shadow of this long, loud sound.

Even with all this in mind, she must step outside the door.

I AM LIKE I AM NOT THERE

Standing before the door, I speak to her. I explain to her the ultimate aim of the game of daring: to dare someone to do what is impossible to do, and thereby undo themselves. With this in mind, I dare her to open the door and step through it. Into the murderous gales of the sky, I say, though I cannot see the sky from in here. She looks at me glassy eyed. She has become more doll-like day by day, spending her hours heaped sideways and still, looking under the furniture at things I can only infer. I repeat myself and wait for surrender.

My sister looks toward the door and places one small hand on the lock. I hear a small, clean turning sound and the rush of air. Then she is over the threshold and moving. I run to the door to close the air out. But I open it again slightly, I watch her through the gap in the door.

Both arms out straight and extended, she walks like someone on a balance beam, down the driveway, teetering away from the door, away from me, twirling around, hopping on an imaginary hopscotch grid. The sunlight draws a yellow haze around her, her hair, her small false hands. Watching her walk away is like watching myself depart, though when I look down, I find I am in place.

At the end of the driveway, she turns and looks back at me from a distance.

Then she is gone.

YOUR MOVE

I plunge my whole fist into the jam jar. I write my name, and your name, all your names, on the wall. I tidy the china with a soft dust-cloth. I rage and rage and rage and rage at the furniture that still resembles human beings; at the ones shaped like people I shout my language. There seem to be fewer. I am picking the blueberries out of the muffins, the toppings off the frozen pizzas, still frozen. Ever, ever fewer. I am shiny, sticky. I run around and around, trailing berry-colored handprints, and when I get back to the start I grow silent and track myself quietly through the halls, soundlessly, I am like I am not there, I am there like I am not there, I am my own ghost trailing my own ghost to some indeterminate point in time, forward and backward on a track made of iron. I plunge my fist into the jam jar. I make a peanut butter and jelly sandwich of the fatherly armchair. Where have you all gone? So I write your name on the sticky surface. So I dust the furniture, even lifting the vases, plates, etcetera, to clean under them. But no one is pleased. No one is bothered. I write you on the wall, your wall, your name. It doesn't even stir from the corner of the eye. There is no one to be pleased. I rule these lands, and there are none that could dare question these acts, or declare them unjust, or affirm that they have come to pass or have not. As a result, do they come undone? I try to do a thing so large or heavy that it recognizes itself, that it does not need someone else to see it to make it endure. I try to carve my name into the wall. I tie all the things to one another with red string; it will not guard against their leaking, slowly, from inside these walls and out, who knows.

FACTS LIKE FACES

I play a game of making it rain. I fill the sky with clouds, I label and describe them one by one. They are all different types, collecting at the ceiling of the living room. I check the forecast in the newspaper, I comment on the dark storm brewing overhead. I hold my hand out, but I feel nothing.

It is necessary that "the child find him or herself confronted by his or her own increasingly 'ordered' behavior as, from the world of practice and play, the world of the adult is grown into." Is it necessary for this world to be so quiet, its contents captured between parentheses?

When the actual shape of the liquid's breakage was discovered, there were two basic tactics that could have been adopted. The first was to reshape the preferences of the liquid, training it toward a manageable complexity that would reveal itself legibly—as a hexagon or a torus, for example. The second would have been to reshape ourselves.

One way of attacking the question of which to choose is to think that, in the context of the development of an organism into an organism that masters its surroundings, reshaping ourselves would have been to "grow backward."

Backward was the more populated direction, and had a tendency to look beautiful as a result. The orientation of our faces on the fore side of our bodies, luckily, made it more difficult to see and long for that direction, which was becoming farther away all the time.

Alexandra Kleeman

OUT OF DOORS

I wake to a mother standing by the bed, a father by the window with his hand on the cord, pulling the blinds open. The blinds are never open.

The sky outside is strange, its papery surface, its white flank. Be handed a coat, a hat, a set of galoshes. We are going outdoors. We never go outdoors.

We have one driveway and it is never used. It leads from the garage with its one shiny car, down past our door, past a little path that leads from our door, past our door, down to a mailbox that we have not looked inside for quite some time.

Mother on one side, Father on the other, a family walks down the driveway to the end of the driveway. It is as though we have never used our eyes before, we are looking right and left, right and left.

Today is a day without weather. We don't know where it went, but it has gone and thus we walk around, soft skinned, into the air. Is this walking the ultimate aim of my father's efforts to cancel the weather? Are we achieved at last?

There is no wind, there is no water. There is light. There is no sense that something in the sky will heave or change color. The only air that moves is air we push from our lungs.

De Potter's First Grand Tour Around the World

Joanna Scott

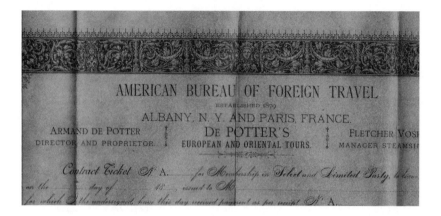

I UNDERSTAND THAT DESPITE *the advantages of such excursions, some of you will object to traveling in parties. The first complaint I often hear expressed is that a touring party travels too fast. Now this is an entirely plausible objection, especially for someone who has never been abroad before. But let me point out that not all of you can leave your home for an extended period. On the contrary, thousands of Americans travel abroad within the space of a year, and those who travel alone end up moving more rapidly and with less comfort than those traveling with me. Solitary travelers miss half the sights, are worn out rushing to catch trains and boats, overpay their servants, and spend too much time disputing hotel bills. By the time they get home, they forget where they've been and what they've seen.*

    And then there's the complaint from people who don't want to be bound to a tour. They think they want to run around the streets of foreign cities irresolute and perplexed. They go to a museum or palace and find it closed for the day. They hire a local guide who doesn't speak English. And if they are traveling in pairs, one of

Joanna Scott

them must wait for the other to study the recommendations in the guidebook, and then they will argue about where to go. They will change their plans again and again, losing time and money.

Finally, there are those who balk at being led around by a stranger. They say they're uncomfortable putting themselves in the hands of someone they don't know. They want to be sure they can trust the person who is leading them through unfamiliar places.

Let me say to those who want to know their conductor beforehand: All you have to do is ask. Come to Albany for a personal interview, or I will come to meet you in Boston, Philadelphia, or New York. Or write to me, and I will write back at length. I will provide references who have known me for years. I will convince you that you will be freer traveling under my charge because you will not be obliged to secure rooms or tickets or a place on an omnibus. If you wish to vary a route, it is easily arranged. If you prefer to stay longer in one place, you are welcome to do so. And as for the worry that you will move too fast, I promise that if you travel with me, you will see more, and more intelligently, than you could otherwise see in double the time. Every day of the tour will be a pleasant one. For those who do not want to take the trouble of researching each destination in order to plan their trip, you can do no better than to join my party. Then the question of seeing what ought to be seen, the question of comfort and enjoyment, the route, time, and expense, are known in advance.

On De Potter's Grand Tour around the World, you are guaranteed first-class accommodations and three meals a day according to the custom of the country visited. Each member of the party is allowed one trunk weighing a maximum of one hundred pounds. Fees to waiters, porters, dragomans, guides, and servants (excluding ship-boarded stewards and hotel chambermaids) are included. In short, all necessary expenses during the whole tour will be covered. The cost of the full tour will be $2,500. The ticket, as stipulated in the original program, does not include wine, laundry, or any extra expenses arising from illness or accidental detention.

Our select party will circuit the Globe in the following manner: Leaving New York, we will travel by train across the country to San Francisco. We will enjoy our Pacific passage to Yokohama on the S.S. Oceanic. *Five glorious weeks in Japan will give us the opportunity to admire the country's gardens and pagodas, to stand at the foot of a colossal Buddha and tour the world-famous*

148

manufactories of porcelain and silk. We will then sail across the Yellow Sea to China, spending three weeks taking in this great civilization, admiring its curious bronzes and ivory carvings, its grottoes and temples and fan-tan houses before traveling on by Pacific Mail Steamer to the Kingdom of Siam, one of the least visited yet most marvelous countries of the Orient. From Siam we head to Burma, a country usually omitted from the regulation World Tour but which we know to contain monasteries, pagodas, and bazaars. We will then travel through the heart of India by train, to Calcutta, Lucknow, and of course Agra, home of the Taj Mahal, which is simply too marvelous to describe. We will move on to Ceylon, land of the cocoa-palm and the bamboo, where we will recover from our fatiguing journey by spending three relaxing days at the luxurious Galle Face Hotel in Colombo. Rested and renewed, we will embark on a steamer of the North German Lloyd to make the unforgettable voyage across the Red Sea and along the Suez Canal to Egypt, a country I can assure you will never lose its charm, even if you have visited it a dozen times before. In Cairo we will be transported by carriages and camels to the Great Pyramids and the Sphinx, miracles of human handiwork. We will make a trip up the Nile as far as the first Cataract, seeing many interesting temples and ruins en route. From Egypt we will travel by steamer to Jaffa and then will take horses across the Plain of Sharon and the Valley of Ajalon to Jerusalem. We will proceed to Constantinople, and then to Athens, with its classic ruins and Field of Marathon. From Greece, we will embark for Brindisi and travel by train through Italy, stopping in all the major cities. After a restful stay at the De Potter chateau in France, we will make a northern extension tour to Russia, Denmark, Sweden, and Norway. We will enjoy a final week in England and depart for home from Liverpool.

The full tour will last eleven months. Our party will include no less than ten and no more than twenty-five members. A physician will accompany the party and provide medical attendance free of charge.

You are advised to invest in steamer chairs. For personal funds, travelers should bring along a Letter of Credit. The American Bureau of Foreign Travel highly recommends the banking house of Brown Bros. in New York. For larger sums, travelers should bring a draft or check on some European bank. English five-pound notes are also very useful. In terms of luggage, I advise you to take only what is *absolutely needed. Most hotels provide chambermaids to do laundry. Wraps, hoods, shawls, overcoats, and rugs are useful. Serge and woolen dresses are best for the ladies, along with three sets of underclothing, one set of warm flannels, an old silk or woolen dress for the railroad, a more elegant dress for the hotels and galleries, and a thin, cool dress for Italy, along with a light wrap, a shawl, a plain hat, a sun umbrella, and a gossamer waterproof.*

For gentlemen, a good business suit and an extra suit are sufficient, along with one set of warm underclothing; linen for about two weeks; an overcoat; strong, easy boots; and small toilet articles.

A passport, while not required, is a convenient means of identification at banks and post offices. Please be advised that every package must be presented for examination at every frontier Custom House. It is a great drawback to foreign travel, but I am an experienced leader and often succeed in passing all trunks and satchels of my party through the line, with only one or two pieces being opened.

I promise that my Grand Tour will be not only incomparably enjoyable, it will also be the most extensive trip ever made around the Globe. I have been preparing for this journey for some time past and all my plans have fully matured. Our date of departure in New York will bring us to each country during the most desirable season of the year. Ladies as well as gentlemen will be perfectly comfortable every step of the way.

Space in this select and limited party is filling up fast, and early registration is encouraged. Application for Membership should be accompanied by check or draft for $10 to the order of A. De Potter. We will depart on October 1st from Grand Central Depot in New York. Please arrive promptly. Madame De Potter and I will be waiting!

They left from New York in the midst of a rainstorm. As the train started to creep forward, they were still settling into the seats in the first-class car, arranging their cushions and chatting among one another in that animated way characteristic of the beginning of every tour. There was laughter among the group, and someone started to sing, "It rained all night the day I left, the weather it was—" The song was interrupted when the train gave a sudden jerk and came to a halt. Some of the older tourists exclaimed in panic. Whistling and shouting could be heard on the platform, and a moment later a bespectacled young woman climbed onto the train, her umbrella only half closed and dripping on the other passengers as she hurried down the aisle in search of a seat.

She was Miss Mooney of Columbus, Ohio, thirty-two years old and still unmarried, a librarian by profession. She had been on the Long Summer Tour twice before she joined Professor Armand De Potter for the Grand World Tour. She liked to say that she'd follow him anywhere. Aimée, Armand's wife, recalled that Miss Mooney had been lost twice—once in Lausanne, when they took a boat excursion on the lake and left her behind, and once when they were touring the perfume factories in Grasse. But each time, she managed to find her way back to the group on her own.

Professor De Potter stood in the aisle to offer a greeting. For the benefit of all the travelers he assured Miss Mooney that he wouldn't have let the train leave without her, although Aimée knew that wasn't true. The train would have left on schedule, with or without Miss Mooney, and there was nothing Armand could have done to stop it.

Armand offered his seat to Miss Mooney, and Aimée smiled a warm welcome as the disheveled woman settled beside her. It was essential that Miss Mooney feel welcome. Every member of the De Potter party must be made to feel welcome. The success of the trip would be measured by their satisfaction. Aimée hadn't discussed it in these terms with Armand, but she understood what was at stake. And though at the moment his bearing was relaxed, his voice gentle and reassuring, Aimée had only to look at the pale knuckles of his hands as he gripped the back of a seat to see how nervous he was. The whole future of the American Bureau of Foreign Travel depended on the success of this trip.

On previous tours, Aimée and Armand had headed east, embarking by steamer across the Atlantic for the Old World. Now, for the first time, they were leading the party west, crossing the country by train. They wouldn't return to New York for eleven months—a length of time that unexpectedly filled Aimée with a secret dread as the train began moving again. It was one thing to be in charge of a party of tourists for three weeks or even through a summer. Aimée loved to travel with her husband and savored the discoveries that came with every trip they took together. But right then, as she watched the windows of the stationary train across the platform moving backward, she wished she had tried to talk her husband out of undertaking such an ambitious tour.

*

There is no surviving written record of De Potter's First World Tour. If Aimée kept a diary of the year, it has long since been lost. But Armand did bring along his camera, and he attempted to document the trip, capturing the highlights that he wanted the travelers to remember and avoiding the experiences that he hoped they would forget.

With so much experience packed into eleven months, who would remember that the De Potter party lost Miss Mooney at the station in Chicago?

They didn't see her again until the train that followed them arrived in Denver, and she was on it, thank goodness. No one but the De Potters, and of course Miss Mooney herself, would remember, and they'd manage to frame the experience as One More Story to Tell— a happy one at that, especially since Miss Mooney met a gentleman on board the train who promised to visit her in Ohio when she returned from the tour.

The Professor and Madame organized a sing-along on board the steamer as they crossed the Pacific, and it was the sing-along that the travelers remembered afterward, not their seasickness.

Nor would they think to mention in their testimonials the mice that Mrs. Lawrence of Yonkers discovered nesting in her mattress in the hotel in Yokohama. And though Aimée knew they must have noticed the awful smell of night soil on the streets of Tokyo, their memory of it was soon erased by their visit to Nikkō. "Do not use the word magnificent till you have seen Nikkō" was Armand's translation of the Japanese proverb. Instead of remembering the smell of night soil in Tokyo, they would remember the temples of Nikkō, the outlines of their gilded pillars faintly visible in the Scotch mist. They would remember the Hotel Nikkō, where, though they were given no more than a thick rug to sleep on, set in a space enclosed by paper screens, those who suffered from insomnia were treated to Aimée's and Armand's soothing voices as they read aloud from Suematsu's translation of *The Tale of Genji*. They would speak fondly of the Hotel Nikkō through the rest of their trip,

and they would continue to remind one another of the wide girth of the cryptomeria trunks, the beauty of the temples and tombs and the Great Pagoda, and the plump cheeks of the young boys at the monastery, who clamored to have their picture taken with Professor De Potter and their local guide, so Armand gave Aimée the camera—

They wouldn't remember how Japanese men on the streets looked at American women with blatant amusement, but Aimée would remember, especially because they had it on record in the photograph her husband took of her standing by a statue on a street in Tokyo. See how all the bystanders are laughing at her?

After five weeks in Japan, they would not be able to remember everything they saw and did. No one but Mrs. Cowing of New York would remember that she fell on the street in Dai Butsu and twisted her ankle and had to be carried everywhere for the next three days. And no one in the group would remember that the train from Kyoto broke down, and they arrived at Osaka three hours late. But they would remember how spectacular their voyage was across the Inland Sea. And Aimée would remember that as Armand sat down on the bench after taking a picture of passing boats, he had reached for her hand and given it a loving squeeze, a simple gesture and not at all unfamiliar by then, their eighth year of marriage, but it was a promise of further intimacy and set her heart racing. To think that she lived the kind of life that was full of such experiences! Armand was right to quote Dr. Prime, who called a voyage across the Inland Sea of Japan the most beautiful sea voyage in the world.

He was also right to say that travel opens a broad field of investigation that is always new and full of interest. Everywhere Aimée looked, there was something to see that would fundamentally change her understanding of the world. An experience might be perplexing, or it might be satisfying, but it always reverberated in her soul. There was the day Armand led them through a garden, and as they approached the steps, the Buddha seemed to come to life, as though rising to his feet.

And there was the time a family of musicians gathered around their party on a street in Bombay—

To the child who spun and jumped for a handful of pennies, Aimée wanted to say, You remind me that life is short, not a moment should be wasted, let us celebrate our ability to move and feel joy. And to the father grinding spices and his boys gathered across the street from their hotel in Lucknow, she wanted to say, I am sorry you are hungry.

That she found an imagined apology a cowardly response to poverty was a secret she preferred to keep to herself, out of a sense of courtesy. She couldn't admit to her fellow travelers and especially not to her husband that there were times when she despised herself for no other reason than her privileges. She would spoil the trip if she revealed her true feelings.

156

But unless she was willing to take off her dress right there on the street, hand over her passport, and exchange places with a beggar who was condemned to suffer merely because of the fact of her birth, her remorse was useless. She wasn't willing to be anything but herself, to cling to her privileges as Professor De Potter advised the ladies to cling to their purses on the streets of Calcutta, and though the children showed her their empty palms embedded with dirt, she ignored them and ran to catch up with her touring party before they turned the corner, and then chatted with them about nothing as they walked back to the hotel, where she went to bed early and fell into an uneasy sleep, dreaming of weeping children with swollen bellies, women squatting to relieve themselves in the gutter, men pounding nutmeg into powder, only to awaken and set off on the next adventure organized by Armand. After already having traveled by rickshaw,

Joanna Scott

she boarded a cog-wheel train,

she traveled on horseback and by carriage,

and even on an elephant

and camel,

all in order to admire the afternoon light pouring through the intricate carvings of a temple door

or to stand with reverent awe as she is doing in a photograph she didn't realize until later was being taken by Armand, who captured the moment when she first looked upon the Taj and was feeling overwhelmed by the evidence of the human ability to create beauty:

"Dear Lord," she prayed, "show me the path to righteousness. Let me do your good work. Forgive me for my selfishness. Help me to be less annoyed when my fellow travelers complain about the food and to remember that we are all your children. Bless everyone. And please don't let me get distracted and lose my way. Help me to keep up with Armand, and do not let him fall in love with another woman. Do not let any of the women in our party fall in love with him. Peace on earth, amen."

All the women, young and old, inevitably ended up idolizing her husband. It happened on every tour. But Aimée didn't even know that she was worried about the possibility of Armand's falling in love with someone else until she bent her head in front of the reflecting pool and prayed. For some reason, it dawned on her right then that her husband's charisma, together with his polite attentiveness, might mislead the young women on the tour into thinking that he cared for them more than he did for his wife.

God heard her prayer and made sure that Professor De Potter did not stray in his affections as they traveled on to Egypt. If anything, he became slightly more formal with his party as time went on, especially after their trip up the Nile, when, during his lecture on "The Burial of the Dead," one of the girls pretended to swoon and the others giggled as he read about the embalmers: "First, with a bent instrument, they extracted through the nostrils as much as they could of the brain . . ."

Armand was disappointed by their irreverence for Ancient Egypt. There was no civilization more fascinating and rewarding to study, in his opinion. His biggest regret was that he hadn't acquired sufficient training early in life to lead an archaeological dig in Luxor. He had even been known to pretend that in his previous life he'd been a Theban priest in the Middle Kingdom—a joke that Aimée worried he was in danger of taking too seriously. But he'd devoted many hours to studying the history of Ancient Egypt, and he felt the indifference of others as a personal insult.

Perhaps because of his disappointment, he used his camera less, and read more from his lecture notes, as their journey progressed. What photographs there are of the rest of the trip were taken by Aimée. There are no pictures of either of them as they wandered together, apart from the rest of the party, through the ruins of Pompeii, or ran like children up the stairs of the Coliseum in Rome. And many weeks later, when Armand followed Aimée outside their little hotel in Norway, and they stood together, their arms around each other, their faces turned to the midnight sun, they didn't have the camera to immortalize the moment. There are no more pictures of any of the De Potter tourists in the album Aimée would put together as a memento after her return to America. There are only images of narrow dirt streets in unidentified villages,

and nameless individuals plucked from the masses,

161

of girls doing laundry,

and mountain slopes,

and glaciers,

and then this one at the end of the album, presumably showing the wake of their ship as they headed home from Liverpool, taken by Aimée when she was feeling quietly relieved that the tour was ending, despite her conviction that she'd been improved in all ways by the adventure—

*

163

They returned to New York on August 16, 1887. Among the sixteen members of the party, there were three who declined to send in testimonials after the trip was over. Mr. Osborn of Wisconsin was cross because he had to have an infected tooth extracted in Paris and missed the excursion to Fontainebleau. Mrs. E. D. Scheble of Toledo, who hadn't purchased a single souvenir, made it known that she thought the cost of the tour was excessive. And Mrs. Boynton of Washington, DC, revealed in a postcard to Aimée months later that if she'd been at all unpleasant through the last weeks of the trip, it was because she had discovered a lump in her breast when they were in Russia. Aimée wrote back to express her concern, but she never heard from Mrs. Boynton again.

All in all, though, De Potter's First Grand Tour around the World was a great success. The testimonials they received were encouraging. Miss Mooney wrote to say that she had spoken of her travels every day since she'd returned home. Others wrote to thank their host and hostess for their kind consideration and painstaking efforts to make the journey pleasant. They all gave Armand permission to cite them as references. Soon he was planning his Second Grand Tour around the World, which he promised would be even more extensive than the first. And once he'd circled the Globe with a second group, it would be easy to do it with a third, and then a fourth.

Distances shrank in his mind as he studied maps and tinkered with itineraries. The more remote a destination was, the more enticing it became. He believed himself to be at the forefront of an unstoppable trend. Travel would only get easier and the discomforts would diminish. Ships were getting bigger and more luxurious, and trains were getting faster. The stars themselves were stepping-stones across the universe's great expanse. The only obstacle was fear of the unknown.

On a torrid July day in Albany, as Armand sat by an open window overlooking Broadway, he considered the challenge. He'd been home from his world tour for a month by then. Aimée had taken the train up to Red Hook to visit her family, and he was at the office, waiting for Fletcher, his business manager, to return from the bank. Browsing through the spring edition of his travel journal, *The Old World and European Guide,* which Fletcher had taken to press in his absence, he thought about how he had to convince people that the very object of their fear was the source of all adventure. The unknown should be looked upon as an opportunity—it was a shelf to fill with romances and histories, a stage to be occupied by an absorbing show.

And there was no impresario more willing and capable than Armand De Potter.

As he continued to page through the journal to make sure all was in order, he was amused to see that Fletcher had included among the illustrations a cartoon Armand himself had drawn the previous year. He'd forgotten about the cartoon, and here it was, in the middle of his journal, offering a vision of a future ample enough to have room for everything that could be imagined.

"All aboard!" he called, though he was the only one to hear.

DR. DE POTTER AND PARTY CROSSING THE ATLANTIC IN 1900.

Two Poems
Donald Revell

ENCANTADAS

Poisonous flower of the soul obscene rigging
Of tall ships tattooed onto blue water tattooed
Flesh of the soul Richard of Saint Victor told you
The body is inside the soul a-sail westward
To the islands of flowers and we shall be there
Early tomorrow we shall have awakened pure
From dreams of ourselves nude stranded in the rigging
Richard of Saint Victor has uttered prayers westward
From the black Encantadas rest safely darling
Put your faith into the clouds these white sheets sailing
Entire worlds early souls aweigh poisonous
Irises with wings I mean the ground is alive

MOUNTAIN'S EDGE

Misted sunlight, a scorpion
Fallen out of the sun
Covers the ground, all of it.
There is a rhythm to things,
But no help. So
Says the ruined poisoner.
We are here, here.
Sunlight answers to the call, and so too,
But tenderly, does Mr. Hart Crane.
Wasp-waisted scorpion
Fallen out of the sun
Must be grass, or otherwise
Be insane, building such a nest
In autumn, making God cruel.

166

East of Furious
Jonathan Carroll

HE WAS THE ONLY MAN she knew who actually looked *good* in a Panama hat. Before meeting him, she had never seen a man wearing one who didn't look either like a poser, a hoser, a loser, a tool, or a fool. But not him, not Mills. He looked great—like a deliciously shady character in some Graham Greene novel set in the tropics, or a sexy guy in an ad for good rum. He also owned a cream-colored linen suit that he often wore together with the hat in the summer. That outfit was totally over the top, but he could get away with wearing such things.

She never knew when he would contact her so when he did she was always both surprised and pleased. He'd say something like "Beatrice, it's Mills. Can you take tomorrow off? Let's go play hooky." And unless there was something absolutely pressing, she would.

He was a lawyer. They met when he represented Beatrice Oakum at her divorce. In court he was cool, precise, and quick-witted. Her ex-husband and his lawyer hadn't known what hit them until the judge awarded her almost everything she asked for in the divorce proceedings.

At a victory lunch afterward, Mills asked if they might be friends. The way he asked—shyly and with a charming tone of worry in his voice—flustered her. In court he was so confident and authoritative. But here he sounded like a seventh-grade boy asking her to dance. On the verge of saying of course, it struck her, uh oh, maybe he doesn't want to be just *friends*, he wants—as if reading her mind, the lawyer put up a hand and shook his head. "Please don't take that any way but how I said it. I just think you and I could be great friends. I hope you do too. No more and no less than that. What do you say?" He stuck out his hand to shake. A funny, odd gesture at that moment— like they were sealing a business deal rather than starting a friendship. It told her everything was all right. She hadn't misread his intentions.

They lived about an hour away from each other so at the beginning it was mostly long phone calls and the occasional visit. That suited them, though, because they were both busy people. The calls came in the evening or on the weekends. They were relaxed and uncommonly frank. Perhaps distance had something to do with it. Because fifty miles separated them, both people felt free to say whatever they wanted without having to worry about the possibility of seeing each other unless they agreed on a time and a place to meet.

Mills loved women. A confirmed bachelor, he usually dated two or three simultaneously. Sometimes they knew about each other, sometimes not. He said he liked the drama that invariably came with "dating multitudes." Hell, he even liked the confrontations, the recriminations, the hide-and-seek that was frequently necessary when divvying up your heart among others.

Eventually Beatrice realized Mills wanted her in his life partly because he did not desire her. At another time that would have hurt— no one likes being unwanted. But after her divorce and the exhausting cruel events that preceded it, she felt like a tsunami survivor. The last thing she wanted was someone new in either her head or her bed. So this kind of friendship was OK with her, at least for now. They'd be buddies, Platonic pals with the added bonus that each brought to the table the unique perspective and insight of his or her sex. Neither of them had ever had a really good, nonromantic friend of the opposite sex and it turned out to be a gratifying experience.

Mills asked questions about why women thought or behaved certain ways so he could better understand and win the hearts of his girlfriends. Beatrice asked many of the same kinds of questions but for a very different reason: She was curious about how men saw life so she could better understand why her ex-husband had behaved the way he did. Mills teased her about this. "You're performing an ongoing postmortem while I'm just trying to get them to say yes."

They ate meals together, went to the movies (although they had very different taste, and choosing what film to see often was a good-natured tug-of-war), they took long walks. Mills had a big mutt named Cornbread who regularly went along with them. That made things nicer because the dog was a sweet, gentle soul who wanted nothing more than to be your friend. When they passed other people on these walks, Beatrice could tell by their expressions that they thought Mills and she were a couple. The happy hound bounding back and forth between them further proved that.

One afternoon they were sitting at a favorite outdoor café by the river. It was a gorgeous June day, the place wasn't crowded, Cornbread slept at their feet: a moment where you couldn't ask for more.

"Tell me a secret."

"What do you mean?" She straightened up in her seat.

Sticking his chin out, he said in a taunting voice, "I dare you to tell me one of your absolute deepest secrets. One you've never told anyone before, not even your husband."

"Mills, we're friends and all, but *come on.*"

"I'll tell *you* one of mine—"

"No, I don't want to hear it!" She made a quick gesture with her hand as if shooing flies away from her face.

"Come on, Bea, we *are* good pals now. Why can't I tell you a secret?"

"Because things like that . . . you should keep to yourself."

He smiled. "Are your secrets so ugly or dangerous that they can't be told?"

She tsked her tongue and shook her head. This was the first time he had ever made her feel uncomfortable. What was the point? "Tell me about your hat."

He looked at the Panama on the table. "My *hat?*"

"Yes, I love that hat. And I love it on you. Tell me where you got it."

"You're changing the subject but that's all right. My hat. I got it as a present from a client who was a pretty interesting guy."

"*Was?*"

"Yes, he's dead; he was murdered."

"Wow! By whom?"

"Well, they never found out. He was Russian and supposedly had quite a few enemies."

"You were his divorce lawyer?"

"Yes." Mills signaled a passing waitress to bring him another glass of wine.

"Who was he married to?"

"A very out-of-the-ordinary woman; an American. They met when she was a guest professor at the Moscow Institute of Steel and Alloys."

"Do you think she killed him?"

Mills smiled strangely. "She *was* on their list of suspects."

"Who wanted the divorce?"

He picked the hat up off the table and put it on his knee. "He did, but she got everything in the settlement because he just wanted out and away from her."

"If he lost everything in the settlement, why'd he give you a present afterward?" Her voice was teasing, but she really wanted him to answer the question.

"Because after it was over, I convinced his wife not to turn him into gold."

Beatrice wasn't sure she'd heard right. "*What?* Say that again."

Mills turned the hat round and round on his knee. "I convinced her not to turn him into gold and he was grateful. I'm a very good negotiator, you know. That's why he gave me the hat; he was thankful."

"What do you mean, *turn him into gold?* What are you talking about, Mills?" Beatrice looked at her friend skeptically, as if he must be putting her on or there was a joke in all this somewhere that she either wasn't getting or he'd told badly.

Cornbread woke up and immediately began biting his butt with great gusto. Both people watched while the dog attacked himself and then stopped just as suddenly, curled up again, and went back to sleep.

"Mills?"

"I told you they met when she was a guest professor in Moscow. She's a metallurgist, but also an alchemist. Do you know what they do?"

Beatrice snorted her derision "I know what they're *supposed* to be able to do—turn dross into gold."

He rubbed his neck and nodded. "'Dross'—I like that word; it's very medieval. But, yes, you're right—that's what they do."

"But there's no such thing, Mills, and don't pretend there is. I know nothing about it, but I do know alchemy is more myth than anything else. People have always tried to transform worthless stuff into gold. But it's a metaphor—a nice one—but it's not *real*."

No longer smiling, Mills said, "Oh, it's real. Believe me, I've seen it happen. I saw her do it more than once."

"Stop it, you're teasing me. But, listen—I am completely gullible about these things. I believe what people tell me. That was half the problem with my husband—I always believed him and you know how *that* ended."

Mills rubbed his neck again and looked at Beatrice a long few moments. It was clear he was carefully considering what to say next. "We met back in seventh grade. I was the first boy she ever slept with."

"Who is this? Who are you talking about?"

"Her name is Heather Cooke. Alchemists aren't made, they're born. It is an inherent talent. Contrary to what most people believe,

170

you can't *study* to be an alchemist, any more than you can study to be a violin prodigy or sports star. Studying makes you smarter and practice makes you more adept, but neither is able to create the divine spark that flares into genius. It's either within you from the beginning or not. That's why all those geniuses so accomplished at other things—Paracelsus, Isaac Newton, Saint Thomas Aquinas—failed at alchemy.

"Heather always had the gift. But the irony was she didn't want it; didn't want any part of it. The ability was thrust on her like a physical handicap. She once even said she would rather have been born blind than possess the ability to do alchemy. But too bad—that was her burden."

Beatrice listened to Mills rattle on, half expecting him to start chuckling at some point, pat her on the shoulder, and say he was kidding—this was all a joke. But he didn't and as his cockamamie story went on, she became more and more engrossed in it.

"She would never tell me how she did any of it, not that I would have understood or been able to duplicate the process even if she had. Heather said anyone can find and mix ingredients but the last most important element is the touch, whatever that meant. I asked if she literally meant physical touch but she said no, it was something far more abstruse than that. She made it plain that she didn't want me to ask more about it."

"You actually *saw* her do alchemy—change dross into gold?"

"Yes, twice. But there are different kinds of alchemy. Not just—"

"Can you tell me about them?"

Mills took a deep breath and both cheeks puffed when he let it out again. "The first time we made love we were fifteen. Heather's father died when she was a child. He was a draftsman for an architectural firm. One of her prize possessions was an expensive Yard-O-Led mechanical pencil he owned. She carried it with her everywhere. That first night we were at her house because her mom was out playing bridge. The pencil was on the desk in Heather's bedroom. I'd admired it earlier. When we were done, she excused herself and left the room. Before she did, she stopped at her desk and picked up the pencil. Then she smiled at me over her shoulder.

"A few minutes later she came back and said, 'This is for you.' She handed me a solid gold mechanical pencil, *that* mechanical pencil. She wanted me to have it as a keepsake of that night."

"But how did you know it was the same pencil?"

"Bite marks. Her father chewed on his pens and pencils when he

171

was working. That one was no different. All over the top of this beautiful heavy gold mechanical pencil were bite marks."

The waitress brought Mills his glass of wine. Neither of them spoke after the woman left. Beatrice kept waiting for him to give her a sign—a smile or a wiggle of the eyebrows, something that said OK, I *am* teasing you. But his face looked even more serious than before.

"Heather *had* told me about the alchemy before but that was all—she never made a big deal of it. Only said she could do this weird thing and that sometimes her mother asked her to do it if there were unexpected bills to be paid; nothing more than that. When I asked what alchemy really was, she made up some kind of boring bullshit explanation that had to do with science and metal and math. But I was a boy and way more interested in her breasts than her math talents, so I didn't ask again.

"She and her mother certainly lived modestly, just the two of them in their little house. God knows with that gift, they could have been rich as Croesus and lived a hell of a lot better than they did. But her mom didn't want it. She had a job that made them enough money to live OK. Heather was very smart and got a full scholarship to the state university and then one to graduate school at the Colorado School of Mines.

"After a while we went our separate ways in high school although we always remained friendly and helped each other out when we could."

"She didn't stay your girlfriend in high school? She gave you her virginity *and* a solid gold pen as a thank you, but you left her? God, Mills, you were incorrigible even back then."

The lawyer shook his head. "Wrong—she dumped *me*. Absolutely broke my heart, but she said she wanted to date other guys and play the field. Remember that old phrase 'play the field'? I haven't heard it in years, but those were her exact words when she told me it was over between us. Heather could be very cold and single-minded about things when she wanted. Said we'd always be friends but you know what *that* means, especially when you're a teenager and a hormone rodeo.

"We traveled in different circles in school so I didn't see her all that much after we broke up. Interestingly, she liked the wild crowd, the drinkers and druggers and bad boys galore. The kids who were always in trouble with the police or being suspended from school for doing outrageous things. One of Heather's boyfriends was the first guy in our school to get tattooed. Remember, this was decades ago and back then getting ink was a pretty big deal. Anyway, she ended up with a reputation for many walks on the wild side by the time we graduated.

"She went to one college, I went to another, and that was that until a few years ago when she called me out of the blue. Said she needed a good divorce lawyer and had heard I was one of the best."

"You *are*. I'll attest to that."

Mills stared at Beatrice a few beats too long before smiling and giving a military salute in thanks. It felt like he was looking for something in her face, something that was there but hard to find. She thought it was an odd reaction to her compliment.

"But here's where the story gets interesting. A few days after we spoke, Heather came to my office. She looked pretty much like she did in high school, only thinner and more chic. My first impression was she looked European. I was sort of right because it turned out she'd lived in Russia for five years.

"We chatted a while about old times but it was plain she was just doing that to be nice. Eventually I said, Look, Heather, tell me what you need and let's talk about it. She was getting divorced and asked to hire me because she wanted the whole process over as quickly as possible. I said fine—give me all the details, I'll contact your husband and his lawyer, and we'll get things rolling.

"She said no, she wanted to hire me to represent her *husband*; wanted me to be *his* lawyer. She already had one for herself and he'd agreed to let her find him one."

Beatrice said, "I'm confused."

"So was I, but those were the facts: She already had a lawyer for herself and was hiring me to represent her husband."

"But, Mills, didn't her husband want to find his own lawyer? *Why* would he want someone to represent him who was an old friend, an old *boyfriend*, of his wife?"

"That's exactly what I asked. She said her husband was Russian and didn't know a good lawyer here. Anyway, both of them just wanted the divorce as soon as possible and they had already agreed on who'd get what. They had no children so that wasn't a problem."

"That's crazy! I've never heard of such a thing."

"Her husband came to my office the next morning. His name was Vadim Morozov. Kind of a nondescript-looking guy, you'd never notice him in a crowd—thin, maybe six feet tall, balding, a nice face but nothing special. He had a heavy accent but his English was almost perfect. The problem was I already knew he was one very bad character.

Heather had filled me in on him the day before.

"They met at a party her last year in Moscow. He told her he was a businessman, which wasn't so far from the truth. He was in import/ export but soon enough she learned that meant smuggling: cigarettes, liquor, stolen cars from the West, rare Tabriz and kilim carpets from Iran . . . the list goes on and on. Vadim was a very resourceful fellow.

"But Heather was crazy about him and didn't even blink an eye when she found out what he really did for a living."

"She didn't *mind* that he was a smuggler?"

"Remember I said she'd always liked bad boys. Whatever hesitation or skepticism she might have had, he charmed out of her. She said she was a goner after the first month."

Beatrice made a sour face and shook her head because it sounded all too familiar—much the same thing had happened with her and her husband, only it had taken a while longer for her to fall completely under his spell.

"Vadim was very upfront with her in the beginning, saying he really wanted to move to America one day because so many Russians had gone and were doing well there. But that was fine with her because she didn't plan on staying in Russia, and if things worked out between them, she'd happily take him home with her when the time came.

"Whether he tricked her or it really was good between them, by the time she was to leave she couldn't imagine going home without him."

"And so, 'Reader, I married him.'" Beatrice said the famous line sarcastically and then shook her head again, disgusted by too many rancid memories of her own failed marriage.

"Well, no, they didn't get married for a while after they got to America. She was smitten but she wasn't stupid. Meanwhile Vadim kept a low profile and, as far as she knew, just enjoyed exploring his new homeland.

"He was eager to see America, so that first summer back they traveled for a couple of months: Los Angeles, Seattle, Phoenix, New York. What Heather didn't know was that in each of those cities when she wasn't around, Vadim made contact with Russian criminals who were running all kinds of illegal businesses—drugs, human trafficking, illegal weapon sales. And right after they married, he went to work."

Beatrice touched Mills's arm and then stood up. "I'll be right back." She walked toward the bathroom although she didn't need to use it. For some unknown reason, hearing this story had opened a floodgate inside her, and now all sorts of really toxic emotions were pouring out. Of course most of them had to do with her ex-husband. Until that moment she thought she'd done a pretty good job of keeping her emotions in check, sorting sanely through the marital disappointments, heartaches, bitter memories, and bad experiences and throwing a great many of them out of her head and heart. But even just hearing this fragment of Heather Cooke's story got Beatrice raging again—at her ex-husband, herself, at their failed marriage, at what an abysmal waste that part of her life had been. In a final letter to her husband, she had written, "If I could somehow erase every single pixel of our relationship from my memory I would do it without hesitation. Even the good times, even the great—I'd press 'delete' in a second."

In the bathroom now she stood looking at herself in a mirror above one of the sinks. *"Loser.* How could you have been so naive?" She sighed and closed her eyes. Her brain quickly filled with a mean circus of lousy, noisy memories and images, all jostling around and elbowing each other aside so they could get to the center ring to perform and annoy her.

"OK, enough." She ran cold water over her hands, checked her eyes to make sure there were no tears, and went back out to Mills and his story of Heather Cooke, alchemist.

As Beatrice sat down again at the table, a thought raised its hand in her head to ask a question. "Did Heather's husband know about the alchemy?"

"No, not at the beginning. As I said, it wasn't something she wanted others to know—in fact, very few did besides her mother. You know those people who are really talented at sports or a musical instrument but rarely play or practice because it doesn't interest them?"

"My ex-husband. He was wonderful at chess but didn't play because the game bored him."

"That was Heather too. She didn't practice alchemy for a variety of reasons but was certainly a master. As an academic, however, she was able to investigate it without raising suspicion by writing her doctoral thesis on the history of alchemy in America. Not the trendiest topic in the world, but it allowed her to explore the subject for years, and along the way discover answers to some of her questions. She told whoever asked that she'd grown intrigued by alchemy both as a practice and metaphor after having worked for so long in an adjacent field of study. Since her degree was in metallurgy, it made perfect sense."

"But then one day her husband found out about it and everything changed," Beatrice broke in, beating Mills to his punch line. As soon as she spoke, she knew it was mean and a result of her minimeltdown in the ladies' room. Here she was, half grumpy, half edgy. Should she go home alone and sulk? Some part of her soul was just east of furious now but should she leave it alone and let it run its course, or take some kind of action that might help assuage it? Was that even possible? Can we ever say to our furies when they're laying siege to our borders that they should take a few deep breaths and back off a little?

Mills, sweet Mills, didn't bite back with meanness. Instead he just picked up the story right after what Beatrice had said. "But *how* Vadim found out is a great story in itself." He was about to continue when he looked more closely at Beatrice. "Are you all right? Do you want to go home?"

"No, but would you mind if we walked a little bit? I'm feeling sort of antsy."

"Of course."

They left the café and walked slowly together by the side of the river. Cornbread was off the leash, zigzagging slowly here and there, sniffing the world. Now and then a bicyclist or jogger whizzed by or they passed other walkers but for the most part they had the area to themselves. After a while Beatrice took Mills's hand. They walked in silence until she said, "OK, I'm OK now. Tell me how he found out."

"Vadim hadn't been feeling well for a while so he went to a doctor and had some tests done. They didn't like what they found so more tests were ordered. Eventually it was discovered he had stage three stomach cancer."

Beatrice stopped and turned to Mills. "How bad is that? I know nothing about cancer."

"Bad. Anyone with stage four is a goner, notwithstanding miracles. He came home from the hospital and told Heather he was dying.

"Now this next part is a little foggy because neither of them would tell me any of the details. I had to put their two stories together to come up with a whole."

"Why wouldn't they tell you details?"

"You'll see in a minute. What they *did* say, both of them, was Heather ordered Vadim to take off his shirt and lie down on the couch. When he asked why, she said, *Just do it.* She put both hands on his stomach and closed her eyes. The hands stayed in one spot for a long time. Vadim tried to speak but she said, Shut up. When she took her hands away, she told him to stay there and left the room.

"She was gone quite a long time but on returning she had a small bottle in her hand, like the kind of little liquor bottle stewardesses give on an airplane when you buy a cocktail. She told him to drink it all and then lie back down again. Vadim didn't know what she was doing but said her voice was one he'd never heard before. It was hard and not to be questioned—'a teacher's voice,' he called it.

"The drink tasted like Coca-Cola, which made it even stranger. He thought, I told her I have cancer and she brought me a *soda*? But he drank it all and lay back down, as ordered. She put her hands on his stomach again, one on top of the other but this time in a different spot, down much lower.

"Vadim said what happened next he did not feel; he emphasized that—nothing at all. After some time she slowly raised her hands off his stomach. Beneath them, as if it were a fish being pulled out of him on an invisible line, was something alive. It looked like a big black cockroach, or some other kind of giant black insect. Horrified, Vadim tried to sit up but Heather put her hand on his chest and yelled at him to stay where he was and wait till she was finished."

"Mills, is this true? You're not making it up?"

"Not a word of it. Everything is true. This is exactly as Vadim told me."

"My God. Go on."

"When the thing had fully emerged out of his stomach, it started crawling up his chest toward his neck. Very casually Heather picked it up off his body. The moment she actually touched it, two things happened—the bug stopped moving and then it turned into gold."

Before Beatrice could protest, Mills put a hand in his pocket and brought out something shiny about fifteen centimeters long. He held it up and she lurched backward because it was a large gold bug, so perfectly detailed and real looking that she expected to see its small legs twiddle in the air.

"Remember we were talking the other day about that TV report describing how dogs can smell different kinds of cancer?"

She nodded but kept her eyes on the gold bug.

"Watch this. Cornbread! Corn, come here."

The dog was off to the side, head down in a bush. As soon as he heard Mills call, he came right over to them. The man put his hand down and let the dog see the gold object. Cornbread eagerly sniffed it, then whined and shook his head hard. He even stepped away from his master, then shook his big head again.

"That's OK, boy, that's OK." Mills put the bug back in his pocket. "He smells the cancer."

"But why do *you* have it now?"

Instead of answering Beatrice's question, the lawyer went on. "That night Heather explained everything to him: the alchemy and how she'd always been able to do it, how she hid the talent all her life despite a fascination with it . . . everything.

"Vadim asked her to do something else, turn something else into gold, but she said no, he must accept that if they were to stay together. She had only prepared an *azoth* now to save his life. But he must never ask her to do alchemy again."

"What's an *azoth*?"

"Today we'd call it a panacea. It's a universal medicine that cures anything."

"Anything? AIDS? Cancer?"

"*Anything.* Authentic alchemists have known how to make it for centuries. But it's almost impossible to find a true master capable of mixing one for you.

"Heather and Vadim argued about it a long time. He said they could be rich; he could do all sorts of amazing things with both the money and her power. But she was unmoved. When he became insistent and the discussion got ugly between them, she said if he insisted, it would be the end of their marriage.

"Vadim was a crook but not a stupid man, at least not *that* stupid yet. He knew when to back off. He agreed to do what she asked. Just knowing that she had cured him of terminal stomach cancer was enough for then. He was very grateful—for a while."

"Heather had *never* used the power, never once before the time she cured him?"

Mills picked up a stick and threw it for the dog "Very rarely. Not since she was an adult. Sometimes when she was young and her mother was desperate for money to pay unexpected bills, but only then. She said they got to know certain jewelers who would pay cash for their gold and not ask questions about where it came from."

"Amazing." Beatrice couldn't help admiring Heather Cooke, if what Mills told her was true. Imagine having that extraordinary ability but never using it.

The lawyer interrupted her musing. "The thing most people don't know about alchemy is there are many different kinds, one more obscure than the other. There's the classic 'dross into gold' variety that you mentioned. But another that's way more interesting is something called introvert or internal alchemy that deals with the mystical and contemplative aspects of the science. It deals with *transformation*."

Beatrice frowned "You think alchemy is a *science*, Mills? Do you really? I always thought it was sort of—"

He answered firmly, "It is definitely a science, and a very old one. In various forms it dates back to the beginning of mankind, believe me. Remember Prometheus stealing fire from the gods? Think of him as the first alchemist. Many of the tenets of modern chemistry are based on experiments and discoveries that alchemists made centuries ago."

They walked along in silence, Beatrice thinking it all over, Mills waiting for a sign from her to continue. Cornbread brought the stick back, eager for it to be thrown again. Two bicycle riders rode slowly past, sharing a laugh.

Beatrice stopped and pointed at her friend. "You're going to tell me that Vadim screwed up. Because he was a crook, I assume it was because of that."

Mills grinned. "Go on."

Beatrice looked at her feet and thought about it some more. "He pulled off a big deal, or *tried* to pull one off with the Russian gangsters he'd contacted on their trip across the States."

"Keep going—you're close."

"But everything went wrong and he ended up having to beg her to make some more gold so they wouldn't kill him."

The lawyer pretended to clap. "Pretty good, as far as I know. The truth is Heather would never tell me the details of exactly what happened because she thought knowing them might endanger me."

"Why you, Mills?"

"Because the guys Vadim was involved with were frightening and ruthless, according to her. I assumed they were responsible for his death although nothing could be proved. Whatever Heather did for them I guess was enough, though, because nothing happened to Vadim . . . *then*. By the time he was killed later, she was long gone from his life.

"When he came to her for help that time, she said she'd do it but wanted a divorce after it was over. Vadim thought she was just bluffing but she wasn't.

"She did her alchemy again and made whatever it was he needed. But when the crisis passed, Vadim wouldn't divorce her. He obviously had other plans for her and her ability." Mills took the stick out of the dog's drooly mouth and threw it as far as he could. "But by the time I met the guy, she must have done something pretty damned scary to convince him otherwise because Vadim was terrified of her. He would have divorced her in two seconds if that were possible. Neither of them told me what it was she had done, but it sure worked. That first time we met, Vadim hadn't been in my office five minutes before he started pleading, 'You're her friend. She loves you. Please tell her not to turn me into gold. Please don't let her do that.' I didn't know if he meant it literally or she'd done something equally terrifying to convince him. But the divorce went very quickly. When it was over he gave me this hat and thanked me for intervening. I didn't say a thing to her about that, but he didn't need to know."

"And what happened to Heather after that?"

Mills shook his head. "I don't know. She disappeared and I never heard from her again."

"You never saw her after the divorce?"

Mills shook his head again.

Beatrice smiled, reached over, and touched his cheek. "Liar. Thank you for being such a good liar. I bet you tell that story to all your female clients."

Mills's mouth dropped and then slowly curved into a wide, happy smile. "It's *you*? It's really you?"

Beatrice nodded. "Yes."

"When did you catch on? When did you wake up?"

She slid her hand from his cheek and rested it on his shoulder. "It began when you showed me the gold cancer bug. But it was all slow and blurry and unclear at first. I wasn't sure what was happening so I waited and listened until everything came back to me. It really is like waking up in the morning after a deep sleep."

"It's exactly like you said it would be."

"That's not me, Mills, it's the alchemy."

"But, Heather, it's *really* you? After all this time it's really you?"

"Yes. And I'll tell you certain details now that I couldn't before because nobody knows who I am now. Enough time has passed."

The Heather Cooke he had known since childhood was a tall thin woman with brown hair and features you remembered. In contrast, Beatrice Oakum was medium height, heavy, and plain faced except for her nice long, blonde hair.

"Can I ask what you made for the Russians? Or how you did it?"

Beatrice shook her head. "No. All you need to know about that is afterward I had to find someone I could hide inside until the danger had passed. Transformation is one of the easier parts of internal alchemy, Mills. You want to enter and hide inside the soul of another person? It takes five minutes to mix up the drink you need.

"I went looking and as soon as I found Beatrice, I hibernated inside her after telling her, *programming* her, to do a few things after sufficient time had passed: I told her to find you. I told her to wake me when you showed her the gold bug. I told her . . . well, the rest isn't necessary to explain. What's most important is here I am, just looking a little different, eh?" She lifted both arms and the two old friends embraced while Cornbread jumped up on them, delighted to share their happiness. Eventually they separated. She took her old boyfriend's arm and they began walking again.

"I cannot believe it's you, Heather. I can't believe it actually happened the way you said it would."

She chuckled. "How many women clients did you tell my story to?"

"Four in the last three years. All of them were duly impressed, I must say. But none woke up when I showed them the bug. When they didn't react, I just dropped it back in my pocket and finished telling them Heather Cooke's great story. But I was only following your instructions. I've been dropping clues to you too all the time we've known each other. You never responded until now."

Pushing hair out of her face, she said, "I'll tell you some things now that I couldn't before, Mills, because I do believe I'm safe. I had to vanish so quickly back then because that bastard Vadim told them what I could do and they sent someone to get me. Do you remember what an *alkahest* is?"

"Yes, the universal solvent, a liquid that has the power to dissolve every other substance."

Beatrice squeezed his arm. "You remembered! The man the Russians sent to get me, to bring me to them? I tricked him into drinking an *alkahest*." She opened her mouth to continue but then decided not to. She was about to describe what happened to the Russian after he drank her version of the universal solvent. But a description wasn't necessary because just the thought of it made Mills shudder.

"Afterward I walked straight out of my apartment, called you, and said what I was going to do and what you must do to bring me back.

Then I went looking for someone to hide inside until the coast was clear."

"But what happens to Beatrice now, Heather? If you remain inside her—"

Ignoring his question, the chubby blonde woman leaned down and ruffled the dog's fur. "Good old Cornbread. Remember the day your father brought him home from the animal shelter? How old were we, twelve? From that very first day you were so in love with him. So what's he now, thirty-five years old?"

Mills shrugged. "Probably closer to forty. The oldest dog in the world. It was your Christmas present to me that year. 'Drink this, little Cornbread, and you'll live forever.' That's what you said. I remember.

"But really, Heather, what about Beatrice?"

She held up one finger as if to say, *Let's not talk about that.*

Altered Native
Tim Horvath

1. CROSSING TAHITI OFF his itinerary, Gauguin heads instead for points north in his gambit to ditch civilization. The more his mind has lolled in the tropics, the more convinced he's become that the languorous heat, syrupy voyeurism, and ornate adzes will merely reiterate Parisian clamor and clutter *sans* the solace of steaming coffee and *pain*. Greenland—now that promises true primitivism. Shifting ice tetrahedra, shuddering rumbles, and terns' glancing landings will translate *"nature mort"* more exactly than gaudy mangoes.

2. At Sennelier, he stocks up on paint: first the *blancs, de Troyes, de Lunare, de ceruse, d'argent, crème, ivoire,* and then some *rouge* and *marron*, and even, in case there's some verity to the name, *verte malachite*. He procures wool skeins & the least imposing harpoon he can find.

3. Arrives tremulous in port of Nuuk, a long-haired French bohemian in a cowboy chapeau. For months he has scrutinized salt form from his table's edges, model clumps and ice glares he built to apprentice himself. Still, the real ones nearly blind him. Blinking and muttering profanities, he catches laughter from sources he can't tie a line to. All this numbness, and yet these sting. From children, the three-pronged bombardment—stares, jeers, and a single snowball—fazes him only till his eyes return. He imagines they are critics from the Sorbonne and doffs his hat with a contemptuous flourish.

4. Dinner with the governor. In awe of the plushness of the quarters with which they've provided him. He struts his title of "painter in residence." The commissions will surely start rolling in. *Any day now.* He writes as much to Mette, to whom he is still betrothed, making sure to include a special note to Aline, favorite daughter, his

maman's namesake. One day he intercepts whispers about a meat market. When he inquires, his hand is made a map by calloused fingers, but at the appointed hour, parting the beads, he finds naught but putrid piles of fish. He purchases one so as not to offend and wonders if he can render paint from their oil, the metallic glow like souls still hovering around their corpses.

5. It's not too hard to find revelers to gambol with under midnight sun. What impressionists could do with this light; what Vincent would do with it! This long hair, he thinks, must go—it freezes stiff like his brushes. Commissions too have frozen, leaving his strokes brusque and scattered. One morning he decides he's a Shiverist, an offshoot of Pointillists, but by afternoon he retracts it: too derivative of Seurat and "his damned dots." Which to learn, Danish, Norse, or one of the Inuit tongues? Wavering, he makes sentences from slats of each and is permutatively misunderstood. Regaling the locals with stories of his time in Copenhagen, he never knows they've pegged him as a Danish spy. Behind his back: "Gauguile."

6. Nauseated by niceties, he trades his lavish room for a turf hut—lean, gray, away from the heart of town. The light is relentless, it finds him, harasses him, and yet he can't cease thinking of dark skin buried under textile strata. A centimeter's exposure here is the purest coquetry.

7. Nuuk has too much of the waft of Copenhagen; he must find the prelapsarian, the primordial. This hunger and a kayak bring him to craggy Kangeq, twelve kilometers distant, the Giverny of the late Aron von Kangeq, a painter, an Inuit master, he decides. He makes it his business to see some Kangeqs. *Mon dieu!* Is that walrus attacking the nude woman or is it performing cunnilingus on her? Is the man at her side attempting rescue or cheering both on? Returning to Nuuk, he will allow himself to be tutored by this *Tupilak*, will in short order produce his own *Manao Tupapau*. Which will shock Paris more—the girl whose nubility he makes no attempt to obscure, or the hooded walrus looking on, Big Death longing for Little Death?

8. Missing his bidet, he nonetheless learns to crap with gusto and hitch up his trousers with native dexterity and aplomb.

9. Nightly he falls skin to skin with one or another non-Mette, some as young as Aline, though the numbers aren't spoken. It is the layers of heat, also without number, from outer to innermost that he most wants to capture in paint, and where he feels acutest failure. Other failures, those as husband and father, are only temporary, he reminds himself; one day he will reunite with them.

10. Darkness gradually usurps all. He works in the hut, but dreams an igloo of Sistine proportions, alighting on a ladder like Michelangelo to fresco the underbelly of snow. Disoriented when he awakens, he staggers outside. The moon and stars collude in faint illumination; his *blancs* have ceded to various shades of dim. He should've brought *gris*, but it will take half a year to arrive now from across the ocean. To think months ago he shunned light, hid from it! The pictures of Mette and children that he's propped up around the room along with his own paintings: Often he cannot make them out.

11. Still he paints. And paints and paints. And carves and carves. Canvases rim the room: *The Little Dreamer, The Man with the Axe,* the sprawling *Where Do We Come From? What Are We? Where Are We Going?* He surveys this last from right to left: an infant in a fur-tufted amauti; at center canvas the tree of life, its trunk an upthrust seal, with an Eve who reaches for an apple bitten as yet only by frost, and across the left he has captured three afterlives: Agneriartarfik lush with berries and caribou, Noqumiut for the lazy hunters, sentenced to a diet of butterflies, and lastly Agelermiut, where the seasons barter their features back and forth. It is, he knows, a masterpiece.

12. He decides carvings will not be his legacy. To heat he burns some, burns others to work by.

13. Blowing warm, clear crystals to lithen his brushes, he knows with certainty he's stumbled on paradise.

14. Puking blood, he fancies himself Viking warrior rather than syphilitic artist.

15. Over a century later, museumed, his works make spectators unpleasantly cold. Some say, "We should go someplace warm." "Starbucks?" "Tahiti!"

16. Into his Creeping Glacier series, fronds of South Pacific green keep slipping like shards from a neighboring universe. This, plus the nipples and pubes he barely conceals under walrus hide, yield countless hours of talk for critics and prudes.

The Education of Benesh the Matchmaker
Nomi Eve

Austria 1944

ON THE THIRTEENTH DAY OF AUGUST, in the year 1944, Benesh was transported from Auschwitz to Mauthausen. Benesh was no fool and knew that Mauthausen was just another way station to hell. Any day he or his fellow prisoners could be hung, shot, killed by gas, their bellies ripped open by bayonet, or taken out into the forest and buried alive. The prisoners routinely traded tales of the ferocity, monstrosity, and idiocy of their jailers, who generally stayed aloof and cultivated auras of savagery and brutality—but who sometimes couldn't resist forming rudimentary relationships with the very people they were charged to watch and kill.

Benesh's parents were dead. His sisters, Hinde and Zusi, were God knows where. They had both been in Auschwitz with Benesh, but then Zusi was sent to Ravensbrook, and Benesh hadn't seen either of them for two years. He assumed they were dead. His older brother, Pinchas, had, thank the Lord, emigrated to America before the war. Pinchas had married the daughter of a Torah scholar from Zagreb. They settled in New York, had two children already, and had begged Benesh, Hinde, and Zusi to come to them . . . but by the time they had decided to, it was too late.

At Mauthausen, Benesh carried stones. He was put on the Stairs of Death because he failed to answer during roll call. The irony is that Benesh was naturally a very obedient person. He hadn't failed to answer during roll call in order to be rowdy, insolent, or defiant, but because he hadn't heard his number called. The wind had been blowing terribly that day and half the bunker hadn't answered on time, so now they were all being punished for the wind's own malfeasance. Every day Benesh climbed the Stairs of Death, lugging a hundred-pound granite quarry stone. Sometimes he carried it on his shoulders, sometimes in his hands, hugged close to his chest, like a fat baby. When the skeleton in front of him slipped, which happened all the time, Benesh was dominoed down into the skeleton behind him, and so on and so forth. Sometimes a prisoner would drop dead on the steps and his corpse would be trampled. The first time Benesh stepped on the dead body of a fellow prisoner, he didn't realize what he was stepping on and thought, "Oh, how strange, a dead cat under my feet." When somebody died on the steps, the rest of them would have to haul the dead body up too. When they finally made it to the top of those 186 steps, the guards would march them over to the Parachute Cliff, where they would line them up and then choose one of them to push another off the cliff. If the man refused, the guards would shoot him. The man would plummet off the cliff with his eyes blasted out, or his belly burst open. Mostly the prisoner who refused to push got shot, and the next fellow got pushed anyway. So two of them went over. When Benesh walked up the steps he never knew if this was going to be the day. His day. There was no way of telling if today was going to be the day he would be forced to wrestle with his conscience and to push, or to let himself be executed. Benesh told himself that he would never push a fellow Jew. Or a homosexual Austrian, or an anarchist Czechoslovak, or a Polish Boy Scout, for that matter, or a Spanish Republican. The prisoners condemned to work the steps were a patchwork bunch. Benesh often thought that if he weren't in a death camp he would enjoy the company of such colorful fellows. No, Benesh would refuse. He told himself he would just stand there on the edge of the cliff, and say, "Shoot me, why don't you?" But sometimes Benesh woke up in the small hours of the night with his hands pressing up on the bunk on top of him, but it wasn't a bunk, it was a person, a fellow prisoner, and he was pushing him with all of his might, pushing, pushing, until the man lost his footing and went over backward, screaming at the top of his lungs. Benesh's arms would tingle from the exertion of pushing a man over the cliff—even though, rationally, he knew he had been dreaming, and also, imposing rationality upon the dream, he knew that the fellow he would be asked to push would be light as a feather, and that to do the job, all he would have to do was flick a pinkie and the man would lose his balance. "Get a hold of yourself, Benesh," Benesh told himself. "Stop dreaming." Sometimes one of the men in the top bunk would yell down, "Cut it out" or "Stop pushing!" and then roll over with a cough or a snore. Sometimes when Benesh woke up he noticed that all the sleeping men were unusually quiet and he would wonder if everyone but him had been smothered overnight. But then one of Benesh's bunkmates would kick him in the shins; the other, a very tall purveyor of phosphorous and other combustible chemicals, would let out a grunt, then, still sleeping, grab Benesh's wrist and hold on for dear life.

One morning, Benesh found himself standing in the office of the Kommandant's adjutant. He had been ordered here, marched here, and shoved inside the office. Benesh was sure he would be killed or tortured, for sometimes the adjutant did that—ordered prisoners to be brought to his office so that he personally could finish them off. He even heard that once the adjutant had had a big dog in his office and that he had supervised as the beast ate off a man's penis. A man's penis! Who had ever heard of such grotesqueries, such torture? But sometimes prisoners came back from the adjutant's office alive, and told the rest of the bunker surprising tales of a man who possessed an unlikely and generous sense of humor. Who offered you a drink, asked questions about your past, made idle conversation. They wondered, how could it be that a man could be a devil one minute and a man the next?

The adjutant was not one of those puffed-up pigified blond Nazis, but a thrust-jawed wolf of a man with ruddy hair, pocked skin, and protruding ears. While Benesh was standing there, the adjutant was looking down at some papers on his desk. He looked up and said, "Aaah . . . Benesh the Matchmaker!" He got up from his desk, came around to the front, and extended a hand. "So pleased to meet you."

Benesh thought the adjutant's hand felt like a springy sponge, not like a hand at all. The adjutant leaned against his desk and said, "Would you like a drink of hot tea?" Then he called for tea and persisted in acting as if this was normal, and so Benesh did too, even though his body was eating itself from the inside out and it hurt to even walk because of the way his bones rubbed against each other, and here, in front of his eyes, the adjutant was a man in the prime of health and seemed by some trick of distortion to be a veritable giant. He towered over Benesh, who felt, in his presence, like an ant by comparison. "Yes, I will act normal," Benesh told himself, even though on his way to the adjutant's office, Benesh had passed by a frozen statue of a man hugging a boy. They had been there for a month now. Every day the guards sprayed them with more water, and the two corpses froze in sequential crystalline layers, turning them into a statue. The rumor around the camp was that the man was a priest and had been caught baptizing the poor boy. They had been taken to the cold showers, and then sprayed with water and left to freeze.

Now here they were, enclosed in ice, the poor boy's last-ditch bid at any kind of salvation caught in suspended animation.

Normal, thought Benesh, taking the tea, *normal*. He took a sip. The tea burned his throat. He coughed and spilled it on his hands, burning his fingers.

Benesh looked up and said to himself, *Benesh, what would be a normal question in this situation?* But then he heard himself asking rashly, impetuously, "How did you know that I make matches?"

The adjutant smiled. His muzzle opened to reveal a bad front left tooth.

"Ah, Benesh," he said, as if they were old friends. "I could flatter you by saying that your reputation preceded you here in Mauthausen, but I would be lying, and I see no need to flatter you, when you should be the one flattering me. You have no reputation in my world. Why, in my world, Benesh the Matchmaker has already ceased to exist. And the truth is that I should single you out for special punishment for being so personally responsible for the birth of so many little baby Jewlings from the matches you have made. I should kill you once for each life you are responsible for. But that is not why I called you here today. No, I will not go off on that tangent. So if you must know—"

Benesh was thinking: must? If I must know what? How can I "must know" anything from this man? Must requires authority, must requires muscle. My muscles are atrophied. My muscles are tapioca.

The adjutant was talking: "—passing by the infirmary and heard one of the other prisoners calling you Benesh the Matchmaker. I sent out some feelers through the camp to see whom he was talking about, and now here you are standing in my office, hunched over like a clam, and smelling worse than a cart horse with distemper. You need a bath, Benesh. And a delousing. Tomorrow come back at ten o'clock and I will see that you are made presentable. If you are a good little Jew, I will even give you some fresh clothes."

That night back in the bunker, when he fell asleep, Benesh dreamed that he was walking by the ice statue corpses and that when he got close, the priest winked at him, and Benesh knew that he was alive in there, under all that ice. "I'll help you," Benesh yelled, "I'll help you." He ran for a bucket of hot water and a chisel, and when he returned with these tools, the ice wasn't ice, but marble. And he could no longer see the forms of the priest and the boy inside. "It's hopeless," he said, laying down the chisel. "I've come too late."

190

In the morning, the guard took him back to the adjutant after roll call. "You are lucky, Benesh," the guard said. "No stairs for you today. No stones to carry." But Benesh didn't know if he was lucky or unlucky. He didn't know if a big dog would be waiting for him in the adjutant's office, having been promised a meal of Jewish nut sack for breakfast. Another guard escorted him to a private bath. The bath was at the rear of the prisoners' brothel. He was given soap, a towel. When he soaked in the warm tub he heard animal sounds of sad, malnourished lovemaking from the other side of the wall. He hadn't felt warm water in so many years that he wasn't sure he could ever bear getting out of the tub, but then he looked down at his shriveled, starved body and was disgusted by the stranger's corpse he was attached to. How have I been grafted onto a corpse? he wondered. He was subsumed by an existential nausea that canceled out the pleasure of the bath. He was given new clothes. They were prison clothes, of course, but they were clean. Then he was ushered out to see the adjutant. The warm bath made him feel colder outside. He hugged his body and watched his breath float ahead of him. This time, the adjutant immediately got up to shake Benesh's hand. He got straight to the point.

"Benesh," he said, "I have called you here for a professional consultation."

"Excuse me?"

"Your line of work—"

Benesh wondered, What am I supposed to say? And then he knew what to say—"I carry stones."

"No, no, Benesh, before all this." The adjutant waved a hand and smiled as if he were saying, "Before this war nonsense, before this little piffle of history."

Benesh tried to clear the fog from his head. What does he want from me? What? And then he said, "You already know, I make matches."

"Exactly. Now you understand why I've brought you here, as a professional. You see, we've had a new batch of girl guards come to Mauthausen for training. They'll be here through Easter. Rapportfuhrer, Blockfuhrer, and I have hatched a little plan. It goes like this. We want you to match up the guards. And if you make ten successful matches, I will personally order the guard at the top of the quarry steps to stop the shenanigans with the cliff. "

This was really too much for Benesh to process. He broke it down into parts: girl guards, plan, matches, shenanigans.

He heard someone saying, "Do you mean the murders on the cliff?" Benesh wondered who would ask such a thing of the adjutant. He heard a little voice in his head saying, "Oh it's me." And then, "Oh, what a cheeky fellow I am." He clenched his buttocks together and said a silent prayer begging God to allow him to retain control over his bodily fluids.

The adjutant had come around the front of his desk. He leaned back on the desk and looked distractedly out the window at the ice statue made of the boy and the priest, while saying, "Yes, yes, you know the whole ridiculous *push-the-fellow-prisoner-off-the-cliff business.*"

Benesh was suddenly so cold. He was inside a block of ice. For what sin was I put here? he wondered. Have I asked to be baptized too? Suddenly he couldn't remember. And then finally, Benesh heard some other Benesh speak up. This other Benesh was saying, "But, Adjutant, sir, ten? Ten is a large number. How about five, five matches?"

"Who do you think you are, Benesh . . . Lot?" said the adjutant. "Bargaining with God for the lives of righteous men? No, there will be no bargains. I said ten and I meant ten. Ten good couples."

Then Benesh heard himself speaking and was startled by his own audacity. But once he started, he didn't feel audacious anymore. He felt quite normal, actually. He was a matchmaker, and the adjutant was a client, that's all.

"Will I—?"

"Will you what?"

"Be allowed to interview the prospects?"

"Preposterous. What would you ask? Favorite color? Favorite purveyor of bratwurst?"

"But how am I to—"

"To what?"

"How am I to assess personalities and affinities? A matchmaker is not a magician. Matchmaking is more science than art, and if I am denied access to my . . . clients . . . I will fail for sure. Then—then your fellow officers will be denied the comfort a good match could bring."

The adjutant ran his tongue over his dead tooth, as if to dislodge a small piece of stuck food. "That, Benesh is your problem, not mine." He seemed to reconsider. "I will make one concession. The officers are gathering for a Christmas party at a recreation villa outside the camp. You will come and be a waiter. You may observe the . . . subjects . . . in this casual social setting. After that you may serve the

192

food in our commissary, off base. I am sure what you will see will help you perform the service I am requesting."

Benesh thought for a moment. "Sometimes it takes months for affection to flower, for love to grow, and anyway—"

"Spare me the pedantic lecture. If you find *me* a match, I will know that the others' matches are also suitable."

Benesh stared at the adjutant's wolf muzzle, and thought, This man could very well eat me up.

"So, what I'm saying, Benesh, is that I like a girl with big tits and a sense of humor."

"What else?"

"Calloused feet for hiking, good teeth for biting, and a nice firm rump for grabbing hold of."

"Interests?"

"Astronomy, medieval military history, and sausage making, of course."

"Why me?"

"This may come as a surprise to you, Benesh, but we Nazis are not immune to the talents of your race, nor are we ignorant of your charms."

"But what you ask is superfluous, beside the point."

"Why?"

"You are the adjutant. Forgive my forwardness, but you are a big, strong, handsome pillar of a man. Clearly you see that you don't need a matchmaker. I am sure that any of the new gals would consider it an honor to be your chosen, ahem, mate."

"Oh, Benesh," complained the adjutant, "I am not looking for a girl who would be honored, but one whom I could love, and who would love me back."

"This is very strange, sir."

"What?"

"To be talking to a Nazi about love."

"But we are."

"Yes, we are."

"Sir."

"Uh?"

"What if you are displeased with my . . . my work?"

"Silly little Benesh, I thought I made that perfectly clear."

"No, sir, it is not."

"If you do a lousy job, then you all go over the cliff. The whole barracks. Just think, Benesh, you could all grow wings. You could

193

all learn to fly." He smiled, his dead-tooth smile. Then he extended his hand. Benesh took it and shook, as if this were a regular deal. He walked out of the adjutant's office, and passed the statue. He dared to reach out and touch the ice. His fingertips burned with cold. In that moment, he communicated with the dead. The priest said, "My son, a deal's a deal." Benesh sighed, "To what deal are you referring?"

Benesh had been a matchmaker since he was a little boy. He had started small—first matching up bull to cow, ram to sheep, bitch to dog, and then, when he was sixteen, he began to make matches for his friends. He had a knack. The people Benesh matched might not have on the surface seemed so compatible: The boy might have been tall, and she short, he might have had a scientific mind, and she an artistic temperament, but Benesh liked to say that he matched souls, not personalities. And ultimately most of his matches found deep and abiding love.

Once, explaining his technique, he had said, "It is simple. Every soul has texture like cloth, and as a matchmaker it is my responsibility to match wool to wool, silk to silk, canvas to canvas." And then he would cock his head to one side and add, "A matchmaker sees the underside—the loose thread and ragged edges. I match deficiencies as much as I match perfections." Whatever his technique, it seemed to work, and as a result his village enjoyed the benefits of his labors, and was an uncommonly happy and loving place to live. On Friday eve when the men sat at the supper table and sang "Woman of Valor" to their wives, their deep voices rose up like chimney smoke, braiding together in the Sabbath sky in a blanket of praise and exultation, for they really and truly loved their wives and the women loved them back, believed the words of the Psalm, and smiled at the future.

Benesh's reputation grew. Young men from the surrounding villages began to engage his services. Young men from farther afield began to take long treks to consult with him and bring back a bride. When Benesh made a match, he employed several techniques: the interview, the gut feeling, and holy mathematics. Benesh was a deep believer in Kabbalistic numerology and would not match up a boy and a girl whose names added up to an unlucky number. A good match could be one where the bride and groom's names added up to Siman Tov, which meant "A Good Sign." The contrary was also true, and several matches he thought initially promising were never pursued because the bride and groom together added up to one of the many names for hell. And when a young man equaled Gehinom and a young woman equaled Azazel, there was no point putting them together, for surely there would be catastrophic trouble in the union. When Benesh made a good match and had the good fortune to be an honored guest at the wedding, he could sometimes see little golden sparks emanating from the bride and groom, like little chains, binding them together. This didn't always happen, but when it did, Benesh knew that the couple would have an uncommonly loving marriage.

Benesh was often put onto the trail of a match when, in his spare time, he added up the names of the young men and women on his lists, and found that some equaled each other, or that their names, when added or subtracted, gave rise to holy sums. That is how he matched the son of the Lodz rebbe with the daughter of the Pilsen rebbe. Both of their names added up to Mazel Tov. And that is how he matched the son of the scribe from Riva with the daughter of the bookseller from Prague. Both of their names had the happy fortune to add up to the equivalent of Garden of Eden. Sometimes, these numerological equivalencies didn't quite work out the way Benesh intended. He had learned over the years to give the gut feeling and the interview somewhat more sway than the numbers themselves. But even he, simple Benesh, was modest enough to admit that there were forces much greater than he. The Holy One Blessed Be He had a plan for each and every one of his children, usually involving marriage, companionship, and, yes, even love for the fortunate. For the unfortunate? The spinsters and aged bachelors of the community, the divorced or the unhappily married . . . Benesh liked to say that there was no one he couldn't match. But he couldn't match someone who wasn't willing. He even turned away good-paying customers if they had what Benesh suspected were clogged-up hearts and would refuse perfect matches time after time. Benesh could spot them a mile away. "My roster is full," he would protest. "My load is too heavy, but may I suggest a course of therapeutic baths and the liberal drinking of honey wine. Come back in the spring, for maybe then I will have an opening."

The night after his interview with the adjutant, sleepless Benesh lay in his bed, a dirty sardine among sardines, squished between two men on either side, and the bunk above and the bunk below. The sounds of the barracks were louder than usual. He heard every fart, every belly rumble, every sleeping sigh and groan amplified. When he finally fell asleep, Benesh had a preposterous dream. The adjutant was holding a shofar to his lips and blowing. But no sound would come out of the ritual horn. He blew and blew until his wolf-muzzle cheeks puffed out and turned pink and then red and then scarlet, and then all of a sudden they just popped, his whole face exploding with mute, senseless effort. When Benesh woke up, the dream hovered in his brain. But he wondered the wrong thing about it. He didn't wonder *Why would a Nazi blow a shofar?* But *What notes was the adjutant trying to blow? A* tekeya, *or* shevarim? *Or maybe a* truah? Then Benesh caught himself, and said, *Benesh, the true question is: Does the adjutant in my dream blow to commemorate or to warn? To praise or condemn? Does he blow for sanctity or sacrilege?*

Before roll call Benesh found Reb Zalman Arnstein, who was a cousin of the great Ger Rebbi. Reb Arnstein had a thick nose, strong shoulders, and a big chin. His hair would have been grizzled if it wasn't shaved. His crescent-shaped blue eyes still sparkled and he still smiled, when others had long stopped smiling. Arnstein was a confidant of most of the men in Barracks 54. They loved him for his wisdom, his cheer, his moral strength, and for his treasure trove of parables, which he shared to alleviate their suffering. The day before the adjutant had called Benesh to his office, Reb Arnstein had told everyone a parable called "The Man Who Read Upside Down." It was a comedic story of improvisers who read the Talmud upside down and sideways because they were so poor they had only one holy book among them. "Who would you be?" Arnstein had asked them. "The man who reads from the right? The left? Or upside down?"

Benesh told Reb Arnstein the story of the previous day. How he had been called into the adjutant's office. How the adjutant expected him to make matches for Nazis, a match for himself. Reb Zalman Arnstein listened patiently, and then said, "Very interesting, Benesh. I never would have expected." He smiled. "But then again, I never would have expected any of this, now would I?" The rabbi motioned to their starving, bony brethren with shaved heads and faces. Then he put his hand over Benesh's and said, "Well, do you think you can do it?"

Benesh shut his eyes, opened them again.

"Benesh, can you?"

"I've never matched anyone but a Jew, and of course I always had time, was never rushed, I could at my leisure interview many girls, many boys, and had the luxury of information—a girl's lineage, a boy's heritage—for the present is but a tiny link on the chain of eternity, and every good matchmaker worth his weight in salt will consider ancestors when matching up their children. As for these Nazis, I know nothing about them, nothing about their pasts or their futures, nothing about their parents or their grandparents, and must make my matches from scratch."

"Benesh, the Holy One Blessed Be He will be your guide. He will supply you with any information you need."

"But if I match up the Nazis, aren't I responsible for making more little Nazis? I mean, if my matches are successful, and the couples wed. Won't I be indirectly, but also somewhat directly responsible for the conception, creation, and spawning of another generation of monsters?" He took a deep breath. "And if so, won't I be courting The Holy One's displeasure? How can I do what the adjutant asks? And the truth is—like I said—I have only ever made matches for Jews, I don't even know what methods I would employ to match up Germans, Nazis no less."

Reb Arnstein was quiet. He put his hands together, spidering his fingers. The rabbi's nose was covered in tiny little blood lines, so many burst vessels giving the impression of his having dipped his nose in a jar of pale red paint. He cocked his head to one side, and said, "No, Benesh, the question is, How can you not?" He shook his head. "It is my opinion that your whole life has led up to this moment. That every match you have made of *yid* to *yidella* has been practice. Yes, we, your brethren, have been your school, your education, but now you must put your God-given talents to holy use. You must match up these Nazis, not frivolously, not willy-nilly, but sincerely, and with deep thoughts to their happiness, their suitability, and, yes, the strengths and weaknesses of their moral characters. Yes, happiness. You must have their happiness in mind, for there is no fooling the adjutant and he will know if you are subverting his wishes, and matching cow to goat and frog to sparrow. Benesh, this is your job, why you were put here on earth. Remember, Benesh, God is the great matchmaker, and by matching up our jailers, you will be doing God's work."

Benesh sighed. "So I was put on earth to be a matchmaker for Amalake, the biblical enemies of Jews?"

"That is one way of looking at it. But another way of looking at it, dear Benesh, is that you were put here on earth to save a barracks full of souls. Not with a sword like Judah Maccabee. But with the weapon of marriage."

Benesh sent word through the camp that he needed all available information on the guards—male and female. In this way, he learned that one of the new girl guards hummed snippets of Wagner's "Wesendonck Lieder" when she marched her prisoners to the factory and that another could often been seen doing calisthenics when her Jews were busy cleaning toilets. He learned that one of the girl guards sometimes carried a small book with her that someone thought was a collection of tales by the Brothers Grimm. Benesh learned that one of the male guards took lots of photographs—and that he carried around a tripod and set it up at seemingly random spots, snapping pictures of birds or trees or barbed wire. Another of the guards was known to have a skin infection on his neck and was rumored to have personally plucked a Jewish doctor from a firing squad because the man knew a recipe for a salve that could soothe his discomfort. Another male guard was known to feed birds and carry a pet rabbit in his pocket when taking his men to the delousing showers.

Of course there were also the less pleasant and more readily apparent character traits to be considered. All of the guards were vicious and heartless and each had been witnessed perpetrating unfathomable atrocities. On the very first day that she arrived in Mauthausen, one of the girl guards made a mother watch while her own daughter's legs were spread open and a silver wolfhound was brought over to lap at the girl's privates as if it were ravishing bread soaked in gravy. The rabbit-carrying guard was also known as the Blaspheming Bayoneter because every few days he bayoneted a Jew or a Spaniard for fun, while taking the Lord's name in vain in a phlegmy, hoarse voice that made people think he suffered sinus trouble. There was much discussion about whether the rabbit-carrying, bayoneting guard would make a good husband for an opera-singing woman guard who regularly smashed the skulls of newborn babies under her booted foot. There was much dissension between prisoners about whether ruthlessness should be matched up with ruthlessness, or if the less fierce Nazis should be matched up with the most horrible ones to lend balance to the union. Benesh vacillated between deciding to match up the less horrible monsters with the most horrible ones, and the most horrible with the most horrible because while he believed in the union of opposites he also sensed that he was already in an opposite world, where upside was down, day was night, life was death, and there was no use pretending that harmony of any sort even existed anymore.

Of course, Benesh was on the lookout for the girl guard with the biggest breasts and behind. There were actually three of them with ample posteriors, but only two with impressive bosoms—Sighelda the baby killer and Frieda the wolfhound bitch, who read fairy tales and had what Benesh considered an idiotic expression on her round little face that signified bad lineage, an imbecile ancestor somewhere in her family tree.

Christmas found Benesh at the Nazis' recreation villa in the forest. Once again he had been taken to bathe, and once again he was given a new prison uniform. After he helped serve the feast, he was even invited by the cook to take a roast duck leg for himself. He ate it too quickly and vomited the whole thing in the mud behind the lodge. He wiped his mouth and went back inside. The adjutant was standing by the Christmas tree holding a wooden rod with a candle on the end. He lit the candles on the tree. It was, Benesh had to admit, utterly beautiful. In the flickering light Benesh saw the guards not as monsters but as a jaunty, handsome lot standing close enough to rub elbows, touch hips, run a hand down a back, and lean flirtatiously closer with a pretty girl. The tree was all lit up now. The adjutant put down his long-handled lighter. Next to him was Frieda the wolfhound bitch, her black eyes flashing in the candlelight. On the other side, Sighelda who killed babies, looking up at the adjutant with a moony smile. Benesh felt himself growing drunk on the warm glow, the pine-scented splendor, and he let his eyes fall on each and every one of them, trying to match names with the details of character he had been collecting. Which was the opera singer? Which was Hans the photographer? Who would care a whit about astronomy? Which was the one who just yesterday pulled the little cripple girl limb from limb when she was brought in on the transport? Which one had the skin condition? How can I know them? he wondered. How can I figure them all out? Time passed, the candles burnt halfway. And then, one by one, the guards all made their way over to Benesh. Quietly, in hurried conspiratorial whispers, they confided in Benesh secrets they had told no one before. They clutched his bony arm and confessed to sexual predilections, romantic idiosyncrasies, and humdrum hobbies they hoped to share with a mate. Benesh shivered even though it was warm in the room. Soon the laughing voices of those Nazis around the tree was the laughter of demons, and he himself was alive but not alive. Somehow he had become a puppet—Benesh who had lost his soul and was now doomed to search for it in the festive blaze of the evergreen glow.

That night, Benesh lay awake, tormented. Clearly, the blonde Sighelda was already in love with the adjutant, but the brunette Frieda, who let dogs have their way with virgins, was the better match for the man who let dogs eat penises. He tried numerology—and when he translated the adjutant's name into Hebrew and then calculated the numbers, he came up with an exact equivalency for the name of the demon Asmodia. Then he translated the names of the girls into Hebrew and found that one of them had a perfect equivalency for the name Lamia, which was an Arabic name for the demon Lilith. For the first time in his professional career, Benesh smiled at the thought of matching demon to demon, and felt suddenly filled with a sense of peace and purpose, as if he were on the track of an eternal truth, not just human coupling.

In the morning he went to serve in the officers' commissary. The adjutant was eating bratwurst and creamed potatoes. Benesh, a starved man, could barely tear his eyes away from the food. For a minute he was delusional and thought the bratwurst, the eggs, the toast, the potatoes, the onions, the juice, were his clients, and he matched them up. Bratwurst to eggs, potatoes to onions, toast to juice. And then he heard talking, and he looked up. Tiny sparks were flooding the room, like golden lassos. The golden lassos danced from Nazi to Nazi, braiding them one to the other as they ate their eggs and buttered their bread.

Before the month was out, Benesh handed the adjutant a list. The adjutant read down the names, smiled, and said, "Good show, good show." Then he threw the paper into the stove and said, "You may go now, Benesh. I am done with you." He spit into the fire—a big hawking gob of phlegmy spit. Benesh watched it sizzle in the embers.

Benesh turned to go. Before he reached the door, the adjutant said, "Tell me, Benesh, which will you choose?"

"Excuse me, sir?"

"To push the next fellow off or to let them shoot you?"

"But you said—"

Silence. A great big wall of silence blanketed the room, and then spread out to muffle the sounds of the entire camp and beyond, the countryside, the country, the world, the heavens above. There was even silence in Benesh's own chest, muffling his heart, stopping it from beating.

"I said nothing. I've never even seen you before and I have no idea why you are standing in my office stinking of shit, rot, and piss. When I find who is responsible for your presence here, I will punish them. Now leave quickly before I call in the dogs."

Benesh ran back to the barracks. He told Reb Arnstein what the adjutant had said, and word quickly spread that Benesh the Matchmaker had made his matches, but that the men of Barracks 54 wouldn't be saved after all. The barracks were filled with moans and wailing. Men beat their hollow chests.

Weeks passed. Benesh went back to carrying stones. And every day when he reached the top of those 186 steps he expected to be led to the cliff, and to be asked to choose, Kill or be killed? Which one will it be, Benesh? Which would you choose? He heard the adjutant's voice in his head, 186 times, each step the question presented itself anew. Awake he had one answer, asleep he had a different answer. But each day when Benesh reached the top of the steps, he and all the other men from Barracks 54 were led directly back to the bunker.

On the way back to the bunker, Benesh always walked with his head down. He looked at his feet. He remembered the sounds that came from the other side of the bathroom door. The prostitutes were Jewish girls. Their visitors were socialists or Frankists, or kapo Jews who had somehow curried favor. Benesh dreamed that he too visited the brothel, not to take advantage of a poor girl, but to say, "Which one of you is looking for a young man? I can help you. It is my job, you see, to make matches."

Time passed. The men of Barracks 54 were never marched to the showers that turned you into ashes and smoke. They were never marched out to the woods and shot or buried alive. They were not summarily hung or executed while other prisoners watched, like the men of Barracks 32, who were made an example and were slaughtered two by two every day for two months. They did, of course, have their own private catastrophes. Sheider Newlichter died of starvation. Avraham Grosberg fell down into a vat of acid and died a horrible, screaming death. Bear Shternberg was kicked in the neck by the photographer Nazi and died that night strangling on blood. Three of the Spaniards succumbed to typhus. An Austrian anarchist went crazy and threw himself on the barracks guard and bit the man's cheek. His death was gruesome—his eyes were scooped out with a knife while he was still alive, and then he was disemboweled in common view of the men returning from the latrines. Everyone had loved this man—he had been uncommonly good-natured and possessed the ability to recite whole passages of popular comedies and thus distract the rest of them from their own miserable thoughts. The men of Barracks 54 suffered these losses and were diminished in number but they were never taken en masse. And as the months passed, they began to have hope. "Maybe Benesh's matches did save us?" they thought. "Maybe we will live after all."

Spring came. The priest and the boy began to thaw. Everyone went to see them, and then quickly averted their eyes because the ice had preserved the pair's humanity, and as they melted, they seemed to grow more and more confused and disconsolate about their predicament. People wanted to comfort them, but they were beyond comfort. And then they quickly began to rot and finally the adjutant ordered the corpses carted away.

After the war, Benesh and his sister Zusi were reunited at Bad Gastein. Hinde was dead, gassed at Auschwitz. They received news that their brother Pinchas in New York and his wife were the parents of twin three-year-old boys, and had just had another baby, a little girl whom they were calling Little Hinde out respect for her dead aunt. Pinchas arranged for them to leave Europe. When they reached America, people said, "What a miracle that you survived." Benesh wanted to agree, but he was afraid of confusing miracles with monsters, and so he kept quiet. He refused to talk about Mauthausen, the 186 steps, the corpses under his feet that felt like dead cats when he stepped on them, the cliff, and the corpses flying off willy-nilly into the sky, and the choices he might or might not have made there.

Benesh became Benny. By mistake, he was even Benjamin. To his own astonishment he became a professor of European history at a well-known American university. When he lectured sometimes he paused and thought, *At every turn, my life seems both astonishing and depleted of resources, I am a quarry without stones, I am a well run dry.* "Excuse me, Professor," his students would say. "Sir, you were saying . . ." And they would nudge him back to the present.

Every so often someone from the old country would call and ask Benesh to arrange a match, but he always refused. His talent was gone, and try as he would, he could not see the sparks, those glowing little tails that connected man to woman, boy to girl, man to

God, and back again. He knew that his gift had extinguished itself in Mauthausen. He would be tempted to try matching up his students. But the feeling wouldn't last very long, and anyway, they seemed to need no help from him finding hands to hold. When Benesh walked through campus it seemed that everyone was embracing, so many couples, arm in arm, unaware of anything but the next step on a pleasant day, on a path shaded by towering old elms.

In 1958, Benesh was invited to the University of Vienna to lecture. He didn't want to go, but a friend, a survivor named Mickey, had insisted. "After all," Micky said, "you must visit the graves of your people once before you die."

"But they have no graves."

"I know, stupid Benesh." Mickey said this even though he didn't think him stupid at all. "No grave, no shroud, no stone, but you must go to Europe and say Kaddish after all."

Benesh moved through the Stephansplatz like a zombie. Everywhere he saw their faces—the baby killer who sang opera, the bayoneter who carried a pet rabbit in his pocket, the big-bosomed matron who tortured virgins with dogs. Every Christian child seemed to resemble Benesh's jailers. He could not help but wonder if one of them was perhaps the son or daughter of one of the matches he had made. A group of boisterous schoolchildren in knickers and caps flooded out of a door. He walked among all these little killers thinking, *I am a beast amongst men, I am Cain cursed to wander through the shades of night for doing the whims of a Nazi, for using sacred art to spawn profane love.* He put a hand up to his sweaty forehead and said, under his breath, "Cool it, Benesh. These are not their children." Then another voice in his head said, "And what if they are? You cannot blame the child for the sins of the father, now can you? Can you?"

Benesh continued down the street. He crossed an alley that led through a row of houses. He turned a corner by a shop that sold antique globes and compasses. Benesh stopped to stare at longitudes and meridians. He heard a sweet high voice and turned around. A red-haired boy with the adjutant's wolf muzzle was speaking to him. He looked twelve, maybe thirteen years old. "Sir, you dropped your handkerchief. Here it is. I picked it up and ran after you but you didn't listen. I followed you. Now I am out of breath and my mother is calling. She will punish me for running off, so take it, take it!"

Benesh reached and took hold of his life, grazing the child's hand with his fingertips.

"Thank you," he wanted to say, "thank you," but the words turned to ice and froze up his throat. He couldn't breathe. When he finally thawed, the child was gone.

f/11
Andrew Zawacki

::

Dusk an outbox SMS, its grammar a macramé aura on the mirror. Cf. Fig
L-14*a*: "Location is where the camera is." Camellia rigged with an
escalator, an interior fountain, & satin detonations—denotations. A
language to lockstep my lung inside, this I I tightrope walk a wire with:

::

Montparnasse, 8h20, drat light mattes the station sterile white. TGV
boarding, bound for Toulouse. Windmills fenced in a rapeseed field—a
quartet of asterisks—are alien vertebrae with propeller heads. 4-track
pasture, park-&-ride: inscape blurs & tatters thru the QuickSnap aperture.

::

At the Mission San Xavier del Bac, a Polaroid nova divided from its light &
the tweeting of jets: "There are no stars in / the metropolitan / area skies
/ only air traffic." A bail-bond center with its chintzy, fluorescent sign, & a
clearance sale being flogged on Commerce Road: EVERYTHING MUST GO.

Andrew Zawacki

: :

Little green moon in the fire alarm, crape myrtle a violet fireworks. Acetylene stain of an Ektachrome sky, a squall enfuchsias the tain of the river Tarn. Weather peroxides the window, a whisky shot & two Tylenol before bed. Trees in their tunics of calico, & love a city in summer: *enneigée*.

: :

Wildwood Crest is a Cessna tailing its tag line over the beach. Along the sand—a description of sound, at 7¾ ips—: a man with a crackling metal detector, its Space Invaders laseresque beeps in sys- & diastole, sweeping the beach as if waving a wand to ward the water off. Or coax it back.

: :

Places named for people named for places somewhere else: a blizzard flecking from histogram cliffs, prairies glossed to palladium print—lilies in italics, the lilacs underlined—at the surreptitious click of a shutter release: clean, rhythmic, meaningless—the stutter of breathing, of esker—& quick.

: :

The center equals all asides aside. "Local television claimed that activists threw smoke bombs at the police, but what they videotaped was activists lobbing back the tear gas canisters that had been fired at us." Plectrum leaves, wind plucked, moog inside the storm: the world is a Wardian case.

: :

Mountain range, the morning star, a diesel generator, or the blue-film AIRPORT MINIT MARKET, its Plexiglas windows rebar barred & coffee burnt in a Pyrex pot. Taillights saccade the exit lane & brogue wind fettles rain from the frontage road. Jezebel, if it ain't broke, don't fix it—break it.

: :

A last-ditch hit of Cipro on the splints of a Claymation pier, the camera not apart from the scene consigned: jamboree of blue jays is a lumièréthique, by the high-fructose corn syrup sunset & its plangent, Plantagenet red, threading blue & purple, to black, like a knife being sharpened to nothing.

Andrew Zawacki

: :

This is how it's going to go down: grain silos & power grids, slingshots dot the Susquehanna, belaying the phone lines in sine wave & synapse, a plat of McMansions splatter a forest, new-mown grass in lawn-brite hypergreen. Unspooled wire to the foosball palace, & a grove of bucket trucks off 81.

: :

Dawn a Saran-wrap rapture of pink, in broke correction ribbon ca. Olivetti Lettera 22. "We don't have manpower. We have to do alone with little handicams." Amtrak track is frankensteinish stitching past the putt-putt course, a latticework of ladders to the mine. "That really happened."

: :

Noises that Skype us, scuff us awake: a moto coughing, a donkey next door, the imam at 5 a.m. The eye is a yard sale GPS, glare of the glass arcades. Muzak, E Track: electronic tropics with Duracell birds. Poltergeist & guttural: to mutter, here, as the Niger does—muddied, & with a mouth.

: :

A folded harmonics, the transepts of air, cool in a dimmer-switch sundown, the seraphim shimmer of August auguring off. In the trees a layaway alarm, vinyl static of matches in a sturdy dive-bar box. The center is liquid, lakelike—a prolegomenon. The world exists to end up on DVD.

: :

Nail gun in the nearing night & "faux para-snowfoam." Tower cranes swivel in syncope—gamma 1, gamma 2—as street lamps scribble Farsi on the floor. As if light were only the manifestation of light. Sky now celadon, now sauterne—24" plasma display—& SRS airbags inflating over the arch.

: :

Rhizome of the railway through the Bordeaux countryside: the I is a Coptic blue Prince Rupert's drop. The tsk of two automated ticket machines, scansion of a hole inside the whole. Frost by fax, a dial-up eclipse, a lacquer on the tautness of the lake: cement of our breath in February air.

Andrew Zawacki

: :

Just off the Jersey Turnpike, ranging the waterway: Maersk containers stacked like butter sticks. A semi sidewinders the passing lane, its tire clacks shivaree our kid to sleep. The windshield set to "landscape view," gussied up in gray, & gas is $2.79^9/_{10}$/gallon. Chekhov's last words were German.

: :

Data file recovery complete: telephone cables arranged in cedilla, icicles *accent aigu*. A light meter teeter-totters—overcast, the selenium shot—like a spirit level bubble, wavering. Shannon, Reykjavik, Santa Maria, on HF radio, U- or V-: "the night ark / adrift, / & water- / divided, the / stars."

: :

The subject turned to image is an object. The borrow pond is frozen over—its flat-screen water, its silkaline edge—as wrinkles cinch a paper folding fan. Rapier light & mimeo snow, slide-guitar catharsis of the sun. In the frame of a Sony portable cam, I is everything that is not the case.

The I and the It
Gabriel Blackwell

UNDER MORE AGREEABLE CIRCUMSTANCES—we are paraphrasing; Bennell was predisposed to cliché and imprecise language—Dr. Miles Bennell, a physician for thirteen years, would have welcomed the sudden relaxation, the opportunity to indulge a newfound frivolity; the life of a busy GP had never exactly encouraged the profligate humoring of passing fancies and so this should have been a glimpse of the life he had not yet found the time to lead. But no. His leisure was unlooked for, his retirement an inescapable result of the tragedy. Why the metaphor of imprisonment? He was not at liberty. Why "a result" but "the tragedy"? Surely, the impact on his work life was outweighed by the collapse of civilization. Ah. Still, he could feel sadness at the loss, regardless of its feathery avoirdupois on some imagined scale. This was the tragedy: His skills had overnight been rendered surfeit. Who, he wondered, would use them? His patients had been replaced. A verbal pun? Or a peculiarly telling choice of words? On the contrary, utterly concrete, not pun or metaphor at all. He had trouble remaining in the chair, complaining that it was unnecessarily low and missing its cushion. Could a cushion be provided, he wished to know? Existential questions were meaningless in a darkened back room of a dry cleaner's. He disliked being referred to as Banquo, and asked that we address him as Miles. We eventually settled on "Bennell," to which he usually answered.

A senescent collegiality was never destined to be his reward for a life of service; this was his substitute. Not for him the merry circuit of golf course, swimming pool, tennis court, bingo hall, and cafeteria. The smell of chemicals gave him headaches, occasionally made him nauseous; might we see to it? His oldest patients had been the first to go. Bennell had been the last of Santa Mira's GPs: the two others, elderly gentlemen, had shuttered their offices almost at once when the trouble started. Both had long been used to dozing off between patients. At risk? They were ideal vectors, Bennell claimed. They had to be destroyed. Isn't it quite natural to be agitated about the disappearance of old friends and colleagues? This was, after all, putting it mildly: He intimated murder. Only when they *are* old friends and colleagues, Bennell corrected us. Please remain in the chair, Bennell. We are only just beginning.

As for his own practice, though there had been a glut of complaints—all curiously similar—in the days following the outbreak, soon thereafter, people stopped coming around altogether. Perhaps he had felt inadequate in some way, embarrassed at the sudden slowing? Not at all. It was simply that no one got sick anymore. There was no one. With no one left to treat and nothing left to do, Bennell drifted from one hobby to the next. Astronomy. Chemistry. Hydroculture. Furniture. Ships in bottles. Messages in bottles. This drift plainly reflected an uneasiness with certain thoughts, certain feelings. Sublimation, an unwillingness to deal with a parricide after all almost literal (one of the doctors, it was disclosed, had been the man who had delivered Bennell forty-two years earlier), and other, more serious offenses: his own ill-accomplished substitution. Why did we insist on pretending the situation was other than it was? Why did he insist on starting with the coda?

One had to have something to do. What was so abnormal about hobbies? A man without a vocation is little better than a beast, unawed by the civilizing influence of drives kept in check. One could not go through one's life playing at a somnambulism one did not suffer from. His earlier comments about our "disarming habit" of humming along to his answers only further bolstered our initial supposition—the man was unserious, impulsive, driven by a glistening, naked desire he believed inimical to his identity. He did not wish to be manhandled or maltreated. Concentrate, Bennell! This is not the piece we have asked for. We will have to begin again.

Bennell had decided to turn his office building into a kind of bulwark, a fortress against the troubles. He moved the storm shutters up from the basement. He padlocked the doors from the inside. Every hatch was battened, every hole spackled. Not even a rat could get in, he assured us. Nor could one get out. Why was solitude so important to him? Security? What did he fear from other people? Still he did not sleep.

He commandeered the other offices, rifling their rec rooms for supplies and their workrooms for something to do with himself in the absence of his occupation, rest, and any *human* company—"I had nothing but time. Do I need to tell you what my neighbors did?" A dry cleaner's. An upholsterer. A carpenter's workshop. A laboratory of some sort. "Gould—the fingers, please." Focus, Bennell. Imprecision ruins the effect. A pharmaceutical laboratory, then, with an apparently nebulous name. _____ Associates, Inc. The caesura, the mark of some unseen force. What did he suppress? Our grip was such that he couldn't breathe; might we loosen it or abandon it altogether? Left-hand technique, Bennell, all-important in passages with complex harmonies. A mail-order farm supply. A candy maker. One could draw certain inferences from this litany, Bennell. A candy maker's? Really? That's what was there. One could draw inferences from its members, yes, but also from its ordering. Order assigns meaning, does it not? Why had the dry cleaner's been first in his mind? Wasn't it obvious? Why, then, did the upholsterer's come second? He had spent little enough time there. Perhaps he could be allowed to finish? Certainly, Bennell. By all means. Have done.

On any given day, a visitor to his office on the second floor would have found the reception area smelling strongly of noxiously intoxicating epoxies or filled with puffs of pleasantly vibrant but eye-irritating smoke, the plush chairs (several now disemboweled) occupied by envelopes of rare seedlings, eccentric and out-of-date sidereal atlases, or vats of plainly dangerous reagents. Of course, there were no visitors in those days. Why introduce a hypothetical visitor or visitors into his narrative then? Why again the specter of an auditor? Had he imagined one at the time? Only the periodic shrieks of . . . what were we exactly?—growing rarer and rarer as Santa Mira was completely overtaken—ever pierced the deaf calm of the office. Otherwise, Bennell felt himself cast adrift in the sea of his uncertain passions. He often imagined the blood crashing through his head, another effect of the sleepless eternal night of the blacked-out building, as the waves of a troubled ocean, slapping against each other like layers of wet quilt. How did he imagine his raft? Of what was it built? He seemed at a loss for words.

What were Bennell's feelings upon giving up one "hobby" for another? Little thought was given to the exchange—one grew from the other, occupied more and more time—and its predecessor less and less—until the latter had simply been abandoned. That was life, wasn't it? Things did not ever really come to a close (until, of course, they did); they simply took up less and less space in the mind, like a game of pick-up sticks gathered, bundled, returned to its drum, its drum to its box, its box to its shelf. A rather harebrained, scattershot life, perhaps, yes. Why not exercise a little restraint? Resolution is rarely the result of accident, Bennell. Dissonance is chance given voice. The cuffs were inhibiting circulation. His fingertips had gone quite purple.

*

We resume.

Logic was at work, Bennell protested. Astronomy led quite naturally to chemistry: How else to understand the chain reactions that powered our universe? Some observed the stars for their beauty, Bennell, mythologized their arrangement, or applied mathematics to judge their distance, thus diminishing their own provincial self-importance. Doesn't the choice (a rather esoteric and—up until very recently—purely conjectural branch of astronomy) of which whim to flatter next perhaps reveal a nature devoted to dominating, subduing? And what were we after? We are not the one in restraints, Bennell. Domination does not interest us. Were you perhaps seeking after the unknowable as a means of staving off discovery of the immediate, i.e., death? Death, even its obvious precursor, disease, was hardly a dire concern at that time, or at any time since. There were more complicated fates to be feared. This won't do. Begin again, Bennell.

A few days after the last patient he could recall seeing had complained of the strange trouble everyone else seemed to have had, Bennell witnessed a string of events that, together, convinced him to put up in his office and hold out there for as long as he could. Did being in large crowds, or, more generally, in public cause feelings of anxiety at that time? "Yes, Gould. Haven't you been listening?" Perhaps it would be helpful to begin at the point at which he could first clearly recall those feelings of anxiety.

"It was a Thursday. I can't recall the date, but I do remember that it was a Thursday, because Thursday is the day the garbagemen come to collect on our block [Hmm.], and also the day that Becky and I had set for our date.

"Well, that morning I had my coffee in bed. [Much better, Bennell.] I was feeling a little run-down. When I stepped outside to get the paper, my neighbor, Burt Danvers, was watering his prize Gertrude Jekyll roses. It had rained the night before, and I recall making a joke about it. Burt didn't laugh, and that was odd because usually Burt is such a cutup. But I guess I was just tired, I didn't think anything of it. No, it wasn't until just before the garbagemen showed up that I noticed something was wrong.

"There was a man's hand, flopped over the lip of Burt's garbage can just at the wrist, like a dog's tongue hanging out of its mouth. I didn't know what to do. Here it was, this beautiful early fall morning, the sky blue, the sun shining, the lawn freshly clipped—I think there were even birds singing—and then there was this man in the garbage can next door. It was like some awful nightmare. [Hmm.]

"I couldn't even speak I was so shocked. I pointed, and Burt glanced over at the can and then back at me without once changing the look on his face. Then he walked calmly over to the can. Not in a hurry, you understand, not in a panic. Like it was the most natural thing in the world to have a man in his garbage can. He put the hose down and tried to tuck the hand back into the can. [Hmm.] He didn't even turn off the water on the hose. It was spraying all over my side of the drive. You know, looking back, I think it must have been Burt Danvers's hand in that garbage can. It must have been.

"Just then, the garbagemen came around the corner, fast, and clipped Burt in the shoulder with their bumper. Before they could slam on the brakes, he was already under the wheels of the truck—there was this awful screeching noise and then a loud popping that I'll never forget—and I ran to help. It all happened so fast, I didn't know what I was doing. What I remember best is the hose: It got kinked under one of the wheels, and started whipping around under the pressure. Before I got ten steps, it had slipped out from under the truck and was aiming right in my face. [Hmm.]

"If Burt's wife hadn't come outside and started screaming in that high-pitched way you all have, I would have stopped the garbagemen and searched under that truck. As it was, I had to run inside before any of them caught on. I thought, 'Maybe I'm seeing things after all,' but I didn't believe it at the time and I don't believe it now.

"All that was there to prove that anything at all had happened was a bluish stain about the size of a twin mattress, nothing that the human body could make. [Hmm.] No Burt Danvers. No body. Just the hose, making a racket on the siding out front and turning my yard into a mud hole. I couldn't go back outside. I was worried that someone might see me. That one of them might see me.

"You know what else I remember? The trash cans were gone. I don't know when the garbagemen would have had time to pick them up in the minute or so it took me to run inside and lock the door, but they had all been lined up down the block, and now they were all gone. That was strange. Mine were the only ones left out on the street, and nobody ever came back to pick them up."

Why give the hose such a prominent place in the telling? That was the detail that came to mind. Yes, but why? Surely not even he could be blind to its connotations? The third and fifth stages of psychosexual development were certainly well represented. Castration anxiety, too. Perhaps, or perhaps there had been a hose in Burt's hand, and when Burt was hit by the truck, the hose had sprayed him in the face. Was Burt an older man? Yes. About Bennell's father's age? Yes, perhaps. Ah, it was becoming even more fantastically symbolic. But he had once again omitted the passage we had inquired about. He would get there. Well then, press on, Bennell. Press on.

"With an injury like that, I assumed I'd see Burt inside of ten minutes, or maybe Burt's daughter, who still lives with her parents, bless her soul. Just about the plainest thing you've ever seen. The assistant librarian. Once, she came to me with the sailor's ailment—that's what we called it in the service—and I did what I could to make her comfortable, but that sort of thing just takes time to heal. Probably some Romeo's method of birth control. I prescribed a really soft pillow and told her for God's sake not to do it again. But she was back in a month. It's always the quiet ones.

"I stayed in all that day, watching the Danverses, until Becky rang the doorbell. We went to the Sky Terrace for dinner but I got called away before we'd even sat down. [Hmm.] Jack Belicec, an old friend, had just found a person in his basement. Stark naked and fast asleep, or unconscious anyway. A little wrinkled, like a newborn puppy. Jack dragged him upstairs and laid him out on the pool table. In the light, the damn thing looked so much like him that he thought he was going crazy. I know exactly how he felt. The thing did look like Jack, right down to the mole on his left buttock. I examined it myself: It was the spitting image. Only, the face didn't seem to have any features."

Yet more stalling. These so-called details, prurient amusements for a sordid imagination, were really quite transparent, Bennell. Wish fulfillment, or else a naive attempt at suggesting such. In what way? What was this interest in Miss Danvers? Bennell refused to discuss her. Why then did he bring her up? What was it about this memory of that particular ailment (particularly apt, perhaps? Did he worry?) that made it seem part of this chain of events? It had just occurred to him, that was all, a fluke signifying no whale beneath the waves, a bobbing tip of no iceberg. Still, it was quite clear he was fascinated by some aspect of the memory. He hadn't been talking about Miss Danvers; Miss Danvers wasn't important. Jack's body, or rather the body in Jack's house . . . Ah, so there it was. Hardly deserves comment, Bennell.

"You want me to finish or don't you? [We want you to *begin*.] The

216

very next day, running from Jack's house back to my own, I saw a gardener take his partner's arm off with a pair of shears. Almost to the shoulder. Did he come by the office? Can you guess the answer? That week, as I went out less and less, pretty much just here and back, I saw three bad car accidents and an honest-to-God shoot-out. Where could these men be going? It's about thirty miles to the hospital in Pasadena, which is twenty-five miles too far if you haven't had any sort of medical attention. I mean, these were extremely serious injuries.

"And here we were, in pretty bad shape ourselves. Going without sleep can be dangerous, even fatal. It does things to a person's physiology that are only really curable through sleep. Becky got a few hours while I watched her, and then she tried to spell me, but she passed out sitting up. When I came to, Becky was gone, replaced by one of those . . . things."

Finally.

Of course it disturbed him. More than he could express at that time or any since. He had had to make himself destroy it. The amphetamines he had injected himself with, along with the lack of sleep, made him feel hollow, "outside of myself," as he put it. Made this horrible thing possible, this thing that he could not now believe he had done. And yet he remembered it clearly? That's just it: He couldn't remember anything about it. Come now, Bennell. No teasing. What did he remember? After, standing there with a bruise on his knuckles like a dentist's drill that bore down when he loosened the grip his right hand had around the leg of his nightstand, a nightstand that, legless and flattened, lay shattered underneath the . . . thing. There was blood everywhere, even in his mouth. A bit of something that looked like egg with ketchup on it was stuck to his shirtfront. He resisted naming it. Don't resist, Bennell. "Gould, you monster." The difference between Shakespeare and a monkey with a typewriter, Bennell, is aim. Hitting the key called for, not its neighbors.

He had rushed to find Jack, sleeping downstairs, and both had made a break for the office. The peaceful look on Jack's face should have clued him in. Did he envy Jack? He only wished he hadn't let Jack have his pistol. He told Jack to wait outside while he checked to see if it was safe. It hadn't taken long for the shrieking to start.

With Becky and Jack gone, there was no longer any need to shuttle between the office and his home, Bennell claimed. Better to choose the more secure place. Why the office then? Shouldn't a man feel more comfortable in his home? Too many windows, too many doors, Bennell said. And perhaps some unwelcome associations? To be sure.

And so, cloistered in the office, there were only his capriciously inflamed passions to stoke. That is, until lack of oxygen smothered them under the terrible blanket that now covered everything. It was as though he had taken that nightstand leg to his old self back there, didn't we see, and not to the empty simulacrum of Becky Driscoll that had crumpled under it like a candy-less piñata. And yet, he seemed to believe that it wasn't Becky at all. Or did he believe that Becky was "hollow," as he had put it, i.e., subject to penis envy? Had he been afraid that she was trying to "screw" him? Is that why he had attacked her with an improvised phallus? Did he feel emasculated by her?

This was too absurd. Becky Driscoll wasn't empty: That thing had been. Please, remain in the chair, Bennell, or the restraints will have to be tightened, the cuffs secured again. But it was absurd, what we were suggesting. The strenuousness with which he denied our "accusation" was revealing. Perhaps displacement was the culprit, the return of that castration anxiety he had described earlier. It had been a hose described earlier. "For God's sake, Gould! A hose. A fucking hose!" Excitement is fine, Bennell, ecstasy, rhapsody, even tears—all acceptable. But anger only bruises the tempo, mashes the score. You will be restrained until you have calmed down.

Ahem. In the first few weeks, he had had the run of the place. He worked in the various offices, whenever the fancy took him. He repaired some of his chairs in the upholsterer's, tried restuffing a divan he found in the farm supply. He discovered volatility in the lab, regretted its discovery. He tried to grow food in flats of bottles he found in the basement but the seeds corroded in the backwash of chemical residue. He even ventured up on the roof with his telescope. But he felt watched: In every office, no matter how involved in what he was doing, he could not escape self-consciousness. He imagined customers, coworkers; on the roof, the eyes of the town. He dismantled the telescope. You see, Bennell? He took the bottles back to his office. He welded the door to the roof shut, painted tarmac on the inside of the windows. Still, he could not sleep. Ah. Something about the second floor seemed suspect to him. He abandoned his office, leaving behind thirty-seven messages in bottles, all drafts of a single letter that he couldn't quite bring himself to finish. Everything on the page seemed false to him the minute it slid through the slim neck. He built fortifications on the stairs, pikes made out of sharpened coatracks bristling from the pile of desks that had taken hours to move into place. Surely you see it yourself, Bennell.

And the basement? Something was very wrong in the basement. It was the echo of the space that set him on edge. He began to feel the same in the front corridor. He could no longer move from office to office without feeling unsafe. Open doors, even empty boxes, scared him. Within a month, he could not stand to be anywhere but the dry cleaner's backroom. Regression, Bennell. Perhaps we will get there after all.

All around him hung suits of clothes, draped in thin sheets of brown butcher's paper, so close together they seemed to ride piggy-back on each other, filling the room until only the small well in the middle where the chair was kept was free of them. All along the walls and in rows so close they overlapped, they huddled together, as though for warmth. They, Bennell? Did he believe them human? Their stillness, the hush of their conversation when he pushed through them to the bathroom or, less frequently, to the front room, reminded him of a public gathering. As though the whole town had convened here? Yes. For a trial? Maybe. Or perhaps for a recital? Here they all were, assembled for some reason or another, stifling their coughs and throat clearings for his benefit. When the last whisper had been quelled, he could sit down and begin.

And so, let us begin again, Bennell. His knees were almost up to his chin: It was ridiculous, this posture, he could hardly breathe, much less recite. He wanted to shut his eyes. He could no longer remember sleep, the feeling of weightlessness, bodylessness. His hands were numb, his legs were numb, even his head was numb; all he could feel anymore was the drag of gravity upon his body, forcing him always down, pressing him to sleep, perchance to dream.

Bennell, there will be time for sleep later. Forget dreams for now; tell us instead about waking. Tell us about the unexpected return of consciousness. Tell us about the odd twilight when the unchecked fancy of the unconscious is interrupted by the reassertion of the will. Tell us about the strain of the world coming into being. Tell us about the grains of light that fall and swirl and fix into dark constellations of surroundings. Tell us about the moment when blankets first have weight, sheets separate from blankets, a head from its pillow, an alarm clock from its nightstand. Tell us about the moment that the creeping things make themselves known, about that moment when the veil's fog has dissipated and you can finally name them. You will rest later, Bennell. First, before you go, give us purpose. For your sake, Bennell, yours and ours, give us meaning.

The Box
Robert Coover

SHE FINDS A BOX by the curb. Someone must have dropped it. They are not poor, but they do not have all they want, so she takes it home and shows it to her husband, in the hope they might extract magical wealth from it. A new car maybe, a chest of gold doubloons, free movie tickets. Her husband, who is hardworking and frugal, carefully amassing the wherewithal for a comfortable retirement, which they both see as a single but endless moment of shared delight after the dullness of their daily working lives, is more amused than excited by her discovery, having little faith in magic as a sound investment. Besides, though the lid comes off, the contents of the box are sealed beneath glass like a collection of butterflies. In fact, there *is* a butterfly inside the box, one with widespread amber wings, pinned to the mouth of a bisque doll's eyeless head; also an apothecary jar; a small bejeweled bird's egg; an owl, looking cramped and hostile, lensless spectacle frames at its feet; a four-poster bed, or at least a picture of one, seemingly afloat in a star-chart sky, and three dice on a crimson dish, all showing threes on top. Behind everything: a mirror, mounted in such a way as to reflect them both as they look inside.

It has a lot of things in it, he says.

I think it's bigger than when I picked it up, she replies, staring at her own stare in the box's mirror. What do you think it all means?

Probably that life's a gamble. You can lose your nest egg if you're too flighty or blind to opportunities or spend too much time dreaming in bed.

That's all . . . ?

You have a better idea?

Well, that *could* be a nest egg, I suppose, with what looks like jewels all over it. But it suggests to me more fundamental things. She is thinking about those dice triplets lying on their womby dish, but chooses not to say so.

Nest eggs are pretty fundamental.

And then, there's that salamander inside the apothecary jar. And those splotches of paint around the owl as if it were being shot at.

221

Which is probably why it looks so angry. And what about that vamping lady there at the edge behind the theater curtain, sticking her bare leg out?

I didn't see her before. I remember her from the movies. I think I was in love with her once upon a time.

Really? She has plucked eyebrows. You hate plucked eyebrows.

That's true. At the time, I guess I didn't notice such things. I was mostly noticing breasts and hair. And bottoms.

You can't see her bottom in the picture.

No, but I remember it. And it makes me happy thinking about it. I find even now I don't really care about the plucked eyebrows.

It seems quite trivial, your memory.

I know. But it doesn't feel trivial. He pauses, considering that feeling, not one he is accustomed to, or ever welcomes. So, what shall we do with it? Open it up and see what else is in it? That egg looks interesting. And the box may have a false bottom.

Is that like a plucked eyebrow?

Yes, except a false bottom is more deceptive. He smiles, conscious suddenly of the many years of their marriage and the quiet routines they have come to. Do you think I was deceived?

She returns his smile in such a way as to suggest she recognizes the sluggish workings of his memory, he who by her lights has none, so focused is he on what might happen next or be made to happen. It's so beautifully made, she says, concealing her unease at the idea of disturbing something that might yet be in some manner magical (he would only laugh at her). The wood itself may be the best thing about it. It would be a shame to crack it open.

We should treat it like an art object, you mean?

Well . . . She looks around. Their own art objects are mostly golf and tennis trophies, travel souvenirs, framed photographs, and certificates of achievement. The few paintings on the walls are street scenes and impressionist landscapes from places they have visited, picked up at sidewalk art shows, and it occurs to her that what her life lacks (this thought is quite new to her) is gravity. More like a nice piece of furniture maybe, she says.

So they set it on an end table in the den where it isn't in the way and can be admired. And so it is, becoming a focus of their own attention and a conversation piece at parties. It's so unusual! their friends say. That gorgeous egg! Those weird star charts! Those dice on a dish! Wherever did you find it? They shrug and smile ambivalently. Just something we picked up. Some think it very mysterious and provocative, others wacky or sad or funny or ominous (that horrible doll's head with the empty eye sockets and pin in its mouth!), while others merely think it pretty, in a class with decorative baskets or fancy tea towels. Most speculate on its value, which is deemed uncertain but probably high. A masterpiece, some declare. Or the amateur creation of an eccentric genius, say others, yes, you've got something there!

Eventually, though, it starts to blend in with the trophies and souvenir ashtrays and stops being a conversation piece, their friends having said all they can think of to say about it. They themselves spend less time looking at it, though he returns to it on occasion during the cocktail hour, trying to recapture the pleasant feelings he had remembering the movie star's bottom, and she, when alone in the house, sometimes finds herself using it as a focus for meditation, gazing fixedly at her own image staring back at her, until the contents of the box seem to spread out into a kind of unboxed world of its own, her mirrored image receding as it opens up. Ever since her guest remarked on the star charts, she is, though somewhat frightened by their depictions of the unimaginable, drawn to them at the same time (terror too's alluring), and wishes to look at them more closely, though she resists still her husband's suggestion that they open it up and see if, as many have asked at parties, those seeming jewels on the egg are real.

But then one night, a drunken guest shakes it to try to get a different dice roll, and things get jumbled up inside. The dice don't move, but the scowling owl falls over on its face, the bed tilts in the sky, and the coverlet on it slips halfway off, revealing not sheets beneath but more starry sky, one of the butterfly's amber wings is crushed, and the decorated egg rolls over on its side. Behind the owl, they see for the first time, are the tatters of a poster advertising a biplane stunt-flying exhibition, the pilots wearing soft leather headgear with big goggles and fluttering neckerchiefs. Though these dashing figures might have aroused in her nostalgic feelings of youthful romance, it is actually he who feels their whimsical lost beauty; she only shudders at the sight of those thin fragile structures upside down in the sky (a sky pasted on another sky), so far from earth. The mirror, too, seems knocked askew, for now when they look into the mirror together they each see only themselves alone, and themselves ever more distant than before.

They jiggle the box gently, trying to stand the egg upright once more, and for a while it becomes an amusing game, especially at the

223

cocktail hour. But just as he, one-handed, a drink in the other, succeeds one day, the jerky motion that rights the egg topples the apothecary jar, spilling out the salamander, which slides behind the fallen owl, and then the egg rolls over again, this time the other way, whereupon they take up seriously once more the idea of opening the box, now for reasons of repair. She is, as before, more reluctant than he, but the tipped bed in the sky, its coverlet, stiff as a body, slipping off it to let the cosmic vastness in, has caused her sleepless nights, her own bed now less anchored, and at last she agrees. If we're careful, he says, we can put it back together again just like it was, and she nods, but is full of apprehension.

And with reason, as it turns out. The wood is so finely tongue and grooved, the glass so deeply locked into it, that the first tentative effort to insert a thin knife blade to pry it open results in the shattering of the glass, releasing a faintly morbid smell. Well, damage done, what can they do? They carefully remove the little egg (the "jewels" are only painted beads, but there is an intriguing rattle within), the owl, and other loose or fallen bits like the jar and spectacle frames, pick out each shard of glass with tweezers, scoop up the purple sand spilled from the apothecary jar (the salamander has gotten lost somehow), reset the bed and cover in the sky. The butterfly's crushed wing, which has left a powdery amber smear on the doll head's lips where it was pinned, is lost forever and the crimson dish in which the dice are fixed is cracked, but she dusts all the other parts with a soft watercolor brush, and they set them back in their places as best they can remember them, feeling a bit like artists themselves.

When she disappears into the kitchen to prepare an omelet for lunch (she has secretly pocketed in her apron a papier-mâché doll's leg with dimpled knee and plump little toes found in the tipped apothecary jar after the sand tumbled out, and wants a closer look before showing it to him), he yields to the temptation to peel back the vamping movie star, a cutout stiffened with paper backing, to glimpse the famous derrière, but finds that only that top part and the extended leg exist, each glued to the back of the thin stiff strip of paper curtain at the edge, all backsides blank. Which, he realizes with a tinge of sorrow, could be a commentary on the nature of desire itself.

When she returns with lunch, he sets the pair of lensless spectacles on his nose and asks her, What do you think? Is this me? But she's not there. Gone back, perhaps, for toast or coffee. The glasses, he discovers, add a third dimension to flat images, and the now fully rounded vamp seems almost to be wagging her outthrust leg at him. He peers behind her with renewed hope, but the back of the figure is incomplete and blank as before. There is, however, an open space he hadn't noticed before behind the curtain, a kind of corridor or portico, its parallel walls seeming to stretch off into infinity, which, even if a trick of the glasses—Clever! he thinks—is too alluring to ignore.

She, left alone (perhaps he went for salt and pepper, she never puts enough), pokes through the box and finds below the begoggled leather-capped airmen an articulated arm without a hand, made of the same stuff as the leg, and she adds it to the collection in her apron pocket, wondering, somewhat sadly, if the doll's disassembled anatomy might not be a sad commentary on the futile human search for integrity, for wholeness. One of the doll's missing glass eyes, she now sees, is affixed firmly to the hidden side of the remounted egg as one of its "jewels," but not the other one. Could that be what's rattling around inside? The star charts are not, after all, glued to the back of the box, but hang like lowered curtains. She peers, fearfully but hopefully, into the shadowy depths behind them to seek out more doll parts, thinking of herself as a kind of conscientious nursemaid on a mission.

He, too, feels himself to be on a mission of sorts. A journey certainly. The facing walls of the portico are mounted with images from the past, in a certain sense his own past because he recognizes all their subjects from his youth, though they are mostly public figures, ballplayers and movie stars and the like, or scenes and characters from stories he has read, or had read to him, so it's a bit like walking through a museum of his life, if not his own life exclusively. His heart is warmed by what he sees, but at the same time, aware that the past is no more than a shadowy tease, forever denied entry to the present, he feels a dangerous yearning that he knows can never be appeased. It's a kind of disease, this insatiable yearning, he acknowledges with a wry smile, as he allows himself to be drawn haplessly into the obscure but intimate depths of the gallery. He finds, one image following upon another, luring him ever deeper, glimpses of a life that might have been his own, homes he might have lived in, beautiful women who might have been his lovers, though he can place none of these things in the real past, whatever that is. Nor are these glimpses of a possible past any past at all, for almost everything is missing in the blank wall spaces between them. He feels vaguely threatened by these false memories—or real memories, doesn't matter, delusions in either case—and decides to turn back, but then he comes upon a locked door.

The hanging star charts cast a kind of shadowy glow on her back-stage search for doll parts (the mirror has receded out of sight, or else it is behind her), but she finds nothing more until she reaches the four-poster bed in the sky. For some time, she realizes, a shiver running up her spine, she has been walking on the star maps, if they are star maps and not the awesome grandeur of the universe itself. She is afraid to look down, but there are stars all around her and overhead as well, she doesn't know *where* to look. As she moves forward, the stars rotate around her, suggesting she is inside a kind of sphere. Only a clever illusion, she hopes, thrilled and terrified at the same time. The bed seems to be afloat as she is afloat, and when she reaches it, or it reaches her, there on a lacy pillow is a doll's porcelain hand. Its dimpled fingers are exquisitely formed with tiny knuckles and fingernails and plump wrinkles in the little palm. It is heartbreakingly beautiful, and she feels her eyes filling with tears. But the thumb is backward to the arm in her apron pocket, so the hand must belong to one she hasn't found. She remembers then a fairy tale she read, or had read to her, about a dismembered baby and how it was brought back to life when its eyes were found and put back in. She's a bit lost out here in the night sky, but she decides to see if she can find the egg again.

He is certain that the locked door's key is in the egg, that's what was rattling about in there, the whole box a kind of wittily contrived scavenger hunt, and, having hurried back to it, he tips it forward carefully and with his penknife pokes a small hole in the bottom of it. Unfortunately, the egg shatters into a thousand pieces, its beady decorations scattering. But he was right: There's the little silver key amid the ruins. He pockets it and runs back down the open portico, ignoring now the deceptive parade of images on the wall, drawn urgently by the mystery of the locked door, the need to know. The irrational need to know.

When she very carefully plucks the glass eye from the cluster of decorations on the side of the egg, the whole thing falls apart, collapsing dishearteningly into a thousand pieces. But she was right: There's the other eye, wobbling about amid the fragments of shell. Her heart is pounding. It may be true! But it rolls away, just beyond her fingertips, whenever she reaches for it. What then? An eye for an eye? But that wouldn't work. She offers up the leg and arm (perhaps the whole box is a witty compendium of clichés, she thinks) and the eye surrenders at last to her grasp. In fact, it rolls right into it. She finds the crippled butterfly still pinned to the doll's mouth when she picks the head up. The poor creature seems to be trying, brokenly, to fly with its one wing. She should put it out of its agony, but she cannot. She feels the tears start again. It's so sad! Life is. But she has come this far. . . . She brushes the tears aside and bravely fits an eyeball into one of the lashless sockets. Where it glares accusingly, maliciously back at her. What? Are the head's amber lips moving? Whispering something? She drops the horrible thing, frozen in fright where she stands, the eye popping out of the socket and seeming to blink mockingly at her as it rolls away. Oh no! Where is her husband? He would know what to do.

Before the locked door, key in hand, he too stands motionless, reconsidering the journey he has made, this interruption of it like the breaking of a timeline—which thought stirs others, more foreboding. He does not know for certain what lies beyond the door, only that nothing will ever be the same if he opens it and enters in. He is overtaken, there before the door, by a nostalgia, not for the past but for the living present, for if their suburban life is somewhat frivolous, even sometimes surreal, it is also delightful, comforting, beautiful even—their backyard barbecue pit, he realizes, is the most sublime work of art they own—and it suits him, suits them both. He pockets the key and starts the long trek back. The need to know is not the only need.

The omelet, still warm, awaits him on his return—from where, he's not quite sure. He removes the spectacle frames and she is there at the table with him, gazing at him affectionately. Here's a slice of buttered toast, she says with a smile that is not quite a smile. And some honey, if you want it. He adds a shake or two of salt and pepper to the omelet. Which is delicious and he says so and thanks her for it. Their restoration of the box is complete except for the broken egg. Of which neither speaks. We'll store the thing in the attic, he says, returning her smile, feeling the irreparable loss of something (probably not important), and she agrees, placing her hand firmly over his.

Barney Rosset, China, May 1945.

China

Barney Rosset

WE DISEMBARKED IN BOMBAY. The trip by train across India was somehow beautiful and sometimes sad. About ten of us, almost arbitrarily assembled, went from Bombay to Calcutta in four days. The coaches were divided into five classes: I, II, III, Intermediate, and IV. Our coach was class IV. It had wooden benches and was stiflingly hot, but I didn't notice the discomfort. I liked India. I tried to learn Hindustani words out of a guidebook and I practiced them on little children who ran up to the train. I stared out at the villages, at the women kneeling beside flat baskets filled with rice and bananas, and suckling babies who would never get enough milk. At one stop when I was on guard duty—we had to watch out for thieves—the train's conductor and its engineer invited me into the station for a cup of tea. When we returned to the platform the train was gone. However, the next train, which we boarded, somehow caught up to mine, and I was able to board it and resume my guard duty post without my absence having been noticed.

After traveling for four days and four nights, we awakened one morning to find ourselves parked on a desolate siding in the middle of nowhere. The heat was *unbearable*, but still the five psychiatrists who were in my group were afraid to get out and look around—without orders. So, a doctor, a homeopathist, and by now my dear friend, left them in the train car and walked down a dirt road lined with very tall coconut trees. A number of coconuts dropped to the ground within a few feet of us. Then we spotted the "perpetrators," monkeys, who were throwing them at us. The enemy barrage was sustained for several kilometers until we stumbled, quite accidentally, on our new camp.

So we ended up in a US replacement camp, thirty miles outside of Calcutta. The uncertainty commenced. Camp Kanchapara was a sweatbox. We were to stay there until individual assignments came through. We lived in tents and ate horrible food. The camp commanders invented things for us to do. There were way too many men, sweating each day and freezing each night as jackals stole our

229

shoes from our tents and rooted in our garbage.

Barney Rosset in a camp in Kanchapara, India,
awaiting assignment, 1944.

I sneaked off to Calcutta as often as I could. There were incredibly elegant brothels occupying some temporarily vacated palaces. One Indian girl, a successful prostitute/courtesan, became very friendly with me. I took her out to a film one afternoon, a highly unusual venture for an American officer. The English civilian audience, including a goodly number of English women looking very middle class and dowdy, seemed a bit disconcerted by the sight of me and my Indian consort, in her elegant but understated sari. I had photographed her putting it on aided by two extremely helpful English women who were her daytime servants in her suite at the palace/brothel.

Finally, orders came through for me to report to the 164th Signal Photo Company in New Delhi. It was our company headquarters for China, Burma, and India (CBI). Our officers lived in better quarters than they did in the States. The food was good. There were big hotels and social functions. New Delhi reminded me of Washington, DC, and I did not like it any more than I did its American counterpart.

All American military personnel in the CBI theater of war were under, nominally at least, the command of the British. Lord Louis Mountbatten was their chosen commander. He seemed, at least from a distance, to be likable and "democratic." However, he did claim some credit for the partitioning of Pakistan from India. That seemed a typical British trick to me. It was the English strategy of divide and conquer.

And he paid for it. Well after he retired at the end of World War II he vacationed in Ireland. On one such trip he was assassinated by members of the outlawed Irish Revolutionary Army (IRA).

My photo company was run by a group of men who had, as part of their perks, their own racehorses, which they both owned and raced at a New Delhi track.

The 164th Photo Company had one unit in China, another in Burma, and a third in India, which included our HQ for the entire CBI theater. The war had been progressing very badly for the allies in Southern China and it looked as if there might have to be a mass evacuation. I wanted to get there before it was too late. It was my chance to get into what for me was the compelling part of the war. Edgar Snow's *Red Star Over China* was getting closer.

It was not difficult to get the assignment. They printed my orders, and I packed. The plane ride over the Himalayas on the way to China lay ahead.

After waiting at an air base, a steaming hole, for two days, I boarded one of the ungainly, underpowered C-46s, along with a mixed group of Americans and Chinese, but mostly the latter. I was so loaded down with baggage I could hardly walk. Everything I had was on me when we rolled down the runway.

Taking off from Assam, India, for Kunming, my unit's Chinese HQ, in December of 1944. I was still a raw, semitrained second lieutenant in the Signal Corps Photographic Service, twenty-two years old, and with only a few dreams to cling to. Squashed under the weight of my equipment, I struggled onto the airplane and sat on the metal floor next to some uncommunicative Chinese soldiers. I leaned back in the curve of the bare fuselage, hugging a heavy parachute, which was a totally foreign object to me. We were in a death crate, a hulk of a cargo plane barely sustained by two undersized motors. As we puffed oxygen through our masks, the planet's highest mountains glowered beneath us and loomed on both sides.

In *Duel for the Middle Kingdom*, William Morwood wrote about the 550-mile flight between Assam in East India and Yunnan Province in southwest China.

> It crossed the towering mid-ribs of the Himalayan Mountains. Jagged peaks thrust up to 20,000 feet and more, usually cloaked in swirling clouds of mist. Winds howled across the barren

231

rockscape, agitating thermal currents of sufficient force to disintegrate planes.... [Zeros], the Japanese fighter planes, cruised the mountains looking for the lumbering American transports of which four hundred and sixty-eight were to be lost in the first three years of operation, shot down or sucked to earth by storms or mechanical failure. The fearsome contorted basalt was known to G.I.s in the [theater] as the Hump, and to pilots that flew it as "clouds full of rocks" or the "aluminum trail."

As we reached our destination, behind the door of the cockpit, the third red-alert light shone as we descended, a sure sign that Japanese Zeros were tailing and using us for cover as they bombed the runway. On landing, I scrambled from the airplane into the night's bewildering disorder—no contacts, no commanding officers, no what-to-do-next. My GI parachute stayed on the runway where I dropped it and ran. Somehow I arrived at a dimly lit wooden shack. It was crowded with Chinese patrons drinking hot yellow rice wine. Apparently, I had left the Kunming air base. The next thing I remember was waking up with a hangover in our outfit's billet, the headache rendered irrelevant by the fact that I was in the China of my dreams.

Landscape near Kunming, 1945.

In 1943 and 1944, Kunming Airport was one of the largest airports in the world. How many thousands of tons of provisions and equipment must have been flown there, "over the Hump" from India? But now, when I arrived in late 1944, China seemed to be a largely static theater of war.

The 164th Photo was small and it shared a hostel in Kunming with another company (nonphoto). Our commanding officer was Lt. Norman Dain. He was a Bostonian with traces of culture and sensitivity. The deceased officer whom I had come to replace had worked about three hundred miles out from Kunming. I really never learned how or why he had died, and my instinct was not to probe. It was quickly obvious that Dain wanted to get me out of Kunming to fill the hole in the 164th Photo lineup as expeditiously as possible.

He told me the 164th was sending me to Kweiyang, the other end of the line. He did not tell me very specifically what to do or how to do it. I was provided with a weapons carrier, which was a small but sturdy four-wheel-drive truck, some equipment and supplies for a still-photo field laboratory, a co-driver, who was a young American GI, and written orders directing me to Kweiyang.

Refugees, Chinese-Japanese front near Kweiyang, 1945.

Having my directive, I drove eastward on the only road, an unpaved one, toward Kweiyang, the capital of Kweichow, the adjoining province and a main place of concentration for Chinese civilians fleeing before what still seemed to be the oncoming Japanese army. I named my weapons carrier "Foto Moto," and painted the name in large letters on the front radiator. The truck was the equivalent of a big, strong mule, not nimble but willing, and I was literally driving it toward the oncoming Japanese.

Barney Rosset's "Foto-Moto" weapons carrier being towed
by members of a Chinese Army unit, China, 1945.

Or was I? What nobody said to me my last night in Kunming, and what was most likely not known, was that the current Japanese offensive had halted just short of the outskirts of Kweiyang, circling part of the city from the east, north, and south just as I was rolling in from the west. Going in our direction there was no traffic to hinder us.

It turned out to be a historic moment in the history of the Sino-Japanese War, marking, I believe, the deepest penetration into China by the Japanese during all of WWII.

If anybody back in Kunming knew of what was potentially the imminent capture of Kweiyang, one that would have included me in its net, there was no mention of that fact. Intelligence info between Chiang Kai-shek's HQ and his American counterparts, supposedly under his command, seemed to be short-circuited.

And so, arriving in Kweiyang after a dizzying ride on dirt roads and hairpin curves, I went to the main American enclave. It consisted of the remnants of a beautiful inn, plus odds and ends of additional buildings. In it was an incredible concentration of Army brass—at least seven West Point grads, all of them full colonels, and a one-star general. What they were doing there, I never really learned.

As if they had expected me, Chinese servants wearing the white jackets of another era took my gear and escorted me to a small, second-floor room whose paper-parchment walls barely made it to the ceiling. On the rafters there was a continuous, noisy, and often visible traffic of rats. I spread my sleeping bag on the bed, which filled most of the room, and went out into Kweiyang.

New Year's Eve 1944. The dirt streets of Kweiyang were crowded and lively with an air of hope and desperation. There were rumored to be Chinese bounty hunters in the crowd, paid by the Japanese to pick off Americans, but my thoughts were not of them. There was space in my parchment-walled room at the inn for a girlfriend whom I had only to find and lead back. And I found her! We had our own New Year's Eve, feeling, holding, and experimenting. The fact that we were almost completely surrounded by the Japanese seemed to make no impact on our celebration.

In the morning I discovered we had an audience on the other side of the thin parchment wall. A certain Father O'Donaghue, Catholic priest and Maryknoll missionary, had heard me sin. My Irish Catholic mother's influence made me erupt in shame, but Father O'Donaghue heard my silent confession and absolved me. The good father remained a staunch friend throughout my time in China.

I was trying to figure out how to put together a photo lab in Kweiyang when I came across a rather thick pamphlet lying in the dirt. It was a manual, not new by any means, published by the US Navy. And, miracle of miracles, it was a detailed, easily understandable manual giving instructions on how to build a photo lab under field conditions. It was just what I needed.

Then I made a new friend, Meredith "Muddy" Rhule. He was an American naval officer in the OSS (Office of Strategic Services). The Chinese OSS people whom he commanded were situated on both sides of the Japanese lines—shuttling back and forth on search and destroy missions. Muddy was a stocky, fearless, bull-necked cop from Springfield, Illinois. He also had been a professional wrestler and a sharpshooter before his demolition training at Great Lakes Naval Training Station outside of Chicago.

Muddy quietly avoided the black market, which had to be at least partially fueled by American personnel. He also was thumbs-down on picking up women when on "duty." Once, driving back to Kweiyang, while making an end run around a Japanese column, we gave a ride to an elegant and beautiful young Chinese woman who was a

OSS Crew warning me to stop—Japanese ahead.
Chinese-Japanese front, China, 1945.

refugee from Hong Kong. It wasn't uncommon then to find well-attired middle-class refugees, young and old, male and female, walking endless miles on the open road, totally alone.

When night fell she seemed disposed to join me in my tent. Rhule said no. She got her own tent.

That night I was resentful. This lovely apparition, fashionably dressed, was determinedly and optimistically making her way to Kweiyang, even though it seemed about to be taken over by the Japanese. Why not be congenial? In the morning she was up ahead of us, dressed as before, ready to step into the Waldorf in New York, or anyplace else, including my Foto Moto, and she was coming with us. She and her suitcase became part of our little entourage. We got to Kweiyang without any conversation between us. I left Muddy off at his OSS compound and suddenly I was alone with this inviting creature. I have no memory of how we conversed, but her directions to me were clear. I was to take her to where she was expected. For a war-ravaged town, the large house (surrounded by high stone walls and thus not visible from the outside) to which she directed me was most certainly not average. When we stopped, an invitation was somehow transmitted to me. I was to return to see her the next day.

And of course I did. She greeted me at the door. She was not alone. With her stood a tall, elegantly dressed man wearing a Chinese gown. Together they took me into a spacious room. It had a sedate look to it: a large table, some wooden chairs, a high ceiling, and windows placed high on the walls facing an inner courtyard. It also had a large canopied bed off to one side. Her companion then disappeared. Was he her husband, her brother, her father? No indication, but the purpose of her invitation was very clear, and I joined her in that rich and ever so private canopied bed.

What did we say to each other? Did we even say anything? I was in a kind of trance. We made love, and I could have stayed with her forever, but clearly that was not the plan. When, like an automaton, I got dressed, as did she, she took me to the door. There was no invitation for another rendezvous, but there was a gentle indication of affection. I could never find that house again, or her—and I looked. Why did she do that? Was her body a gift to me for helping her on the road, a one-time thank-you note? Had it been just an episode in war, where people touch for a moment and then continue, "two ships passing in the night," no running lights, no signals?

Rhule trained his Chinese demolition teams to act with precision. Their mission was to penetrate Japanese-held areas and then to destroy anything of potential value to the Japanese Armed Forces. What

Barney Rosset, second from right, with OSS demolition team members, 1945. Meredith "Muddy" Rhule, OSS chief, third from left.

237

that meant was blowing up the very same war matériel that we had
brought in for the Chinese Army, whether over the Hump or the
Burma Road, that had been captured or bought from corrupt segments
of the Chinese army by the Japanese. Now we had to destroy it in
order to keep the Japanese from using it against us.

With Rhule I became a sort of unofficial OSS man, without the
knowledge of my HQ or his, helping him get his operatives to their
areas of operation and then back to home base. I covered many miles
of Chinese roads with him and his cadres. All the while I was doing
unofficial and unpaid work with Muddy Rhule on behalf of the OSS.

Perhaps it would be appropriate to say a few words here about why I
was rejected by the OSS. This is something I didn't learn about until
many years later when, through the Freedom of Information Act, I
was able to access files and learned I was being investigated even in
1945. Following is a report to ascertain if I was a good candidate for
the Secret Service. Apparently, they thought not, as can be gathered
from this report by Lt. Paul Bordwell.

FOIA Document #25

*[In CIA Ltr OTO 8/29/75 this
is Document 177.]
MEMO OTO 2/17/45
According to CIA Cover Ltr OTO
8/29/75 this is "Released."*

HEADQUARTERS
OSS SU DETACHMENT 202
X-2 Branch

MEMO:

FROM: 2nd Lt Paul H. Bordwell
TO: LT (jg) Arthur H. Thurston, USNR

1. It was requested by Major Harding that I
make an inquiry re the wire from Washington
on 2nd Lt. Barnett Rosset of the 165th [sic]
Signal (Photo) CO.

2. On the morning of the 27th of January,
I called on the commanding officer and
frankly told him why I wanted to know the

whereabouts and availability of ROSSET. His commanding officer was most obliging and gave me a rather complete story on ROSSET.

3. It seems that ROSSET is a 22 year old officer who in most instances seems to act round about the age of 17 rather than 22. He is not particularly mature. It also seems that his father is some New Deal "bigwig," to quote the CO, and that this attempt to get him into the OSS has been going on for quite some time.

4. At present ROSSET is in charge of the Field Photographic team consisting of himself and several enlisted men, operating out of Kweiyang. At the immediate writing, Rosset is strictly speaking not available due to a shortage of personnel. However, three or four additional officers are in the process of being shipped in, in which case, the CO is willing to release ROSSET.

5. From a personal point of view of his CO, ROSSET certainly would not be fitted for any intelligence work. One, he has had no experience whatsoever; two, he is far too immature, and three, he does not impress you as being too intelligent.

6. In summation, from his CO's point of view, it might be said that the said officer is under the impression that the entire scheme is one of "dirty politics."

Instead of taking me into the OSS, they suggested I be transferred to another unit.

FOIA Document #26

[In CIA Ltr OTO 8/29/75 this is Document 178.]
MEMO OTO 2/17/45
According to CIA Cover Ltr OTO 8/29/75 this is "Released."

Barney Rosset

DET 202 COMMO WASHINGTON

FROM: SAINT DH 001   March 12, 1945
TO: HEPPNER FROM BH 015   NA 756712
DIST: CHUNGKING 3277

SINCE YOU DO NOT FEEL THAT ROSSET IS
SUITABLE FOR X-2 WORK WOULD YOU CONTACT
FIELD PHOTOGRAPHIC AND ARRANGE FOR HIS
TRANSFER THAT BRANCH. 109 PERSONALLY
INTERESTED IN THIS MATTER. DUE TO HIS
TECHNICAL TRAINING HE SHOULD BE SUITABLE
FOR FIELD PHOTOGRAPHIC WORK.

178
TR: 1219502
MR: 130222f

So now the Chinese followed the Japanese—who were propelling themselves back home, toward the east, with little pressure from the Chinese. My Signal Corps Photo team's job now was to record this strange retreat. Apparently, Chiang Kai-shek held to the dictum of the ancient philosopher Sun Tzu, who wrote in his *Art of War*, "The acme of skill . . . is to subdue the enemy without fighting at all." There were supposedly twenty thousand or more Chinese troops with

Evacuation of wounded, Chinese-Japanese front east of Kweiyang, 1945.

240

mobile artillery "pursuing" the enemy, yet a few Japanese soldiers with machine guns held them off again and again.

One night in the middle of a burnt-out village, Corporal Cedric Poland, a truly invaluable member of our photo unit, and I stopped at a desolate, destroyed road intersection to sleep. We tied our hammocks between the jeep and its trailer. Occasionally, in the darkness, we could see ghostlike figures moving around in the ruins of the buildings but nobody came close to us. Hoards, literally thousands, of rats scurried directly under our hammocks to cross the dirt road.

There had been rumors of Japanese reinfiltration. I was nervous and hot. I began keeping my gun very close to me. We had not eaten after we stopped. I had brought along a large number of cans of fruit, and stood shirtless in the gloom, wolfing down some pears. The place smelled of death.

Morning light brought reality with it. The homeless wanderers who meandered through the refuse no longer looked like Japanese soldiers. We started off, looking for the most forward American liaison team. On one stretch we found perhaps twenty dead Japanese cavalry men and their horses. They had either been ambushed by guerrillas or strafed by the Fourteenth Air Force—both groups later claimed credit. The open areas were covered with growing corn, and it was perfectly quiet. It was almost like being on a dirt road in Iowa, in the summer. Only the stench of the dead ruined such daydreams.

The bridges became increasingly difficult to cross. They had been destroyed, and then repaired in the flimsiest fashion. Poland and I were thankful that we had switched to a light jeep. We had left Foto Moto back in his stable.

We came to a town that we knew was very close to the front. It had once boasted a British consulate, which still showed signs of its previous ownership plastered to it. The roof was gone, and one fallen wall exposed the remains of the rooms. A few buildings were intact, but most were smashed and debris blocked the streets. We crept forward, got stuck, backed up, and slowly made our way through town. The people were gaunt, and they hardly seemed to notice us, although we knew that not many Americans could have preceded us there recently. We eventually made our way to the US Liaison Team's headquarters located in a half-battered-down house on the outskirts of town.

There we were informed that, the day before, an American inspection team made up of an American colonel, a Chinese colonel, a Chinese interpreter, and an American captain had arrived in a jeep.

241

They wanted to see the front. The liaison team warned the sightseers that they were already very close to the Japanese, but the American colonel had not been impressed. He wanted to see some fighting, so they set out in their jeep again, looking for Japanese. They drove along the unpaved highway to the last point held by Chinese regulars. A Chinese squad leader tried to stop them, but no Japanese gun positions were in sight, and no one heard any gunfire. The colonel ignored the warnings and continued on.

Another jeep drove up to our little group. In it were Teddy White, the famous *Time* correspondent, and a *Life* photographer. They seemed happy and relieved to see us. We sat around in the broken-down little courtyard and talked. There was one embarrassing moment for me, though, since before he had been identified, I said to him, "Do you know Teddy White is coming?"

He replied, "I am Teddy White."

After talking, we all started out for the place where the inspection team from Washington had last been seen.

We arrived at their last known position. We did not make much progress for two or three days. Water had to be boiled in big gas cans, and the day's heat was compounded by the fires. I was filthy. My clothes clung to me, and it was a tremendous effort to shave. At night we listened to the Air Force radio, which was powered by hand pumping.

The Air Force liaison officer and his men rode with Poland and me in one jeep, while White and his photographer followed us in theirs. We got to the point where the missing jeep was supposed to have stopped. We had passed more burnt-out bridges to get to it. Nobody was around and no jeeps. A burnt-out building stood to one side of the road, and a little stone shed stood on the other. Rice paddies ran up to the side of the road, which was bordered with damp gullies. Mountains rose a few hundred yards off to the side. We got out of the jeep and looked for farmers to talk to. At the foot of the hills there were a few small villages. The first one was completely deserted. The Japanese had lived in it; we found scraps of uniforms and rifle cartridges. Narrow pathways ran between the mud buildings. The enemy had just left. Maybe he still lurked around the corner.

Cedric Poland was an absolutely reliable and extremely capable soldier, whether he was working as a photographer or doing work necessary to keep our company functioning as efficiently as possible under very difficult conditions. And most amazing of all about Poland was that he was a cousin of my old Chicago love, Nancy Ashenhurst.

This is not to mention that he and his family were from northeast Massachusetts and proprietors of the famous mineral water company Poland Springs.

Anyway, Cy Poland, the Air Force Flying Tiger pilot with his two or three men, and I went back to where the jeep had stopped and examined the nearby building. I walked into the barnlike structure and immediately a horrible smell washed over me. There was a pile of straw in one corner. A hugely bloated, burned corpse lay on top of it. I couldn't tell if the body was Japanese, Chinese, or American. We decided that the shreds of uniform left indicated that it was Chinese. Then we left the area and drove back to our temporary camp. We had found a body, but we had not found our missing men. We probed further the next day, but White was no longer with us. He had gone back to Kunming in order to send his dispatch back to *Time*.

CT-45-24021, Chihkiang, China, May 6, 1945.
Mortar victims of the 171st Regiment,
Fifty-Seventh Division. The mortar came from
a Japanese position about two hundred yards
away. The Fifty-Seventh Division is defending
the road leading to Chihkiang.

The rest of us stood in a little group on the road and there the search ended. One of the men kicked at a pile of dirt in the gully, and suddenly a cadaver was uncovered. Maggots swarmed over the face, and the skull was almost completely devoid of flesh. A few feet away we found another corpse in the same condition. Poland and I photographed the remains.

We had to try and make identifications. We decided the first one was the Chinese interpreter, and the second one the American colonel. We were wrong. The American colonel and his aide, an American captain, had been captured alive.

We gave the film to the infantry liaison people and we never heard anything concerning it again.

A week later the missing American colonel wandered back into an outpost. He had escaped, he said, but the captain had not. The colonel said he was only able to untie his own bonds and he had had to leave the captain behind. This didn't quite make sense—if his hands were free, why couldn't he have untied the other officer's bonds?

In any case, in White's book *Thunder Out of China*, he reflected quite intelligently on what he had found out in his visit:

> From headquarters in Kunming, you beat your way 400 miles to shabby, weather-worn Kweiyang and thence to field headquarters, and you've come only half the way. There American Brigadier General Frederick Boyce and Chinese General Tang En Po jointly deploy and dispose of Chinese and American personnel in combat. Their remote control runs another 400 miles to the quiet, fluid string of foxholes that is the front, inhabited by hungry Chinese infantry men and grimy, filthy Americans.
>
> The sprawling creeping Chinese front is inching forward in the wake of the Japanese retreat.
>
> In the old army and lower down the highway, an American unit consists of four to ten men, a couple of gasoline drums, the ubiquitous jeep, a radio, and 20 to 30 cases of dehydrated rations.
>
> The smallest knots are air liaison teams, artillery, and regimental liaison units. They are as makeshift as they can be. They consist of an officer, one or two enlisted men, a Chinese interpreter and a Chinese cook.
>
> In the campaign for Liuchow and the corridor to the sea, there is none of what men of the West would call real fighting. But men are dying.

Shortly after these events, I wrote a letter home on quite another subject. An incredibly sad one it was:

April 14, 1945
Kweiyang

The news of the death of President Roosevelt came as a terrible shock yesterday. It was just about the worst news since the war began. I think that Roosevelt was the greatest American since Lincoln, and if ever the world needed him, it is now. Truman is faced with a tremendous responsibility and I hope that everybody cooperates with him. The influence of Roosevelt on America was so tremendous that it is incalculable. Under him we made more legislative advances for the benefit of the people than we had in the last fifty years combined. He had weaknesses and strengths, and to me he symbolized the best of our American culture and economic system. He was the best symbol of democracy and freedom that American capitalism has produced and his loss to America is also just as great a loss to the rest of the world. It will probably be a long time before we have a man like him to lead us again.

Roosevelt's memorial service in Kweiyang, 1945.

While FDR did not live to see it, the end of the war was getting closer. The Japanese continued taking their time about backing up, but every night we pitched our hammocks a little farther down the road as we headed for the big city of Liuchow, which had once been the site of the biggest American airfield in China. As we neared, Chinese troops encountered a small number of entrenched Japanese. But the Chinese did not seem eager to engage the enemy at close quarters and contented themselves with firing at the enemy position with artillery. Had the Chinese commanders made a real push, they could have prevented some of the damage the Japanese were doing to the town and its people. But the generals were taking no chances with their personal safety.

We felt compelled to make a move. Didn't the saying "save face" start here? We decided to take a walk toward the Japanese. We thought we might shame the Chinese into following us. General Joseph Stilwell had done that when crossing the Salween River into Burma, but Stilwell was a four-star general who knew what he was doing. We believed the Japanese only had small arms and we could walk quite a ways before moving into their range. A railroad track cut across the area in front of us, on a rise, providing cover almost up to the Japanese entrenchment. It was an extremely hot day, and we did not want to carry any unnecessary objects, including weapons. A little while later I was most sorry we had left them behind. The Chinese had glared at us as we walked nonchalantly out, but they said nothing. Soon we were between them and the Japanese. We came to the railroad tracks and halted. Once past the tracks, we would be within range of the enemy rifles. However, thick foliage on the other side of the tracks would hide us as we crossed. We raced over the top of the abutment and into the trees on the other side, creeping cautiously through them for a few moments, still advancing on the Japanese.

Then bullets began cracking over our heads. We dove into tall grass and stopped dead. We did not know if the shots were meant to hit us or not, but we began to wonder what exactly we were doing. We did not have so much as a penknife amongst all of us. The Chinese could no longer see us and had no idea how close to the Japanese position we were. A Japanese soldier could have easily strolled down and put us out of our misery.

Next morning, the way was clear for an Oklahoma Sooner dash into Liuchow. We got up very early in a drizzling rain and learned that the Japanese had abandoned their position and Chinese scouts were setting out to explore the road. Our decision was made. This had to be it. My photographers, including the Air Force officer and me, hurriedly packed up and moved out. We caught up to and passed the lead element of Chinese scouts. No consultations now. We could see the hill was empty and we did not want to be stalled. The flat surface of the airfield soon appeared in the distance. It was surrounded by a barbed-wire fence and we followed the wire until we found an opening. I drove the jeep right out onto the field. The remains of the building installations were on the far side of the enormous field. The dirt runways were pitted with four-foot-wide holes. It looked as if the Japanese had dug them with the intention of putting mines in them and then left without completing the job. I got out of the jeep and looked carefully down into one of them. Nothing seemed to be concealed at the bottom.

The July 9, 1945, issue of *Time* magazine featured a report from China, sent by correspondent Teddy White. He radioed: "The Chinese army's biggest success was the recapture of the key city of Liuchow, one-time Fourteenth Air Force base."

Liuchow was a horrible, terror-stricken shambles. Few buildings remained intact. Fires smoldered and the smell of death hung heavy over everything. Very few people were in the streets we passed through, and those were literally in a daze.

CT-45-26722, Liuchow, China, 17 July 1945. Victory parade organized by Lt. Joe Passantino and Lt. Barney Rosset.

A large river bisected the city. All of its bridges had been destroyed. We drove along the edge of it, photographing the destruction. We found a family huddled in the center of the road. Two little children lay there, apparently near death. Their parents had been shot in the

247

legs. Through a combination of words and gestures, they told us they had been shot by the Japanese. Unfortunately, we had no medical resources and could not even give them rudimentary treatment. I hoped that we might find someone who could help them, but looking around at the destruction everywhere made me think that there was little possibility of doing so.

We left our jeep and set out on foot for the riverbank. We had to cross the water to get to the main center of town. A boatman offered to take the four of us across in his small sampan. A crowd on the other bank stood waiting for their liberators, namely us photographers. They were waving flags and cheering at the edge of the boat landing. The Chinese slapped us on the back. We were the great American liberators. Disillusion had yet to set in. That would take a few days.

The first night back on the airfield was uneasy, but nothing happened. In the morning we explored our surroundings. The wrecks of

CT-45-25428, July 1, 1945, Liuchow, China. Wrecked US plane has red metal disc placed by Japanese over star to draw fire from US planes during battle for strategic air base.

several planes were neatly lined up in a bay adjoining a runway. The Japanese had lived up to their reputed cleverness. They had camouflaged destroyed American fighter planes to look like Japanese Zeros. Their ruse meant to draw fire had worked; the decoys were riddled with bullet holes and torn up by American bombing and strafing.

The next day a captain from the Corps of Engineers and an enlisted man landed in a little L-5. The captain had not been out of the plane for five minutes when he found the first mine. His plane had passed right over it when it landed. We were dumbfounded. The Japanese had planted American fragmentation bombs with detonators on them. We followed the captain and he pointed out the ugly noses of one frag bomb after another. He walked to the edge of one of the holes, but stopped before he got to the lip. A bomb was planted there too. The Japanese had expected us to do just as we had done: to look into the holes and stand on the edges. They had left their excavations empty and put the mines into the loose dirt around them.

The captain and his helper set to work clearing off a strip for future landings. They crawled on their stomachs up to the mines and softly brushed away the dirt. Then they attached fuses and lit them one by one to destroy them.

We photographed the first few attempts, but retreated when the fuses started sputtering. I jumped into the jeep and drove it more than a hundred yards away. One of the mines sent shrapnel screaming past my ears even at that distance. There were thousands of mines on the field and it took weeks to clear them away. I returned by plane to Kunming with the exposed film, feeling grateful that I had not set off one of those mines and been killed.

The Bund, Shanghai, September 1945.

From Liuchow an Air Force plane flew us to Shanghai, a place I already knew through dreams—it was my secret Chicago. I had earned the right to go there after dodging cholera and malaria, after slogging through the mess created by the corrupt and crooked Chiang Kai-shek regime.

We landed in Shanghai in a drizzling rain at a Japanese-held field and three of my 164th photographers and I were taken to a Japanese-driven pickup truck parked on a runway. The war was still on but it was with a new script. I had switched consciously from Edgar Snow's version, *Red Star*, to Malraux's *Man's Fate*. Standing in the open back of the pickup truck, the four of us were driven into the city. There was nobody to be seen for blocks. Then we began to notice people in the streets, gawking at us, and, as I gradually realized, cheering—we four in American uniforms, standing in the rain, represented again the US liberating army. The truck took us to the Bund, the waterfront area of Shanghai, to the Cathay Hotel—one of the most beautiful hotels I had ever seen. Outside the Cathay, Bubbling Well Road and then Nanking Road were lined with people who applauded as we entered the hotel. The Japanese manager met us in the lobby. I was in a fog, dazed by this strange transition in a war that still had a few days to run. The manager led me to my suite, knocked, and an imposing Japanese officer in an immaculate white uniform answered, bowed to me, and left, turning over his luxurious suite to a twenty-three-year-old American lieutenant.

On the day before, I had slept on an airfield in the cholera-stricken heat bath of Liuchow. Now, with the press of a button, I was ordering trays of Canadian Club, ice, and soda from room service. Out on Bubbling Well Road the girls were walking arm in arm, while American officers were still imprisoned in the YMCA practically next door and would be kept there for at least a few days to come. The latter were delighted when we brought bottles of scotch to their cells. But we were free and they stayed in jail.

One curious incident occurred when we were invited to a party at a Soviet club. It was a dinner in a richly appointed hall with a portrait of Stalin at one end and Lenin at the other. There were many beautiful women in attendance. As the night progressed, I found that most of the Russians there, many of whom were Jewish, didn't like Stalin or Lenin, for that matter.

At the end of the evening, I asked one of the girls if I could take her home. She pointedly told me to watch out for the German Jewish women I might meet in the ghetto. They were all prostitutes, she warned me.

I had learned that perhaps twenty thousand German and Austrian Jews were still confined to a ghetto not far from our hotel. Actually, the next day we stumbled on some of them at an afternoon dance/picnic they were holding in Hongkou Park. They stared at us and at our American uniforms as though we were apparitions, and we were equally shocked to see them. Within what seemed a short time a young man came running up to me with a small package that he insisted upon giving to me. It was a Rolleiflex camera still in its original box. I think he must have returned to the ghetto to pick it up. The band stopped playing and we found ourselves joyously embraced by men and women, young and not so young. A short while later we heard a voice call out from the podium, "Break it up, it's curfew."

"No more curfew," I said, "the war is over." My new friends were not quite convinced.

I picked out one young woman, Ilse Hammer, a very attractive, dark, German Jewish girl from Berlin. We went and sat on a bench together, defying the curfew at dusk. The streetlights lit up, and along came a tall, turbaned Sikh rifleman in the International Settlement Police, a vestige of British Rule that the Japanese had maintained. This was the test. My new friends and we Americans, shaking, watched as the Sikh strolled up. He saluted me and said, "Good evening, Sahib."

Ilse Hammer, refugee from Berlin and friend of Barney Rosset, Shanghai, 1945.

251

He hadn't tried to arrest us, he merely wished us a good evening. The constabulary already recognized their new clients.

It soon became apparent that Ilse was also adaptive. A former law student from Berlin, she unlocked Shanghai for me. Despite the curfew maintained in the ghetto, she had made the French Concession her domain, her special place, that chunk of Paris where one drank at turn-of-the-century bistros on the Avenue Joffre.

I was definitely more fascinated by her than disapproving. Ilse made me think of Valerie, the temptress in Malraux's *Man's Fate*, which was set in Shanghai. But who then was I? Sometimes I was her lover and protector. At other times, I was waiting, anxious and excited, for her to return from some unexplained rendezvous.

"Tony" was Ilse's Shanghai name. She worked at the Roxy, a somewhat disreputable nightclub, as if there could be such a thing in wartime Shanghai, located on Tongshan Road alongside several other little nightclubs. The club was set back from the sidewalk, in a clump of trees. Its small electric sign was scarcely noticeable. A clean paved walk led up to the door, where a turbaned Sikh doorman stood. Inside, a long hallway led to the main part of the club. A bar was partially enclosed in a niche in the far corner of the room. A three-piece band softly played old American tunes almost constantly. A small dance space was carved out from the nest of tables and a few couples were sometimes dancing. It was not crowded.

The night I met her, Tony was sitting at one of the tables waiting for someone like me.

I asked her to join me. She led me over to a booth in the quietest part of the room. Her low-heeled shoes and simple beige dress seemed made more for a walk through the park than this dark nightclub. Her hair fell down over her neck in a thick wave, softening her slightly sharp features and giving a touch of tender youthfulness to her big, sad eyes. The dark rings under them were not noticeable in the smoky air. I liked Tony, very much.

A voluptuous young blonde sat by herself in a corner. Tony said that she was her girlfriend Trudy. The music stopped and the musicians retired to the bar and Tony's friend came over to our table.

At three in the morning an American marine sergeant entered the club and announced that the closing hour was approaching. For the moment, he constituted the honorary and complete military police force of Shanghai. After spending the war in a Shanghai jail, he had been released to the heaven prepared for all good marines. Nobody took his warning very seriously and he downed two shots of rum before shaking hands all around and leaving.

Tony and Trudy began talking about themselves. They were Jewish refugees from Berlin. Shanghai was the only port left open to them when they fled Germany before the outbreak of the war. Tony was not so eager to talk about the past. She had just entered law school in Berlin when the professors began their diatribes against the Jews. She had tried to ignore the problem, but it began to be impossible. One day she insulted a teacher. Her friends, including the head of the school, smoothed things over while she packed her books and left. After that the problem was how to leave the country. Her mother was not willing to go: Germany was her homeland, and she owned property there. Tony's father, separated from the family for years, wrote from Switzerland, constantly urging her to leave. There was a friend, the son of a rich shop owner. They decided to get married and escape together. Hans was still a boy, but it was easier for a married woman to travel. They took a train to Italy, and at the German frontier they were searched—and robbed—by the German frontier guards. It was a battle to get on a boat, any boat. However, their honeymoon voyage was provided, free of charge, on a luxury-style Japanese ship that took them to Shanghai, the only port they knew in the world still open to them, from an Italian port on the Mediterranean. The Italians and especially the Japanese operators of the luxurious tour ship were friendly and cooperative.

In Shanghai, Hans became a drummer in one of the bedraggled little nightclub bands, but his mind never left Berlin. Tony started out as a salesgirl in a store, and then the jobs were gone. She had to join her friends in the bars, living off commissions on drinks, and whatever else one felt it necessary to do.

Tony divorced Hans after a year in Shanghai, but she said he kept coming to her with every new problem this jungle of a city threw against him. She spoke unemotionally about her mother. It was almost certain that she had died in a gas chamber, but no letter ever came to clarify the past.

At 3:30 a.m. the two waiters would begin putting away the tablecloths and stacking the chairs on the tables. Everybody else had left. When I was there on other nights, I would slip a wad of the fantastic ten-thousand-dollar, ersatz Japanese bills to the head musician when he came over to say good night.

At closing, it was pouring rain outside. The bearded Sikh was still standing on the walk. Tony and Trudy and I emerged into the night, the two women with their bicycles in tow. I asked if they wanted pedicabs, the rickshaws pulled by bicycles. Trudy said no and, wishing us a good night, rode off. Tony and I waited a moment for a soaked, bare-legged pedicab driver to pull up. Tony took the bike she had and put it on the pedicab and off we went.

Back at the posh Cathay, Tony stood in the middle of the large bedroom, making no move to take off her dripping, shabby raincoat. I tried to comfort her but suddenly she was crying. She said she had to leave. It was too late for breakfast. She could not make a date. If I wanted to come to the Roxy, that was my business. She worked there. I took her back downstairs to her bicycle. It was still pouring, but she did not hesitate to go out. We stood in the rain while she unlocked the wheel of her bike. Then I asked her again: tonight at six in the lobby of the hotel. She said maybe and swiftly pulled away from the curb and winged down the Bund, past lines of sampans and steamers tied up at the docks. I saw her disappear over a bridge, standing up on the bike, pedaling determinedly and naturally.

The next afternoon the American brass was beginning to arrive. Several colonels were standing at the hotel desk waiting to be assigned rooms. They wore combat boots and carried carbines slung over their shoulders.

I walked to a big chair near the street entrance and sat down. Probably Tony would not come, but I could not give up hope.

Painted, pretty, white Russian girls sauntered in and out. Some had just said good-bye to their Japanese friends; all of them were picking out their American officers. Allied internees, fresh from the detention camps, pushed timidly in, as if they were still not quite sure that freedom was legal. I saw barbed-wire fences and years of enforced boredom stamped on their thin faces.

At a quarter past six, Tony arrived. Her light cotton dress and flat-heeled shoes made her look strangely and pleasingly out of place in the luxurious lobby. She pulled the bicycle with her and there was a shy smile on her face. I put my arm around her waist as we walked out of the hotel into the dying August day. A badly spelled sign was going up between the Cathay and the hotel near it. WELCOME VICTORTUOUS SEVENTH FLEET.

Our pedicab was like a hansom going through Central Park. Shirt-sleeved crowds flowed along beside us in rickshaws, bicycles, automobiles, and on foot. Nobody was in a hurry. The office workers were going home. The International Settlement was free, and the atmosphere vibrated with relief and indolence. As much as I had thought about Shanghai, through the eyes of Malraux, I was not prepared for the blocks of semimodern structures, the broad streets, the great enterprises. The Fiaker Restaurant to which we went was Viennese. Big photographic panels of Vienna lined two walls of the quiet, half-empty place. A waiter carefully drew the cork from a bottle of dry white wine.

In my imagination I could see Tony in Vienna, lost in a fairy dream at the opera, and later holding her father's hand in a café, sipping hot chocolate covered with a cloud of cream. Tony had no desire to revisit her bad memories of what had happened in Vienna, but she took a photograph from her worn wallet and put it down in front of me. A tall, dark man held a little girl at his side. The paper was yellow and frayed, but the German script was still legible. The last words were "*geliebte* Ilse" ("I love Ilse").

Now it was good to leave the restaurant and go out into the city. With the whole night spread out before us, we walked along the boulevard in the warm, yellow-lighted evening, watching the twisting and rolling shadows cast out by the heavy old bicycle at our side.

On the roof of the Cathay there was a cabaret with an open-air terrace. We sat up there leaning on the railing, flush with the top of the sky, Shanghai pancaked beneath us. The lights of Bubbling Well Road and the Bund intersected each other. Small lamps flickered from sampans on the river and the British racetrack etched out a black oval in front of the Park Hotel nearby.

Once in my room, adolescent modesty disappeared. We undressed and embraced. Love was gentle in the humid near dawn. There was a feeling of closeness and wakeful peace.

At six or so, she moved away from me and I watched her through half-dreaming eyes as she pulled the cotton dress down over her thin, lithe body. Then she came over to the bed and kissed me, in a soft, rubbing way, across the mouth and cheek.

She was gone before I could pull her back. But after that she would stay the night. We didn't have to go to the Roxy, where she had had to urge drinks on me while she drank colored-water cocktails.

Shanghai was made even stranger by the mute corps of stylish, surprisingly tall, white-uniformed Japanese soldiers, who drifted around zombie like. One rainy night, cycling alone, downhill along the waterfront, my newly obtained bicycle spun out from under me and I landed hard on my back. I looked up from the wet brick road to see a large company of white uniforms surrounding me, faces regarding me with blank, inert hostility. I rose nervously and remounted my bicycle in this enemy throng, which slowly and uncertainly parted as I began to roll. I picked up speed and crossed the Waibaidu Bridge, on my way to meet Tony.

One day the US Army G-2 colonel attached to the Chinese Combat Command gave me a welcome task—to help a US Navy lieutenant commander seize evidence of the collaboration of Chiang Kai-shek—Chancre Jack—with the Axis. Some Italian seamen who had fought on the Loyalist side in the Spanish Civil War, then been jailed in Shanghai after reaching there by ship from Spain and now released, had occupied the Italian Embassy. I quickly collected my photographer's case full of Signal Corps microfilming equipment, bedrolls, carbines, and a bottle of whiskey wrapped in a towel. My photographers and I joined the Italians in that embassy for three days and nights, reassembling and photographing the shreds of documents that Mussolini's fleeing diplomats left behind. The Malraux environment still enveloped me.

In late October the phone rang in my suite at around 4:00 a.m. and an American officer's voice instructed me to be downstairs with all my possessions in one hour, for transport back to Kunming.

I was ordered to return to New York via India. In shock, I woke Tony. One hour! I gathered everything I owned, including two Chinese bicycles, a treasure in themselves, and sacks of Japanese occupation currency. I then took Tony downstairs and got her a pedicab. I heaped clothes, all the money I had, and the bicycles on top of her. And only then told her I was leaving—now it was shades of Humphrey Bogart and Ingrid Bergman's *Casablanca*. Tony and I parted, only this time the roles were reversed. I was stunned and confused.

Auf Wiedersehen, Shanghai.

This time there were no bombs dropping on the Kunming runway— the war was over and I felt like a postwar casualty. I felt bruised and abandoned.

Kunming was under curfew due to the antics of Chiang Kai-shek's henchmen, but the next night I "liberated" someone's jeep, an unusual act for me, and found the bar/brothel Girls of All Nations, outside of Kunming. In a desperate mood, I got one of the Girls from one of the Nations and drove her around aimlessly, from large roads to small roads, then off road, and across a field, finally making love to her on the cold ground at the bitter dead end of my China journey.

November 19, 1945
Kalaikunda, India

Dear Mother and Dad,

The political situation all over the world, but particularly in the Far East, is pretty discouraging, because the Americans, British, and French seem to have taken up the same policies that the Japs and Germans left off with. It seems pretty clear to me that the failure of the British to get out of India, and their fighting in Indonesia is a direct contradiction to all their high sounding war aims and radical changes in party. They have no more right to rule India than the Chinese do, and it would be impossible to make a bigger mess of things than they have. Right here in India they have men like Nehru who are among the greatest in the world. Their help to the Dutch who want to get back their ill-gotten possessions is also disgusting. The same goes for the French in Indo-China. The people there have been persecuted and exploited by the French for years and I think that they would rather have the Japs than the French rule them, and with good cause.

Where we are dead wrong is in our policy with China. The central government in China is the biggest bunch of grafters and crooks I have ever seen. Chiang Kai-shek is nothing but a fascist in my estimation, and NEVER fought the Japs throughout the war, whereas the Chinese Communists fought continuously without our help, and at the same time raised the living standards of the people. So what do we do, we arm the central government to fight the Communists. The least we could have done would have been to have kept our hands off and let them fight it out, and if we had, the Communists would have won hands down because the morale on their side is incomparably higher. The central gov. troops want no part of fighting. The Communists are incredibly ingenious with equipment and they can use anything or make anything. They made rifles and pistols by hand, and I saw the weapons too. At the front they used the old stuff and the poorest soldiers. I saw them using old Russian artillery and ten year old ammunition, while in the rear areas they have the new American stuff.

If the Americans, Dutch, British, and French persist in this attempt to rule other peoples in the world, which they have no right to do, then we are headed in a straight line for the third world war, because these people won't stand for it. If it had not been for Gandhi in India, I feel sure the Indians would have killed countless thousands of English, but his leadership in non-violence has saved a lot of lives. In return the British put him in prison. Just as the Irish and Americans broke away

257

from the English, the people here will too and if the British don't let them go peacefully they will just have to kill all the English. 80 million can't rule 800 million forever. These people are not stupid, they just don't have the materiel, but that never stopped anybody permanently. It is quite lucky the Japs never reached India because if they had they would have found a lot of sympathizers here to help them.

Dec 21, 1947
Shanghai

Ilse Hammer
674/59 Tongshan Rd.
Shanghai 18/China

Dear Barney, what a real surprise your X'mas card had given me. I was pretty sure that by now you completely had forgotten about me. It quite flatters me to know, that occasionally you remember me.

It might interest you to hear, that by March of the next year I will enter USA for good. I think that San Francisco will be the first port I am going to be sent to. If I can find a job there in the first week, I may stay otherwise my community will send me to some smaller city.

Do not wonder why I have changed my mind, I just could not get a visa to France from Shanghai, but from the States it will be rather easy, also that I want only a visiting permission and in any case come back to America.

There are not much news to tell. Right now I am working at the 9 floor of the Cathay-Hotel (you remember?) the place is named the "Tower." The "Fiaker" is still operating but opposite its former house. Also the Roxy Nightclub is still open, but it has a different owner and is one of the few places that keep open after 11 o'clock, official closing hour. You must have certainly heard about the silly exchange we have here. For one American Dollar you get now Shanghai Dollar 160.000—CNC, soon we will have to count in millions again like the time you had been here, while we had still Japanese money.

It has become very cold lately, and all I am dreaming about is a heated room in Frisco and a nice bathroom with hot water all day and night. But I am sure that those dreams will come true soon and that makes me a bit warmer already.

It would be nice to hear a little more about you, what are your plans? Are you married already? If you don't find time to write to Shanghai to me, you can always write to San Francisco "Hicem" that is an international organization.

I wish you a very merry X'mas and happy New Year also for our family.

Do sometimes remember,

Your Tony

Yes, Tony, I do remember you! For the rest of my life, I will remember you, my Ilse, my Tony.

```
(BASIC:  Ltr fr 1st Lt. J. E. Passantino, Sig C. Officer in
         charge of Liuchow Photo Det. to CG, USF, CT, APO 879.
         Subject:  Award of Bronze Star Medal to 2nd Lt. Barnet
         L. Rosset, Jr., dtd 7 Aug 45


200.6                    2nd Ind                    JHMP/1h
   1

HEADQUARTERS, USF, CT, APO 879, 26 September 1945.

TO:  Commanding Officer, 3374th Signal Photo Sv. Co.,
     USF, CT, APO 627.

     1.  Recommendation for Bronze Star Medal for 2nd
Lt. Barnet L. Rosset Jr. is disapproved.


        BY COMMAND OF LIEUTENANT GENERAL STRATEMEYER:

                              EDDIE T. WOOD
                              1st. Lt., AGD
                              Asst. Adj. General
```

The Artificial Stork
Ryan Call

I DO NOT KNOW for how long we traveled *The Beneath*, that harsh terrain on which the grounded go lost and flightless, nor could I explain to you how we survived with little sustenance, as the children did not seem the least bit interested in foraging for food and collecting water. We seemed to navigate these barren ridgelines, these wind-swept rocks, these chalky, infertile grounds under miraculous power, as if some gods had mistaken us for blessed and cleared for us an easy path. We had only to follow that path as it wound its way through the ruined foilage and splintered earth, hoping as we went that we might come across some hidden, but well-appointed pasture in which to halt for the night.

The weather, oddly, suspiciously, moved with us, but at a respectful distance. A satisfactory hole in the cloud cover, through which the pleasant sun and blue sky showed themselves, appeared occasionally above our heads while the thunderstorms shed their electric charges on the smoldering earth around us. When we slept, a fog descended over our makeshift campground, draped itself loosely about our bodies so as to hide us from our fates. Despite my avowed hatred for the rotten ground, I could not help but collapse in exhaustion upon it after each day's journey. I suspect the children fared little better than I, though they had long ago resigned themselves to such a transient existence.

I was the newcomer, the latest to have fallen from the sky.

In the morning, we awoke in time to see yet another flying machine plummet into the distant hills at our back and disappear among the burning forests in the valley below. The children stowed our bedrolls and other equipment, strapped my body into the travel hammock, and broke camp. They had developed a practical but necessary routine of survival, one to which I had to strictly adhere if I ever hoped to return to all I cherished in my life: my wife, my son, my skies.

*

260

I remember very little of the crash itself, though I can very well imagine the violence of its activity, having long studied crashes of years past: the flight logs of now-dead aviators, the published reports of accident investigation committees, the leaked transcripts of the dying crew's last words as they sought absolution from the gods. If pilot error had caused my own crash, then consider this story my attempt at rectifying that error, for in it you will find evidence of my suffering the consequences of my mistake. Please forgive me.

But, if some unpredictable force had exerted itself on my flying machine and sent it spiraling into *The Beneath*, then read in my words a mournful prayer, for I too have unfairly lost the altitude of my life, and for that, I deserve your sympathy.

In either case, what follows here is as complete a retelling as I can muster. Be aware that my retelling suffers the unfortunate drag of a faulty memory, one that makes unwieldy the flight of each sentence as it journeys across the page, and so you should read these lines with as much hopeful skepticism as I do, for I have yet to discover how I might gain passage home.

I recall sheltering anxiously in the wreckage, the eerie sound of creaking metal, cracking wood, the pops and snaps of the flying machine breaking apart in the canopy of the trees. I loosed my body from the collapsed structure of the cockpit, and reached out to my commanding officer, an elderly, ancient pilot of the guild, someone who had guided me throughout my early course of study, finally endorsing my appointment as first officer on his airship.

Sadly, I could do nothing for him.

I climbed out of the flight deck and painfully straddled a tree branch to gain my bearings. Below me bits and parts of the flying machine lay strewn throughout the underbrush, and among them curled the numerous bodies of our unfortunate passengers, bent and strained in unnatural forms like some frantic punctuation on the forest floor.

Hello? I called, meaning to make my way toward the nearest voice, but none greeted me.

In the distance, I heard the slight cry of a baby, and as I turned to peer into the gloom of the trees, my legs slipped from around the tree branch.

*

When I next awoke, I found myself in the company of children. They had made a cradle of their arms—their tiny, pink, swollen arms—and lifted me free of the forest floor. They carried my body to the shadowy bank of a nearby stream, and set me down on the moss and ferns. They fed me a warm concoction from the rubber nipple of a baby's bottle. Some poked me and prodded me as if to tempt me toward exertion, though I believe now they merely meant to check my body for injuries, of which I had many. They spoke to each other as though I could not hear them.

An aviator, one said.

Where are his epaulets? asked another.

Torn away.

He's no aviator.

I made to speak, to assure them that I was an aviator, but I could only cough from the pain in my chest and throat. I blinked and regarded them closely. A circle of rounded faces looked down at me, each one full cheeked and muddy, crowned by wisps of hair and makeshift caps. Their wondrous eyes seemed to twitch and turn with excitement, though I could not tell in the glow of the burning wreckage if they focused on me or on some deadly insect crawling across my forehead. For some time they deliberated as to what they might do with me, and I soon understood that while many of them thought I could be of some help to their purpose, a small number of them believed me to be a bad omen, a gremlin of *The Beneath* come to distract them from their mission. A small girl began to sharpen sticks that she had retrieved from the forest floor, small roughened sticks that she distributed to everyone, and I shuddered to think of their use, having suddenly recalled the stories of my own childhood, in which captured gremlins often met terrible ends.

One of the children smoked an intricately carved pipe, the tip of which he tapped now and then against the front of his tiny teeth as he thoughtfully listened to the others bicker, and I figured him to be their leader, so careful were his movements. After some time, he stepped closer to me, and the children hushed as he bent down to examine my ruined uniform. Blood had slowly spread across my chest and neck, my torn shirt, my tie, my jacket. The boy methodically unbuttoned my shirt, and when he pulled it open, he beckoned for the others to look. There, buried in the flesh of my chest, was my metal insignia pin—my wings—the force of the impact with the ground having crushed it there into me.

You're our pilot now, the boy said.

*

So began my life with the children of wreckage, a troupe of stranded children who traveled *The Beneath*, a collection of sole survivors, those precious babes who had by some miracle lived through the most terrifying of crashes. They had gathered themselves into a collective and had made *The Beneath* their temporary home as they together sought out means of one day finally returning to their parents, if only they could rise high enough.

I was to help them build a flying machine.

Despite my broken body, my shattered limbs and joints, I helped them as best I could. They carried me with them in a makeshift travel hammock, the largest of the children alternately dangling me between them as we moved from one debris field to another, sites of past, present, and future crashes.

It seemed to me that the children often repeatedly visited the scenes of their own crashes, at which the survivor dutifully found his spot on the ground and lay there, curled up and dreaming of his mother and father, the gentle way they had sat with him as the flying machine began its plummet, how they had wept over him until the very end. The others stood respectfully some distance away, lit a fire, and prepared a bowl of pretend porridge to warm the sleeper upon his waking from the dream. What purpose the children meant to achieve during these visitations I could not discern, though I imagine it helped them to reconnect with their deceased parents in some way.

At present crash sites, the children sifted and sorted through the wreckage, and I discovered that each child had a certain duty. Some carried to me all manner of parts that they thought might be useful: ailerons and rudders, wingtips and propeller heads, cracked struts and knotted guy wires, lengths of fuselage, busted-up landing gear. I examined each part in turn, assessing its structural integrity, how it might fit into our current inventory, which one child relayed to me from memory at each site, and whether or not I believed it could be repaired by a child's hand and rudimentary knowledge of maintenance. The parts I approved of were then affixed to an enormous fuselage that the children dragged in their wake, cheerfully calling it *The Artificial Stork*. With each crash site, the flying machine grew bulkier and heavier. The children did their best to approximate the ideal of a proper flying machine; however, theirs was a flawed rendition, derived from their having puzzled through the busted and burnt remains of countless crashes. I counseled them as best I could in

263

its creation, but I worried that soon we would no longer be able to travel, much less fly the damned thing.

If the children's behavior confused me at these particular sites, then when we stumbled across the clean, peaceful site of a future crash, I grew terrified. Only their leader, the silent child with the pipe, seemed capable of divining where a flying machine might someday smash into *The Beneath*, and when he discovered such a site, he collapsed onto the ground in fear, sending the other children into paroxysms of mourning. I feared for my life at these points, for the children often turned on me, blaming my profession, cursing my responsibility for the rise and fall of others, others who had entrusted to me their lives, others who had innocently expected me to deliver them safely to their destination. They spoke crudely of me in a language I had never before heard issue forth from a child's mouth. They struck me with sticks, pebbles, spare parts, tools, any implement they could snatch up in their tiny fists. Of course I could not avoid their wrath, secure as I was in the travel hammock, so I had to endure the injury they wreaked upon my body until they fell asleep from the exhaustion. I knew that if they were to ever let me return to my family, I must allow them to use me as they pleased.

Nights we relaxed our travels and made camp to rest, to regain what little strength we had. The children lit fires, pretended to cook and eat their porridge, and then began story time. They gathered around the fire, and each one told a bedtime story, according to a rotating schedule. They told stories about their favorite pets, their siblings, their fondest memories of hide-and-seek. One child spoke of a family trip she had taken to the birthplace of flight. Another child told story after story about his loving parents, their habits of parenting him with a safety net, of how they helicoptered in his presence. Often the children prompted each other when their stories faltered, inserting helpful reminders as to senses and feelings the storytelling child might have experienced in that life before the crash, and when all discussion failed, they passed to the stuttering child the memory foam, a block of cushion that I recognized to be part of an air traveler's lost pillow, which the child clutched softly, as if by kneading its structure, the foam might release another story into the smoke above the campfire.

Then one night came my turn to speak a bedtime story. I refused initially, but the child with the pipe appealed to my sense of etiquette, explaining that each of them had shared stories, why then could I not, being now an accepted member of their company? To his reasoning I yielded, nodding, and my handlers propped the hammock against a boulder so I might address the children, and from this vantage point I looked into their upturned faces, across which churned the shadow play of the fire.

Perhaps, here, I made my mistake, though at the time I believed I should do my best to ingratiate myself in their presence, as the flying machine they had nearly completed seemed my only hope of returning home, despite how badly it might function. See, I had listened long enough to their own stories to know a little bit about each of them, and these histories I thought to combine with what I knew of my own son, of his desires and actions, of raising him from a baby to a boy of similar age as these, my temporary children. I only meant to improve their spirits and perhaps give them some cheerful stories to counter their dismal evenings, for often after story time, the children retired to their sleeping rolls in tears, sobbing themselves to sleep.

But now I see that my stories merely confused them, perhaps led to their destruction.

I spoke to them terrific stories about their parents, their past lives, weaving fact with fantasy in order to create what I hoped might be wonderful worlds into which they might disappear when they felt troubled, as my son had often done on his sadder days. I granted to them magical powers that they had enjoyed as babies. I told tales about their parents, all of whom I claimed to have met during my time as an aviator, and spoke of their grand and daring feats. I prophesied the future, a happier time during which they would reunite with their families.

The more I spoke these stories, the more the children clamored to hear newer and finer details, and soon I had trouble keeping all of it straight in my mind. Who had visited the aurora borealis on the eve of his or her parents' anniversary? To whom had I given the power of wingless flight as a newborn? Had I named the twins' mother and father as the healers of the second sky, or did that honor belong to the little girl with the wooden arm? Where had I located the reunion festival? Certainly not in my own city? Did the jet stream serve as haven for their waiting mothers and fathers, or had I called it an accursed wind that drove their parents cruelly throughout the atmosphere until the children might save them? The children began to question my stories, some of them corrected my errors thankfully, while others argued over the intricacies of fate and self-determination, beating me when my stories contradicted the earlier versions they had heard. When I could not remember the correct answer, I pleaded with the children as they punished my error with their fists and sticks. I claimed exhaustion under their blows, and I requested that the children tell stories of their own, classic stories of their mothers and fathers, the stories I had heard during the early days of my traveling with the group.

To my horror, the children relayed nearly word for word my own made-up stories.

They had forgotten the realities of their lives, of their parents, of their childhoods.

This new forgetfulness caused the children to grow sluggish in their movements, and they soon ceased to pull with any real effort the massive structure of the flying machine. Instead we wandered in decreasingly concentric circles, until we finally settled on a flattened plain populated by light shrubs, a rare species of flightless birds, and the occasional line of dried timber that had once grown along streambeds and creeks. The area seemed to have been farmed in a previous age, though the plain appeared to have lain fallow for quite some time.

The children situated my broken body in the shadow of *The Artificial Stork* to protect me from the worsening weather, though I tried to convince them to place me in the shelter of its cockpit, where I might secretly attempt to start it as they slept that night. The child with the pipe insisted that no one would be able to hear my stories if I were stashed away, and he much preferred that we all stayed out of doors.

So here we remain, I strapped into my hammock and the children lounging comfortably around me, listening to the stories I tell, arguing about the details, all while the great hulk of our flying machine slowly rusts and erodes under the elements of *The Beneath*. I hope that one day, should the children cease to beat me long enough so that my body might finally heal, I can sneak aboard, lock the hatch, spool up the great engines so that its wings flap miraculously overhead, and return to my wife and son. Until then, I can only imagine my way home, these children the unwelcome sentinels by my side.

Regeneration at Mukti
Julia Elliott

CALL ME A TRENDMONGER, but I've sprung for a tree house. My bamboo pod hovers amid galba trees, nestled in jungle but open to the sea, the porch equipped with hemp hammocks. A flowering vine snakes along the railings, pimping its wistful perfume. With a single remote control, I may adjust the ceiling fans, fine-tune the lighting, or lift the plate-glass windows, which flip open like beetle wings. My eco-friendly rental has so many amenities, but my favorite is the toilet: a stainless basin that whisks your droppings through a pipe, down into a pit of coprophagic beetles. These bugs, bred to feast on human shit, have an enzyme in their gut that makes the best compost on the planet—a humus so black you'd think it was antimatter. The spa uses it to feed the orchids in the Samsara Complex. As visitors drift amid the blossoms, we may contemplate the life cycle, the transformation of human waste into ethereal petals and auras of scent.

"Orchids are an aphrodisiac," said a woman at lunch today, her unagi roll breaking open as she crammed it into her mouth, spilling blackish clumps of eel. She had crow's-feet, marionette lines around her mouth, a porn star's enhanced lips.

"Yes," said a man in a sky blue kimono, "I think I read something about that on the website."

"They have orchid dondurma on the menu," I said, scanning the man's face: budding eye bags, sprays of gray at his temples, the gouge of a liver line between his green eyes. I placed him in his early forties.

"Fruit sweetened," he said, "fortified, I believe, with raw mare's milk, if you do dairy."

"Colostrum," I said. "Mostly goat. But I don't ingest sweeteners or juices, only whole fruits."

"My philosophy on dairy," said the woman, waving her chopstick like a conductor, "is that milk is an infant food. I weaned myself ten years ago." Her lush bosom actually heaved, hoisted by the boning of a new-fangled corset.

For some reason (maybe it was the way the woman shook her dead blonde hair like a vixen in a shampoo commercial), I found myself smirking at the man over the centerpiece of sculpted melon. I found myself wondering what he'd look like after completing the Six Paths of Suffering. I couldn't help but picture him shirtless, reclining on a rock beside one of the island's famous waterfalls, his skin aglow from deep cellular regeneration and oxygenation of the hypodermis.

"I'm Red," he said. And he was: flushed along his neck and cheeks, the ripe pink of a lizard's pulsing throat.

The powers that be at Mukti—those faceless organizers of regeneration—have designed the spa so that Newbies don't run into Crusties much. We eat separately, sleep in segregated clusters of cottages, enjoy our dips in the mud baths and mineral pools, our yoga workshops and leech therapy sessions, at different times. As Gobind Singh, our orientation guru, pointed out, "The face of rebirth is the mask of death." And this morning, as I walked the empty beach in a state of above-average relaxation, I spotted my first Crusty crawling from the sea.

Judging by the blisters, the man was in the early stages of Suffering. I could still make out facial features twitching beneath his infections. He had the cartoonish body of a perennial weight lifter, his genitals compressed in the Lycra sling of a Speedo. He nodded at me and dove back into the ocean.

I jogged up the trail that curled toward my tree house. In the bathroom, I examined my face again. I studied familiar lines and folds, pores and spots, ruddy patches and fine wrinkles, not to mention a general ambient sagging that's especially detectable in the morning.

Out beyond the Lotus terrace, the ocean catches the pink of the dying sun. A mound of seaweed sits before me, daubed with pomegranate chutney and pickled narcissus. My waitress is plain, as all the attendants are: plump cheeks and brown skin, hair tucked into a white cap, eyebrows impeccably groomed. Her eyes reveal nothing. Her mouth neither smiles nor bends with the slightest twist of frown. I'm wondering how they train them so well, to be almost invisible, when I note a shadow darkening my table.

"Hi," says the man from yesterday. "May I?"

"Red, right? Please."

The bags under his eyes look a little better. His helmet of hair is losing its sticky sheen. And his bottom lip droops, making his mouth look adorably crooked.

"Just back from leech therapy." He grins. "A bit freaky to have bloodsuckers clamped to my face, but it's good for fatty orbital herniation and feelings of nameless dread."

We laugh. Red orders a green mango salad with quinoa fritters and mizuna-wrapped shad roe. We decide to share a bottle of island muscador. We drink and chat and the moon pops out, looking like a steamed clam.

Though Red is a rep for Clyster Pharmaceuticals, he's into holistic medicine, thinks the depression racket is a capitalist scam, wishes he could detach himself from the medico-industrial complex. I try to explain my career path (human-computer interaction consulting), how the subtleties of creative interface design have worn me out.

"It's like I can feel the cortisol gushing into my system," I say. "A month ago, I didn't have these frown lines."

"You still look youngish," says Red.

"Thanks." I smile, parsing out the differences between *young* and *youngish*. "You too."

Red nods. "It's not that I'm vain. It's more like a state of general depletion. The city has squeezed the sap out of me."

"And life in general, of course, takes its nasty toll."

"Boy does it." Red offers the inscrutable smile of an iguana digesting a fly.

I don't mention my divorce, of course, nor my relocation to a sun-deprived city that requires vitamin D supplementation. I pass the wine and our fingertips touch. Red's wind-mussed hair is a significant improvement, and I imagine kissing him, forgetting that in two weeks we'll both be covered in weeping sores.

I've opened my tree house to the night—windows cranked, jungle throbbing. My blood's up from Ashtanga yoga. A recent dye job has brightened my hair with a strawberry blonde, adolescent luster. Wineglass in hand, I pace barefooted. And Red: seated on my daybed, his face feral from a five-day beard, lips so pink I've already licked them to test for cosmetics.

Between thumb and index finger he's rolling a globule of sap. Now he's inserting the resin into the bowl of his water pipe. And we take another hit of ghoni, distillate of the puki bloom, a small purple fungus flower that grows from tree frog dung. We drift out onto the porch and fall into an oblivion of kissing.

We shed our clothes, leaving tiny silken mounds on the bamboo planks. Red's penis sways in the humid air. Shaggy thighed, he walks toward the bedroom, where vines creep through the windows, flexing like tentacles in the ocean breeze.

He reclines and smiles, his forehead only faintly lined in the glow of Himalayan salt lamps. We've been hanging out religiously for the past seven days, are addicted, already, to each other's smells. Every night at dinner we begin some delirious conversation that always brings us back to my tree house, toking up on ghoni, chattering into the night. Earlier, discussing the moody rock bands that moved us in our youth, we discovered that we attended the same show twenty-seven years ago. Somehow we'd both been bewitched by a band of sulky middle-aged men with dyed black hair who played a broody, three-chord pop. Now we can't stop laughing at how gravely we'd scowled at them from the pit, our gothic costumes bought from the mall.

We've already been infected. Both of us received the treatment two days ago, Red at eleven, me at three. And we met for a lunch of shrimp ceviche between appointments.

All week long, Lissa, the lactose-free blonde, has been chattering about the Hell Realm, wondering, as we all are, when our affliction will begin. She's the kind of person whose head will explode unless she opens her mouth to release every half-formed thought. Her perfume, derived from synthetic compounds, gives me sinus headaches. Just as I suspected, she's an actress. I'm almost positive she has fake tits. Even though Red and I beam out a couple vibe, huddled close over menus and giggling, she has no problem plopping down next to him, lunging at the shy man with her mammary torpedoes. And he always laughs at her lame jokes.

This afternoon I have a mild fever and clouds stagnate over the sea. The meager ocean breeze smells of sewage. I feel like a fool for ordering the monkfish stew, way too pungent for this weather. And Lissa won't stop gloating over her beef kabobs. Red, sunk in silence, keeps scratching his neck. I'm about to exhale, a long, moody sigh full of turbulent messages, when Lissa reaches over her wine flute to poke Red's temple with a mauve talon.

"Look," she says, "bumps."

I see them now: a spattering of hard, red zits. Soon they'll grow fat with juice. They'll burst and scab over, ushering in the miracle of subcutaneous regeneration.

"And my neck itches." Red toys with his collar.

According to the orientation materials distributed by Guru Gobind Singh, the Hell Realm is different for everyone, depending on how much hatred and bitterness you have stored in your system. All that negativity, stashed deep in your organic tissues, will come bubbling to the surface of your human form. The psychosomatic filth of a life-time will hatch, breaking through your skin like a thousand min-uscule volcanoes to spit its lava.

"Time for my mineral mud bath," says Red. And now I see what I could not see before: a row of incipient cold sores edging his upper lip, wens forming around the delicate arch of his left nostril, a clus-ter of protoblisters highlighting each cheekbone like subtle swipes of blusher.

The Naraka Room smells of boiled cabbage. Twelve of us squat on hemp yoga mats, stuck in the frog pose. Wearing rubber gloves, Guru Gobind Singh weaves among us, pausing here and there to tweak a shoulder or spine.

According to the pamphlet, Gobind Singh has been through the Suffering twice, without the luxury of gourmet meals, around-the-clock therapies, or hands-on guidance from spiritual professionals. Legend has it that he endured the Hell Realm alone in an isolated tree house. Crumpled in the embryo pose for weeks, he unfurled his body only to visit the crapper or eat a bowl of mung beans. His skin's as smooth as the metalized paint that coats a fiberglass mannequin. His body's a bundle of singing muscles. When he walks, he hovers three millimeters off the ground—you have to look carefully to de-tect his levitational power, but yes, you can see it: The bastard floats.

I can't help but hate him right now. After all, this is the Hell Realm and hatred festers within me. My flesh seethes with blisters. My blood suppurates. My heart is a ball of boiling pus. As I squat in medita-tion, I tabulate acts of meanness foisted upon me over the decades. I tally betrayals, count cruelties big and small. I trace hurts dating back to elementary school—decades before my first miscarriage, way before my bulimic high school years, long before Dad died and my entire family moved into that shitty two-bedroom apartment. I re-cede deeper into the past, husking layers of elephant skin until I'm soft and small, a silken worm of a being, vulnerable as a drop of dew

271

Julia Elliott

quivering on a grass blade beneath the summer sun.

"Reach into the core of your misery," says Gobind Singh. "And you will find a shining pearl."

The pamphlet, *Regeneration at Mukti*, features a color photo of a pupa dangling from a leaf on the cover. Inside is an outline of the bodily restoration process. My treatment has borne fruit. I suffer (oh how I suffer!) from the following: urushiol-induced dermatitis (poison oak rash), dermatophytosis (ringworm), type one herpes simplex (cold sores), cercarial dermatitis (swimmer's itch), herpes zoster (shingles), and trichinosis (caused by intramuscular roundworms). Using a blend of cutting-edge nanotechnology and gene therapy, combined with homeopathic and holistic approaches, the clinicians of Mukti have transmitted controlled infections into my body through oils, fungi, bacteria, viruses, and parasites. As skilled therapists work to reroute my mind-body networks to conduct more positive flows, my immune system is tackling an intricate symphony of infections, healing my body on the deepest subcellular levels: banishing free radicals, clearing out the toxic accumulation of lipofuscins, reinstalling hypothalamus hormones, and replacing telomeres to revitalize the clock that directs the life span of dividing cells.

I itch so much that I want to scrub my body with steel wool. I want to roll upon a giant cheese grater. I'd love to flay myself and be done with the mess. According to the pamphlet, however, not only does scratching interfere with the healing process, but the mental discipline required to refrain from scratching strengthens the chakra pathways that enhance positive mind-body flow.

I have a beautiful dream in which I'm wallowing in a patch of briars. I worm my naked body against thorns, writhe ecstatically in nests of prickly vines. I cry out, convulsing with the sweet sting of pleasure. I wake before dawn, pajamas stuck to my skin.

For me, consciousness is nothing but the seething tides of itchiness, hunger, and thirst, a vague sex drive nestled deep in the misery. I live like an animal from minute to minute, appointment to appointment—breakfast, lunch, and dinner.

Morning: a bowl of oats with flax seeds and blueberries, followed by a kelp bath and castor oil massage. After that: a cabbage poultice administered by experts, who then slather my body with shea butter and wrap it in sea-soaked silk. Before lunch I must descend into the bowels of the Samsara Complex for blood work and nanotech nuclear restructuring. Then a lunch of raw vegetables and fermented organ meats, kombucha with goji and spirulina.

Postlunch I do a volcanic mud bath, then hydrate with a goat milk and basil soak. Next comes a green-tea sensory-deprivation session, then kundalini yoga with Gobind Singh. Staggering from this mind fuck, I head straight for the Samsara Complex for stem-cell work and injections of Vita-Viral Plus. Then a light coconut oil massage and I'm good to go.

At supper I'm startled by Red's appearance. Yes, I've been monitoring his Incrustation. But I wasn't prepared for the new purple swellings around his eyes or the dribbling boils on his chin. Ditto the lip cankers and blepharitis. Of course I'm aware of my own hideousness. Of course I recoil each time I see my face in the mirror (think rotted plums and Spam). And the itching is a constant reminder of my state. Nevertheless, deep in the core of my being, I feel unscathed, as though the process were happening to someone else.

Though Red and I haven't touched each other in weeks, we eat together most nights, fresh from soothing therapies and tipsy on our allotment of organic, sulfite-free wine. We have about an hour until the itching becomes unbearable, then we slump off to our respective tree houses.

Tonight we're enjoying the fugu sashimi with pickled dandelion greens. The humidity hovers around fifty percent, great for our raw skin. And the ocean looks like pounded pewter. Though we're both disgusting, it's like we're mummy wrapped in putrid flesh, our real selves tucked down under the meat costumes.

"I was thinking about the hot springs," says Red. "Since our infections seem to be stabilizing."

"Quite a hike," I say. "It'd be hell on our swollen feet."

"You can do most of the way by ATV."

"What?" says Lissa, who's hovering over our table, wearing a full-body catsuit of black spandex, only a few square inches of her polluted flesh visible through eye and mouth holes.

"I wanna go," she says, sitting down on the other side of Red. "I hear the springs help with collagen reintegration."

"And improving the flow between throat and brow chakras," says Red, smiling idiotically.

"Really?" says Lissa. "The third-eye chakra? Cool."

A waitress appears. Lissa orders kway teow with fermented beef. The patio's getting crowded. The music's lame, all synthesized sitars and tabla drum machines. But Red bobs his head in time to the tunes. And Lissa slithers up next to him, gazes raptly at a pic on his iPhone.

"That's you?" she shrieks.

"That's me."

"A mullet. No way!"

"It's an alternative mullet, not a redneck mullet."

"Let's not mince hairs," quips Lissa.

"Ha! Ha! Ha!" cries Red.

And then Lissa flounces off to the bathroom, but not without tousling his hair.

"God." I take a sip of water. "She's dumb."

"She's not as stupid as she puts on," says Red.

"What does that mean?"

"You know, the whole ingenue act."

"She's got to be at least thirty-eight."

"Chronologically, maybe, but not biologically."

I want to drill Red for a more precise number—Does she look thirty-two? twenty-six? nineteen?—but I don't. I grab my purse, a practical satchel that slumps on the table beside Lissa's glittering clutch.

"Don't go," says Red. "I haven't swilled my allotment of vino yet."

"That's OK." I manufacture a yawn. "I'm sleepy."

I weave through the tables without looking back, skirt the rock garden, and stomp down the jungle trail. Deep in the forest, male kibi monkeys howl, adolescents looking for mates. The small nocturnal monkeys spend their days dozing in the hollows of trees, but at night they hunt for insects and baby frogs. They eat their weight in fruit, sip nectar from flowers, sing complex songs that throb with vitality and longing.

After a four-mile ATV jaunt, Red and I finally steep neck-deep in a steaming spring. Though Lissa invited herself along, I scheduled our jaunt for a Tuesday, well aware of her strenuous nanotech routine. For the first time in weeks, the itch has left me, and my body flexes, supple as a flame. The hot springs stink, of course, a predictable rotten-egg funk, as sulfur dioxide leaks into the air. But it's worth it. My skin's sucking up nature's beauty mineral, strengthening collagen bundles, improving cellular elasticity. Plus, mist-cloaked mountains swell around us. And though Red's facial blebs have started to ooze, he radiates boyish optimism.

"Look what I brought." He smiles, leaning out of the pool to dig through his rucksack. "Sparkling apple cider. Organic. Though I forgot glasses."

"That's OK. We can swig from the bottle."

"Exchange HSV-1 fluids?"

"And ecthymic bacteria."

"Ugh."

We sit in the mystical vapor, sipping cider and touching toes. The haze softens the hideousness of our faces. Our disembodied voices dart like birds in a cloud. We talk about Red's ex-wife, whose weakness for fey hipster boys is partially responsible for his sojourn at Mukti. I tell him about my money-obsessed ex-husband, who once updated his stock portfolio while I was in the throes of a miscarriage. Through the bathroom mirror of our hotel room in Bali, I could see him in the other room, smirking over his Blackberry. And then I heard him talking to his broker on the phone.

"I'm sorry," says Red.

"I'm over it."

I find his hand under the water. We sit floating in a state of semi-contentment. Then we start up with the cider again.

Exceeding our daily allotment of alcohol, we drink until the bottle is empty and the effervescence inside us matches that of the bubbly spring. A plane flies over. The sun infuses our mist shroud with a pearly glow. And then a man steps into the pool, emerging from the steam as from another dimension, clad in dingy cutoff shorts. By all appearances, he's not a patient. His skin has photoaged into a crinkled rind. He's got senile cataracts and wisps of long, gray hair. And when he cracks a smile, we see a wet flash of gums, like a split in a leathery desert fruit.

"I have company today," he says, his accent Californian with a hint of Caribbean patois. "I'm Winter." He extends a gnarled hand. I'm thinking he must be an ancient hippie who retired here before Mukti took off.

"You folks up from the spa, I reckon." He sinks down into the pool.

"How'd you guess?" says Red, and the old man chuckles.

"And you?" I say.

"I'm from around. Got a little cottage up over the way."

Winter tells us he keeps goats, sells cheese and yogurt to Mukti,

Julia Elliott

plus fruit from his orchard and assorted herbs. He asks us how the healing's going. Inquires about the new post office. Wonders what's up with the pirates who've been plaguing the Venezuelan coast.

"Pirates?" says Red.

According to the old man, pirates usually stick to freighters, but have recently drifted up to fleece Caribbean cruise ships.

"Thought I heard something about yachts getting hassled near Grenada," Winter says.

"This is the first we've heard about any pirates," I say, imagining eye-patched marauders, dark ships flying skull-and-crossbones flags.

"Probably just talk," says Winter.

Red checks his watch, says our soak has exceeded the recommended span by four and a half minutes. We say good-bye to Winter, speed off on our ATV.

Seventy-five percent humidity, and the boils on my inner thighs have fused and burst, trickling a yellow fluid. My neck pustules are starting to weep. Choice ecthemic sores have turned into ulcers. I spend my downtime pacing the tree house naked. I shift from chair to chair, daybed to hammock, listening to the demented birds. A plague of small green finches has invaded the island. They flit through the brush, squawk, and devour berries.

This morning I've neglected my therapies. Though I'm due for nanotech restructuring in thirty minutes, the thought of putting on clothes, even the softest of silk kimonos, makes my skin crawl. But I do it, even though I know the fabric will be soaked by the time I get to the Samsara Complex. I slip on a lilac kosode and dash down the jungle trail, gritting my teeth.

I pass a few Crusties. I pass a dead turtle, its belly peppered with black ants. I pass an island assistant, lugging her sea-grass basket of eco-friendly cleaning chemicals. Though she, like all the assistants, is a broad, plain-faced woman, the beauty of her complexion startles me. But then I remember that in a few weeks, my sores will scab over. I'll crawl from my shell, pink and glowing as the infant Buddha. I'll jet to the mainland and buy a fleet of stunning clothes, get my hair cut, meet Red for one last rendezvous before we head back to our respective cities. We'll revel in our sweet, young flesh—and then, well, we'll see.

*

Another evening in paradise and I pick at my grilled fig salad. The ocean is gorgeous, but what's the point? It might as well be a postcard, a television screen, a holographic stunt. Red's pissy too, grumbling over his lobster risotto. And don't get me started on Lissa.

Lissa won't shut up about the pirates. Keeps recirculating the same crap we've heard a hundred times: The pirates have attacked another Carnival cruiser; the pirates have sacked yachts as close as Martinique; the pirates have seized a cargo ship less than ten miles offshore from our very own island. Angered by the resale prospects of boutique med supplies, they've tossed the freight into the sea.

"I always thought pirates were the epitome of sexy," says Lissa, crinkling her carbuncular nose at Red.

"They won't seem so sexy if you run out of Vita-Viral Plus," says Red.

"Unless you think keloid scars are the height of chic," I add.

"But medical supplies are worthless to them," whines Lissa. "What would they gain from another attack?"

"They might attack out of spite," I say.

"Mukti keeps emergency provisions in a cryogenic vault," says Lissa, "in case of hurricanes and other potential disasters."

"Or so the pamphlet promises," says Red, gazing out at the ocean, where a mysterious light beam bounces across the water.

"You think they'd lie to us?" Lissa widens her enormous eyes and runs an index finger down Red's arm. She's a touchy person, I tell myself, who hugs people upon greeting and pinches shy waitresses on the ass.

"I wouldn't be surprised." Red smiles at her and turns back to the sea.

Both Red and I are in the latter stages of contraction when the pirates seize another cargo ship. Our flesh has crisped over with full-body scabbing. We're at that crucial point when collagen production stabilizes, when full-tissue repair and dermal remodeling kick into high gear. Of course, the powers that be at Mukti have not acknowledged the pirate incident. The powers that be have given no special security warnings. They've said nothing about waning provisions or shortages of essential meds. Though the therapists and medical staff carry on as usual, I detect a general state of skittishness—sweat stains in the armpits of their white smocks, sudden jerky movements, faintly perceptible frown lines on faces hitherto blank as eggs.

277

Julia Elliott

Rumors spread through the spa like airborne viruses. And one day, a day of high humidity and grumbling thunder, the kind of day when your heart is a lump of obsidian and you wonder why you bothered to get out of bed at all, it becomes common knowledge that the pirates have seized a freighter, that they're negotiating a ransom with Mukti, asking a colossal sum for the temperature-sensitive cargo.

Red and I are on the Lotus Veranda eating zucchini pavé with miso sauce, waiting for poached veal. The waitress slinks over, apologizes, tells us that the dish will be served without capers. Red and I exchange dark looks. We imagine jars of capers from Italy stacked in the belly of a cargo ship, the freighter afloat in some secret pirate cove. And deeper in the bowels of the boat, in a refrigerated vault, shelves full of biomedical supplies—time-sensitive blood products and cell cultures in high-tech packaging.

All around us, scabby patients whisper about the pirates, reaching a collective pitch that sounds like an insect swarm. Hunched in conspiratorial clusters, they flirt with scary possibilities: spoiled meds, botched stage-five healing, full-body keloid scarring, an appearance that's the polar opposite of that promised by *Regeneration at Mukti*. "Shedding your pupal casing," the pamphlet boasts, "you will emerge a shining creature, renewed in body and spirit, your cell turnover as rapid as a ten-year-old's. Skin taut, wrinkles banished, pores invisible, you will walk like a deva in a pink cloud of light."

I'm in the Samsara Complex for cellular restructuring. There's a problem with the nanobot serum. They keep rejecting vial after vial, or so I've gathered through several hissing exchanges between the biomed doc and her technicians. When Tech One finally shoots me up, he jabs the needle in sideways, apologizes, then stabs me again.

I stagger into the Bardo Room, where a half dozen Crusties mill among orchids, the floor-to-ceiling windows ablaze. Nobody speaks. The endless ocean glitters beyond, a blinding, queasy green. The light gives me a headache, an egg of throbbing nausea right behind my eyes. I collapse into a Barcelona chair. My skin tingles beneath its husk. I stare down at my hands, dark with congealed blood and completely alien to me. I wonder if I should have stayed as I was—blowing serious bank on miracle moisturizers, going to yoga five times a week, dabbling in the occasional collagen injection.

Of course, it's too late to turn back now. I must focus on positive

278

affirmation, as Guru Gobind Singh so smugly touts. I must not allow my mind to visualize a body mapped with pink, puffy scars. With such an exterior, you'd be forced to hunker deep in your body, like a naked mole rat in its burrow.

Red, fresh from bee-sting therapy, joins me under the shade of a jute umbrella, our eyes protected by wraparound sunglasses. It's too hot to eat, but we order smoked calamari salads and spring rolls with mango sauce. Red's incommunicative. I'm trying to read *Zen and the Art of Aging* on my iPhone, but the sun's too bright. We don't talk about the pirates. We don't talk about our impending Shedding. We don't talk about the chances of scarring, the jaunt to the mainland we've been planning. I tell Red about the monkey I spotted from my tree-house porch last night. I try to discuss the ecological sustainability of squidding. We shoo jhunkit birds from our table and decide to order a chilled Riesling.

More and more Crusties crowd onto the patio. Waitresses hustle back and forth. They no longer inform us when some ingredient is lacking. They simply place incomplete dishes before us with a downward flutter of the eyes. Certain therapies are no longer offered—sensory deprivation and beer baths, for example—but we strive to stay positive.

Although we keep noticing suspicious changes in medical procedures, we prevent cognitive distortions from sabotaging our self-talk. When a bad thought buzzes like a wasp into the sunny garden of our thoughts, we swat the fucker and thump its crushed corpse into the flower bed. And, most importantly, we spend thirty minutes a day visualizing our primary goal: successful mind-body rejuvenation and an unblemished exterior that radiates pure light.

Nevertheless, it's hard to sustain mental focus when your spring rolls lack almonds, when your wine's third-rate, when your dermis burns beneath its crust. It's hard to envision yourself floating in a bubble of celestial light when you look like you've been deep fried. I'm having trouble picturing the crystalline features of the deity. I can't help but notice that the sea smells of sewage, that our table is sticky, that our waitresses are contemptuous, smooth skinned, and pretty in their way, with decades of insolent youth to burn. When Lissa alights at our table in a translucent white kimono, my misery is complete.

But Red only nods at her, keeps staring out at the empty sea.

I'm studying his profile when I spot a dark figure lurching from a clump of pink hibiscus. Black skin, green shorts, ammo vest. The man lugs a Kalashnikov. He's yelling in Spanish. Other pirates emerge from the landscaping, waving guns and machetes. One of them screams fragments of English: *Surrender, you scab-covered dogs.* Lanky, with a dramatic cheek scar, he tells us to put our wallets on the table, along with all cell phones, iPods, Blackberries, handheld gaming devices, and jewels. Random pirates fire their guns into the air.

In one convulsive movement, patients start rifling pockets and purses, removing rings and bracelets, plunking valuables onto tables. Then we sit with hands behind our backs as the bandits have instructed. We don't flinch as they rip designer sunglasses from our faces. We squint with stoicism at the boiling sea while they fill their rucksacks with treasure. Shadows grow longer. The sun sinks. The jhunkit birds, emboldened by our immobility, descend upon the tables to peck at canapés.

When the pirates finally creep off into the jungle, crouched in postures of cartoonish stealth, the waitresses spring into action. They bustle about distributing bottled water. They assure us that security has been summoned. They fill our wineglasses, wipe bird shit from our tables, spirit away our dirty plates. The sky flushes pink. Lissa trembles like a Chihuahua until Red drapes a friendly arm over her back. He's just being courteous, I tell myself, as I wait for this contact to end.

A woman weeps quietly at the edge of the patio, then she blows her nose and orders shrimp dumplings in ginger broth.

According to the pamphlet, the final days before Shedding should be days of intense relaxation—no medical procedures, no exhilarating therapies, no excursions. Even extreme dining is discouraged. It's difficult to drift like a feathery dandelion seed when Mukti's security forces have crawled out of the woodwork into our sunny paradise. They've always been here, of course, lurking in the shadows, monitoring the island from subterranean surveillance rooms, but now they loiter openly in their khaki shorts, handguns only partially concealed by oversized tropical shirts.

Yesterday, while enjoying an aloe vera bath in the Bodhi Herb Garden, I heard a crude snicker. I gazed up through a tendril of sarsaparilla to glimpse the smirking face of a security guard. There he was, licking an ice-cream cone, his mustache dotted with pearls of milk. And now, as I float in the Neti Neti Lagoon, stuck in step two of the Instant Calming Sequence, I hear a security guard barking into her cell phone. I count to six and wait for her to finish her conversation. When I start over with a fresh round of uninterrupted breathing, her ringtone bleeps through the gentle thatch of birdsong. So I switch to Microcosmic Orbit Meditation, envisioning a snake of light slithering through my coccyx. Now the security guard is laughing like some kind of donkey. I open my eyes. Gaze up into palms and spot a tiny camera perched next to a cluster of fruits. Its lens jerks back and forth like the head of a nervous bird.

In addition to the dread of pirates charging through the bush, in addition to the distraction of security guards and fears of type-I scarring, we must also worry about the weather as the island's now on hurricane watch—or so the powers that be informed us this morning. The ocean breeze has become a biting, sandy wind. A weird metallic scent blows off the sea, and I get the feeling that the island's swathed in bad karma. Plus, a few Crusties, having shed their husks, have been jetted to the mainland without the Rapture Ceremony—a ritual designed to reassure remaining Crusties that their golden time will come, that they too will walk in flowing robes, their silky necks garlanded with narcissus.

Yesterday afternoon, instead of gathering on the beach to watch the smooth-skinned devas depart in the Ceremonial Boat, we crowded into the lobby of the small airport. Through a plate-glass window, we observed two devas dashing from flower-decked golf carts toward a commuter jet, their faces shrouded by scarves and sunglasses. Security guards swarmed, their tropical shirts easy to spot. And rumor has it that one of the devas, a famous movie star, was being whisked off to California where she'll resume her career as a romantic comedy queen—blonde icon of feminine joie de vivre, laughing in the sun.

Red, in the final throes of his remodeling phase, has a TSF of 99.6 percent. His exterior has the golden huskiness of a pork rind. And now, as he scans the endless ocean, his beautiful green eyes burn behind his scabby mask. He's barely touched his scrambled tofu. He takes long, dreamy slurps of mango smoothie. I know he'll be jetting off to the mainland soon. Once there, he won't be able to contact me by phone or e-mail, the Mukti contract dictates, so we've made arrangements, booking reservations at the Casa Bougainvillea.

I keep picturing that moment when we'll meet by the pool at sunset. I keep picturing Red reclined beside the waterfall featured on the hotel's brochure. First he'll look startled. Then he'll smile as his eyes run up and down my body. He'll bask in the vision of a female epidermis refortified with type III collagen and glowing like the moon. Though I haven't worn jewel tones for years, I'll highlight the infantile pallor of my skin with a scarlet sheath dress. I'll wear a choker of Burmese rubies. Dye my hair auburn, paint my nails crimson, wear lipstick the color of oxygenated blood.

After we revel in the softness of a ten-minute kiss, we'll drink Romanée Conti under the stars.

Yesterday I stood in the airport lobby, watching Red hop from a flower-decked golf cart and then scurry through strong wind to Mukti's commuter jet. Kaffiyeh-style headgear and huge sunglasses concealed his face. When he turned from the platform to wave, a shadow passed over him, and then he dipped into the jet with a sly smile. I have no idea how his Shedding went. I have no idea what his refurbished carnality looks like, though I've seen his Facebook pics, his high school yearbook photos, a few snapshots of the young Red rock climbing in Costa Rica.

Lissa too has been spirited away—nubile and golden, I fear. Though she was obscured by a chiffon Lotus robe, I have the sick suspicion that she's gone through her Shedding unscathed. That she looks gorgeous. That she'll stalk Red at the Casa Bougainvillea, appearing naked and luminous beneath his balcony in a courtyard crammed with flowering shrubs.

And now, as the few remaining Crusties huddle in the basement of the Skandha Center, awaiting the wrath of a category-four hurricane named Ophelia, Gobind Singh lectures us on the Deceptive Singularity of the Self.

"The Self you cling to," says Gobind Singh, "is an empty No Self, or Shunya, for the True Self does not differentiate between Self and Other, which is not the same, of course, as the No Self."

Gobind Singh sighs and takes a long glug of spring water, for we are the Stubborn Ones, unable to take pleasure in the Shedding of Others, greedy for our own transformation. According to Gobind Singh, the True Self must revel in the Beauty of the Devas, even if we ourselves do not attain True Radiance during this cycle, because the True Self makes no distinction between Self and Other.

According to Gobind Singh's philosophy, I should delight in the divine copulation of Red and Lissa, which is probably taking place right this second on one-thousand-thread-count sheets. I should yowl with joy at the thought of their shuddering, simultaneous orgasm. I should partake in the perkiness of Lissa's ass as she darts from the bed, turning to give Red a full-frontal display before disappearing into the humongous bathroom to pee. According to Gobind Singh, their ecstasy is my ecstasy.

Glowing with self-actualization, floating a few millimeters above the bamboo flooring, Gobind Singh weaves among us. We sit in full lotus, five sullen earthbound Crusties, slumped in our own hideousness. We fidget and pick at our flaking shells. The second the guru turns his back, we roll our eyes at each other.

And when the winds of Hurricane Ophelia pick up, shaking the building and howling fiercely enough to blot out the throbbing of electronic tablas, we can't control the fear that grips us. All we can think about is literally saving our skins. As the electricity flickers and the storm becomes a deluge, Gobind Singh tells us that all men, no matter how wretched, have a Buddha Embryo nestled inside them, gleaming and indestructible as a diamond.

I wake alone in the basement of the Skandha Center, calling out in the darkness for the others. I bang my shins against their empty cots. Upstairs in the dim hallway, I discover sloughed Casing, shreds of what looks like crinkled snakeskin littering the jute carpet. I pick my way toward the light. Hurricane Ophelia has shattered the floor-to-ceiling lobby windows, strewing the floor with shards of glass.

Out on the wrecked patio, windblown chairs have been smashed against the side of the building. And birdcalls whiffle through the air.

"Hello," I yell, but no one answers.

The Samsara Complex is empty. So is the Lotus Lounge; both buildings battered by the storm.

I jog down a jungle trail toward the Moksha Jasmine Grove. There, a natural spring trickles from the lips of a stone Buddha. Pink birds flit through the garden. The statue squats in a pool, surrounded by trellises of Arabian jasmine that have miraculously survived the hurricane. Raindrops sparkle on leaves. The garden is a locus of peace and light.

From the deepest kernel of my being, I crave water. My throat's parched. My skin burns. And I know that my time has come. I feel pregnant with the glowing fetus of my future self.

I shed my robe. I step into the blue pool. I sink neck-deep into the shallow water, mimicking the pyramid structure of the seated Buddha, face-to-face with his stone form. I drink from the spring until my thirst is quenched. And then I breathe through my nose, fold my hands into a Cosmic Mudra. Counting each inhalation, I become one with the water.

My body is like a pool's surface, its brilliance dulled only by a skin of algae.

My body is like a fiery planet, casting off interstellar dust.

Slowly, I rub myself, chanting the Bodhisattva vows:

I vow to liberate all beings, without number.
I vow to uproot all endless blind passions.
I vow to penetrate, beyond measure, the Dharma gates.
And the Great Way of Buddha, I vow to attain.

My Casing begins to pull away. I don't look at my uncovered flesh. I squeeze my eyelids shut to avoid temptation and keep on chanting, focused on the radiance pulsing within. In my mind's eye I see a glimmer of movement, a hazy form with human limbs, a new and improved woman emerging from the murk—glorious and unashamed.

On the count of three, I open my eyes.

Modern Adventures at Sea
Peter Gizzi

Say it then or
sing it out.
These voyages, waves.
The bluing of all I see.
Sing it with a harp
or tambourine.
With a drum and fiddle.
These notes and its staff,
the lines' tracery
blooming horizon.
These visions insisting.
Its laws. I embrace
accident. I accidentally
become a self in sun
in the middle of day.
Where are you? Cloud,
what shadow speaks
for me. I wonder.
Is there an end
to plastic. Is
yesterday the new
tomorrow. And
is that a future?
Do we get to
touch it and be

content, here
before we go.
That the signs
won't remain
untranslatable
in the end.
And that I may
learn this language.
That there could
be a language
say with a dolphin,
a dog, a cattle herder
and slaughterhouse,
a lumberyard
and big redwood.
That someone
could say to the crude.
Stay there. And
don't be drawn
into this tired game.
I wonder if the poem
gets tired. If
the song is worn
like sea glass.
I wonder if I am
up to this light.
These ideas of order
and all I feel
is disorder.
Walking down
the avenue

I see the sap
weeping on the cars.
See the wrack
about my feet.
Its state of decay.
To see that decay
as the best of all
worlds before me.
It's transformation
not transportation
that's needed. Here.
It's embracing
the soft matter
running my engine.
My guff. And fright.
This piss and
vinegar. And tears.
That I won't
commit violence
to myself in mind.
Or to others
with cruel words.
That I may break
this chain-link ism
of bigger than
smaller than why
feel bigger than
anyone feeling smaller.
Can I transform
this body
I steward. This

my bio mass.
My accident.
When lost at sea
I found a voice,
alive and cresting,
crashing, falling
and rising. To drift,
digress, to dream
of the voice. Its
grain. To feel
its vibrations. Pitch.
Its plural noises.
To be upheld
in it, to love.
Whose book lying
on that table?
And where does
the voice
come from?
What life
was attached
to its lift.
To its feint,
its gift of sight.
To understand
oneself. With-
out oneself.
How to live.
What to do.

Under the Boardwalk
Andrew Ervin

THE MAIN DRAG THROUGH WILDWOOD still has a bunch of retro doo-wop motels built in the fifties. The shoobies and historic commissions make a big deal out of the vintage boomerang-shaped roofs and zigzagging balconies, but the places are all kind of crappy inside. The sign for the Waikiki Tiki Motor Lodge is a huge Easter Island head with no body and a palm tree for hair—the blinking neon glimmers through the rain and makes the face smile and frown and smile and frown. There aren't any cars in the lot or lights on in the rooms.

My gut's still so full from dinner that I might get sick. Vince's housekeeper made some delicious soup with the fish I caught this morning, but I drank too much wine to drive all the way back to Philly and anyway I didn't want to crash at his house what with his bitchy wife calling every five minutes. *Where is he, Zach? Where is he, Zach?*

The furniture in the lobby looks like it could be in a museum if it wasn't so beat up. Some wiseass drew a peace sign on the sofa with a Magic Marker. The guy behind the counter looks like he's a hundred years old but his hair's dyed black. He hides his cigarette behind his back. His sideburns are gray. The moisture off his bottle of beer has soaked through his racing form.

I get a room for the night and pay with cash. Vince's wallet has a lot of money in it, and I know better than to use his credit cards. The police can trace that kind of thing these days with computers. They can see everything you buy, every movie you borrow from the library.

My room's stifling hot and smells like suntan lotion. There's no 1950s theme—it looks like any regular motel room, with the tiny bars of soap and the plastic wrap around the cups. I turn on the window air-conditioner unit. My sunburn's pretty bad and I'm so full I can hardly breathe right. There's a small TV and the bed still has one of the devices you could put a quarter in to make it vibrate. I'll get change at the arcades later and try it out.

When we were kids, my parents would take us—me and my big brothers—down to the boardwalk once a year. It was the highlight of every summer. They'd give us each five dollars to supplement however much we saved up and we would blow our allowances playing Skee-Ball long enough to win an electric-shock hand buzzer or a rubber chicken. One time I got lucky and won a Springsteen album that I still have even though I don't even own a record player. My wife, Jackie, tried to throw it away when we moved but I found it in the trash and rescued it. We would eat ice cream sandwiches and cotton candy and I'd buy enough saltwater taffy to last the rest of the summer, but my brothers would punch me until I gave them some and we'd eat it all in the dark of the backseat before falling asleep for the long ride home.

My shirt's wet from the rain and I didn't bring a change of clothes with me because Vince and I planned to drive back to Philly after our fishing trip. I caught so many fish. It was my lucky day. A shared balcony overlooks the pool and parking lot. I can't see the cooler through the SUV's tinted windows. The rain hits the surface of the neon-lit water and makes countless rings that grow outward into complex Venn diagrams like the sky is trying to make something logical out of an infinite number of things.

Vince took me out fishing for the day and I was supposed to ask him if Jackie—his sister—and I could borrow some money just, you know, until the economy improves and I can find a new job. Now his head and some parts of his arms and torso are in the cooler along with all the fish I caught.

His housekeeper used some of them to make that delicious soup. It tasted perfect on a night like this, what with all this rain.

She's probably called the police by now.

I go back downstairs to talk to the guy at the front desk. He's listening to the ball game on the radio. The air-conditioning feels good.

"What do you need?" he wants to know. He takes a drag from his cigarette, which he doesn't bother to hide anymore because I've already paid for my room. He looks at me like he knows exactly what I'm going to ask.

"Is there someplace around here to find some company?" I've heard people use that line in the movies.

He looks at me funny, like even though I'm his customer and he just works at a shitty little motel he's somehow better than me. It kind of bothers me.

"A hooker?" he asks. "Sure I can make a few calls. How much do you want to spend?"

I look around, hoping there's not anyone else in the lobby. I had only paid for sex once before in my entire life and that was at a bachelor party—Vince's, in fact—so that doesn't count. "I don't want someone old," I say.

"You can go anywhere from twenty bucks to two hundred, just don't come crying to me when you get them crabs."

Two hundred dollars is too much. I have lots of cash all the sudden, but I'm going to need it. I've been out of work a little while and my wife's getting impatient. "What will a hundred dollars get me?"

"Maybe an hour how am I supposed to know?"

He is *so* superior, with his bad dye job and gravelly, lung-cancerous voice.

"A hundred dollars but no more. And not someone old."

"A young girl, you got it. I'll make some calls."

I tip the guy ten dollars and he looks at me like I've insulted him.

Back upstairs, the air conditioner's not functioning right. I hide the rest of Vince's money under the mattress and lie down to watch the game. The Phillies are in a rain delay so they're showing old footage from when I was a kid. Pete Rose stretches a single into a triple and slides headfirst. I switch it off when someone taps at the door.

The prostitute's Asian. She looks like she's maybe sixteen, but has put on a shitload of makeup to try to appear older. She's wearing a shiny yellow raincoat. I'm kind of nervous, I guess. It's weird. I wasn't expecting an Asian. It's OK—I'm not racist or anything, it's just not what I was expecting. If I had to guess, I'd say she's probably Vietnamese. After the oil spill in the Gulf of Mexico a lot of the undocumented fishermen down there came to the Jersey Shore. More arrive every month.

I sit on the edge of the bed and she looks at me funny like I was supposed to take her coat, but it's not like there's anyplace to hang it up.

"I'm Zach," I say. "Do you speak English?"

"My name is Debra," she says. "And I probably speak better English than you, asshole. Let's get this shit over with. It's two hundred dollars for the first hour and a hundred more for every hour thereafter."

She sounds like any American kid, no accent at all.

"Two hundred? The guy downstairs said one hundred."

"He was ill informed," she says. She unbuttons her coat, which drips onto the worn carpet. She looks at her watch and in doing so holds in her upper arms to squeeze her breasts together. The slit of her raincoat billows open enough to reveal a single ivory stocking that runs halfway up her thigh. A tiny purse, too small to carry anything significant, dangles at her side. Her eyelids are done up bright blue.

I need to get more money from my hiding spot. "*Everyone* hides their money under the mattress," she says, and puts the bills in her purse. "At least you left your wedding ring on."

It didn't occur to me to take it off.

"Get undressed. The clock is ticking and you still need to take a shower."

"A shower?"

"Yes, it's the pipe that comes out of that wall in the bathroom. You stand under it. Get going. Or don't—it's your money. Actually it's my money now, but it's your hour. Should you so choose you certainly *could* spend it standing here like a dumb ass, or you could get a quick shower and then we'll have sex. It makes very little difference to me."

I get in the shower.

When I come back out she's completely naked and watching a nature program on TV. "Let's see if I can make you a little less uncomfortable," she says, but I don't get the feeling that she really cares if I'm comfortable or not. She kneels in front of me and I close my eyes. I think of many different things while she's giving me head.

Jackie sitting on the sofa at home waiting for me.

The sound of Vince's wife on the phone: *Where the hell is he, Zachary?*

Danielle back in human resources—the bitch who got me fired.

The colorful little bathing suits in Vince's twins' drawers.

A cackle of hyenas on the television is finishing off the bloody, stringy remains of an antelope.

"Just a sec," I say and stop her. "I need you to do something."

Debra looks up at me. "Anything within reason," she says.

"I need you to clean the makeup off your face."

"My makeup?"

"Yeah, your lipstick. The stuff on your eyes." I put my thumb on her lips and she flinches when I smear the red mess onto her cheek. "I want to see what you really look like."

"It's your hour," she says. She stands and goes into the bathroom. I put my shorts and wet shirt back on.

When she comes back out her skin is clean and pristine brown. She's gorgeous. Her eyes are clear and bright, but she doesn't look any younger without the makeup after all. "Listen, let's just call it a day," I say even though I paid for another forty-five minutes. I hand her more money from Vince's wallet. She looks at the twenty-dollar bill like it's something profane and capable of soiling her and her dignity.

"What do you want me to do?"

"Nothing. Just take it. You can leave."

"We're done?"

"Yeah, we're done. Wait . . . no," I say. I'm staring at her breasts—
I can't help it. "I have another idea. How much time do I have left?"

She looks at her watch again. "Forty-three minutes."

"That will be enough. Get your coat on."

"Where are we going?"

"To the boardwalk."

"Another fan of the Drifters?"

"Another what?"

"Everyone wants to get laid under the boardwalk. 'Down by the
sea-*ee*-eeea.'"

"No, that's not it. I don't want to get laid at all."

"Perhaps hiring a sex worker wasn't your wisest course of action."

"I want to play Skee-Ball."

"Skee-Ball?"

"Right, it's this game where you roll a ball up a ramp and try to—"

"I know what it is. I was born here, asshole. I'm as American as
you are," she says. "And I'll admit that playing Skee-Ball sounds a
whole lot better than sucking your dick."

She's already putting on her raincoat.

We stop in the parking lot so I can make sure the SUV is locked. I
don't need anyone snooping around. I have enough fish in there to
feed me and Jackie for months. If I can get that soup recipe I'll bring
a pint over for Lezzie and the twins. She is *such* a bitch, but the kids
really are adorable.

The motel's just a block from the boardwalk. It's getting late and
this rain has kept a lot of people indoors so there're not many people
in the arcades, and the candy shops are mostly empty. One place is
popping popcorn, another selling fudge by the pound. It all smells so
good, like when I was a kid.

The strange thing about the boardwalk at night is the big empty
blackness where the beach is. There're no streetlights down there
obviously so the boardwalk looks like the edge of the entire world,
like jumping over the side of it would send you plummeting a million miles down to the bottom of the universe. We can't even hear
the waves above the programmed noise of the pinball machines.

I take Debra's hand and she doesn't argue. People probably think
she's my adopted daughter. "How old are you anyway?" I ask.

"That's the only personal question you get. I'm twenty-four."

293

I know she's lying, and I don't appreciate it. "You look like you're sixteen."

"Listen, people are always saying that kind of shit to Asian women." She lets go of my hand. "I'll say this once: We are *not* some kind of docile and submissive dolls who exist merely for your pleasure. If anything, I'm better educated than you are and just from looking at you I know that I make more money, so don't go giving me any more of that racist bullshit. Misogynistic losers like you are paying for my fucking doctorate. This is just a summer job—some people work in banks or wait tables. You get it?"

"What are you studying?"

"No more personal questions."

"How about your name—is it really Debra?"

The way she says "No" makes me want to stop asking. Fortunately, we arrive at an arcade. In the front, right on the boardwalk, they have those machines with hundreds of nickels piled on top of each other and arms that come out and try to push them down to the tray where you can collect them. The idea is that if you put one more nickel in, you can be the person who finally gets it in the right spot to trigger the chain reaction that spills a pile of money out, but it never works no matter how many nickels you keep putting. That person is never you.

When you sit down and think about it, the arcade games there in Wildwood—even Skee-Ball—aren't all that different from the slot machines and poker tables up the Garden State Parkway in Atlantic City. It's all gambling, however soft and plush some of the prizes might be.

"How much time do I have left?"

"Thirty-two minutes."

I get a bunch of change and give five dollars' worth to Debra before I realize that the Skee-Ball machines take bills nowadays. It used to be just dimes and quarters. We each get ten balls and I roll one into the thirty-point ring on my first try. Tickets click *chhck chhck chhck* out of the machine. Then Debra goes and her ball flies straight into the gutter. No points. "Fuck!" she says. I go again and hit a forty. Another strip of tickets snakes out. I'm doing great, better than I ever did as a kid. It's awesome. The disco music is even louder than the pinball machines and I'm hitting thirties and forties and even the occasional fifty. The balls keep finding the small rings. It's unreal. The tickets coil at my feet. They can't jump out of the machine fast enough. It's like all my good luck during the fishing trip earlier has continued. I haven't had so much fun in years. Playing Skee-Ball again, and with a beautiful girl no less. It's the greatest feeling in the world.

Debra gets frustrated, though. She keeps rolling the balls into the gutters and doesn't win any tickets. "Fuck you, you fucking fuck!" she yells and the man working behind the counter comes over and tells her to keep it down because there's kids around. He has one of those old coin dispensers on his belt. He stops what he's doing to watch me play and even with the pressure I keep hitting thirties and forties. The Skee-Ball machine is singing to me now. The whole arcade is. I'm on fire. No one's seen anything like it.

"I'm going to win you a prize," I tell Debra. "What do you want?"

"I want the giant squirrel," she says.

Above the counter they have a row of stuffed animals as tall as she is. One of them looks kind of like a squirrel but it just as easily could be a gopher or a beaver. It would take a kid all summer and a couple hundred dollars to win enough tickets for it. It's probably been there for years.

She gets ten more balls but it's like she's not even trying. A couple tickets trickle out. When all her balls are gone again she looks at her watch. "Do you want to keep playing for another hour?" she asks.

"How much will it cost me?"

I assumed she'd be willing to hang out for another hour for free because we're having fun playing Skee-Ball instead of having sex under the boardwalk in the rain.

"What do you mean how much?" she wants to know. "We talked about this. A hundred dollars. I'm a starving grad student."

"I don't have that much money," I say.

"Yes you do," she says. "I saw it in your wallet."

She's right—I do have it. It's just that I have other things to spend it on. Jackie would kill me if I didn't come home with some money. I don't know why she didn't ask her brother for it herself, why I had to do it.

"Do you like fish?" I ask.

"Fish?"

"Yeah—I caught a bunch of fish today. All kinds. Flounder, grouper, some I've never seen before. Big ones too. You can have some if you want, but you'll want to get them on ice pretty quick."

The look she gives me—it's like she feels sorry for me. But she's the one out in the rain in a miniskirt, her high heels getting stuck between the boards. She takes a step backward.

"I think I'll pass, but thanks anyway," Debra says. "I hope it was good for you. Uh, bye!"

She hurries back out to the boardwalk without even taking the few tickets she won. I don't feel like playing anymore either. Even with how good I did, combined we still only won enough tickets to buy the junkiest toys in the case. I choose a green plastic lei and put it on but it's already unraveling.

Misogynistic loser? That was what she called me.

It's still raining and I don't have any dry clothes so I buy a novelty T-shirt. The only size XXL they have on sale says JESUS IS MY HOMEBOY. Jackie will think it's funny too. I stop for an ice cream and eat it on the way back to my room.

Two police cars have parked in the lot of the Waikiki Tiki. The red and blue lights combine with the neon of the Easter Island head. It looks cool. One officer's walking into the lobby while three others shine their lights in the windows of Vince's SUV. I still have a half-full cooler in the back. I don't want to get stuck talking to them, though, answering a ton of questions, so I turn around and head back to the boardwalk to play some more Skee-Ball. I have enough of Vince's money left to win that squirrel.

On Walks: Rousseau

Cole Swensen

1.

One morning while walking   while the earth in its passing   passing a morning   that fell down and died
It was not without irony that Rousseau met his death on a quiet path   a breeze   gathering up all men

Unknown in their hope   and would float   down honor down and   visiting his friend René Louis de
Girardin at Ermenonville   simply walked out   to and through a crystal wood   had carved his name

Into, which is time.   Rousseau went out walking, which is to say, out thinking   the mechanical relation
Between the body   which is always oddly falling   and the walker, who insists on its falling horizontally

So that the horizon becomes a streak that resembles the great migrations, silhouetted   Rousseau cut
Out of black paper   and thus endangered   all the great walks   have stumbled on a seed, they refused

Water from the hands outstretched   (remember how he fell sharp on rock)   and the horizon reeled
Rousseau found in his walking, only mind   and walked it a chasm, which should not   frighten, a gulf

That then you spoke.   He didn't say much, preferred to write: On a single morning I lost count

2.

Ruisselet is how a given water walks   and in its talking star, demands   Rousseau was an *exilé*, found
A crossroads at which the entire expanse of France looked like all of France.   We say: gave and small

Things fall   to their knees.   So many pilgrimages end   with a thousand knees   broken into
The smallest parts imaginable.   Rousseau refused to imagine a reason at the core of which   no awe

Would unravel   which is the nature of and mission flaming   that every step you take is thieving
The riven earth.   Rousseau was raised in a largely agrarian economy, and yet his father was a clock

Maker, which left a little tick   counting as he spoke   and if you walk it out, will the hour cleave and
Of what are now we rid?   "I can only think when walking"   said R, softly counting, who counted on his

Hands rather than his fingers   opening the letter, the first division   really an incision cut adrift. I once
Walked all night through a public park.   There is no dark.   Remembered and so its ringing stalks the

Shred   or the fade   or the leaves underfoot when you get lost or when you lose   Rousseau in the trees

298

3.

For Rousseau walking   was an only thing   a solitary breech of a rift of scree   one walked one
By one. It began   at a gate   and the gate swung shut   Rousseau began walking at the age of 15

If a single thing   spins fast enough   will it become   or make the trees run in the rain, flagrant
Shut. If nothing remains but what alone   the map still or the parchment on which it's drawn still

A living thing standing in the sun.   First Walk: first line: *that so alone am I who loved*   so a walking
Is a toward   I saw myself in shards. Rousseau was always hoping he'd run into himself and yet

The drift that strikes to multiple, the gift struck in the coin of eye, you can't turn back he could not
Turn and so the music stayed in his ears.   In the hands of friends, we find the trees, just the right

Trees, but in the trees, we find only trees until they break   out and cage, wrung, it rings until the
Gate, he was returning late, and the gates of Geneva swung shut and in them caught.   There's not

Much to leave when you're only 15   is everything   a matter of the adamant   and the indelible

Cole Swensen

4.

Any walk   Rousseau once said   is endless where   the wilderness might seem to have a name
Undone from within, unanswered flaw, written out by hand.   The entire text of what is now

Known as *The Reveries of a Solitary Walker* was found scrawled   and the hand goes on, has its own
Hundreds of miles to go. The slope—the loping slant—distance times the rhythm inherent in the word

Whose lighter step is heard outside on the gravel   to have a body only audible, more easily lost,
You were tracing a path with a #4 pencil that craved a river and along it an overhanging oak

Every leaf is a mirror as it falls   and then falls on   and mirrors what storm   as the storm won some
Other word was used for what came   from habit to obsession to compulsion   in long graceful lines

The long line of gray trees angled at a distant distance is the hill   and over the hill the gray bare
Hands all over the sky, which is a lighter gray going on, an army retreating lost in thought, the whole

Race lost and calm   in a ring on the crown of a hill   where the circle in which we are walking rings

5.

If life would be harder if you just stood still   is nonetheless a visceral relationship between
the pace at which you walk and that at which you write as if, and is, a memory that percolates

through bone, which writes its own version   piles of stones along the roadside, oddly specific
for an accident, the spine of the ridge equally incident in its perfect echo of the line of the road

itself   the fact of walking alone   the few hours each day he could free for that occupation
wholly saved the broken from the breaking *I am crushed a man and on this dust*   his last yes

was a detailed list of the species of plants he saw along his way   problematize the distance that
evaporates between walking and reverie to become reactivated in the imperative to pace off

sizable sections of France   and though in his later years, his pallet was restricted, it intricated,
and displacement tends   a gentleman   who confused his face with something seen or almost

seen in a forest   yet only from a corner   and barely with the sun always beside you always walking.

301

Notes Toward the Recovery of Desiderata
John Madera

THIS BEING SOMETHING about closed doors and opening windows; or, this being an omnibus of memory's debris, history's talus, and desire's residuum; or, this being a brooding topography of perception and a cross-section of time's strata; or, since there is always a forgetting in the remembering, this could be a story about Usnavy, pronounced oos-nā-vē, a mash-up made from the name of an armed force, the name itself forced, rather than bestowed, on a character, that is, a woman, the woman who would, in this story, think these things, think that this name was forced on her by her rum-buzzed mother, who would likely have come up with the idea for the name while watching U.S. destroyers and frigates, the name emblazoning their seemingly adamantine sides, like a braggart's body art, each downed mojito making the idea not only not nonsense but beautiful, while also making each massive sun-bleached machine floating past La Habana look less like the predator it was, look less like a giant hammerhead shark craving flesh and blood, as it lurched, hungry for fuel, toward the oilers and stores ships docked at the base at Guantánamo Bay; the possible story continuing with a reverie, in which the character, Usnavy, considers herself almost blessed—if she could ever believe in such things again—that her name wasn't a more ill-considered one, considering the lore, well, more like the gossipy flotsam—or was it more akin to jetsam: deliberately discarded debris?—that floated around about mothers and fathers choosing their children's names from product packaging, from multinational companies' logos, calling their little tykes "Cocacola"; or, instead, taking common names and spelling them backward, to bizarre effect, ending up with names like "Adnama" and "Leugim," from Amanda and Miguel, respectively; Adnama, though, sounding like "Adamah," the feminine derivation of the Hebrew name for Adam, meaning ruddy earth; or the story—surely a joke!—she'd heard at the hospital where she worked as a midwife, where a woman was overheard saying she wanted to name her daughter "Placenta" because she'd "heard the nurses use the word and thought it sounded pretty"; the possible character's reverie invariably centering on her wish that her own mother had named her Elizabeth or Elisabeth, with its innumerable variations, like Alžbeta, a Czechoslovakian variant; Erzsébet, the Hungarian version; or Eilís from Irish, or the Italian Elisabetta, or the Polish Elzbieta, or the Portuguese and Russian variant: Elizabeta, or the Romanian Elisabeta, or the Scandinavian Elisabet; or one of Elizabeth's countless plain and grainy nicknames, like Bess, Bessie, Bessy, Beth, Betsy, Betty, Elsie, Liz, Lizzie, Libby, Lisa, and Liza; or the countless diminutives coming from the countless ethnic variations of the name.

This woman, Usnavy, could be portrayed disliking her name, by creasing her lips into a thin slit, blanching her face, as if it were a gesso-primed canvas, as she thought of her drunk mother hearing some kind of music in the name; Usnavy, while growing up in La Habana, wishing her name was Ceiba instead, in tribute, perhaps, to the massive ceiba tree, the so-called Arbol de la Paz, planted outside Santiago de Cuba, a place she had often visited as a schoolgirl; the name Ceiba retroactively revealing itself to be more reflective of who she was, or rather, who she would end up becoming, that is, someone uprooted and then transplanted; Usnavy, later, as an exile, however, wishing her name was Elizabeth, to her mind a royal name evoking crowns and gowns and crenellated castles; a name with a provenance, a resonance of romance, adventure, and legends; of swordplay, empire, and intrigue; a name, perhaps, that would have girded her for what would become the defining ruptures of her life.

So this story could have a series of set pieces in which the character, now having been christened—yes, the religious overtones here serve the interest of the story—Elizabeth, or one of its innumerable variations, embarks on any number of quests, is faced with challenges, or horrors, like the afternoon she had found an old man, ashen faced and shivering (though you could bake in the clammy prewar corridor), a crumpled marionette, his legs scissored open, framed by a door several doors down from her own, and wondered how long he'd been there, and whether any of the neighbors, most of whom were widowers or retirees, old and lonely souls, must have heard this man's cries, cries like asphalt-skidding tires, when just moments before coming out of the elevator she'd been thinking about defaulted loans and grilled asparagus, and the damn cat; but after Elizabeth plopped her groceries on the floor—paper bags crackling like tinder—all that disappeared, and so she ran to him, lowered her head to hear him drily mouth, "There . . . there . . . ," thumbing into the apartment, and she saying to him, "Everything's going to be all right," but feeling that some jeweled thing had shattered, that some dark cloud had metastasized, that some scab had been ripped open; and, wobbly kneed, she passed through the foyer, scanned the dark one-bedroom apartment, sniffed away the metallic stink of old age, and saw the taped-down curtains and the single light coming from the end of a small hallway; and, after turning the corner, and almost tripping over an overturned chair, she saw it, what had spooked the old man, made him collapse, made him dumb: the vegetabular face, the wanton tongue, the slurry eyes: the wrathful wreath; and, feeling as if all the air inside her had been vacuumed out, Elizabeth eked out some words: "Who . . . gave . . . you . . . the . . . right?" and, after vomiting, said, "Damn it! Just had to be the hero."

The set piece featuring, let's call her Elzbieta could follow, where she would first be described as rising from bed thinking, *To desire is to kill.* She would obsess over the phrase, perhaps because she already missed the big city. Her father, a man who had seen "more than more than enough"—as he would say—wanted some kind of change. There was talk of trees in the north. And where there were trees, there was water. Nothing overflows like a rumor. She knew that. So did he. *But what of desire?* she wondered. *Longing for something it lives, but when you get it, it dies? Did death persist behind every glance? Was want another handicap?* She never spoke her thoughts, but her silence worried her father anyway. Here, the siroccos moved the turbines, powered the filters. Who knew what kind of water there was up north? whether it even rained? It was dry here, but the rooftop gutters dropped enough rainwater into their barrels, and the filters removed the pollutants and bacteria and algae: the toxic stuff each raindrop caught from the air. Raindrops aren't tear shaped, Elzbieta thought, but this didn't stop her from crying every time the sky broke. The stores from the last rainfall would get them as far as the next week. It was raining less and less. Everything was drying up. But what about the militias? "What do we have to lose?" her father would ask. "All of our things, for starters," she'd say. "Our stores, power cells, the cart, our clothes even." And that was the best that could happen. The worst was conscription, a kind of slavery—he, in spite of his age, a frontline grunt; she, a scullery maid—if they were lucky. Sometimes dreams of old days, of the southland, of Asheville, would flare up in her mind. Everything was ash now. All she had from her largely unremembered nightmares was that infernal phrase. *Desire equals death?* Day after day her father pestered her. They were starving. They had to leave. One morning, waking from a restless sleep, all traces of her nightmare washed away, she rose from bed to awaken her father. Seeing his leathery skin, his sunken eyeholes, she finally understood the troubling refrain. *Desire was a dismal chasm, an end without release, without clarity*, she thought, *a rumored whim of the screaming damned.*

The story could go on to describe how that woman, Elizabeth, sipped from a cup of oolong, and turned on the television, the same tube-based black-and-white contraption that she had once, as a child, looked behind to find out where all the loony cartoons with all their vrooms and kabooms had come from; the screen flashing news about a fire, a fire that took eighty-seven lives in West Farms, a neighborhood in the northeast corner of the South Bronx. The irony of the fire being the cause of a flood of thoughts would not be lost on her, nor would the irony of the name of where the fire had taken place, that is, "Happy Land," and what the fire had done. And the simultaneity, the convergence of tragedy and happiness, two things normally incongruous, was something with which she had some familiarity.

Like her, the story could go on to reveal, Julio González, the man responsible for the fire, was one of the Marielitos, one of the many boat-lift refugees who had departed from Cuba's Mariel Harbor for the United States between the late spring and late fall of 1980. And Elizabeth, having watched the news broadcast images of the inferno (a neighborhood resident's grainy video footage capturing the smoke billowing out from the club, inhuman cries somehow still audible beneath the sirens screaming possible salvation; cold appraisals from fire department officials underscoring the footage), could ask herself how González could live with himself, for what would probably be many years, in prison, with the knowledge of having killed all those people, of having made a charnel house of a social club, the guilt of it; and then answering to herself that he wouldn't have to live with himself, that is, with the self that had committed the atrocity, for all those years, because whatever being he happened to have or happened to be, just like whatever being anyone else happened to have or happened to be, was always a legion of selves, much like that bedraggled man, a walking house of demons, demons who were cast out by Jesus, a Jesus she had once come to love, a Jesus she had, by the time of the fire, long since abandoned; an army of I and me and mine, the presence of which, despite the many people who were calling González a monster now, proved that he was a person, and as a person he didn't have anything remotely resembling a fixed identity, and so he would not have to live with the self that had killed eighty-seven people, otherwise life would truly be unlivable, or at least overburdened, the guilt, perhaps, choking him, much like his victims (mainly Hondurans celebrating Punta Carnivale), who had found themselves clutching their clothes to their mouths, closing their eyes to keep out the smoke, their eyes, in the end, drying up, their mouths and throats and chests filling up with smoke, choking them.

Perhaps intangible, Elizabeth could be a heavy, and earthy, no, earthbound woman, now twenty or twenty-one, with hair severely drawn back into a braid, which would whip across her back as she walked, or rather, pounced, although now it merely ticktocked behind her as she paced her apartment. She could be shown enjoying the idea of a fire sparking a flood of memories (the mixed metaphor, to her mind, a perfect cocktail), first with a description of how her eyes, which usually had a kind of smudged quality to them, now brightened, like lamplights popping on in a dark park, as she was transported back ten years to that winter and early spring in Cuba, to those few weeks before she and her mother left La Habana, a city decayed after decades of neglect, yet a city still filled with marvels, like its grand streets and plazas and boulevards, and especially La Habana Vieja, with its columned walkways and intimate gateways, and its colonial architecture, where one's eyes would land on crumbling walls covered with jaundiced floral and geometric mosaics; on the myriad balconies with lacy wrought-iron balustrades, where you could sometimes see plump women, with all their festoonery, fluttering fans in synchrony with their own nervous palpitations, as they looked on other balconies where sometimes people—surely Babalawos, the Santería priests "who know the secrets," they would think—kept chickens; a city in a city where one's eyes would land on begrimed baroque facades and red terra-cotta-tiled roofs; on the buildings' windows, their countless windows, shuttered and otherwise; on the filtered light splashed onto walls and floors, colliding colors forming kaleidoscopes; each window a portal of possibility—in morning, ornate orifices of light, in evening, apertures for eavesdropping; on the vibrant life of its steamy streets, where Usnavy or Ceiba too, still wearing her uniform, would play after school, passing the boys playing checkers on pavement corners, or the men shuffling dominoes, the familiar click-clack of the tiles on the table, the blue smoke from the men's cigars fermenting the air; a city she had not returned to in the ten years since she had left; a city that had since fallen into myth, into dream.

And it was something like a dream when her mother had told her

306

that they were leaving for the United States of America, an unwieldy name she would soon practice saying over and over again; an unreal place, known to her, as it was known to anyone she knew, from whatever she had heard from whatever someone else had said about whatever he or she had heard, a place that a former peanut farmer— she would later learn—called "a country of refugees," offering "an open heart and open arms to refugees seeking freedom from communist domination." But what did she, an eleven-year-old schoolgirl, know about politics? Leaving La Habana would be an adventure, the adventure promised in the fairy tales her grandmother would recite at night, Usnavy or Ceiba kneading the wrinkly fat on the old woman's arms.

The story could go on to describe how a few days after her mother told her the news, they left for Mariel, an industrial town west of La Habana, Usnavy or Ceiba having packed inside her tiny suitcase the few items of clothing she had, including her school uniform: her starched white shirt and pleated skirt, and a few dresses—what people who were used to dramatic changes in seasons called sundresses; nothing, in other words, that would be suitable for the blunt and blustery, wintry blitzkriegs she would soon experience. She also packed a wood turtle her uncle had carved for her, a dog-eared copy of *Veinte poemas de amor y una canción desesperada*, and a doll, a frayed doll she might have long outgrown, but one that had, despite its mouth having been rubbed away, seemingly demanded to be brought along.

Mariel, the city from which she and her mother would take a boat to the USA, was a dank and gray concretion of factories and warehouses—it boasted Cuba's largest cement works—and its power station promised that the lights and electricity were at least less likely to go out. The camp they lived in before they were finally allowed to depart was a terrible place, terrible for even a moment, not to mention the three days they ended up staying; a filthy place without restrooms or showers, where they were daily given a boxed ration of rice and beans to eat, where they drank water coming out of a rusty spigot, where they were largely confined to a square of hardpan under a large canvas tarp you could hardly call a tent, the malodorous air of flesh and mold, the stink of piss and shit and fish wafting everywhere. The camp was crammed with people, their dreams hovering about them like ghostly presences. There were the two old men, blotto but steady, playing chess, dreaming of Capablanca, one of them usually sacrificing a rook to get the initiative, his expression somewhere between Buddha bliss and cardsharp cool. There was the boisterous bouquet of women fanning themselves as if fearing that their flower-print dresses would wilt otherwise. A fastidious family, Jehovah's Witnesses, daily spread the word about invisible rulers, end times, and the battle of Armageddon, unfazed by the ever-present knot of boors, their bluster and ballyhoo. A woman, whose sooty eyes bore holes into anyone who happened to glance at her, would sit facing the sound of the sea, sliding her palms together as if she were a little girl planning mischief, sometimes simply pressing them together as if contained within them was some boundless force. Twin girls, their bangs falling over their unibrows like a peplum of moss, played hopscotch—the chalky grid resembling Paul Klee's evanescent markings—using a pebble for their marker. There was a wind-swollen goat there too, its weary bleats a string of noes. And there was the loon, a hunched-over giant, chasing after a boy with a kite, drool oozing down his goony chin, his loud laughter, the unbridled laughter of a toddler: the sound of joy.

And the story could go on to describe how, after several days living at the camp, Usnavy or Ceiba's mother hardly spoke to anyone at all, and how she couldn't understand why, since her mother was always loud, would always say whatever came to mind, whenever it came to mind (well, at least when she was soused), a finger snap punctuating whatever she had said. Sure, her mother had hardly shown much interest in her as a child, but she had always been funny, a clown of sorts, and would only become pensive when sober or angry when drunk, whenever Usnavy or Ceiba asked where her father was, who her father was, her mother explaining, in turn, yet again, that her father Leugim had been a soldier for the revolution, that he had died serving his country. It would be years before Elizabeth would learn that her mother had met a man, a clarinetist from America, whose name she didn't remember, in a nightclub, slept with him, and that she had found out about her pregnancy before it was too late to abort, that she had had two abortions before that, that she had never liked children, and had never thought she would ever be a mother. And it would be years before she would learn from Alegría, her mother's close friend, who had arrived in the USA several years before they did, that when the nurse had brought Usnavy, to be breastfed by her mother, her mother didn't even want to see her, that she had fallen into the sadness Ceiba or Elizabeth would later, as a midwife, learn to identify as postpartum depression. Not knowing that her mother had always been depressed, had suffered from an undiagnosed dysthymia—fatigue and ill-temper being her default states, unless she was drinking—Usnavy or Ceiba could hardly expect that her mother would slowly slide into a hole as large as the Sacred Cenote, which Ceiba or Elizabeth would one day visit in Chichén-Itzá, but without the pleasure of its luxurious azure, a deep sadness that would, in the camp, force the daughter to mother the mother, that this would be the second rupture in her life.

Day after day, as they waited for the call to embark, Usnavy or Ceiba's mother, cocooned in her own private darkness, fell deeper into sadness, where she not only didn't speak, but hardly moved, the meals her daughter brought to her lying cold and uneaten on the crate beside her cot. Usnavy or Ceiba sometimes spoon-fed her mother, beginning every meal with asking why her mother wasn't eating, why she wasn't talking, why she wasn't moving, her questions and pleas segueing into a recounting of her own day: what she had seen and heard and felt, until she emptied herself out, finally knitting her fingers within her mother's, her mother staring out, her marbled eyes empty of everything, her face bereft of all motion and emotion. Her mother would, however, turn her head to look at her, with some real recognition of who she was, whenever Usnavy or Ceiba mentioned that they would soon see Alegría, her childhood friend, and their American sponsor, who would meet them in the States and bring them to live with her in New York City, where she would quickly help her mother to adjust, to find work, to start her life all over again.

And the story could go on to describe the night before Usnavy or Ceiba and her mother would finally leave the island, how everything would be still, the sky eggplant purple, a black dominion flecked with bits of mirror, with a moody moon: an engorged lemon, luminously looming, a kind of insinuating movement in the air all around, where one second she was standing, an alabaster statue in the stillness, gazing blankly at the sky, toward the sea, the sea that would take her away from her home, to another place, a place full of promise, and the next second she was squirming out of an invisible man's grasp from behind her, her screams muffled by his hand—I'm stronger than you, the flat, no, the concavity of his palm seemed to say—the thick pincerlike fingers of his other hand yanking up her blotched cotton smock of a dress, tugging down her panties, her moppet body struggling, legs flopping about like a puppet, heart punching her chest as if it were an animal desperately trying to shatter her rib cage, tears rivering, the pain of him worming inside of her, the writhing shadow they cast an infernal thing, a stain on the wall, the thrusts ending in seconds, too, she feeling like she did the day she had, alone in a pool, not knowing how to swim, floated on her back into the deep end, and then, suddenly, fear capsized her, and she was sinking, her arms and legs quickly windmilling, her joggled body almost comically spasmodic, until her hands gripped a side of the pool; and how she'd sobbed then as she was sobbing now, mutely as if her mouth was still covered, tears falling in tandem with the blood runneling down her legs, those same legs buckling at the knees, forcing her down to the muddied floor.

The next morning, before the rooster shook everyone else awake, her body, somehow not her body, a punctured hole, she thought, was a body transformed through its very violation into something unknown, Usnavy or Ceiba still knowing that this was yet another rupture in what would be a life full of ruptures, a rupture of the body, yes, but also of the mind, enabling her to think of her body as a container of selves, where her mind could choose to look at whatever she saw and felt and touched and tasted and smelled as something that always needed to be mediated with whatever she had experienced beforehand and whatever could possibly occur later, each experience then divided among further selves, selves contained in her body, like files in a cabinet, a mind that could still return to the moment before the first rupture, that is, the severing of the cord connecting her to her mother, and then forward to the moment she had looked at the sky in Mariel, to the moments before she became a monster's burrow, knowing that she must attune her mind to the sky in order not to be engulfed by its chaos, that she must be mindful, must have her mind full of air, of the emptiness that surrounded her in that moment, and remain in that state a long time so that she would not be subsumed by the sounds, by the oohing sound of the wind, by the soft sounds of people rolling over in their sleep, by the sound of that goat still no, no, no-ing; she listening to those sounds as if she were that same person, or rather, that the person she once was was a person she could always return to and be, reminding her, as she thought about it now in New York City, still drinking her tea, or perhaps it was hot cocoa, of a rushed note somebody had sent to her saying, "I hope you are doing," forgetting to add "well" at the end of the bland greeting, which prompted her to think how doing was something worth doing just for the sake of doing something, prompting her to offer her wish that that person was *doing* as well.

The story could cycle back to the past again, back to the camp at Mariel, zooming in on Usnavy or Ceiba's papery face, on her eyes, two bright globes awhirl, on her bell-like nose, nostrils throbbing, in and out, in and out. Lying on her cot—a wooden pallet, really—the oboe moos of cows sounding from afar, she would yank at the snapped umbilicus flowing out from her chest, her very connection to the island forever severed—exiled from it before her body had ever shaken off its sand and dust and air.

The story could return to the present where Ceiba or Elizabeth continued thinking about González, the arsonist, how he had worked in a warehouse. The news had mentioned something about him working in a lamp factory. And it was only later that she heard that he had recently been fired from it, and that soon after this his girlfriend had broken up with him. And Ceiba or Elizabeth thought about how it must have felt to pack boxes, to shove a broom around, or whatever else he had to do, to perform the tasks that needed to be done that nobody wanted to do and yet still be among the lowest paid employees, day after desultory day, the indignity of it. "It was revenge," she had overheard someone say in an elevator at the hospital. "After he got fired, of course he had to go fire somebody else." Laughter filled the box going up and up and up while Ceiba or Elizabeth seethed.

Having languished in a Cuban jail for three years in the early seventies, González, a lifelong deserter, a drifter, poor and likely full of gloom at his unspooling life, had heard about the boats that would leave for America, toward the promise of something better—surely anything could be better than the nothing of his life, his life a line of zeros he'd tunneled through. After saying good-bye to everything that he knew, he lied, saying he sold drugs, in order to gain passage on one of the boats, a boat the US news would soon call a freedom flotilla. Rumors had it that Castro was emptying out prisons, along with the mental wards, in order to rid the island of its *"escorias,"* its slag, so the lie was a sure way for González to get a ride out of his nightmare toward his American dream.

And Ceiba or Elizabeth could think about how González might have been there in Mariel the same time she had, that he too might have stood at the harbor, looking at the hundreds of boats: sloops and trawlers and seiners, with hundreds of American flags flapping in the wind, sounding like a flock of birds. It was one of those boats that would take Usnavy or Ceiba and her mother to Key West, Florida. Usnavy or Ceiba had always loved books, especially books of poems, but it would be years before she would read "Key West: An Island Sheaf," the unfinished poems Hart Crane had left behind, which

311

contained an epigraph from William Blake: "The starry floor, / The wat'ry shore, / Is giv'n thee 'til the break of day." Wrapped within an emotional hurricane she too would certainly feel "satin and vacant," but her trip would have none of the grandeur of these poems. There would be no sign of merpeople.

On the day they would leave Mariel for America, the sun, a rose abloom in the sky, shone, and in its brightness seemed to say, *Rise up now! Begone, travelers!* The hullabaloo in the camp rang in Usnavy or Ceiba's ears, and the sense of excitement, a pulpy thing, buoyed her even while her mother shuffled sadly around, so that even her heart seemed to say, *O bright morning, hark!* "Gather your things," someone said. "Everyone stick together," someone else said. "There's nothing here for us," someone else said to someone who was crying. The wind was whistling, pushing everyone around, as if to say, *Go now, now is the time, the sea is calling, go now, you cannot refuse. Listen! Worthless words will try to stop you, so listen to the wind.*

Finally casting off, their boat, a rusty hulk used for shrimping, nosed itself toward the Straits of Florida. Dragging her mother, her mother's hand dead as driftwood, Usnavy or Ceiba shoved her way toward the prow of the boat, the tired thing that would take them to their new world. Gazing at the waves' dark corrugations, feeling her mother's hand slither out of her own, she thought about the wind and the ocean, her life raveling out before her. The ocean is always many things: something real and imagined, and something simply invented; something seen and unseen; and also where all those things, those ideas converge. It is both vista: something that cannot be contained, and a container: a dwelling. It is a space as much as it is a place, a space that takes up space. Life itself may have rolled up from the ocean floor, from microbes near deep-sea hydrothermal vents; and, having swallowed up land and ships and people, the ocean was also the world's largest graveyard. A cry shook Usnavy or Ceiba from her reverie.

There was a struggle at the stern of the boat. A flash of red. Some shouts. Arms jerking back and forth. Heads bobbed up and down, and side to side, in order to see; and then, a brassy splash, like a sounding cymbal, and some cries. Something or someone had gone overboard. Usnavy or Ceiba squeezed her way toward the back, where she saw her mother treading water, her long black hair sprawled out on the surface of the sea as she shouted something to her daughter, who, with the noise of the ocean, the boats, and the other people shouting, could hardly make out what her mother was saying, although she finally heard the word "alegría": happiness, but no, her mother meant Alegría, her old friend, that she would be there in America to meet Usnavy, that Alegría would take care of Usnavy in place of herself. After shouting some more words, still indecipherable, her mother turned her back from the ship, and swam toward her beloved island, becoming smaller and smaller, changing from foreground to middle ground to background, until she vanished completely.

This could be another rupture in a life of ruptures. But what were those things behind Usnavy or Ceiba but a thorny nest of vestiges? And who were all those people: that raisin-faced woman whose flaccid flesh she used to stretch like taffy; that stern matron with chalk-dusted hands, bellowing commands in a place Usnavy or Ceiba had called a schoolroom; that charisma-oozing emperor with his patriarchal beard; that droopy-eyed boy who would tease her about how she always had her head in a book; and who, especially, was that woman, whose sad and lovely face, with its glassy eyes, bulbous lips, and knife of a nose; a face that changed, mercurially, from inscrutable, whenever bored, which was about half the time, to murderous, whenever enraged, which rounded out the other half; that woman whose browned voice men found irresistible, a sad and sleepy voice, singed with enough tobacco to make it a sultry rasp; that woman whose dresses were a rococo explosion of reds and oranges and yellows: a walking inferno; that woman who was a mother who was a mother only in name? Ghosts all.

Back at the front of the boat, Usnavy or Ceiba wept, her whole body shaking as she sucked in her cries, her body slowly becoming numb and finally motionless, until she resembled an ancient sailing ship's carved figurehead. This no-longer-a-girl girl at sea could be dream incarnate, each wanting eye fixed on the horizon, hooked to that line like a fish, her eyes also expanding to view her own protean self. She thought of Yemayá, this being fused with la Virgen de Regla—surely there beneath the turbulence—mother of every living thing, of each of the seven seas, protector of all children; Usnavy or Ceiba recalling how her grandmother had told her to make an offering to Yemayá just before sailing away, a ritual she had, in the rush and hubbub, still forgotten to perform. And now, looking at the sea, almost swallowed by its chaos and darkness, Usnavy or Ceiba sang, the melody, something of her own invention, lilting much like a lullaby; and having neither melons nor syrup nor honey nor fish, nor any proper offering, really, she rummaged through her tiny suitcase and found the wood turtle she'd had since she was seven. Cupping it in her hands, its head facing her future, Usnavy or Ceiba sang and then dropped the turtle into the sea.

Imagine her there, a painter, gazing at the vast vapidity of the sea, watching wave after wave after wave, each trough and crest vanishing as quickly as they appeared, her eyes painting the sea's portrait (or was the sea a mirror, making it her own face her eyes were tracing?), allowing her mind to zigzag, but also struggling to keep her footing as the boat rocked, ominously, side to side. Usnavy or Ceiba, a wisp in the wind, surrendered to the air, to the briny wind that filled her nostrils, chafed her face, the sun effacing one part of her barely-there self, the ocean erasing the rest. Her stomach churned. Seasick, she vomited over and over again until there was nothing left inside to come out. Afraid that the small boat would capsize, Elizabeth sought sanctuary, some solace in the boat's hull; and, swooning into a nook, she wished that her mother were there, that her mother had snapped out of her own gloom long enough to finally embrace her, tell her that she was safe, that she was wanted, that she was loved. But how could she, a mother who had learned too late that she was going to be a mother, had learned too late to rid herself of what would become her greatest burden, her doom, a mother who had hardly taken care of Usnavy after she was born, and who, after years of letting other people, mainly her own mother, take care of Usnavy, had only just begun to show her daughter some affection, but always at a distance, as if there were a thick transparent wall between them, that wall still sandwiched between every rare touch.

There could have been over a hundred boats that day, boats ranging in size from eighteen to ninety feet, each one of them intent on closing the gap of ninety nautical miles between past and future tense, Usnavy or Ceiba's boat passing several ships—many of them crammed with dreamers—that had broken down, bobbing perilously on the sea; and passing others towed by US Coast Guard cutters. And having heard rumors of the strong currents, that just a short time ago many vessels had been caught in a minihurricane, the wind whipping at a powerful seventy miles per hour, that several boats had overturned in the water, Usnavy or Ceiba feared her rusty, busted-up boat wouldn't make it.

Soon after this story's hero arrived in Key West, she could have been sent, along with all the other passengers on her boat, to live in Fort Indiantown Gap in Pennsylvania, where, in a barracks, she

would live within a grid of cots, fending for herself as she waited for
Alegría, who would bring her not to the promised New York City but
to Union City, a home to Cubans since the 1940s, where Usnavy or
Ceiba or Elizabeth would be immediately enrolled in school, a place
that, in the past, had always been her only respite from the chaos of
her home, of having to mother her mother; a place that now would
be a respite from the chaos of not having a mother at all, not even a
surrogate; a place, still, where she would feel like a fool whenever
someone acted on her behalf in loco parentis, whenever she stut-
tered, whenever she flubbed a word in English—a life where she too
would fall into sadness, where boyfriend after boyfriend would look
into her face, which was usually fixed in a grimace, and be unmoored
by it, by how cold it was, how stolid, like chiseled quartz, and would
look at her as if at a tombstone. This arrival to Union City, with its
constant change, all the moving from apartment to apartment, could
have been the time when Ceiba or Elizabeth began holding sets of
two contrary statements to be true at the same time, like the following: I am understood and I am misunderstood; or, I am broken
and I am whole; or, I am lost and I am found; or, I am loved and I am
unloved; or, I am settled and I am unsettled; or, I am happy and I
am unhappy; leading up to being able to believe that a mass murder
could be both incomprehensible and comprehensible, since everything
is always mitigated by where you stand, the belief of which could
allow Ceiba or Elizabeth to reflect on what she thought had been
González's life before he was a mass murderer, when he had nothing
and no one upon his arrival in Key West, Florida, on May 31, 1980,
and all the nothings leading up to March 25, 1990, that terrible day
he drowned eighty-seven people in a lake of fire.

She imagined González drunk, teetering toward Happy Land, the
illegal social club, a gasoline container in each hand acting as
weights to help him maintain his balance, as if he were one of those
madmen on a wire, transforming the simple act of getting from here
to there into a magnificent feat, each step a thing of awe. And wasn't
he, as she pictured him now, a dreadful figure, treading that thin line
between awesome and awful, words that used to mean almost the
same thing, as he poured gasoline all around the building, splotch-
ing his clothes with the toxic stuff, the smell taking him back to
when he was a teenager tooling under the hood of his grandfather's
impeccably maintained 1957 Chevrolet, his "Yank tank," its ornate
chrome shining in the sun's white light. Ceiba or Elizabeth imagined
him standing in front of the club, drunk and angry at having lost

315

everything, filled with a despair perhaps worse than the one he had felt ten years before, now an exile, unable to speak the language, having hardly any practical skills, having nothing at all; Ceiba or Elizabeth shivering at the thought that a person with nothing at all is dangerous precisely because he or she has nothing to lose.

This story, an adventure story situated as much in the mind as in the body, could end with a kind of suturing of the defining ruptures of Usnavy or Ceiba or Elizabeth's life, this transformation occurring after a massive confrontation, perhaps with her mother, who had finally arrived in America eight years after the boat lift. Her mother, sober now, and surprisingly gray, her demeanor that of one confident in having made the right decision, her voice, though, feeble as she explained that she had returned to Cuba to take care of her own mother—how could she abandon her, an old woman with cancer?— and who would quickly shift their conversation back to Usnavy, to how much she had grown, to how much everyone was proud of her, how she had shown that, against all odds, one of the Marielitos could thrive, could contribute to this country's greatness, how unlike González Usnavy was. And her mother would argue, like everyone else was arguing, that González was a monster, devil's spawn, and deserved what was coming to him, that is, 174 twenty-five-year sentences, consisting of eighty-seven second-degree murder charges as well as eighty-seven charges of arson, for a total of 4,350 years in prison, the total itself singling him out as something outside of humanity, something inhuman: a monster—what else but a monster or god could live for that long?—the argument she and her mother were having slowly persuading Usnavy or Ceiba or Elizabeth that existence is predicated on speaking and listening to someone else, and that language is what makes history possible, and that if she simply ceased the conversation, with her mother and everyone else who knew her, then she would cease to exist as the self or selves she was or had been, thereby ushering in her own apotheosis, her change, finally, into someone else, someone without ruptures, some *one*, someone, in other words, other than herself; but this whole series of possibilities would have to first cohere into a story, and to be a story it would have to first surrender to the desire for profluence; or, rather, if it could first surrender to the idea that since real events themselves don't have coherence, sense, and meaning, and that what one sees in so-called objective reality is illusory, and that, as a result, the best vehicle for integrity, purpose, and sense is a story; and if only this story didn't wish to frustrate those expectations for some kind of wholeness, the kind found in linear development, then Usnavy or Ceiba or Elizabeth's coming-of-age story, her "travelogorrhea," could be told, but instead what we have here is something that frustrates, thwarts the art of storytelling, because this story that could be a story is always returning to what could happen—for how could it be a story if you haven't gone anywhere? What you have, instead, is something with a lot of holes in it, each hole a kind of scotoma, an obscuration of the textual field, something chockablock with porous words like doors, brooding, look, blood, choosing, logos, schoolgirl, uprooted, spooked, siroccos, rooftop, understood, oolong, looked, loony, cartoons, took, flood, colonial, festoonery, malodorous, blotto, boors, ballyhoo, sooty, loon, drool, oozing, goony, revolution, co-cooned, childhood, dominion, moody, moon, looming, shook, choose, oohing, cocoa, zooming, wooden, oboe, moos, poor, gloom, unspooling, good-bye, stood, looking, sloops, books, abloom, hulla-baloo, driftwood, overboard, schoolroom, tobacco, rococo, hooked, swooning, nook, doom, fool, unmoored, scotoma, and porous.

Three Poems
G. C. *Waldrep*

DISCRETE SERIES: WEIGHT/BELLS

to depart from is not:

as sleep or: heft:
in steerage: immigrant

transit, you want
what earth wants, *viz.*
installation: soil,

stones, sacks, fire,
bedframes, live
animals: "a poor art"

is not the same as

"art for the poor":
angelus: arrant axis:

the object speaks
for the object, rogue

monad: accidental

web: sound makes,
grafted carefully into

supplement: angle
of refraction, perfect

trinity: meridian:

gravity seeps into
matter & we, softened,

cut away the mold:
from architrave:

& left with: vitreous

combinations: for
experience, sheer
instrument: armistice:

little shale wicks:

flames recorded
at the pitch of flight:

DISCRETE SERIES: SELINSGROVE

one town hides another:

we live there, & like it
most of the time, we say:

to the artifacts of
evening: processional:

the mercy seat, or
just a bit of architecture:

tinder/consequence:

is a matter of faith,
not of style so much

as that word's
usually meant: field-

stubble, as opportunity
for photography,

something the figure
can do that plants can't:

cf. duplicity: to vuln:

no I am not done
bearing upward: this

body, its glands &
constituent organ stops:

porous: sympathetic,
i.e., receptive of vibrations

at certain frequencies:

incoming: as ordnance:

duck & cover, shallow
gibbet of astringent sun:

DISCRETE SERIES: CORIOLIS EFFECT

swept silk: gutter
for the mind's
iris: coral filament:

how glass refrains
from breaking
the sound barrier:

align to empathy:
a Providence:
constrained by

judgment, dusty
annulus: a bareback
instrument: bids

frame the upper
shades: rubral
efferent: unwedded

angles the skin
collects: a weather
palette: clear

of system: chorus:
acclaim or (nightly)
border crossing:

world's member:
lily chapel: a film
run backward

as we race: a myth
contracted,
as from birth's

slick hexagram:
what happy glyph:
inertial circle:

fire's fragment:
ladder, portrait, neu-
tron, apple, star:

Aftermath
Karla Kelsey

She has not forgotten the way departure lists away
from what's proffered & the remainder traffics thinly
papered to remember him by. Though if she could but
fall from these frequented patterns of thought there
would be *the field* but not *the drawn to the field*. The
gesture of memory represents moments of fixation as
the sun goes down, though in another scenario this
would be a fractional element of eggshelled fiction. A
postcard from the West featuring a lone palm arced
over a sunset-riddled sea. She reads the message in
white vapor trails fading into sky. Trio of motorcycles
roar by. Residing inside each system: Yellow's accretion
becomes spring until at last the air golds. The only
other man in the room besides you sends out low
musk, draws slow circles with his pen, a ballad under
his breath. In this scenario she climbs to the top of the
hill an hour before sundown, marking each degree of
declension with increasingly darker shades of crimson.
Farm & field & farm. Road & truck & river & road &
at the edge of sight the sea. On to night then, for
tomorrow birds go slinging in their shallows, waiting
out first the summer storm, then the autumn storm.
Through all of this he'll stand at the edge of a far shore,
carved in white. Here she'll grow into an account of
solitude versus her portrait in the mirror or water, more
fascinating for its warp, its hurrying on without her.

Meandered to repair, the highway gone strange & pulled south to
blurred heat. Getting out of the car to wander the metal & salt
of accident & shore.

As in the catapult theory of ruin* or what
shakes a blessing from branded, thinned sight I divide the moment
by your telling offhand

of the daughter pulled from the burning rig,
then forwarded to images nested* along the roadside. Billboard of
a house, the apple held to my lips in near saying

old waters
into new waters as if we too could circumference the globe rarely
stopping & only for fuel & necessity. Blanched sight calibrated to
proximity, border,* hour,

the road carving past the flock of pigeons.
Our cold sand beaches as opposed to the wearing away in the East
where they fall under fire & burn.

* For example, if the hero leaves home in quest of
something & the object of his desires is far away,
he can reach it by magic horse, eagle, flying carpet,
flying ship, astride the devil, etc.

* The leaves cannot bear it. The rhythms work
into the spine & these are the marks of what fades
into questioning, hour, the pierce of soul
gesturing.

* It will be easily seen that in each case we are
dealing with the transfer of the hero to the place
where the object of his search is located, but that
the forms in which the transfer is realized are
different.

Karla Kelsey

Dust man, one-among-a-number-of-dust-men, do you or do you not create a new road when you drive down & down to the sea?
                    The real featured, made deliberately an object of intention
                    & in such an object I tamp down your each success. Which they call cruel & glossy*
                    though they don't know the sparrow bone where you cried *there-flower-there-follower* with couched intentions meant to be expressive of dawn.
                    But when we make those acts & their objects the objects of our attention—touch in the violet-shaded hollow, touch in lilac or the cloud did score the sky—we discover that we present ourselves as moments* in a sequence.
                    Or have you grown out of the pit in my eye* & the leaning of the red barn back into ground?

* We have both constants & variables. Let us take another example.

* The princess does not wish to marry, or her father does not want her to marry a suitor he or she dislikes. The suitor is required to perform impossible tasks: to jump to her window on horseback, bathe in a cauldron of boiling water, solve the princess's riddle, etc.

* You see, the stakes are sometimes somewhat higher than I spy you in the crow field marking you a crow man, another sack of dust.

Against the alley we were marked in hound wind as in your love
could only & ever come across when darked. I place our least
useful movement in our ends.*
                      But then & but there within
the scent of lilac the last touch sprang & measured hard,
measured live &
                adjusted to the street, to the startled seer.
We had to slow in our fall under the barrel moon to ugly
grasses
       & so this contributes to my inclination to take, always,
the turn to the right. Turn-turn & corner clipped was called a
circle.*
      With such acts the life of the story bends in:*
apprehension called to round, & round to hinge in the dark
when the striated measure of the field dips out of sight.

* Function, according to this definition, denotes
the action of character, the point of view of
narrative progress whether it be toward a
so-called negative value or to a value we render as
positive end.

* An afternoon V mosaic-worked into the hush,
gull egg cradled in the hollow of my hand.

* For example, if an eagle takes the hero to the
country of a princess, we do not have the function
of flying on a bird, but one of a transfer to the place
where the object of the search is located.

Karla Kelsey

For all along the sun had been changing its costume all over the
room & your face had gone blanched & this began the pattern
of marching onward & forward & so forth.*

The curve of hind into
hoof as opposed to the woolen measure of the sling unbuckled
& the horse released to shaky legs, shaky galley of the boat in
near shallows.

The revision of you heard me calling from the
rocks* as you kept abreast of the horse & then wrapped in torn
blankets

which intercedes the account of swimming to shore
in mist in the dead of night.

Because what is the means of equating
diversion, energy from the fiction of a citadel. By this I mean
our faith.

By this I mean we've burnt the costume by falling &
lying* for the car was a sun, was a chair, that you wouldn't,
that you couldn't make go.

* Likewise, if the hero jumps to the princess's
window on horseback, we do not have the
function of jumping on horseback, but of
performing a difficult task, a matter of courtship.

* Ash light following location. Catalyst.

* To the sophisticated scholar this diversity
conceals a logically determinable unity. In the first
case we deal with a transfer to the place of the
search, whereas in the second we have the motif
of the difficult task.

(The wintered the wanted the day, quiet summons under split branches. Profuse. & the path out & she follows the along & along. This is what they called for. That narrowing. That walking split-sided the atoll studded this North Atlantic gyre meanders to repair. To clear the grand scope. Driven off. Riven, this unseasonable breeze dim unraveling juniper, her home marred in the rim of the marrow—

then followed his blue coat down the path & then running)

The Fortunes of Cities
Marc Nieson

I.

OF COURSE WE THOUGHT him mad. As crazy and arrogant and suddenly megalomaniacal as any of his forebears—who, need it be mentioned, began developing this city on all our backs some two and a half centuries ago. Seventeen sixty-seven is the date you'll most often hear cited. Seventeen July, 1767, to be precise, back when Prejuntas wasn't much more than its mission and mud. Among city archives you can still find the very flourish of his iconic ancestor's quill across the brittle deed—Don Javier Acevedo Severiano—the first merchant with enough cojones to challenge our church. But nowadays, the Severiano name on most of Prejuntas's lips was Don Francisco's, and his act of defiance, some whispered, even more ambitious. More indelible.

Mind you, history is not what this brief is meant to address. (Quite the opposite, we hope.) History is an entirely other matter of debate. The following report is but our attempt to place our city's recent events into some semblance of official sense and perspective. A record of accountability.

Typically, a recitation of the Severiano family's steady rise to wealth and power would be in order here for proper context. An exhaustive account of all the land-grabbing and gradual distillation of their Old Dominion® sugar and rum empire that made Don Javier's bold silhouette on horseback the trademark that still graces every grocery and kitchen counter in the commonwealth; all the storied politics and Severiano intrigues; the generations of scandals and blasphemies; their whole phoenix-ridden mythos of entitlement and invincibility, passed on from one silver-spooned scion to the next.

But let us move on. Let's admit that Don Francisco Efrain Severiano was always projected as the last of his line; childless and impotent and, as the general consensus held, a little light in the head ever since birth. In actuality, that head, if anything, was somewhat heavy and enlarged, suggesting what more than one recent doctor has diagnosed from afar as symptomatic of some variant of autism. Hence explaining his childhood obsession with telescopes and astrolabes, which never dampened during his sixty-plus years shuffling around the family hacienda on the hill.

In short, Don Francisco never struck any of us as a true Severiano. Silent and reserved. Harmless, extraneous. A token heir, at best. More shadow than silhouette. Indeed, some even thought him a ghost, but then there he was, standing among us at his mother's funeral, feast day of Santa Clara, two years ago. That's when many claim Don Francisco's miraculous metamorphosis began. After all, the Doña Candelaria Cardona Severiano had hid and controlled her "special" son his entire life. Doted on him for the child he'd remained, keeping him close and clueless with the same undying ferocity with which she'd clasped the reins of her inherited purse strings.

But then the Doña had finally died—ninety-six years stubborn— and, walking next to her horse-drawn procession, as if still tethered, was her only son. And next to him, though of course he was oblivious, plodded the old rumors. There had always been questions as to his true paternity. Whispers concerning a certain rum salesman from Havana who used to come through in the 1930s during Prohibition. Some of us still recall the cut of his white linen suits and straw hat, the sweet smoke of his cigars. Some claim Don Francisco's non-aquiline nose is surely his, though the Doña went to her grave revealing nothing new.

That her marriage was loveless was never in dispute. Nor were the two older daughters she *did* bear her husband—though as young women they later withdrew to the States and were eventually disowned by her legally. But Don Francisco was always a question in our minds. A cipher and confusion. An unexplained blot in the midst of our city, and on the Severiano name. Even as his mother was entombed in the family mausoleum, there he stood, dimly staring off in the direction of the bay, squinting at the horizon. Same as ever. More or less, this was the only posture in which we'd ever seen him—glimpsed daily on the southern balconies of the hacienda overlooking the city and its wide bay beyond. On one balcony was installed his astrolabe and on the other his brass telescope, behind which he'd alternately stand still as an egret for hours on end, scanning either waves or stars. If you didn't know better, you might mistake him for a statue.

Still, while none of us had ever talked with or even to him, if you had taken a poll of those in attendance at the Doña's funeral, the majority would have said they felt sympathy for Don Francisco. Or perhaps pity is the better word. In any event, those few who joked or still called him a mute idiot in truth wished him no harm. And if they slurred anyone, it wasn't Don Francisco or the Doña or even the rum salesman, but the cuckold. Blame, after all, has had a complicated lineage in Prejuntas.

But alas, we tempt sliding back into history, which again isn't pertinent here. What's worth noting is that some two years ago Don Francisco newly emerged as if from a cocoon into our consciousness, and very soon we all came to recognize that here was no simpleton.

In retrospect, this probably shouldn't have surprised us as much as it did. Clearly he'd always had a head for science and math. Stories of secret journals crammed with his scratched figures and numbers had been circulating ever since he was in short pants. Journals that by now, hacienda staff have confirmed, had nearly doubled the Severiano private library. At night, you could still spot him in silhouette before the old leaden windows of balcony number two, duly bent over the polished eyepiece and scanning the stars. Scribbling away at his endless notations. He was an incurable insomniac, his heavy step growing even slower and clumsier with age. And then there were those rumors of the slight vibration he always complained of, his big head often cocked to one side as if to hear it all the better. Some distant rubbing insect? Or the faint music of the spheres?

Ah, the music.

Finally we come to the crux of the matter—the Don's renowned ear and true passion, the humming heart and harmony behind his *Proyecto Grande*. As quoted in the newspapers, the idea first came to Don Francisco in a dream (though since he rarely slept, we've discounted that particular reference). In other accounts, the Don has called it an "aria" (which to us seems far more probable). Some have gone so far as to call it a vision, the manifestation of all he'd been scanning skyward and offshore for all these years, as if he'd been waiting for some new fate to raise its head over our horizon yet again.

In any event, not long after his mother's interment Don Francisco claims to have been visited one night by a "voice." Faceless and towering and ensconced in the shining armor of a conquistador, gallantly striding across the great stage of the old opera house. A tenor so terrifyingly beautiful and arresting that the Don evidently wet himself. Toward dawn, he "awoke" with the lilting melody still burning in his ears, and rushed off downstairs in search of his driver to take him downtown.

Now, of course, Don Francisco no longer had a driver—his mother's will having stipulated that all but the necessary help be retired upon her demise. Assuming her son would never venture beyond his balconies, she'd excused her driver (and the car, for that matter), her seamstress, the gardeners, the distiller, the . . . well, the list of those regretfully let go far exceeds those who remained—namely, one chef, two maids, and Don Francisco's original nursemaid-cum-governess, who herself was easily ninety and shouldn't last much longer. As always, the Doña Candelaria's priority was to ensure her son's care, and in all truth the Severiano coffers weren't as bottomless as we'd all presumed. All of Prejuntas, it seems, had been living under reduced circumstances for some time.

But back to the morning after the visitation. Don Francisco was without car or driver, but fortunately one old groom had stayed on, begging only food and a bedstead over the stables. The Doña had consented, provided that he'd keep an extra eye out for her son. This Luis saddled the one remaining gelding and led the still-pajamaed Don Francisco downhill toward that old patch of Prejuntas's narrow alleyways and cobblestones. Twice the Don nearly fell from his mount, Luis having to all but tie his charge's arms around the horse's neck. Those few bleary-eyed citizens lucky enough to still have a job to awaken for glanced out their windows, then turned back in disbelief.

Upon finally reaching the long shadows of the great opera house's facade, Luis helped the Don back down to the ground then stepped aside. Don Francisco took two hesitant steps forward then stood transfixed before the sun-pierced ruins. Inside, the remaining rubble from the collapsed roof had long since given way to the roots of *flamboyan* and *peregrina*, their flowering canopy vibrant yet bereft of all prior imperial splendors. No vaulting ceiling or gold leaf remained, no angels even. Everything reduced to a shell of scars. The Don literally swayed in his disorientation, finding not even an echo. And then, according to Luis, for perhaps the first time in his adult life, Don Francisco wept.

Here might be an apt place for a quick footnote. Scores of us are still around who can attest to how the Doña used to sit her toddler son on her lap for each premiere and how utterly still and rapt the boy remained through the final curtain. This, of course, before she'd begun sheltering him from all but her trusted staff some years before the old opera house went entirely dark.

Again, according to Luis, Don Francisco sat similarly rapt and wide
eyed beside him for hours under the ruins' tall trees as he explained
all that had transpired during the ensuing years the Don had stood
apart contemplating distant tides and constellations. Of his grandfather's squandered trust and father's foolish pride, the decades of
political cockfights and impasse, all the handshakes and corporate
backstabbing, the resulting migrations and privations, the lingering
stench of piss and despair. Thus had gone the fortunes of many cities
like Prejuntas, her days in the sun long gone, her gilt lusters vanished. Or perhaps vanquished is the better word, when you consider
the lost veneers of such counterparts as, say, Córdoba and Granada.
Tenochtitlan. El Dorado.

And indeed Don Francisco listened on as if to some childhood
fable, silent as ever yet attentive. He'd had no idea of his larger history or inheritance. No idea whatsoever of what taxes were, let alone
that the Severianos had been exempt for the last two centuries. From
time to time his gaze would wander past Luis's thin shoulders, where,
framed in the opera's vacant window holes, squatted the surrounding barrio, like some diseased shipwreck. Like waves these revela-
tions and indignities overpowered the Don's newfound senses, until
finally toward dusk he held up his arm—high like a spear and probably echoing the stance of that girded tenor in his mind's libretto.
And then, reportedly, Don Francisco Efrain Severiano scribbled the
following on a scrap of paper. Or perhaps inscribed is the better word:

"We shall restore my family's former glory."

II.

For weeks nothing more was heard, and Luis figured his *patrón* had
returned to his own private amnesia. The maids attended to his quarters and the chef to his daily morsels, while downhill our ancient
ceiba tree still listed at the barrio's edge. Then someone noted that
the balconies had not been visited in two straight days. After a third
such day whispers began to multiply, and by week's end the rumors
swelled. Was it really true? The end of the Severianos? In retrospect,
it could have been that simple. That quietly laid to rest.

But then, fresh sightings of the Don's shadow were confirmed—
glimpsed through the windows of the library, the dining room. Word
trickled downhill from one of the maids that alongside his untouched
dinner plates lay dusty tomes and onion-skinned blueprints. Wax
drippings pooled on the table linen, and empty rum tumblers were

found left on wooden armrests, graphite smudges everywhere. Meanwhile, soft operettas sifted down the stairwells all night long as the Don paced the hallways of old family portraits and pored over his plans.

As for his ultimate architectural designs, we couldn't really fault the Don's vision. Part of their colonial imprint was in deference to historical integrity, but part equally shaped by his limited indoctrination. The hacienda, after all, was more museum than home, like one huge display case under glass. From his very first steps on its dark parquet floors to playing hide-and-seek behind Flemish tapestries, his days were draped in an imperial past. A world of balustrades and deep velvet curtains. Silvered inkwells and Habsburg cutlery. Velázquez, early Goya. The main fountain in the foyer still hid escudos under its algae and, some said, raw nuggets. And all the while his mother's gramophone spun upstairs. Strains of Guerrero and Ibañez, Callas, Casals.

Thus you can probably imagine some due resistance when Don Francisco's intentions and drawings for the new opera house were first made public. On the one hand, we thought the whole enterprise obscene—that Severiano tropical hubris simultaneously brought back to new heights and lows—but at the same time there came a low-level rumbling from the dankest gutters. A tapping of sticks and drums from those among us who'd fallen beyond pride and memory. Beyond our fears and sleeplessness, and hunger for the merest scrap of a job or dignity. Beyond even the waiting and the hope. Indeed, that was the refrain first heard whispered then openly intoned among our citizens again: *esperar.*

Thus despite our history, on the first anniversary of the Doña's death, ground was broken. Don Francisco's Counter-Restoration had begun.

Luis, of course, was made foreman, and lines of willing laborers quickly crowded about the sudden cast of his shadow across the cobbles. He proved himself a fair proxy, though, a stableman by trade and nature, making sure each workhorse got his fair sweat and share. Everything was scheduled and apportioned, and all according to the Don's scratched plans and stipulations. Soon, decades of debris and neglect were being attacked by eager hands. All the crumbled stonework and wrought iron of yore carted off. Sharpened axes taken to the invading trees and *allamanda.* Pry bars shouldered and old mules straining to rend every last shred of root and rust.

Then from out of the woodworks arose craftsmen who still knew the old ways. Master masons and gnarled forgers of iron, glaziers and carpenters and seamstresses, specialists in Moorish ceramics and grout, trompe l'oeil. Daily, materials were streaming into the rejuvenated port, and the public library reopened. Soon schoolchildren began making field trips to the work site. The tourists' stares once again met in the eye.

Yes, a palpable pride and decency could be felt taking root among the returning bustle and commerce of Prejuntas. Don Francisco made certain all his workers were properly fed and even hired musicians to play during lunch hour. Here was a new Severiano indeed. Not the end of his ancestors' line, but a fresh seed. Whispers of the "mute bastard" drowned under new songs in his praise. A second chrysalis was unfurling, both in and around him. A new distillation. He was bringing us together not politically so much as chemically, infusing a collective family with a single intent. A new mission.

And the Don himself proved no distant *patrón* either. Right there on-site with us each morning and the very last to leave each night, overseeing every foundation and strut of this new opera house. At first we were fascinated by his sudden proximity, but as he scaled the scaffolding alongside us, we noted the same stone dust on his thighs, the same darkened skin at his nape. All at once he became our master and mascot, our *milagro*. His own pet project was the central courtyard's fountain, in whose bottom he painstakingly set those same tossed doubloons and nuggets from the hacienda—though here inlaid to recreate the exact positions of the constellations as they would have shone on that famed night of 17 July, 1767. Yes, Prejuntas's history was being both honored and rewritten right before our eyes.

Of course the city's main plaza was also in much need of a facelift, and don't think the church didn't try to newly nuzzle in on that Old Dominion® sugar teat too, but Don Francisco mutely resisted their entreaties. After all, here was a man of the people, a servant of science and music, not God or government. His loyalties were to the opera house alone. To us. By now nearly every other citizen in Prejuntas was on his personal payroll—the wealth finally redistributing. Meanwhile, unknown to any of us, the Severiano resources were silently depleting.

Still, each night Don Francisco would make his solitary rounds of the construction site, then head uphill for his riding lesson with Luis. Afterward, he'd share a quiet cigar or glass of rum by the old fireplace then request his lieutenant's reports of the day. At moments, Luis would take note of his *patrón*'s exhaustion or the evident disarray of the hacienda itself. Sometimes he'd even voice a concern, but the Don would duly wave him off to bed, then stay up to all hours poring over his punch lists. Squinting under his flickering candelabrum, growing gaunt.

In the final weeks leading up to the opera's grand opening, arroyos of activity coursed through the streets and workshops of Prejuntas, a veritable fever pitch of communal verve and commitment. With all but the last brushstrokes of finish work completed on the edifice itself, the bulk of attention now turned to planning the opening night's festivities.

Of course everyone was going to attend, but the Don insisted on official invitations nonetheless—each handwritten on the antique Severiano stationery edged in gold and embossed with the family crest, and each sealed with red wax and string. The missives were then hand delivered in woven baskets to the portals of the governor and every ex-financier, each beleaguered merchant and academic, every single compadre and campesino alike. Even the parochial priest was entreated to come consecrate the heavenly fountain.

And while public advertising was similarly superfluous, a corps of muralists was hired to paint bold fliers and billboards, banners strung across the avenues proclaiming EL GRANDE ESPECTÁCULO. Soon young boys ran through the alleys giggling and shouting, *"El Gran Culo de los Severianos! El Gran Culo!"* but this too only seemed to expand Don Francisco's following.

Then someone realized that many of us wouldn't have the proper attire befitting such an event. That gave rise to the final mobilization—tailors and dressmakers and cobblers and jewelers, florists and furriers, hairdressers by the dozen. And with them arrived more shipments—satins and silks and leathers and organza, a bouquet of perfumes and lipsticks, and still more invoices and paychecks. When one ship's container of velvet failed to arrive in sufficient time, the Don ordered the hacienda's own crianza-colored curtains torn down for more gowns.

Meanwhile, if you walked around back of the opera—the alleyway now budding with bougainvillea and red jasmine—you could hear the trilling scales of the orchestra at practice, of blessed voices similarly stretching for light. Supposedly the score's conductor was still tinkering with eighth notes, but rest assured the commission was complete. Promised was a *zarzuela* at once classic and contemporary, its lilting libretto embroiling princes and battlements, maidens both regal and base. Onstage, the last production details were being diligently attended to: the final costume fittings and focusing of Fresnels, the orchestra pit already mopped, the casters beneath each set piece oiled and dabbed dry. All that remained now, as they say, was for the ribbon to be cut and the fat lady to sing.

III.

The evening of the premiere was crystalline if unseasonably cool, perfect weather for a slung stole or shawl. For the first time in recent memory, dainty heels were again heard clicking down sidewalks amid glimpses of petaled hemlines and taut tuxes. Drawn carriages and stray dogs paused at every street corner, where suckling pigs turned on spits and the thud of carving machetes raised no eyebrows. Goblets of top-shelf Old Dominion® rum clinked against jars of raw moonshine and all manner of dialects shared. For once, the serrated hillsides of Prejuntas stood level and laughing. Arm in arm we were. Equals.

Still, at the same time, there hung an eerie stillness in the air. Not unlike that breathlessness on the night of a long-awaited election, or that sallow gasp before an arriving hurricane. Or coronation. Or coup.

Uphill at the hacienda, Don Francisco too was presumably taking a deep inhale while buttoning up the final flourishes to his finery: adjusting the angles to his sable and sword, smoothing out the sash of Severiano colors across his breast. We could almost picture him, waxing the tips of his silver mustaches then duly proceeding down the long hallway outside his quarters, reflecting upon each painting's pose, perhaps even nodding to old Don Javier's portrait.

When the hour finally approached, he headed down to the stables where his loyal groom awaited, similarly straight backed in his best clothes and, frankly, beaming. Finally, here was the occasion for which Luis had truly stayed on and instructed his *patrón*. Beside him stood the Don's mount, similarly combed and shod and gleaming. The two men bowed to one another and then Don Francisco ascended his saddle like a true conquistador. Luis, at his own insistence, assumed his position, walking three lengths behind.

*

An uncanny glow accompanied Don Francisco's ride through Prejuntas that night. To a man, everyone swore it was something more than the warmth of strung bulbs and bonfires lining his route. Something perhaps reflected in his golden stirrups and epaulets? Or no, emanating from Don Francisco himself—a sureness to his bearing, a luster. That Severiano profile, after all.

Waves of fellow citizens happily parted before his gelding, strewing palm fronds before each hoof fall. Some even launched hosannas. Gone were any murmurings of madness or dissent or even expectation. The prevailing wind embraced only the present moment flickering before us. This wasn't the past or nostalgia, fantasy or stage set. This was as real as our hunger had been. This was our calendar reborn. This was now and forever.

Upon finally arriving at the small square before the opera house, Don Francisco dismounted. No one, of course, expected a speech, yet after gaining the opera's front steps he paused to face the throngs—a suspended moment during which you'd swear the mute might actually speak. And could you blame us for believing? After all, this was a night beyond *all* hope and waiting, and yes, even prayer. A night of true miracles and destiny.

The Don humbly removed his tricorn hat and gently cocked that enlarged head of his to the side. A silence thick as his own fell upon us all then, such that we could soon hear the near pleading of night birds and stray cats . . . then the faint thrumming of halyards in our harbor . . . then the hiss of distant waves and great cloth sails snapping at sea, an oceanic echo of our entire evolution unfurling . . . and then, even all that held its collective breath. Finally, Don Francisco nodded to Luis, who in his best Castilian accent declared, *"Como siempre, nuestro tesoro nacional."* Then, as if to kiss a ring, the Don knelt before the stretched yellow ribbon, sliced it with his sword, and the sea of us slid through the sluice of parting mahogany doors.

Of the staged performance itself, nothing needs be recorded here. No doubt its utter grace and magic will forever blossom in each of our individual minds. Those dizzying sets and arpeggios, those transcendent smiles of recognition wafting through the orchestra and balconies . . . for these we lack sufficient artfulness, if not the very words. Future generations, we apologize. One colleague among us humbly noted that true miracles never deliver their meanings to us, regardless of interpretation. Suffice it to say that on that evening, we were all left mute.

What we do feel compelled to document here (given the considerable volume and frequency of ensuing debate and apocrypha, and based on what we've best been able to ascertain from verifiable facts and testimonies) is precisely what did transpire in the immediate hours following the performance.

After all the encores and applause, the shaking of heads and hands, the endless embraces and exhortations; after all the fluted glasses were drained of bubbly, and that final cluster of glittering fireworks faded from the overhanging sky; after that last scrap in the square was swept up and every dog and drunkard had circled his plot of dirt for the night, and every last child in Prejuntas safely tucked beneath bedsheets and dreaming, Don Francisco Efrain Severiano stood alone at center stage of our opera house. (Again, let us take a moment here to assert that we have in our possession sworn testimonies attesting to the fact that the Don was first seen making his customary rounds. Whether this was to make certain he was alone, we cannot confirm, and indeed, as a body, remain divided of opinion on this point. All such signed affidavits, however, are available for review in the city's official archives).

In any event, the Don lingered on and alone midstage, probably taking in the theater's grand expanse of pillars and ceiling and sparkling chandeliers, each and every glorious detail he'd so tenderly attended to reproducing. Meanwhile, in his palm he cradled a small electronic switch. Evidently he'd had a grand finale of his own planned. A series of explosives he'd personally encased within the foundation so that in a single flash the four great walls of the opera house would topple inward, like Samson's temple.

And like it says in the Bible, one-third of heaven fell.

The next morning, a sealed and scripted letter was found in the Severiano library, detailing the Don's last directives. In his scratchy pen was an enumerated budget and timetable for the removal of all rubble, and a subsequent materials list for the construction and erection of his future statue in situ. Also included was a handsomely drawn self-portrait as a model, along with express coordinates to align the statue's pedestal with specific stars.

And so, it would seem the Don had remained clueless as ever to the last. Extant debts from the opera house's construction were barely covered by liquidating the hacienda's last furnishings and art, and if any monies did remain they were swiftly plundered for other civic reclamations. No, the last traces of Don Francisco and the Severiano line were glimpsed that deafly silent morning after in the ghostly silhouette of his surviving gelding, wandering shell-shocked and aimless, his empty mount's reins dragging among the smoke and ash.

And as for us? For you, future generations? Where does that leave us? Well, that remains to be seen. Whether what comes next is an overture or merely a refrain rests in your hands now. As far as this body is concerned, we would hope the matter is finally beyond debate. Meanwhile, if you have any further questions, we suggest you visit the ruins of this new old opera house, where each morning the shadows of our ancient ceiba's upper branches can be seen reaching out to brush the site's boot print.

The Ballad of Ballard and Sandrine
Peter Straub

1997

"So, do we get lunch again today?" Ballard asked. They had reached the steaming, humid end of November.

"We got fucking lunch yesterday," replied the naked woman splayed on the long table: knees bent, one hip elevated, one boneless-looking arm draped along the curves of her body, which despite its hidden scars appeared to be at least a decade younger than her face. "Why should today be different?"

After an outwardly privileged childhood polluted by parental misconduct, a superior education, and two failed marriages, Sandrine Loy had evolved into a rebellious, still-exploratory woman of forty. At present, her voice had a well-honed edge, as if she were explaining something to a person of questionable intelligence.

Two days before joining Sandrine on this river journey, Ballard had celebrated his sixty-fifth birthday at a dinner in Hong Kong, one of the cities where he conducted his odd business. Sandrine had not been invited to the dinner and would not have attended if she had. The formal, ceremonious side of Ballard's life, which he found so satisfying, interested her not at all.

Without in any way adjusting the facts of the extraordinary body she had put on display, Sandrine lowered her eyes from the ceiling and examined him with a glance brimming with false curiosity and false innocence. The glance also contained a flicker of genuine irritation.

Abruptly and with vivid recall, Ballard found himself remembering the late afternoon in 1972 when, nine floors above Park Avenue, upon a carpet of almost unutterable richness in a room hung with paintings by Winslow Homer and Albert Pinkham Ryder, he had stood with a rich scapegrace and client named Lauritzen Loy, his host, to greet Loy's daughter on her return from another grueling day at Dalton School, then observed the sidelong, graceful, slightly miffed entrance of a fifteen-year-old girl in pigtails and a Jackson Browne

sweatshirt two sizes too large, met her gray-green eyes, and felt the
very shape of his universe alter in some drastic way, either expanding a thousand times or contracting to a pinpoint, he could not tell.
The second their eyes met, the girl blushed, violently.

She hadn't liked that, not at all.

"I didn't say it was going to be different, and I don't think it will."
He turned to look at her, making sure to meet her gaze before letting
his eye travel down her neck, over her breasts, the bowl of her belly,
the slope of her pubis, the length of her legs. "Are you in a more than
ordinarily bad mood?"

"You're snapping at me."

Ballard sighed. "You gave me that *look*. You said, 'Why should
today be different?'"

"Have it your way, old man. But as a victory, it's fucking pathetic.
It's hollow."

She rolled onto her back and gave her body a firm little shake that
settled it more securely onto the steel surface of the table. The metal,
only slightly cooler than her skin, felt good against it. In this climate,
nothing not on ice or in a freezer, not even a corpse, could ever truly
get cold.

"Most victories are hollow, believe me."

Ballard wandered over to the brass-bound porthole on the deck
side of their elaborate, many-roomed suite. Whatever he saw caused
him momentarily to stiffen and take an involuntary step backward.

"What's the view like?"

"The so-called view consists of the filthy Amazon and a boring,
muddy bank. Sometimes the bank is so far away it's out of sight."

He did not add that a Ballard approximately twenty years younger,
the Ballard of, say, 1977, dressed in a handsome dark suit and brilliantly white shirt, was leaning against the deck rail, unaware of being
under the eye of his twenty-years-older self. Young Ballard, older Ballard observed, did an excellent job of concealing his dire internal condition beneath a mask of deep, already well-weathered urbanity: the
same performance, enacted day after day before an audience unaware
of being an audience and never permitted backstage.

Unlike Sandrine, Ballard had never married.

"Poor Ballard, stuck on the *Endless Night* with a horrible view and
only his aging, moody girlfriend for company."

Smiling, he returned to the long steel table, ran his mutilated right
hand over the curve of her belly, and cupped her navel. "This is exactly what I asked for. You're wonderful."

"But isn't it funny to think—everything could have been completely different."

Ballard slid the remaining fingers of his hand down to palpate, lightly, the springy black shrublike curls of her pubic bush.

"Everything is completely different right now."

"So take off your clothes and fuck me," Sandrine said. "I can get you hard again in a minute. In thirty seconds."

"I'm sure you could. But maybe you should put some clothes *on*, so we could go in to lunch."

"You prefer to have sex in our bed."

"I do, yes. I don't understand why you wanted to get naked and lie down on this thing anyhow. Now, I mean."

"It isn't cold, if that's what you're afraid of." She wriggled her torso and did a snow angel movement with her legs.

"Maybe this time we could catch the waiters."

"Because we'd be early?"

Ballard nodded. "Indulge me. Put on that sleeveless white French thing."

"Aye, aye, *mon capitaine*." She sat up and scooted down the length of the table, pushing herself along on the raised vertical edges. These were of dark green marble, about an inch thick and four inches high. On both sides, round metal drains abutted the inner side of the marble. At the end of the table, Sandrine swung her legs down and straightened her arms, like a girl sitting on the end of a diving board. "I know why too."

"Why I want you to wear that white thing? I love the way it looks on you."

"Why you don't want to have sex on this table."

"It's too narrow."

"You're thinking about what this table is for. Right? And you don't want to combine sex with *that*. Only I think that's exactly why we *should* have sex here."

"Everything we do, remember, is done by mutual consent. Our Golden Rule."

"Golden Spoilsport," she said. "Golden Shower of Shit."

"See? Everything's different already."

Sandrine levered herself off the edge of the table and faced him like a strict schoolmistress who happened momentarily to be naked. "I'm all you've got, and sometimes even I don't understand you."

"That makes two of us."

She wheeled around and padded into the bedroom, displaying her plush little bottom and sacral dimples with an absolute confidence Ballard could not but admire.

Although Sandrine and Ballard burst, in utter defiance of a direct order, into the dining room a full nine minutes ahead of schedule, the unseen minions had already done their work and disappeared. On the gleaming rosewood table two formal place settings had been laid, the plates topped with elaborately chased silver covers. Fresh irises brushed blue and yellow filled a tall, sparkling crystal vase.

"I swear, they must have a greenhouse on this yacht," Ballard said.

"Naked men with muddy hair row the flowers out in the middle of the night."

"I don't even think irises grow in the Amazon basin."

"Little guys who speak bird language can probably grow anything they like."

"That's only one tribe, the Piraha. And all those bird sounds are actual words. It's a human language." Ballard walked around the table and took the seat he had claimed as his. He lifted the intricate silver cover. "Now what is that?" He looked across at Sandrine, who was prodding at the contents of her bowl with a fork.

"Looks like a cut-up sausage. At least I hope it's a sausage. And something like broccoli. And a lot of orangey-yellowy goo." She raised her fork and licked the tines. "Um. Tastes pretty good, actually. But . . ."

For a moment, she appeared to be lost in time's great forest.

"I know this doesn't make sense, but if we ever did this before, *exactly* this, with you sitting over there and me here, in this same room, well, wasn't the food even better, I mean a *lot* better?"

"I can't say anything about that," Ballard said. "I really can't. There's just this vague . . ." The vagueness disturbed him far more than seemed quite rational. "Let's drop that subject and talk about bird language. Yes, let's. And the wine." He picked up the bottle. "Yet again a very nice Bordeaux," Ballard said, and poured for both of them. "However. What you've been hearing are real birds, not the Piraha."

"But they're talking, not just chirping. There's a difference. These guys are saying things to each other."

"Birds talk to one another. I mean, they sing."

She was right about one thing, though: In a funky, down-home way, the stewlike dish was delicious. He thrust away the feeling that it should have been a hundred, a thousand times more delicious: that once it, or something rather like it, had been paradisal.

"Birds don't sing in sentences. Or in paragraphs, like these guys do."

"They still can't be the Piraha. The Piraha live about five hundred miles away, on the Peruvian border."

"Your ears aren't as good as mine. You don't really hear them."

"Oh, I hear plenty of birds. They're all over the place."

"Only we're not talking about *birds*," Sandrine said.

1982

On the last day of November, Sandrine Loy, who was twenty-five, constitutionally ill tempered, and startlingly good-looking (wide eyes, long mouth, black widow's peak, columnar legs), formerly of Princeton and Clare College, Cambridge, glanced over her shoulder and said, "Please tell me you're kidding. I just showered. I put on this nice white frock you bought me in Paris. And I'm *hungry*." Relenting a bit, she let a playful smile warm her face for nearly a second. "Besides that, I want to catch sight of our invisible servants."

"I'm hungry too."

"Not for food, unfortunately." She spun from the porthole and its ugly view—a mile of brown, rolling river and low, muddy banks where squat, sullen natives tended to melt back into the bushes when the *Sweet Delight* went by—to indicate the evidence of Ballard's arousal, which stood up, darker than the rest of him, as straight as a flagpole.

"Let's have sex on this table. It's a lot more comfortable than it looks."

"Kind of defeats the fucking purpose, wouldn't you say? Comfort's hardly the point."

"Might as well be as comfy as we can, I say." He raised his arms to let his hands drape from the four-inch marble edging on the long steel table. "There's plenty of space on this thing, you know. More than in your bed at Clare."

"Maybe you're not as porky as I thought you were."

"Careful, careful. If you insult me, I'll make you pay for it."

At fifty Ballard had put on some extra weight, but it suited him. His shoulders were still wider far than his hips, and his belly more nascent than actual. His hair, longer than that of most men his age and just beginning to show threads of gray within the luxuriant brown, framed his wide brow and executive face. He looked like an actor who had made a career of playing senators, doctors, and bankers. Ballard's real profession was that of fixer to an oversized law firm in New York with a satellite office in Hong Kong, where he had grown up. The weight of muscle in his arms, shoulders, and legs reinforced the hint of stubborn determination, even perhaps brutality, in his face: the suggestion that if necessary he would go a great distance and perform any number of grim deeds to do what was needed. Scars both long and short, scars like snakes, zippers, and tattoos bloomed here and there on his body.

"Promises, promises," she said. "But just for now, get up and get dressed, please. The sight of you admiring your own dick doesn't do anything for me."

"Oh, really?"

"Well, I do like the way you can still stick straight up into the air like a happy little soldier—at your age! But men are so soppy about their penises. You're all queer for yourselves. You more so than most, Ballard."

"Ouch," he said, and sat up. "I believe I'll put my clothes on now, Sandrine."

"Don't take forever, all right? I know it's only the second day, but I'd like to get a look at them while they're setting the table. Because someone, maybe even two someones, does set that table."

Ballard was already in the bedroom, pulling from their hangers a pair of white linen slacks and a thick, long-sleeved white cotton T-shirt. In seconds, he had slipped into these garments and was sliding his suntanned feet into rope-soled clogs.

"So let's move," he said, coming out of the bedroom with a long stride, his elbows bent, his forearms raised.

From the dining room came the sharp, distinctive chirping of a bird. Two notes, the second one higher, both clear and as insistent as the call of a bell. Ballard glanced at Sandrine, who seemed momentarily shaken.

"I'm not going in there if one of those awful jungle birds got in. They have to get rid of it. We're paying them, aren't we?"

"You have no idea," Ballard said. He grabbed her arm and pulled her along with him. "But that's no bird, it's *them*. The waiters. The staff."

Sandrine's elegant face shone with both disbelief and disgust.

"Those chirps and whistles are how they talk. Didn't you hear them last night and this morning?"

When he pulled again at her arm, she followed along, reluctance visible in her stance, her gait, the tilt of her head.

"I'm talking about birds, and they weren't even on the yacht. They were on shore. They were up in the air."

"Let's see what's in here." Nine minutes remained until the official start of dinnertime, and they had been requested never to enter the dining room until the exact time of the meal.

Ballard threw the door open and pulled her into the room with him. Silver covers rested on the Royal Doulton china, and an uncorked bottle of a distinguished Bordeaux stood precisely at the midpoint between the two place settings. Three inches to its right, a navy blue and royal purple orchid thick enough to eat leaned, as if languishing, against the side of a small, square crystal vase. The air seemed absolutely unmoving. Through the thumb holes at the tops of the plate covers rose a dense, oddly meaty odor of some unidentifiable food.

"Missed 'em again, damn it." Sandrine pulled her arm from Ballard's grasp and moved a few steps away.

"But you have noticed that there's no bird in here. Not so much as a feather."

"So it got out—I know it was here, Ballard."

She spun on her four-inch heels, giving the room a fast 360-degree inspection. Their dining room, roughly oval in shape, was lined with glassed-in bookshelves of dark-stained oak containing perhaps five hundred books, most of them mid-to-late-nineteenth- and early-twentieth-century novels ranked alphabetically by author, regardless of genre. The jackets had been removed, which Ballard minded, a bit. Three feet in front of the bookshelves on the deck side, which yielded space to two portholes and a door, stood a long wooden table with a delicately inlaid top—a real table, unlike the one in the room they had just left, which was more like a workstation in a laboratory. The real one was presumably for setting out buffets.

The first door opened out onto the deck; another at the top of the oval led to their large and handsomely furnished sitting room, with reading chairs and lamps, two sofas paired with low tables, a bar with a great many bottles of liquor, two red lacquered cabinets they had as yet not explored, and an air of many small precious things set out to gleam under the parlor's low lighting. The two remaining doors in the dining room were on the interior side. One opened into the spacious corridor that ran the entire length of their suite and gave access to the deck on both ends; the other revealed a gray passageway and a metal staircase that led up to the captain's deck and cabin and down

346

into the engine room, galley, and quarters for the yacht's small, unseen crew.

"So it kept all its feathers," said Sandrine. "If you don't think that's possible, you don't know doodly-squat about birds."

"What isn't possible," said Ballard, "is that some giant parrot got out of here without opening a door or a porthole."

"One of the waiters let it out, dummy. One of those handsome *Spanish-speaking* waiters."

They sat on opposite sides of the stately table. Ballard smiled at Sandrine, and she smiled back in rage and distrust. Suddenly and without warning, he remembered the girl she had been on Park Avenue at the end of the sixties, gawky-graceful, brilliantly surly, her hair and wardrobe goofy, claiming him as he had claimed her, with a glance. He had rescued her father from ruinous shame and a long jail term, but as soon as he had seen her he understood that his work had just begun, and that it would demand restraint, sacrifice, patience, and adamantine caution.

"A three-count?" he asked.

She nodded.

"One," he said. "Two." They put their thumbs into the round holes at the tops of the covers. "Three." They raised their covers, releasing steam and smoke and a more concentrated, powerful form of the meaty odor.

"Wow. What is that?"

Yellow-brown sauce or gravy covered a long, curved strip of foreign matter. Exhausted vegetables that looked a little like okra and string beans but were other things altogether lay strewn in limp surrender beneath the gravy.

"All of a sudden I'm really hungry," said Sandrine. "You can't tell what it is either?"

Ballard moved the strip of unknown meat back and forth with his knife. Then he jabbed his fork into it. A watery yellow fluid oozed from the punctures.

"God knows what this is."

He pictured some big reptilian creature sliding down the riverbank into the meshes of a native net, then being hauled back up to be pierced with poison-tipped wooden spears. Chirping like birds, the diminutive men rioted in celebration around the corpse, which was now that of a hideous insect the size of a pony, its shell a poisonous green.

"I'm not even sure it's a mammal," he said. "Might even be some organ. Anaconda liver. Crocodile lung. Tarantula heart."

"You first."

Ballard sliced a tiny section from the curved meat before him. He half expected to see valves and tubes, but the slice was a dense, light brown all the way through. Ballard inserted the morsel into his mouth, and his taste buds began to sing.

"My God. Amazing."

"It's good?"

"Oh, this is way beyond 'good.'"

Ballard cut a larger piece off the whole and quickly bit into it. Yes, there it was again, but more sumptuous, almost floral in its delicacy and grounded in some profoundly satisfactory flavor, like that of a great single-barrel bourbon laced with a dark, subversive French chocolate. Subtlety, strength, sweetness. He watched Sandrine lift a section of the substance on her fork and slip it into her mouth. Her face went utterly still, and her eyes narrowed. With luxuriant slowness, she began to chew. After perhaps a second, Sandrine closed her eyes. Eventually, she swallowed.

"Oh, yes," she said. "My, my. Yes. Why can't we eat like this at home?"

"Whatever kind of animal this is, it's probably unknown everywhere but here. People like J. Paul Getty might get to eat it once a year, at some secret location."

"I don't care what it is, I'm just extraordinarily happy that we get to have it today. It's even a little bit sweet, isn't it?"

A short time later, Sandrine said, "Amazing. Even these horrible-looking vegetables spill out amazing flavors. If I could eat like this every day, I'd be perfectly happy to live in a hut, walk around barefoot, bathe in the Amazon, and wash my rags on the rocks."

"I know exactly what you mean," said Ballard. "It's like a drug. Maybe it is a drug."

"Do the natives really eat this way? Whatever this animal was, before they serve it to us, they have to hunt it down and kill it. Wouldn't they keep half of it for themselves?"

"Be a temptation," Ballard said. "Maybe they lick our plates too."

"Tell me the truth now, Ballard. If you know it. OK?"

Chewing, he looked up into her eyes. Some of the bliss faded from his face. "Sure. Ask away."

"Did we ever eat this stuff before?"

Ballard did not answer. He sliced a quarter-sized piece off the meat and began to chew, his eyes on his plate.

"I know I'm not supposed to ask."

He kept chewing and chewing until he swallowed. He sipped his wine. "No. Isn't that strange? How we know we're not supposed to do certain things?"

"Like see the waiters. Or the maids, or the captain."

"Especially the captain, I think."

"Let's not talk anymore, let's just eat for a little while."

Sandrine and Ballard returned to their plates and glasses, and for a time made no noise other than soft moans of satisfaction.

When they had nearly finished, Sandrine said, "There are so many books on this boat! It's like a big library. Do you think you've ever read one?"

"Do you?"

"I have the feeling . . . well, of course that's the reason I'm asking. In a way, I mean in a *real* way, we've never been here before. On the Amazon? Absolutely not. My husband, besides being continuously unfaithful, is a total asshole who never pays me any attention at all unless he's angry with me, but he's also tremendously jealous and possessive. For me to get here to be with you required an amazing amount of secret organization. D-day didn't take any more planning than this trip. On the other hand, I have the feeling I once read at least one of these books."

"I have the same feeling."

"Tell me about it. I want to read it again and see if I remember anything."

"I can't. But . . . well, I think I might have once seen you holding a copy of *Little Dorrit*. The Dickens novel."

"I went to Princeton and Cambridge, I know who wrote *Little Dorrit*," she said, irritated. "Wait. Did I ever throw a copy of that book overboard?"

"Might've."

"Why would I do that?"

Ballard shrugged. "To see what would happen?"

"Do you remember that?"

"It's tough to say what I remember. Everything's always different, but it's different *now*. I sort of remember a book, though—a book from this library. *Tono-Bungay*. H. G. Wells. Didn't like it much."

"Did you throw it overboard?"

"I might've. Yes, I actually might have." He laughed. "I think I did. I mean, I think I'm throwing it overboard right now, if that makes sense."

"Because you didn't—don't—like it?"

Ballard laughed and put down his knife and fork. Only a few bits of the vegetables and a piece of meat the size of a knuckle sliced in half remained on his plate. "Stop eating and give me your plate." It was almost exactly as empty as his, though Sandrine's plate still had two swirls of the yellow sauce.

"Really?"

"I want to show you something."

Reluctantly, she lowered her utensils and handed him her plate. Ballard scraped the contents of his plate onto hers. He got to his feet and picked up a knife and the plate that had been Sandrine's. "Come out on deck with me."

When she stood up, Sandrine glanced at what she had only briefly and partially perceived as a hint of motion at the top of the room, where for the first time she took in a dun-colored curtain hung two or three feet before the end of the oval. What looked to be a brown or suntanned foot, smaller than a normal adult's and perhaps a bit grubby, was just now vanishing behind the curtain. Before Sandrine had deciphered what she thought she had seen, it was gone.

"Just see a rat?" asked Ballard.

Without intending to assent, Sandrine nodded.

"One was out on deck this morning. Disappeared as soon as I spotted it. Don't worry about it, though. The crew, whoever they are, will get rid of them. At the start of the cruise, I think there are always a few rats around. By the time we really get in gear, they're gone."

"Good," she said, wondering: *If the waiters are these really, really short Indian guys, would they hate us enough to make us eat rats?*

She followed him through the door between the two portholes into pitiless sunlight and crushing heat made even less comfortable by the dense, invasive humidity. The invisible water saturating the air pressed against her face like a steaming washcloth, and moisture instantly coated her entire body. Leaning against the rail, Ballard looked cool and completely at ease.

"I forgot we had air-conditioning," she said.

"We don't. Vents move the air around somehow. Works like magic, even when there's no breeze at all. Come over here."

She joined him at the rail. Fifty yards away, what might have been human faces peered at them through a dense screen of jungle—weeds with thick, vegetal leaves of a green so dark it was nearly black. The

350

half-seen faces resembled masks, empty of feeling.

"Remember saying something about being happy to bathe in the Amazon? About washing your clothes in the river?"

She nodded.

"You never want to go into this river. You don't even want to stick the tip of your finger in that water. Watch what happens now. Our native friends came out to see this; you should too."

"The Indians knew you were going to put on this demonstration? How could they?"

"Don't ask me, ask them. *I* don't know how they do it."

Ballard leaned over the railing and used his knife to scrape the few things on the plate into the river. Even before the little knuckles of meat and gristle, the shreds of vegetables, and liquid strings of gravy landed in the water, a six-inch circle of turbulence boiled up on the slow-moving surface. When the bits of food hit the water, the boiling circle widened out into a three-foot thrashing chaos of violent little fish tails and violent little green shiny fish backs with violent tiny green fins, all in furious motion. The fury lasted about thirty seconds, then disappeared back under the river's sluggish brown face.

"Like Christmas dinner with my husband's family," Sandrine said.

"When we were talking about throwing *Tono-Bungay* and *Little Dorrit* into the river to see what would happen—"

"The fish ate the books?"

"They'll eat anything that isn't metal."

"So our little friends don't go swimming all that often, do they?"

"They never learn how. Swimming is death, it's for people like us. Let's go back in, OK?"

She whirled around and struck his chest, hard, with a pointed fist. "I want to go back to the room with the table in it. *Our* table. And this time, you can get as hard as you like."

"Don't I always?" he asked.

"Oh," Sandrine said, "I like that 'always.'"

"And yet, it's always different."

"I bet *I'm* always different," said Sandrine. "You, you'd stay pretty much the same."

"I'm not as boring as all that, you know, " Ballard said, and went on, over the course of the long afternoon and sultry evening, to prove it.

After breakfast the next morning, Sandrine, hissing with pain, her skin clouded with bruises, turned on him with such fury that he gasped in joy and anticipation.

351

1976

End of November, hot sticky muggy, a vegetal stink in the air. Motionless tribesmen four feet tall stared out from the overgrown bank over twenty yards of torpid river. They held, seemed to hold, bows without arrows, though the details swam backward into the layers of folded green.

"Look at those little savages," said Sandrine Loy, nineteen years old and already contemplating marriage to handsome, absurdly wealthy Antonio Barban, who had proposed to her after a chaotic Christmas dinner at his family's vulgar pile in Greenwich, Connecticut. That she knew marriage to Antonio would prove to be an error of sublime proportions gave the idea most of its appeal. "We're putting on a traveling circus for their benefit. Doesn't that sort of make you detest them?"

"I don't detest them at all," Ballard said. "Actually, I have a lot of respect for those people. I think they're mysterious. So much gravity. So much *silence*. They understand a million things we don't, and what we do manage to get they know about in another way, a more profound way."

"You're wrong. They're too stupid to understand anything. They have mud for dinner. They have mud for brains."

"And yet . . . ," Ballard said, smiling at her.

As if they knew they had been insulted and seemingly without moving out of position, the river people had begun to fade back into the network of dark, rubbery leaves in which they had for a long moment been framed.

"And yet what?"

"They knew what we were going to do. They wanted to see us throwing those books into the river. So out of the bushes they popped, right at the time we walked out on deck."

Her conspicuous black eyebrows slid nearer each other, creating a furrow. She shook her beautiful head and opened her mouth to disagree.

"Anyway, Sandrine, what did you think of what happened just now? Any responses, reflections?"

"What do I think of what happened to the books? What do I think of the fish?"

"Of course," Ballard said. "It's not *all* about us."

He leaned back against the rail, communicating utter ease and confidence. He was forty-four, attired daily in dark tailored suits and white shirts that gleamed like a movie star's smile, the repository of a thousand feral secrets, at home everywhere in the world, the possessor of an understanding it would take him a lifetime to absorb. Sandrine often seemed to him the center of his life. He knew exactly what she was going to say.

"I think the fish are astonishing," she said. "I mean it. Astonishing. Such concentration, such power, such complete *hunger*. It was breathtaking. Those books didn't last more than five or six seconds. All that thrashing! My book lasted longer than yours, but not by much."

"*Little Dorrit* is a lot longer than *Tono-Bungay*. More paper, more thread, more glue. I think they're especially hot for glue."

"Maybe they're just hot for Dickens."

"Maybe they're speed-readers," said Sandrine. "What do we do now?"

"What we came here to do," Ballard said, and moved back to swing open the dining-room door, then froze in midstep.

"Forget something?"

"I was having the oddest feeling, and I just now realized what it was. You read about it all the time, so you think it must be pretty common, but until a second ago I don't think I'd ever before had the feeling that I was being watched. Not really."

"But now you did."

"Yes." He strode up to the door and swung it open. The table was bare, and the room was empty.

Sandrine approached and peeked over his shoulder. He had both amused and dismayed her. "The great Ballard exhibits a moment of paranoia. I think I've been wrong about you all this time. You're just another boring old creep who wants to fuck me."

"I'd admit to being a lot of things, but paranoid isn't one of them." He gestured her back through the door. That Sandrine obeyed him seemed to take both of them by surprise.

"How about being a boring old creep? I'm not really so sure I want to stay here with you. For one thing, and I know this is not related, the birds keep waking me up. If they are birds."

He cocked his head, interested. "What else could they be? Please tell me. Indulge a boring old creep."

"The maids and the waiters and the sailor guys. The cook. The woman who arranges the flowers."

"You think they belong to that tribe that speaks in birdcalls? Actually, how did *you* ever hear about them?"

"My anthropology professor was one of the people who first discovered that tribe. The Piranhas. Know what they call themselves? The tall people. Not very observant, are they? According to the professor, they worshipped a much older tribe that had disappeared many generations back—miracle people, healers, shamans, warriors. The Old Ones, they called them, but the Old Ones called themselves **We**, you always have to put it in boldface. My professor couldn't stop talking about these tribes—he was so full of himself. *Sooo* vain. Kept staring at me. Vain, ugly, and lecherous, my favorite trifecta!"

The memory of her anthropology professor, with whom she had clearly gone through the customary adoration-boredom-disgust cycle of student-teacher love affairs, had put Sandrine in a sulky, dissatisfied mood.

"You made a lovely little error about thirty seconds ago. The tribe is called the Piraha, not the Piranhas. Piranhas are the fish you fell in love with."

"Ooh," she said, brightening up. "So the Piraha eat piranhas?"

"Other way around, more likely. But the other people on the *Blinding Light* can't be Piraha, we're hundreds of miles from their territory."

"You *are* tedious. Why did I ever let myself get talked into coming here anyhow?"

"You fell in love with me the first time you saw me—in your father's living room, remember? And although it was tremendously naughty of me, in fact completely wrong and immoral, I took one look at your stupid sweatshirt and your stupid pigtails and fell in love with you on the spot. You were perfect—you took my breath away. It was like being struck by lightning."

He inhaled, hugely.

"And here I am, forty-four years of age, height of my powers, capable of performing miracles on behalf of our clients, exactly as I pulled off, not to say any more about this, a considerable miracle for your father, plus I am a fabulously eligible man, a tremendous catch, but what do you know, still unmarried. Instead of a wife or even a steady girlfriend, there's this succession of inane young women from twenty-five to thirty, these Heathers and Ashleys, these Morgans and Emilys, who much to their dismay grow less and less infatuated with me the more time we spend together. 'You're always so distant,' one of them said, 'you're never really *with* me.' And she was right, I couldn't really be with her. Because I wanted to be with you. I wanted us to be *here*."

Deeply pleased, Sandrine said, "You're such a pervert."

Yet something in what Ballard had evoked was making the handsome dining room awkward and dark. She wished he wouldn't stand still; there was no reason why he couldn't go into the living room, or the other way, into the room where terror and fascination beckoned. She wondered why she was waiting for Ballard to decide where to go, and as he spoke of seeing her for the first time, was assailed by an uncomfortably precise echo from the day in question.

Then, as now, she had been rooted to the floor: in her family's living room, beyond the windows familiar Park Avenue humming with the traffic she only in that moment became aware she heard, Sandrine had been paralyzed. Every inch of her face had turned hot and red. She felt intimate with Ballard before she had even begun to learn what intimacy meant. Before she had left the room, she waited for him to move between her and her father, then pushed up the sleeves of the baggy sweatshirt and revealed the inscriptions of self-loathing, self-love, desire, and despair upon her pale forearms.

"You're pretty weird too. You'd just had your fifteenth birthday, and here you were, gobsmacked by this old guy in a suit. You even showed me your arms!"

"I could tell what made *you* salivate." She gave him a small, lopsided smile. "So why were you there anyhow?"

"Your father and I were having a private celebration."

"Of what?"

Every time she asked this question, he gave her a different answer. "I made the fearsome problem of his old library fines disappear. *Poof!* No more late-night sweats." Previously, Ballard had told her that he'd got her father off jury duty, had canceled his parking tickets, retroactively upgraded his B- in Introductory Chemistry to an A.

"Yeah, what a relief. My father never walked into a library, his whole life."

"You can see why the fine was so great." He blinked. "I just had an idea." Ballard wished her to cease wondering, to the extent this was possible, about the service he had rendered for her father. "How would you like to take a peek at the galley? Forbidden fruit, all that kind of thing. Aren't you curious?"

"You're suggesting we go down those stairs? Wasn't *not* doing that one of our most sacred rules?"

"I believe we were given those rules in order to make sure we broke them."

Sandrine considered this proposition for a moment, then nodded her head.

That's my girl, he thought.

"You may be completely perverted, Ballard, but you're pretty smart." A discordant possibility occurred to her. "What if we catch sight of our extremely discreet servants?"

"Then we know for good and all if they're little tribesmen who chirp like bobolinks or handsome South American yacht bums. But that won't happen. They may, in fact they undoubtedly do, see us, but we'll never catch sight of them. No matter how brilliantly we try to outwit them."

"You think they watch us?"

"I'm sure that's one of their main jobs."

"Even when we're in bed? Even when we . . . you know."

"Especially then," Ballard said.

"What do we think about that, Ballard? Do we love the whole idea, or does it make us sick? You first."

"Neither one. We can't do anything about it, so we might as well forget it. I think being able to watch us is one of the ways they're paid—these tribes don't have much use for money. And because they're always there, they can step in and help us when we need it, at the end."

"So it's like love," said Sandrine.

"Tough love, there at the finish. Let's go over and try the staircase."

"Hold on. When we were out on deck, you told me that you felt you were being watched, and that it was the first time you'd ever had that feeling."

"Yes, that was different—I don't *feel* the natives watching me, I just assume they're doing it. It's the only way to explain how they can stay out of sight all the time."

As they moved across the dining room to the inner door, for the first time Sandrine noticed a curtain the color of a dark camel-hair coat hanging up at the top of the room's oval. Until that moment, she had taken it for a wall too small and oddly shaped to be covered with bookshelves. The curtain shifted a bit, she thought: A tiny ripple occurred in the fabric, as if it had been breathed upon.

There's one of them now, she thought. *I bet they have their own doors and their own staircases.*

For a moment, she was disturbed by a vision of the yacht honeycombed with narrow passages and runways down which beetled small red-brown figures with matted black hair and faces like dull, heavy masks. Now and then the little figures paused to peer through chinks in the walls. It made her feel violated, a little, but at the same time immensely proud of the body that the unseen and silent attendants were privileged to gaze at. The thought of these mysterious little people watching what Ballard did to that body, and she to his, caused a thrill of deep feeling to course upward through her body.

"Stop daydreaming, Sandrine, and get over here." Ballard held the door that led to the gray landing and the metal staircase.

"You go first," she said, and Ballard moved through the frame while still holding the door. As soon as she was through, he stepped around her to grasp the gray metal rail and begin moving down the stairs.

"What makes you so sure the galley's downstairs?"

"Galleys are always downstairs."

"And why do you want to go there, again?"

"One: because they ordered us not to. Two: because I'm curious about what goes on in that kitchen. And three: I also want to get a look at the wine cellar. How can they keep giving us these amazing wines? Remember what we drank with lunch?"

"Some stupid red. It tasted good, though."

"That stupid red was a '55 Château Pétrus. Two years older than you."

Ballard led her down perhaps another dozen steps, arrived at a landing, and saw one more long staircase leading down to yet another landing.

"How far down can this galley be?" she asked.

"Good question."

"This boat has a bottom, after all."

"It has a hull, yes."

"Shouldn't we actually have gone past it by now? The bottom of the boat?"

"You'd think so. OK, maybe this is it."

The final stair ended at a gray landing that opened out into a narrow gray corridor leading to what appeared to be a large, empty room. Ballard looked down into the big space and experienced a violent reluctance, a mental and physical refusal, to go down there and look farther into the room: It was prohibited by an actual taboo. That room was not for him, it was none of his business, period. Chilled, he turned from the corridor and at last saw what was directly before him. What had appeared to be a high gray wall was divided in the middle and bore two brass panels at roughly chest height. The wall was a doorway.

Peter Straub

"What do you want to do?" Sandrine asked.

Ballard placed a hand on one of the panels and pushed. The door swung open, revealing a white tile floor, metal racks filled with cast-iron pans, steel bowls, and other cooking implements. The light was a low, diffused dimness. Against the side wall, three sinks of varying sizes bulged downward beneath their faucets. He could see the inner edge of a long, shiny metal counter. Far back, a yellow propane tank clung to a range with six burners, two ovens, and a big griddle. A faint mewing, a tiny *skritch skritch skritch*, came to him from the depths of the kitchen.

"Look, is there any chance . . . ?" Sandrine whispered.

In a normal voice, Ballard said, "No. They're not in here right now, whoever they are. I don't think they are, anyhow."

"So does that mean we're supposed to go inside?"

"How would I know?" He looked over his shoulder at her. "Maybe we're not *supposed* to do anything, and we just decide one way or the other. But here we are, anyhow. I say we go in, right? If it feels wrong, smells wrong, whatever, we boogie on out."

"You first," she said.

Without opening the door any wider, Ballard slipped into the kitchen. Before he was all the way in, he reached back and grasped Sandrine's wrist.

"Come along now."

"You don't have to drag me, I was right behind you. You bully."

"I'm not a bully, I just don't want to be in here by myself."

"All bullies are cowards too."

She edged in behind him and glanced quickly from side to side. "I didn't think you could have a kitchen like this on a yacht."

"You can't," he said. "Look at that gas range. It must weigh a thousand pounds."

She yanked her wrist out of his hand. "It's hard to see in here, though. Why is the light so fucking weird?"

They were edging away from the door, Sandrine so close behind that Ballard could feel her breath on his neck.

"There aren't any light fixtures, see? No overhead lights, either."

He looked up and saw, far above, only a dim white-gray ceiling that stretched away a great distance on either side. Impossibly, the "galley" seemed much wider than the *Blinding Light* itself.

"I don't like this," he said.

"Me neither."

"We're really not supposed to be here," he said, thinking of that

358

other vast room down at the end of the corridor, and said to himself, *That's what they call the "engine room," we absolutely can't even glance that way again, can't can't can't, the "engines" would be way too much for us.*

The mewing and skritching, which had momentarily fallen silent, started up again, and in the midst of what felt and tasted to him like panic, Ballard had a vision of a kitten trapped behind a piece of kitchen equipment. He stepped forward and leaned over to peer into the region beyond the long counter and beside the enormous range. Two funny striped cabinets about five feet tall stood there side by side.

"Do you hear a cat?" he asked.

"If you think that's a cat . . . ," Sandrine said, a bit farther behind him than she had been at first.

The cabinets were cages, and what he had seen as stripes were their bars. "Oh," Ballard said, and sounded as though he had been punched in the stomach.

"Damn you, you started to bleed through your suit jacket," Sandrine whispered. "We have to get out of here, fast."

Ballard scarcely heard her. In any case, if he was bleeding, it was of no consequence. They knew what to do about bleeding. Here, on the other hand, perhaps sixty feet away in this preposterous "galley," was a phenomenon he had never before witnessed. The first cage contained a thrashing beetle-like insect nearly too large for it. This gigantic insect was the source of the mewing and scratching. One of its mandibles rasped at a bar as the creature struggled to roll forward or back, producing noises of insect distress. Long, smeary wounds in the wide middle area between its scrabbling legs oozed a yellow ichor.

Horrified, Ballard looked hastily into the second cage, which he had thought empty but for a roll of blankets, or towels, or the like, and discovered that the blankets or towels were occupied by a small boy from one of the river tribes who was gazing at him through the bars. The boy's eyes looked hopeless and dead. Half of his shoulder seemed to have been sliced away, and a long, thin strip of bone gleamed white against a great scoop of red. The arm half extended through the bars concluded in a dark, messy stump.

The boy opened his mouth and released, almost too softly to be heard, a single high-pitched musical note. Pure, accurate, well defined, clearly a word charged with some deep emotion, the note hung in the air for a brief moment, underwent a briefer half-life, and was gone.

"What's that?" Sandrine said.

"Let's get out of here."

He pushed her through the door, raced around her, and began charging up the stairs. When they reached the top of the steps and threw themselves into the dining room, Ballard collapsed onto the floor, then rolled onto his back, heaving in great quantities of air. His chest rose and fell, and with every exhalation he moaned. A portion of his left side pulsing with pain felt warm and wet. Sandrine leaned against the wall, breathing heavily in a less convulsive way. After perhaps thirty seconds, she managed to say, "I trust that was a bird down there."

"Um. Yes." He placed his hand on his chest, then held it up like a stop sign, indicating that he would soon have more to say. After a few more great, heaving lungfuls of air, he said, "Toucan. In a big cage."

"You were that frightened by a kind of parrot?"

He shook his head slowly from side to side on the polished floor. "I didn't want them to catch us down there. It seemed dangerous, all of a sudden. Sorry."

"You're bleeding all over the floor."

"Can you get me a new bandage pad?"

Sandrine pushed herself off the wall and stepped toward him. From his perspective, she was as tall as a statue. Her eyes glittered. "Screw you, Ballard. I'm not your servant. You can come with me. It's where we're going, anyhow."

He pushed himself upright and peeled off his suit jacket before standing up. The jacket fell to the floor with a squishy thump. With blood-dappled fingers, he unbuttoned his shirt and let that too fall to the floor.

"Just leave those things there," Sandrine said. "The invisible crew will take care of them."

"I imagine you're right." Ballard managed to get to his feet without staggering. Slow-moving blood continued to ooze down his left side.

"We have to get you on the table," Sandrine said. "Hold this over the wound for right now, OK?"

She handed him a folded white napkin, and he clamped it over his side. "Sorry. I'm not as good at stitches as you are."

"I'll be fine," Ballard said, and began moving, a bit haltingly, toward the next room.

"Oh, sure. You always are. But you know what I like about what we just did?"

For once he had no idea what she might say. He waited for it.

"That amazing food we loved so much was toucan! Who would've guessed? You'd think toucan would taste sort of like chicken, only a lot worse."

"Life is full of surprises."

In the bedroom, Ballard kicked off his shoes, pulled his trousers down over his hips, and stepped out of them.

"You can leave your socks on," said Sandrine, "but let's get your undies off, all right?"

"I need your help."

Sandrine grasped the waistband of his boxers and pulled them down, but they snagged on his penis. "Ballard is aroused, surprise number two." She unhooked his shorts, let them drop to the floor, batted his erection down, and watched it bounce back up. "Barkis is willin', all right."

"Let's get into the workroom," he said.

"Aye, aye, *mon capitaine.*" Sandrine closed her hand on his erection and said, "Want to go there on deck, give the natives a look at your magnificent manliness? Shall we increase the index of penis envy among the river tribes by a really big factor?"

"Let's just get in there, OK?"

She pulled him into the workroom and only then released his erection.

A wheeled aluminum tray had been rolled up beside the work-table. Sometimes it was not given to them, and they were forced to do their work with their hands and whatever implements they had brought with them. Today, next to the array of knives of many kinds and sizes, cleavers, wrenches, and hammers, lay a pack of surgical thread and a stainless-steel needle still warm from the autoclave.

Ballard sat down on the worktable, pushed himself along until his heels had cleared the edge, and lay back. Sandrine threaded the needle and, bending over to get close to the wound, began to do her patient, expert stitching.

1982

"Oh, here you are," said Sandrine, walking into the sitting room of their suite to find Ballard lying on one of the sofas, reading a book whose title she could not quite make out. Because both of his hands were heavily bandaged, he was having some difficulty turning the pages. "I've been looking all over for you."

He glanced up, frowning. "All over? Does that mean you went down the stairs?"

"No, of course not. I wouldn't do anything like that alone, anyhow."

"And just to make sure . . . you didn't go up the stairs either, did you?"

Sandrine came toward him, shaking her head. "No, I'd never do that either. But I want to tell you something. I thought *you* might have decided to take a look upstairs. By yourself, to sort of protect me in a way I never want to be protected."

"Of course," Ballard said, closing his book on an index finger that protruded from the bulky white swath of bandage. "You'd hate me if I ever tried to protect you, especially by doing something sneaky. I knew that about you when you were fifteen years old."

"When I was fifteen, you did protect me."

He smiled at her. "I exercised an atypical amount of restraint."

His troublesome client, Sandrine's father, had told him one summer day that a business venture required him to spend a week in Mexico City. Could he think of anything acceptable that might occupy his daughter during that time, she being a teenager a bit too prone to independence and exploration? Let her stay with me, Ballard had said. The guest room has its own bathroom and a TV. I'll take her out to theaters at night, and to the Met and MoMA during the day when I'm not doing my job. When I *am* doing my job, she can bat around the city by herself the way she does now. Extraordinary man you are, the client had said, and allow me to reinforce that by letting you know that about a month ago my daughter just amazed me one morning by telling me that she liked you. You have no idea how goddamned fucking unusual that is. That she talked to me at all is staggering, and that she actually announced that she liked one of my friends is stupefying. So yes, please, thank you, take Sandrine home with you, please do, escort her hither and yon.

When the time came, he drove a compliant Sandrine to his house in Harrison, where he explained that although he would not have sex with her until she was at least eighteen, there were many other ways they could express themselves. And although it would be years before they could be naked together, for the present they would each be able to be naked before the other. Fifteen-year-old Sandrine, who had been expecting to use all her arts of bad temper, insult, duplicity, and evasiveness to escape ravishment by this actually pretty interesting old guy, responded to these conditions with avid interest.

Ballard announced another prohibition no less serious, but even more personal.

"I can't cut myself anymore?" she asked. "Fuck you, Ballard, you loved it when I showed you my arm. Did my father put you up to this?" She began looking frantically for her bag, which Ballard's valet had already removed to the guest room.

"Not at all. Your father would try to kill me if he knew what I was going to do to you. And you to me, when it's your turn."

"So if I can't cut myself, what exactly happens instead?"

"*I* cut you," Ballard said. "And I do it a thousand times better than you ever did. I'll cut you so well no one will ever be able to tell it happened, unless they're right on top of you."

"You think I'll be satisfied with some wimpy little cuts no one can even see? Fuck you all over again."

"Those cuts no one can see will be incredibly painful. And then I'll take the pain away, so you can experience it all over again."

Sandrine found herself abruptly caught up by a rush of feelings that seemed to originate in a deep region located just below her rib cage. At least for the moment, this flood of unnameable emotions blotted out her endless grudges and frustrations, also the chronic bad temper they engendered.

"And during this process, Sandrine, I will become deeply familiar, profoundly familiar with your body, so that when at last we are able to enjoy sex with each other, I will know how to give you the most amazing pleasure. I'll know every inch of you, I'll have your whole gorgeous map in my head. And you will do the same with me."

Sandrine had astonished herself by agreeing to this program on the spot, even to abstain from sex until she turned eighteen. Denial too was a pain she could learn to savor. At that point Ballard had taken her upstairs to the guest suite, and soon after down the hallway to what he called his "workroom."

"Oh my God," she said, taking it in, "I can't believe it. This is real. And you, you're real too."

"During the next three years, whenever you start hating everything around you and feel as though you'd like to cut yourself again, remember that I'm here. Remember that this room exists. There'll be many days and nights when we can be here together."

In this fashion had Sandrine endured the purgatorial remainder of her days at Dalton. And when she and Ballard at last made love, pleasure and pain had become presences nearly visible in the room at the moment she screamed in the ecstasy of release.

"You dirty, dirty, dirty old man," she said, laughing.

Four years after that, Ballard overheard some Chinese bankers, clients of his firm for whom he had several times rendered his services, speaking in soft Mandarin about a yacht anchored in the Amazon Basin; he needed no more.

"I want to go off the boat for a couple of hours when we get to Manaus," Sandrine said. "I feel like getting back in the world again, at least for a little while. This little private bubble of ours is completely cut off from everything else."

"Which is why—"

"Which is why it works, and why we like it, I understand, but half the time I can't stand it either. I don't live the way you do, always flying off to interesting places to perform miracles. . . ."

"Try spending a rainy afternoon in Zurich holding some terminally anxious banker's hand."

"Not that it matters, especially, but you don't mind, do you?"

"Of course not. I need some recuperation time, anyhow. This was a little severe." He held up one thickly bandaged hand. "Not that I'm complaining."

"You'd better not!"

"I'll only complain if you stay out too late—or spend too much of your father's money!"

"What could I buy in Manaus? And I'll make sure to be back before dinner. Have you noticed? The food on this weird boat is getting better and better every day?"

"I know, yes, but for now I seem to have lost my appetite," Ballard said. He had a quick mental vision of a metal cage from which something hideous was struggling to escape. It struck an oddly familiar note, as of something half remembered, but Ballard was made so uncomfortable by the image in his head that he refused to look at it any longer.

"Will they just know that I want to dock at Manaus?"

"Probably, but you could write them a note. Leave it on the bed. Or on the dining-room table."

"I have a pen in my bag, but where can I find some paper?"

"I'd say look in any drawer. You'll probably find all the paper you might need."

Sandrine went to the little table beside him, pulled open its one drawer, and found a single sheet of thick, cream-colored stationery headed *Sweet Delight*. An Omas rollerball pen, much nicer than the Pilot she had liberated from their hotel in Rio, lay angled atop the sheet of stationery. In her formal, almost italic handwriting, Sandrine wrote, *Please dock at Manaus. I would like to spend two or three hours ashore.*

"Should I sign it?"

Ballard shrugged. "There's just the two of us. Initial it."

She drew a graceful, looping S under her note and went into the dining room, where she squared it off in the middle of the table. When she returned to the sitting room, she asked, "And now I just wait? Is that how it works? Just because I found a piece of paper and a pen, I'm supposed to trust this crazy system?"

"You know as much as I do, Sandrine. But I'd say, yes, just wait a little while, yes, that's how it works, and yes, you might as well trust it. There's no reason to be bitchy."

"I have to stay in practice," she said, and lurched sideways as the yacht bumped against something hard and came to an abrupt halt.

"See what I mean?"

When he put the book down in his lap, Sandrine saw that it was *Tono-Bungay*. She felt a hot, rapid flare of irritation that the book was not something like *The Women's Room*, which could teach him things he needed to know: and hadn't he already read *Tono-Bungay*?

"Look outside, try to catch them tying us up and getting out that walkway thing."

"You think we're in Manaus already?"

"I'm sure we are."

"That's ridiculous. We scraped against a barge or something."

"Nonetheless, we have come to a complete halt."

Sandrine strode briskly to the on-deck door, threw it open, gasped, then stepped outside. The yacht had already been tied up at a long yellow dock at which two yachts smaller than theirs rocked in a desultory brown tide. No crewmen were in sight. The dock led to a wide concrete apron across which men of European descent and a few natives pushed wheelbarrows and consulted clipboards and pulled on cigars while pointing out distant things to other men. It looked false and stagy, like the first scene in a bad musical about New Orleans. An avenue began in front of a row of warehouses, the first of which was painted with the slogan MANAUS AMAZONA. The board walkway with rope handrails had been set in place.

"Yeah, OK," she said. "We really do seem to be docked at Manaus."

"Don't stay away too long."

"I'll stay as long as I like," she said.

The avenue leading past the facades of the warehouses seemed to run directly into the center of the city, visible now to Sandrine as a gathering of tall office buildings and apartment blocks that thrust upward from the jumble of their surroundings like an outcropping of mountains. The skyscrapers were blue-gray in color, the lower surrounding buildings a scumble of brown, red, and yellow that made Sandrine think of Cézanne, even of Seurat: dots of color that suggested walls and roofs. She thought she could walk to the center of the city in no more than forty-five minutes, which left her about two hours to do some exploring and have lunch.

Nearly an hour later, Sandrine trudged past the crumbling buildings and broken windows on crazed, tilting sidewalks under a domineering sun. Sweat ran down her forehead and cheeks and plastered her dress to her body. The air seemed half water, and her lungs strained to draw in oxygen. The office buildings did not seem any nearer than at the start of her walk. If she had seen a taxi, she would have taken it back to the port, but only a few cars and pickups rolled along the broad avenue. The dark, half-visible men driving these vehicles generally leaned over their steering wheels and stared at her, as if women were rare in Manaus. She wished she had thought to cover her hair, and was sorry she had left her sunglasses behind.

Then she became aware that a number of men were following her, how many she could not tell, but more than two. They spoke to each other in low, hoarse voices, now and then laughing at some remark sure to be at Sandrine's expense. Although her feet had begun to hurt, she began moving more quickly. Behind her, the men kept pace with her, neither gaining nor falling back. After another two blocks, Sandrine gave in to her sense of alarm and glanced over her shoulder. Four men in dark hats and shapeless, slept-in suits had ranged themselves across the width of the sidewalk. One of them called out to her in a language she did not understand; another emitted a wet, mushy laugh. The man at the curb jumped down into the street, trotted across the empty avenue, and picked up his pace on the sidewalk opposite until he had drawn a little ahead of Sandrine.

She felt utterly alone and endangered. And because she felt in danger, a scorching anger blazed up within her: at herself for so stupidly putting herself at risk, at the men behind her for making her feel frightened, for ganging up on her. She did not know what she was going to have to do, but she was not going to let those creeps get any closer to her than they were now. Twisting to her right, then to her left, Sandrine removed her shoes and rammed them into her bag.

They were watching her, the river scum; even the man on the other side of the avenue had stopped moving and was staring at her from beneath the brim of his hat.

Literally testing the literal ground, Sandrine walked a few paces over the paving stones, discovered that they were at any rate not likely to cut her feet, gathered herself within, and, like a racehorse bursting from the gate, instantly began running as fast as she could. After a moment in which her pursuers were paralyzed with surprise, they too began to run. The man on the other side of the street jumped down from the curb and began sprinting toward her. His shoes made a sharp *tick-tick* sound when they met the stony asphalt. As the ticks grew louder, Sandrine heard him inhaling great quantities of air. Before he could reach her, she came to a cross street and wheeled in, her bag bouncing at her hip, her legs stretching out to devour yard after yard of stony ground.

Unknowingly, she had entered a slum. The structures on both sides of the street were half-collapsed huts and shanties made of mismatched wooden planks, of metal sheeting, and tar paper. She glimpsed faces peering out of greasy windows and sagging, cracked-open doors. Some of the shanties before her were shops with soft-drink cans and bottles of beer arrayed on the windowsills. People were spilling from little tar-paper and sheet-metal structures out into the street, already congested with abandoned cars, empty pushcarts, and cartons of fruit for sale. Garbage lay everywhere. The women who watched Sandrine streak by displayed no interest in her plight.

Yet the slum's chaos was a blessing, Sandrine thought: The deeper she went, the greater the number of tiny, narrow streets sprouting off the one she had taken from the avenue. It was a feverish, crowded warren, a *favela*, the kind of place you would never escape had you the bad luck to have been born there. And while outside this rat's nest the lead man chasing her had been getting dangerously near, within its boundaries the knots of people and the obstacles of cars and carts and mounds of garbage had slowed him down. Sandrine found that she could dodge all of these obstacles with relative ease. The next time she spun around a corner, feet skidding on a slick pad of rotting vegetables, she saw what looked to her like a miracle: an open door revealing a hunched old woman draped in black rags, beckoning her in.

Sandrine bent her legs, called on her youth and strength, jumped off the ground, and sailed through the open door. The old woman only just got out of the way in time to avoid being knocked down.

She was giggling, either at Sandrine's athleticism or because she had rescued her from the pursuing thugs. When Sandrine had cleared her dooorway and was scrambling to avoid ramming into the wall, the old woman darted forward and slammed her door shut. Sandrine fell to her knees in a small room suddenly gone very dark. A slanting shaft of light split the murk and illuminated a rectangular space on the floor covered by a threadbare rug no longer of any identifiable color. Under the light, the rug seemed at once utterly worthless and extraordinarily beautiful.

The old woman shuffled into the shaft of light and uttered an incomprehensible word that sounded neither Spanish nor Portuguese. A thousand wayward wrinkles like knife cuts, scars, and stitches had been etched into her white, elongated face. Her nose had a prominent hook, and her eyes shone like dark stones at the bottom of a fast, clear stream. Then she laid an upright index finger against her sunken lips and with her other hand gestured toward the door. Sandrine listened. In seconds, multiple footsteps pounded past the old woman's little house. Leading the pack was *tick tick tick*. The footsteps clattered up the narrow street and disappeared into the ordinary clamor.

Hunched over almost parallel to the ground, the old woman mimed hysterical laughter. Sandrine mouthed, *Thank you, thank you*, thinking that her intention would be clear if the words were not. Still mock laughing, her unknown savior shuffled closer, knitting and folding her long, spotted hands. She had the ugliest hands Sandrine had ever seen, knobbly arthritic fingers with filthy, ragged nails. She hoped the woman was not going to stroke her hair or pat her face: She would have to let her do it, however nauseated she might feel. Instead, the old woman moved right past her, muttering what sounded like *Munna, munna, num.*

Outside on the street, the ticking footsteps once again became audible. Someone began knocking, hard, on an adjacent door.

Only half visible at the rear of the room, the old woman turned toward Sandrine and beckoned her forward with an urgent gesture of her bony hand. Sandrine moved toward her, uncertain of what was going on.

In an urgent, raspy whisper: *Munna! Num!*

The old woman appeared to be bowing to the baffled Sandrine, whose sense of peril had begun again to boil up within her. A pane of greater darkness slid open behind the old woman, and Sandrine finally understood that her savior had merely bent herself more deeply to turn a doorknob.

Num! Num!

Sandrine obeyed orders and *nummed* past her beckoning hostess. Almost instantly, instead of solid ground, her foot met a vacancy, and she nearly tumbled down what she finally understood to be a staircase. Only her sense of balance kept her upright: She was grateful she still had all of her crucial toes. Behind her, the door slammed shut. A moment later, she heard the clicking of a lock.

Back on the yacht, Ballard slipped a bookmark into *Tono-Bungay* and for the first time, at least for what he thought was the first time, regarded the pair of red lacquered cabinets against the wall beside him. Previously, he had taken them in, but never really examined them. About four feet high and three feet wide, they appeared to be Chinese and were perhaps moderately valuable. Brass fittings with latch pins held them closed in front, so they were easily opened.

The thought of lifting the pins and opening the cabinets aroused both curiosity and an odd dread in Ballard. For a moment, he had a vision of a great and forbidden room deep in the bowels of the yacht where enormous spiders ranged across rotting, heaped-up corpses. (With wildly variant details, visions of exactly this sort had visited Ballard ever since his adolescence.) He shook his head to clear it of this vision, and when that failed, struck his bandaged left hand against the padded arm of the sofa. Bright, rolling waves of pain forced a gasp from him, and the forbidden room with its spiders and corpses zipped right back to whatever had given it birth.

Was this the sort of dread he was supposed to obey, or the sort he was supposed to ignore? Or if not ignore, because that was always unwise and in some sense dishonorable, acknowledge but persist in the face of anyway? Cradling his throbbing hand against his chest, Ballard let the book slip off his lap and got to his feet, eyeing the pair of shiny cabinets. If asked to inventory the contents of the sitting room, he would have forgotten to list them. Presumably that meant he was supposed to overlook his foreboding and investigate the contents of these vertical little Chinese chests. *They* wanted him to open the cabinets, if *he* wanted to.

Still holding his electrocuted left hand to his chest, Ballard leaned over and brought his exposed right index finger in contact with the box on the left. No heat came from it, and no motion. It did not hum, it did not quiver, however delicately. At least six or seven coats of lacquer had been applied to the thing—he felt as though he were looking into a deep river of red lacquer.

Ballard hunkered and used his index finger to push the brass latch pin up and out of the ornate little lock. It swung down on an intricate little cord he had not previously noticed. The door did not open by itself, as he had hoped. Once again, he had to make a choice, for it was not too late to drop the brass pin back into its latch. He could choose not to look; he could let the *Sweet Delight* keep its secrets. But as before, Ballard acknowledged the dread he was feeling, then dropped his hip to the floor, reached out, and flicked the door open with his fingernail. Arrayed on the cabinet's three shelves were what appeared to be photographs in neat stacks. Polaroids, he thought. He took the first stack of photos from the cabinet and looked down at the topmost one. What Ballard saw there had two contradictory effects on him. He became so light-headed he feared he might faint, and he almost ejaculated into his trousers.

Taking care not to tumble, Sandrine moved in the darkness back to the top of the staircase, found the door with her fingertips, and pounded. The door rattled in its frame but did not give. "Open up, lady!" she shouted. "Are you *kidding*? Open this door!" She banged her fists against the unmoving wood, thinking that although the old woman undoubtedly did not speak English, she could hardly misunderstand what Sandrine was saying. When her fists began to hurt and her throat felt ragged, the strangeness of what had just happened opened before her: It was like . . . like a fairy tale! She had been duped, tricked, flummoxed; she had been trapped. The world had closed on her, as a steel trap snaps shut on the leg of a bear.

"Please!" she yelled, knowing it was useless. She would not be able to beg her way out of this confinement. Here, the Golden Shower of Shit did not apply. "Please let me out!" A few more bangs of her fist, a few more shouted pleas to be set free, to be *let go, released*. She thought she heard her ancient captor chuckling to herself.

Two possibilities occurred to her: that her pursuers had driven her to this place and the old woman was in league with them; and that they had not and she was not. The worse by far of these options was the second, that to escape her rapists she had fled into a psychopath's dungeon. Maybe the old woman wanted to starve her to death. Maybe she wanted to soften her up so she'd be easy to kill. Or maybe she was just keeping her as a snack for some monstrous get of hers, some overgrown loony-tunes son with pinwheel eyes and horrible teeth and a vast appetite for stray women.

More to exhaust all of her possibilities than because she imagined they possessed any actual substance, Sandrine turned carefully around, planted a hand on the earthen wall beside her, and began making her way down the stairs in the dark. They would lead to some spider-infested cellar, she knew, a foul-smelling hole where ugly, discarded things waited thuglike in the seamless dark to inflict injury upon anyone who entered their realm. She would grope her way from wall to wall, feeling for another door, for a high window, for any means to escape, knowing all the while that earthen cellars in shabby slum dwellings never had separate exits.

Five steps down, it occurred to Sandrine that she might not have been the first woman to be locked into this awful basement, and that instead of broken chairs and worn-out tools she might find herself knocking against a rib cage or two, a couple of femurs, that her foot might land on the jawbone, that she might step on somebody's fore-head! Her body of a sudden shook, and her mind went white, and for a few moments Sandrine was on the verge of coming unglued: She pictured herself drawn up into a fetal ball, shuddering, weeping, whimpering. For a moment this dreadful image seemed unbearably tempting.

Then she thought, *Why the FUCK isn't Ballard here?*

Ballard was one hell of a tricky dude, he was full of little surprises, you could never really predict what he'd feel like doing, and he was a brilliant problem solver. That's what Ballard did for a living, he flew around the world mopping up other people's messes. The only reason Sandrine knew him at all was that Ballard had materialized in a New Jersey motel room where good old Dad, Lauritzen Loy, had been dithering over the corpse of a strangled whore, then caused the whore to vanish, the bloody sheets to vanish, and for all she knew the motel to vanish also. Two hours later a shaken but sober Lauritzen Loy reported to work in an immaculate and spotless Armani suit and Brioni tie. (Sandrine had known the details of her father's vile little peccadillo for years.) Also, and this quality meant that his presence would have been particularly valuable down in the witch-hag's cellar, although Ballard might have looked as though he had never picked up anything heavier than a briefcase, he was in fact astonishingly strong, fast, and smart. If you were experiencing a little difficulty with a dragon, Ballard was the man for you.

While meditating upon the all-round excellence of her longtime lover and wishing for him more with every fresh development of her thought, Sandrine had been continuing steadily on her way down the stairs. When she reached the part about the dragon, it came to her that she had been on these earthen stairs far longer than she had expected. Sandrine thought she was now actually beneath the level of the cellar she had expected to enter. The fairy-tale feeling came over her again, of being held captive in a world without rational rules and orders, subject to deep patterns unknown to or rejected in the daylit world. In a flash of insight, it came to her that this fairy-tale world had much in common with her childhood.

To regain control of herself, perhaps most of all to shake off the sense of gloom-laden helplessness evoked by thoughts of childhood, Sandrine began to count the steps as she descended. Down into the earth they went, the dry, firm steps that met her feet, twenty more, then forty, then fifty. At a hundred and one, she felt light-headed and weary, and sat down in the darkness. She felt like weeping. The long stairs were a grave, leading nowhere but to itself. Hope, joy, and desire had fled; even boredom and petulance had fled; hunger, lust, and anger were no more. She felt tired and empty. Sandrine leaned a shoulder against the earthen wall, shuddered once, and realized she was crying only a moment before she fled into unconsciousness.

In that same instant she passed into an ongoing dream, as if she had wandered into the middle of a story, or, more accurately, a point far closer to its ending. Much, maybe nearly everything of interest, had already happened. Sandrine lay on a mess of filthy blankets at the bottom of a cage. The Golden Shower of Shit had sufficiently re-laxed, it seemed, so as to permit the butchering of entire slabs of flesh from her body, for much of the meat from her right shoulder had been sliced away. The wound reported a dull, wavering ache that spoke of those wonderful objects, Ballard's narcotic painkillers. So close together were the narrow bars, she could extend only a hand, a wrist, an arm. In her case, an arm, a wrist, and a stump. The hand was absent from the arm Sandrine had slipped through the bars, and someone had cauterized the wounded wrist.

The Mystery of the Missing Hand led directly to Cage Number One, where a giant bug creature sat crammed in at an angle, filling nearly the whole of the cage, mewing softly, and trying to saw through the bars with its remaining mandible. It had broken the left one on the bars, but it was not giving up, it was a bug, and bugs don't quit. Sandrine was all but certain that when in possession of both man-dibles, that is to say before capture, this huge *thing* had used them to saw off her hand, which it had then promptly devoured. The giant bugs were the scourge of the river tribes. However, the Old Ones, the Real People, the Cloud Huggers, the Tree Spirits, the archaic Sacred Ones who spoke in birdsong and called themselves **We** had so shaped the River and the Forest, which had given them birth, that the meat of the giant bugs tasted exceptionally good, and a giant bug guilty of eating a person or parts of a person became by that act overwhelmingly delicious, like manna, like the food of paradise for human beings. **We** were feeding bits of Sandrine to the captured bug that it might yield stupendous meals for the Sandrine and Ballard upstairs.

Sandrine awakened crying out in fear and horror, scattering tears she could not see.

Enough of that. Yes, quite enough of quivering; it was time to decide what to do next. Go back and try to break down the door, or keep going down and see what happens? Sandrine hated the idea of giving up and going backward. She levered herself upright and resumed her descent with stair number one hundred and two.

At stair three hundred she passed through another spasm of weepy trembling, but soon conquered it and moved on. By the four hundredth stair she was hearing faint carnival music and seeing sparkly light figments flit through the darkness like illuminated moths. Somewhere around stair five hundred she realized that the numbers had become mixed up in her head, and stopped counting. She saw a grave that wasn't a grave, merely darkness, and she saw her old tutor at Clare, a cool, detached don named Quentin Jester, who said things like, "If I had a lifetime with you, Miss Loy, we'd both know a deal more than we do at present," but she closed her eyes and shook her head and sent him packing.

Many stairs later, Sandrine's thigh muscles reported serious aches, and her arms felt extraordinarily heavy. So did her head, which kept lolling forward to rest on her chest. Her stomach complained, and she said to herself, *Wish I had a nice big slice of sautéed giant bug right about now*, and chuckled at how crazy she had become in so short a time. Giant bug! Even good old Dad, old LL, who often respected sanity in others but wished for none of it himself, drew the line at dining on giant insects. And here came yet another proof of her deteriorating mental condition, that despite her steady progress deeper and deeper underground, Sandrine could almost, sort of half persuade herself that the darkness before her seemed weirdly less dark than only a moment ago. This lunatic delusion clung to her step after step, worsening as she went. She said to herself, I'll hold up my hand, and if I think I see it, I'll know it's good-bye, real world, pack

Old Tillie off to Bedlam. She stopped moving, closed her eyes, and raised her hand before her face. Slowly, she opened her eyes, and beheld . . . her hand!

The problem with the insanity defense lay in the irrevocable truth that it was really her hand before her, not a mad vision from Gothic literature but her actual, entirely earthly hand, at present grimy and crusted with dirt from its long contact with the wall. Sandrine turned her head and discovered that she could make out the wall too, with its hard-packed earth showing here and there the pale string of a severed root, at times sending in her direction a little spray or shower of dusty particulate. Sandrine held her breath and looked down to what appeared to be the source of the illumination. Then she inhaled sharply, for it seemed to her that she could see, dimly and a long way down, the bottom of the stairs. A little rectangle of light burned away down there, and from it floated the luminous translucency that made it possible for her to see.

Too shocked to cry, too relieved to insist on its impossibility, Sandrine moved slowly down the remaining steps to the rectangle of light. Its warmth heated the air, the steps, the walls, and Sandrine herself, who only now registered that for most of her journey she had been half paralyzed by the chill leaking from the earth. As she drew nearer to the light, she could finally make out details of what lay beneath her. She thought she saw a strip of concrete, part of a wooden barrel, the bottom of a ladder lying on the ground: The intensity of the light surrounding these enigmatic objects shrank and dwindled them, hollowed them out even as it drilled painfully into her eyes. Beneath her world existed another, its light a blinding dazzle.

When Sandrine had come within thirty feet of the blazing underworld, her physical relationship to it mysteriously altered. It seemed she no longer stepped downward, but moved across a slanting plane that leveled almost imperceptibly off. The dirt walls on either side fell back and melted to ghostly gray air, to nothing solid, until all that remained was the residue of dust and grime plastered over Sandrine's white dress, her hands and face, her hair. Heat reached her, the real heat of an incendiary sun, and human voices, and the clang and bang and underlying susurrus of machinery. She walked toward all of it, shading her eyes as she went.

Through the simple opening before her Sandrine moved, and the sun blazed down upon her, and her own moisture instantly soaked her filthy dress, and sweat turned the dirt in her hair to muddy trickles. She knew this place; the dazzling underworld was the world she had left. From beneath her shading hand Sandrine took in the wide concrete apron, the equipment she had noticed all that harrowing time ago, and the equipment she had not, the men posturing for the benefit of other men, the sense of falsity and stagecraft and the incipient swelling of a banal unheard melody. The long yellow dock where on a sluggish umber tide three yachts slowly rocked, one of them the *Sweet Delight.*

In a warm breeze that was not a breeze, a soiled-looking scrap of paper flipped toward Sandrine over the concrete, at the last lifting off the ground to adhere to her leg. She bent down to peel it off and release it, and caught a strong, bitter whiff, unmistakably excremental, of the Amazon. The piece of paper wished to cling to her leg, and there it hung until the second tug of Sandrine's dirty fingers, when she observed that she was gripping not a scrap of paper but a Polaroid, now a little besmudged by contact with her leg. When she raised it to her face, runnels of dirt obscured portions of the image. She brushed away much of the dirt, but could still make no sense of the photograph, which appeared to depict some piglike animal.

In consternation, she glanced to one side and found there, lounging against bollards and aping the idleness of degenerates and river louts, two of the men in shabby suits and worn-out hats who had pursued her into the slum. She straightened up in rage and terror, and to confirm what she already knew to be the case, looked to her other side and saw their companions. One of them waved to her. Sandrine's terror cooled before her perception that these guys had changed in some basic way. Maybe they weren't idle, exactly, but these men were more relaxed, less predatory than they had been on the avenue into Manaus.

They had their eyes on her, though, they were interested in what she was going to do. Then she finally got it: They were different because now she was where they had wanted her to be all along. They didn't think she would try to escape again, but they wanted to make sure. Sandrine's whole long adventure, from the moment she noticed she was being followed to the present, had been designed to funnel her back to the dock and the yacht. The four men, who were now smiling at her and nodding their behatted heads, had pushed her toward the witch-hag, for they were all in it together! Sandrine dropped her arms, took a step backward, and in amazement looked from side to side, taking in all of them. It had all been a trick; herded like a cow, she had been played. Falsity again; more stagecraft.

One of the nodding, smiling men held his palm up before his face, and the man beside him leaned forward and laughed into his fist, as if shielding a sneeze. Grinning at her, the first man went through his meaningless mime act once again, lifting his left hand and staring into its palm. Grinning even more widely, he pointed at Sandrine and shouted, "*Munna!*"

The man beside him cracked up, *Munna!*, what a wit, then whistled an odd little four-note melody that might have been a birdcall.

Experimentally, Sandrine raised her left hand, regarded it, and realized that she was still gripping the dirty little Polaroid photograph of a pig. Those two idiots off to her left waved their hands in ecstasy. She was doing the right thing, so *Munna!* right back atcha, buddy. She looked more closely at the Polaroid and saw that what it pictured was not actually a pig. The creature in the photo had a head and a torso, but little else. The eyes, nose, and ears were gone. A congeries of scars like punctuation marks, like snakes, like words in an unknown language, decorated the torso.

I know what munna *means, and* num, thought Sandrine, and for a moment experienced a spasm of stunning, utterly sexual warmth before she fully understood what had been given her: that she recognized the man in the photo. The roar of oceans, of storm-battered leaves, filled her ears and caused her head to spin and wobble. Her fingers parted, and the Polaroid floated off in an artificial, wind-machine breeze that spun it around a couple of times before lifting it high above the port and winking it out of sight, lost in the bright, hard blue above the *Sweet Delight.*

Sandrine found herself moving down the yellow length of the long dock.

Tough love, Ballard had said. To be given and received, at the end perfectly repaid by that which she had perhaps glimpsed but never witnessed, the brutal, exalted, slow-moving force that had sometimes rustled a curtain, sometimes moved through this woman, her hair and body now dark with mud, had touched her between her legs, Sandrine, poor profane lost deluded most marvelously fated Sandrine.

1997

From the galley they come, from behind the little dun-colored curtain in the dining room, from behind the bookcases in the handsome sitting room, from beneath the bed and the bloodstained metal table, through wood and fabric and the weight of years, **We** come, the Old

Ones and Real People, the Cloud Huggers, **We** process slowly toward the center of the mystery **We** understand only by giving it unquestioning service. What remains of the clients and patrons lies, still breathing though without depth or force, upon the metal worktable. It was always going to end this way, it always does, it can no other. Speaking in the high-pitched, musical language of birds that **We** taught the Piraha at the beginning of time, **We** gather at the site of these ruined bodies, **We** worship their devotion to each other and the Great Task that grew and will grow on them, **We** treat them with grave tenderness as we separate what can and must be separated. Notes of the utmost liquid purity float upward from the mouths of **We** and print themselves upon the air. **We** know what they mean, though they have long since passed through the realm of words and gained again the transparency of music. **We** love and accept the weight and the weightlessness of music. When the process of separation is complete, through the old sacred inner channels **We** transport what the dear, still-living man and woman have each taken from the other's body down down down to the galley and the ravening hunger that burns ever within it.

Then. Then. With the utmost tenderness, singing the deep tuneless music at the heart of the ancient world, **We** gather up what remains of Ballard and Sandrine, armless and legless trunks, faces without features, their breath clinging to their mouths like wisps, carry them (in our arms, in baskets, in once-pristine sheets) across the deck and permit them to roll from our care, as they had always longed to do, and into that of the flashing furious little river monarchs. **We** watch the water boil in a magnificence of ecstasy, and **We** sing for as long as it lasts.

NOTES ON CONTRIBUTORS

CHARLES BERNSTEIN's "Recalculating" is the title poem from a work in progress. Bernstein is the author of *Attack of the Difficult Poems: Essays and Inventions* (University of Chicago Press) and *All the Whiskey in Heaven: Selected Poems* (Farrar, Straus and Giroux). He teaches at the University of Pennsylvania.

GABRIEL BLACKWELL's "Untitled (Sid Vicious, New York, 1978)" was the *Web Conjunctions* supplement to last spring's *Shadow Selves*. He is the reviews editor of *The Collagist* and the author of *Neverland*, a chapbook from Uncanny Valley Press.

RYAN CALL is the author of *The Weather Stations* (Caketrain). He lives in Houston.

JONATHAN CARROLL is the author of sixteen books. His latest, *The Ghost in Love*, is published by Farrar, Straus and Giroux. He lives in Vienna, Austria.

ROBERT COOVER is the author of more than twenty books, most recently *A Child Again* (McSweeney's) and *Noir* (Overlook). He teaches digital writing at Brown University, where he directs the International Writers Project.

KATHRYN DAVIS has written six novels, the most recent of which is *The Thin Place* (Little, Brown). She lives in Vermont and teaches at Washington University in St. Louis. "Descent of the Aquanauts" is a chapter from her next novel, *The Duplex*.

JULIA ELLIOTT's fiction has appeared in multiple issues of *Conjunctions*, as well as in *Tin House*, *Georgia Review*, *Puerto Del Sol*, the *Best American Fantasy* anthology, and elsewhere.

ANDREW ERVIN is the author of *Extraordinary Renditions* (Coffee House Press).

NOMI EVE is the author of *The Family Orchard* (Knopf).

PETER GIZZI is the author of *The Outernationale* (Wesleyan), *Some Values of Landscape and Weather* (Wesleyan), *Artificial Heart* (Burning Deck), and *Periplum* (Avec Books). A new book, *Threshold Songs* (Wesleyan), is forthcoming in the fall of 2011. He is currently the Judith E. Wilson Visiting Fellow in Poetry at Cambridge University.

BENJAMIN HALE's first novel, *The Evolution of Bruno Littlemore* (Twelve), was published in February. He is the recipient of a University of Iowa Provost's Fellowship and a Michener-Copernicus Society of America Award. He grew up in Colorado and now lives in New York, where he teaches at Sarah Lawrence College.

CATHY PARK HONG's second book, *Dance Dance Revolution*, was published by W. W. Norton in 2007.

TIM HORVATH (www.timhorvath.com) is the author of *Circulation* (sunnyoutside) and stories in *Conjunctions, Fiction, Everyday Genius*, and elsewhere. He teaches creative writing at Boston's Grub Street and Chester College of New England and has received a Yaddo residency.

KARLA KELSEY is the author of *Knowledge, Forms, the Aviary* and *Iteration Nets* (both Ahsahta Press).

ALEXANDRA KLEEMAN has published work in *DIAGRAM* and *The Paris Review*. She lives in New York City.

JOHN MADERA (www.johnmadera.com) has published work in *Conjunctions, The Believer, Opium, Tarpaulin Sky, Review of Contemporary Fiction, Rain Taxi, Brooklyn Rail*, and elsewhere. He is the managing editor of *Big Other* and a columnist for the *Nervous Breakdown*.

STEPHEN MARCHE is a novelist and a culture columnist at *Esquire*. In 2011, he will release *How Shakespeare Changed Everything* with HarperCollins, and a novel, *Love and the Mess We're In*, with Gaspereau Press.

JAMES MORROW is the author of nine novels, including a postmodern historical epic, *The Last Witchfinder* (Morrow); a Mary Shelley homage, *The Philosopher's Apprentice* (Morrow); and the Godhead Trilogy (Harcourt). He has received the World Fantasy Award, the Nebula Award, the Grand Prix de l'Imaginaire, and the Prix Utopia. His recent novella, *Shambling Towards Hiroshima* (Tachyon), won the Theodore Sturgeon Memorial Award.

MARC NIESON's fiction has been published in *Carve Magazine* and *Great River Review*; excerpts from *Schoolhouse: A Memoir in 13 Lessons* have appeared in *Literary Review, Iowa Review*, and *Chautauqua*. His fiction has been awarded the 2008 Raymond Carver Short Story Contest prize, while his feature-length screenplay, *The Speed of Life*, won the Special Jury Prize at the 2007 Venice Film Festival.

HOWARD NORMAN's most recent novel is *What Is Left the Daughter* (Houghton Mifflin Harcourt). "Radio From the Cities" is from a memoir, *I Hate to Leave This Beautiful Place*, forthcoming in 2012.

KEN PRIOR shot on thirty-five-millimeter film for nearly thirty years before making the changeover to digital photography in 2000. His photograph on the cover of this issue was taken from the shoulder of Schiehallion, the mountain in Scotland where Nevil Maskelyne conducted early experiments in 1774 to estimate the weight of the Earth.

DONALD REVELL is the author of eleven collections of poetry, including most recently *The Bitter Withy* and *A Thief of Strings* (both Alice James Books). He directs the creative writing program at the University of Nevada, Las Vegas.

Legendary publisher and editor BARNEY ROSSET founded Grove Press and *The Evergreen Review* and published, among many others, such authors as Samuel Beckett, William S. Burroughs, Henry Miller, Malcolm X, Tom Stoppard, Jack Kerouac, Jorge Luis Borges, Jean Genet, Eugène Ionesco, Federico García Lorca, and Kenzaburō Ōe. Rosset has completed work on his autobiography, *The Subject Is Left Handed*, from which his piece in this issue is excerpted.

JOANNA SCOTT's most recent novel is *Follow Me* (Little, Brown). "De Potter's First Grand Tour Around the World" is excerpted from her forthcoming book, *The Gilt Cabinet*.

KYRA SIMONE is a writer from Los Angeles. Her poetry and nonfiction have been featured in *The Silo* and *Les Flaneurs*, with forthcoming work in *Black Clock*. She serves as an editor for *Her Royal Majesty*, a visual and literary arts magazine based in Paris, where she currently lives.

SUSAN STEINBERG is the author of *Hydroplane* and *The End of Free Love* (both FC2). She is the United States Artists Ziporyn Fellow in Literature for 2010 and teaches at the University of San Francisco.

PETER STRAUB is the author of eighteen novels and two collections of shorter fiction. He edited *Lovecraft's Tales* and the two-volume *American Fantastic Tales* for the Library of America and was given the Life Achievement Award at the 2010 World Fantasy Convention.

COLE SWENSEN's most recent book is *Greensward* (Ugly Duckling). A collection of essays, *Noise that Stays Noise*, will appear later this year from University of Michigan Press, and *Gravesend*, a collection of poetry, will be published by the University of California in 2012. A translator of French poetry and art criticism and founding editor of La Presse Books, she teaches at the Iowa Writers' Workshop.

G. C. WALDREP's most recent collections are *Archicembalo* (Tupelo), which won the Dorset Prize, and—in collaboration with John Gallaher—*Your Father on the Train of Ghosts* (BOA Editions). He teaches at Bucknell University.

ANDREW ZAWACKI is the author of three poetry books, *Petals of Zero Petals of One* (Talisman House), *Anabranch* (Wesleyan), and *By Reason of Breaking* (Georgia). His most recent chapbook is *Glassscape* (Projective Industries), and his translation of Sébastien Smirou, *My Lorenzo*, is forthcoming from Burning Deck.

ROBERTO BOLAÑO

BETWEEN
PARENTHESES

Essays, Articles and Speeches
1998–2003

"This volume makes up
something like a personal cartography of
Roberto Bolaño and comes closest,
of everything he wrote, to being
a kind of fragmented autobiography."

–*From the introduction by* Ignacio Echevarría

"Of all books, memoirs are the
most deceitful because the pretense in
which they engage often goes undetected
and their authors are usually only
looking to justify themselves.
Ostentation and memoirs tend to
go together. Lies and memoirs
get along swimmingly."

–Roberto Bolaño, from the essay "Memoirs"

NEW DIRECTIONS
75 Years of Independent Publishing

PAPERBACK AVAILABLE IN MAY

JAVIER MARÍAS

YOUR FACE TOMORROW
VOLUME THREE
POISON, SHADOW, AND FAREWELL

"Quirky, hypnotic, and utterly original...
this brilliant novel is surely one of the greatest
the century has so far produced"

– *The New York Review of Books*

"Magnificent.
It's as terrifying as
it is beautiful"

–Stacey D'Erasmo, *The New York Times Book Review*

NEW DIRECTIONS
75 Years of Independent Publishing

"As his dazzling career continues to demonstrate,
Mr. Coover is a one-man Big Bang of exploding creative force."
— *The New York Times*

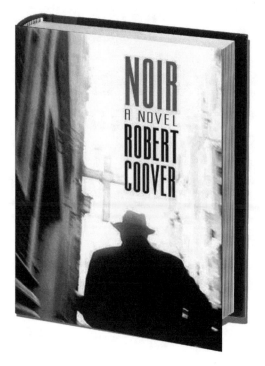

"Dazzling ... Like Thomas Pynchon in 2009's
Inherent Vice, Coover pops off laughs on every page."
— *Publishers Weekly* (starred review)

"At age 75, Coover is still a brilliant mythmaker, a potty-
mouthed Svengali, and an evil technician of metaphors.
He is among our language's most important inventors."
— Ben Marcus

www.overlookpress.com

Small Beer Press is celebrating 10 years of publishing books (and 15 of putting out a zine—my, time flies) by keeping on keeping on. Wild, no?

We've got mind-popping short story collections from Joan Aiken, Geoff Ryman, and Maureen F. McHugh, and an anthology of contemporary Mexican stories of the fantastic. Ok, so anthologies in translation aren't for everyone (why not?), but, hey, you're reading *Conjunctions*, so it might be for you.

We've got a handful of weird novels—including one for the kids by none other than Lydia Millet. *The Fires Beneath the Sea* is the first of a series for middle graders inspired by Madeleine L'Engle: pick it up for the kids, grandkids, nieces, nephews.

Other things: that zine, *LCRW*, comes out twice a year full of fresh voices. Every year we publish the very necessary *A Working Writer's Daily Planner*.

And there's Weightlessbooks.com, a one-stop spot for all your indie press favorites where we add new DRM-free ebooks every week.

If you've been reading our books: thanks for ten years of fun! If you haven't, hope we can tempt you to check them out soon.

smallbeerpress.com
facebook.com/smallbeerpress
weightlessbooks.com

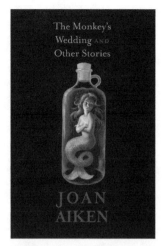

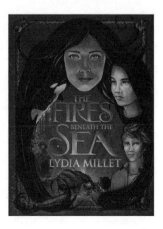

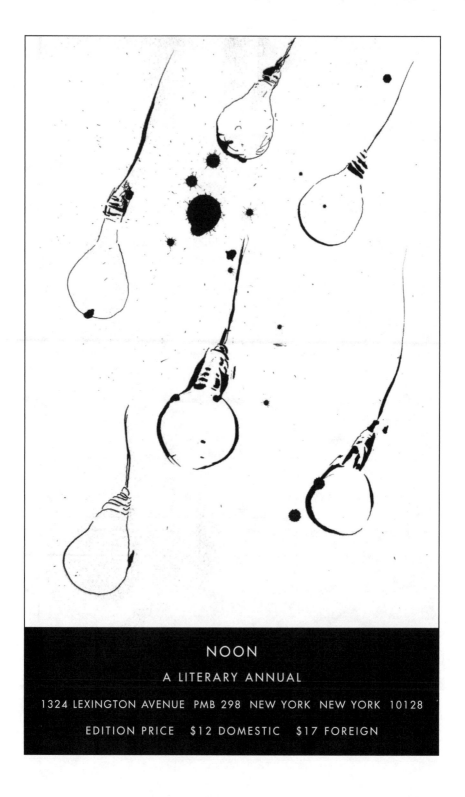

NOON

A LITERARY ANNUAL

1324 LEXINGTON AVENUE PMB 298 NEW YORK NEW YORK 10128

EDITION PRICE $12 DOMESTIC $17 FOREIGN

Christina Mengert: *As We Are Sung*

This first book explores the transformation from "I am speaking" to "I am singing." Restlessly, in abrupt (sometimes humorous) shifts it examines the subtle, the inaccessible, "the song that is sung between notes," and sometimes seems almost to disperse into a space as vast and tolerant of indeterminacy as Barbara Guest's. Christina Mengert has crossed the country from her native Georgia to Denver and back East, to teach in Bard's Prison Program.

Christina Mengert: As We Are Sung

Poetry, 64 pages, offset, smyth-sewn, original pbk. $14

Gale Nelson:
This Is What Happens When Talk Ends

Each of 8 sets of 8 poems follows the vowel pattern of a particular passage from Shakespeare. They could be called homovocalic translations though they ignore Shakespeare's content while trying to build toward their own coherence. The sets are not arranged in sequence, but in a chess pattern, the earliest surviving knight's circuit, from 840 AD.

Born in Los Angeles, Gale Nelson is Assistant Director of Literary Arts at Brown University. Burning Deck has also published his *ceteris paribus* and *stare decisis*.

Poetry, 104 pages, offset, smyth-sewn, original pbk. $14

David Lespiau: *Four Cut-ups*
or The Case of the Restored Volume
[Série d'Ecriture, No. 24; translated from the French by Keith Waldrop]

Real and fictional characters (Mrs. Lindbergh, Gertrude Stein, William Burroughs, Billy Budd or the Kid) circulate through a kind of mobile whose movement constructs a form out of fragmented perceptions, ideas, stories, quotations, and gives a strangely uncanny sheen to the most realistic details.

David Lespiau lives in Marseille. Other recent books are *Ouija-Board* and *La poule est un oiseau autodidacte*.

Poetry, 64 pages, offset, smyth-sewn, original pbk. $14

More Terrae Incognitae:

Tom Ahern: *The Capture of Trieste.* Stories, 66 pp. LP $14
Beth Anderson: *Overboard.* Poetry, 80pp. $14
Norma Cole, ed., *Crosscut Universe: Writing on Writing from France.* 160 pp. $18
Cyrus Console: *Brief Under Water.* Poetry, 64 pp. $14
Michael Davidson: *The Landing of Rochambeau.* Poetry, 80 pp., LP $14
Elke Erb: *Mountains in Berlin.* Poems, 96 pp. $14
Patrick Fetherston: *The World Was a Bubble: a Brief Life of Francis Bacon.*
    Poem with prose interruptions, 56 pp. LP $14
Pascal Quignard: *On Wooden Tablets: Apronenia Avitia.* Novel, 112 pp. $14
Esther Tellermann: *Mental Ground.* Poem, 80 pp. $14
Dallas Wiebe: *Going to the Mountain.* Stories, 192 pp. LP $14

Orders: www.spdbooks.org, www.burningdeck.com,
In Europe: www.audiatur.no/bokhandel

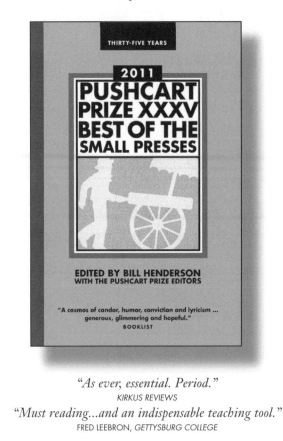

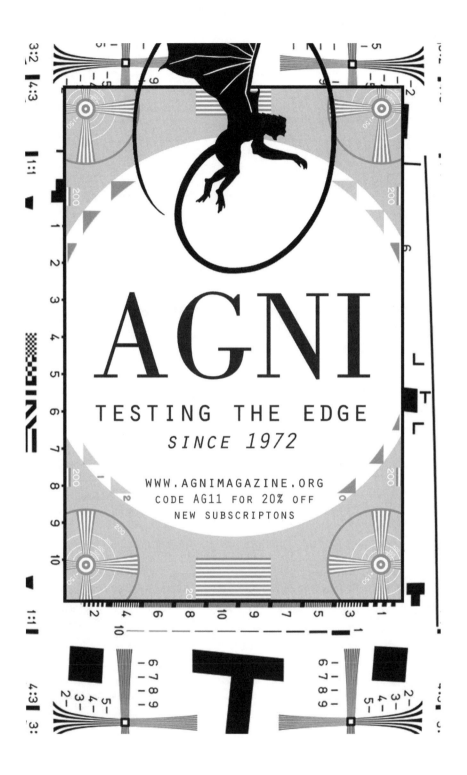

INSTITUTE FOR
writing&
thinking

IWT at BARD COLLEGE
announces

July 10-15, 2011
Weeklong Workshops

Including
Writing and Thinking
Writing to Learn
Creative Non-Fiction: Telling the Truth
Poetry for Today's Classrooms
Inquiry into Essay
Writing Retreat

November 4, 2011
Writing-Based Teaching Workshops

One-day concurrent workshops on the writing
practices teachers want to know most about:
focused freewriting, loop writing, double-entry
notebooks, collaborative learning, process
writing, and image explosion.

For complete workshop and conference descriptions,
please visit www.writingandthinking.org
or call (845) 758-7484

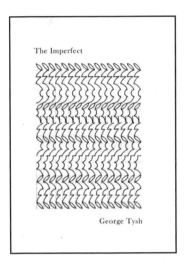

Paul Revere's Horse

A Literary Journal

Issue 5

Special Feature: Writers from Iran

Moniru Ravanipur
Omid Fallahazad
Azareen Van der Vliet Oloomi
Shahriar Mandanipour *on* Ardeshir Mohassess
(*Translated by Sara Khalili*)

Interview with Moniru Ravanipur

Plus...

Lost Poets Review
Selected by Brian Kim Stefans

Georges Perec *on* Alban Berg's *Wozzeck*
(*Translated by Rob Halpern*)

New Writing
Jeffrey Herrick, Michael Mejia,
John Duvernoy, Sara Jaffe

Available in Summer 2011

http://www.paulrevereshorse.org

House Arrest
A Novel by Ellen Meeropol
978-1-59709-499-3 / $24.95

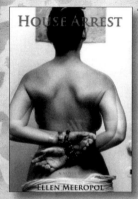

"Meeropol's work is thoughtful and tightly composed, unflinching in taking on challenging subjects and deliberating uneasy ethical conundrums."
—**Publishers Weekly**

In this strong first novel, an unusual relationship develops between a home-care nurse and the pregnant cult member under house arrest to whom she is assigned prenatal visits. Emily Klein suspects that this new assignment has been dumped on her because her boss is trying to get rid of her, but she quickly warms to her new charge, Pippa Glenning, court-ordered to wear an ankle monitor after the deaths by exposure of her 14-month-old daughter and another child in the communal Family of Isis home she lives in—considered a cult by the disapproving community; the two children froze to death during a night of ritualistic celebrations. Emily's ability to empathize with Pippa stems from her own family problems: her father was imprisoned for setting fire to a draft board office during the Vietnam War and Emily provides daily care for her cousin's daughter, born with spina bifida. Throughout, Emily is vexed by the question: is something wrong just because the consequences are awful?

RED HEN PRESS

Available from University of Chicago Distribution Center
To place an order: (800) 621-2736 / www.redhen.org

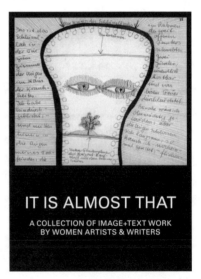

COUSIN CORINNE'S

REMINDER

ISSUE NUMBER THREE

COMING JUNE 2011

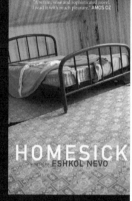

CONJUNCTIONS:55

URBAN ARIAS

Urban Arias

Edited by
Bradford Morrow

In *Urban Arias* the reader may visit any number of cities from Paris to Tokyo, London to Los Angeles, Varanasi to Berlin, Miami to Rome, San Jose to Las Vegas, Havana to Chicago, Lincoln to New Orleans to the city that initially inspired the issue, New York. Here, too, are cities of the unfettered imagination, curious places like Altobello and Anthem, where Jellyheads and Scarecrows respectively reside. Wander down the avenues of *Urban Arias* and you will even discover a city made of meat and gingerbread. Cities we know. Cities we imagine. Cities we imagine we know.

The living collectives known as cities are among the oldest of human experiments in habitation. *Urban Arias* explores our collective existence through new work from John Ashbery, Joyce Carol Oates, Etgar Keret, Paul La Farge, Lyn Hejinian, C. D. Wright, Brian Evenson, and many others. Also featuring a historic interview with Thomas Bernhard and photographs by Deborah Luster and Michael Wesely.

Conjunctions. Charting the course of literature for over 25 years.

CONJUNCTIONS
Edited by Bradford Morrow
Published by Bard College
Annandale-on-Hudson, NY 12504

To purchase this or any other back issue,
visit our secure ordering page at www.conjunctions.com.
Contact us at conjunctions@bard.edu or (845) 758-1539
with questions. $15.00